The Fate of Western Hungary 1918-1921

József Botlik

MATTHIAS CORVINUS PUBLISHERS
BUFFALO - HAMILTON

Translated and edited by Peter J. Csermely

The title of the original book:
Nyugat-Magyarország sorsa 1918–1921
Vasszilvágy, 2008. Magyar Nyugat Könyvkiadó.
ISBN 978-963-8761-23-1
Library of Congress DB955 .B667 2008
Second amended, edited edition

ISBN: 1-882785-24-X

Library of Congress Control Number: 2012947894

2012

PRINTED IN THE UNITED STATES

CONTENTS

Foreword

The writer of these few introductory lines was born Egyházasrádóc in the county of Vas, immediately in the vicinity of the Hungarian-Austrian Trianon defined border. He attended his four years of elementary school in a one room schoolhouse. (Then I became a student of the Reformed Middle School of Csurgo in 1941.) These biographical details were not put here for diversion, or reasons of boasting. Rather, because Jozsef Botlik's harrowing book, based on a mass of *bona fide* fact-supported sources, reminded me – more accurately, 'provoked' them out of me. The first memory invoked by the reading of the manuscript was of the Reformed (and every other) elementary school classroom, where I learned writing and much else, and the administrative map of Vas County hanging on the wall. Beginning in Grade 3, not a day would go by without our teacher calling somebody out to the map and ask: "Describe and point out what our county lost with the terrible Trianon peace" (and what we must, as a matter of course, regain). We said and pointed: Austria took the Felsőőr [now Oberwart] and Németújvár [Güssing] districts, Yugoslavia, the Muraszombat [Murska Sobota] district. Our mutilated county thus had seven, not ten, districts. Also, our faces burned for two reasons: the fluster of answering and the humiliation that befell us.

However, as I was reading the manuscript, the still smoldering indignity was joined by a shocking thought. What would have happened, the thought struck me as a nightmare, if all the goals of the territory hungry Austrian leadership were met in their entirety, as was the case with our other neighbors, the Czechs, Romanians and Serbs. After all, the strongly left leaning politicians of the newly formed Austrian Republic wanted to commandeer all of Western Hungary: Pozsony [Bratislava], all of Moson, Sopron and Vas counties, and the northwestern part of Zala County to the railway line of Celldömölk – Türje – Zalaegerszeg – Lenti – Alsólendva – Csáktornya. Already in early November of 1918, writes the author, they created in Vienna the *Westungarische Kanzlei* [Western Hungary Bureau], under whose auspices and direction, prepare, by armed force if necessary, the annexation of 16,000 km^2 of territory. What made it most repulsive was the immoral Austrian mindset. After all, Austria wanted to take purely Magyar populated areas from an associated country, the other half of the Austro-Hungarian Monarchy, with whom our soldiers shed their blood for four years obeying our common emperor-king. Is there anything more repulsive in the world than to rob someone together with whom we suffered and fell?

What seemingly froze a man such as me: My God, what would have happened to me if such vulgar appetite came to pass? If my village, and the entire county, was given to Austria? Would I have even been born? And if yes, what would have happened to me, become of me? An Austrian citizen? A frustrated, neurotic member of a minority, forced to forget his origins, bury his ancestors; a sort-of assimilated Austrian-German? Too terrible to even contemplate – no matter how the craze of internationalism-globalism propaganda rages today.

The author's book, of course, does not address the fate of individuals (like me) but collectively ours, the Magyars. Of that part of the country, which, through more than three years of serious problems and ordeals, József Botlik documents for us in a precise and factual manner, the Hungarian successes. In the end, the Austrian demands were largely warded off between November 1918 and December 1921, thanks entirely to our efforts. The sole minor success in the appalling mutilation of a country was won here as a sign of the nation's will of the day. It was all thanks to the diplomatic moves following the collapse of Communism in Hungary; perhaps even more to the voluntary resistance, military and civil. Among them, finally, was the compelling of the plebiscite, the demand and resistance of the individual villages that fell into the border zone. Not in last place, the stand taken by the Hungarian armed volunteers (including in the Lajta-Banat) and the strength of the Western Hungarian insurrection, which could successfully effect a change – after the signing of the peace treaty! – from the astounding claim of 16,000 km^2 to a more modest 5,000 km^2?

The book, and its theme, exemplifies: No matter how much of a defeated situation a community finds itself, if it does not give up, if it does not give in, no matter how great its opponents, there always was, or could have, an incentive for resistance, for defiance. What's more, the effort may even bring concrete results. But only if we make, are able to make, the necessary sacrifice, as then in Western Hungary, the greatest one: the brave sacrifice of life. It is thus, even if this heroic example failed to make much of a change in the outcome of the terms of the dictated Trianon treaty or among the Austrians who lost with us. In the newly annexed Burgenland province of Austria, 24,500 people claimed themselves as Hungarians (1910 census and 64,000 spoke Hungarian, too). In our day, the number of indigenous Magyars is around 4,000. By proportion, this represents the greatest assimilation of a Magyar minority, plummeting to 16% of its former number. Not to the great glory of Austrian democracy and minority policies.

The name of the historian-author is known today among a wider public, not just among those in the business. His earlier books and studies deal with another, also annexed, region: Sub-Carpathia. They have found favor for a very good reason. It is predictable that this book will also find favorable reception. It is my belief that this book should not be recommended to the attention of readers, rather, due to its subject, reasoning and good style should become mandatory reading – primarily for our countrymen living in the West of Trans-Danubia. And not just them but it would add to all of us with a hazy grasp of history, to our collective Magyar national consciousness.

Lajos Für

Chapter 1: From allied country to territory claiming neighbor
Austria and Western Hungary (*Westungarn*) in 1918–1919

On the eve of the 'Aster Revolution,' so called after its flover emblem [worn by demonstrating supporters-*ed*.], on the night of October 23-24, 1918, Mihály Károlyi (1879-1955) set up the Hungarian National Council, with himself as president, and unilaterally announcing themselves as the opposition government. On October 31, 1918, Count Mihály Károlyi, the Red count, and his circle forced the takeover of political power in the country. On the same day, the western counties of Hungary – Moson, Sopron and Vas – also formed local Hungarian National Councils, which quickly made decisions to set up similar councils in the towns and villages. In the following days, national councils were formed, even in German speaking settlements, which set as their main tasks: the organization of the feeding of the population and the maintenance of public safety. In Sopron, for example, it was formed on October 31, as a 15-member council, made up of radical, democratic and socialist elements, which officially took power over the city the next day.[1] At this time, the distribution of food for the population was much worse on the Austrian side than on the Hungarian.

Following the military collapse of the Austro-Hungarian Monarchy,[2] the delegation of the Upper House of the Hungarian National Assembly, led by Baron Gyula Wlassics (1852-1937), president of the Upper House, and members: prince Miklós Esterházy (1869-1920), counts Emil Széchenyi and Emil Dessewffy (1873-1935) – left on November 12, at the request of prime minister Károlyi for a hunting lodge in Eckartsau, on the bank of the Danube between Vienna and Hainburg. Their mission there was to brief Charles Habsburg IV, King of Hungary (1916-1918), of the revolutionary situation in Hungary, as well as consult with the monarch about a "temporary retreat

---

[1] Környei, Attila: Az osztályharc néhány kérdése Sopron megyében a polgári demokratikus forradalom időszakában (1918. november – 1919. március) [Several questions of the class warfare in Sopron County during the period of the civic democratic revolution (November 1918 – March 1919)]. In: *Soproni Szemle*, 1969. Issue 1, p. 5.

[2] Irinyi, Jenő: Az osztrák–magyar hadsereg összeomlása. (A volt főparancsnokság okmányai alapján) [The collapse of the Austro-Hungarian army. (Based on the documents of the former headquarters.)]. In: *Új Magyar Szemle,* year I, volume III, issue 2–3, December 1920, pp. 180–198; Baron Sarkotič, István: Az összeomlás Boszniában és Hercegovinában [Collapse in Bosnia and Herzegovina]. In: *Új Magyar Szemle,* year II, volume I, issue 2, February 1921, pp. 168–177. (Infantry general Sarkotič was the last commanding officer of the Austro-Hungarian forces posted to Bosnia-Herzegovina, until Nov. 6, 1918.); General Baron Arz, Arthur: 1914 – 1918. A központi monarchiák harca és összeomlása [1914-1918. The battle and collapse of the central monarchies]. Budapest, 1942.

declaration."[3] The basis for the declaration was the Lamasch government's Schönbrunn Proclamation, prepared the previous day, November 11, in which Charles IV stated: "In advance, I recognize German-Austria's decision regarding its future state organization." Although the proclamation did not contain a reference to his abdication from the throne, in light of circumstances, it essentially meant the end of 700 years of Habsburg rule.

As a result of the visit and urging of the representatives of the Hungarian Upper House, led by Gyula Wlassics, on the following day, November 13, king Charles IV issued the Eckartsau Proclamation, which was essentially a repeat of the Schönbrunn Manifesto and announced: "I resign from all participation in the affairs of the state and agree to whatever form of state Hungary will decide." Subsequently, the decision of the Hungarian National Assembly announced on November 16, according to which, henceforth Hungary was a "sovereign and independent people's republic." The so-called Eckartsau proclamation made use of the same form which the ruler accepted on November 11 as Charles I, Emperor of Austria, not abdicating from, or renouncing all claims to, the throne. After these two proclamations, the ruler and his family moved to Switzerland. During his later two attempts to regain the Hungarian throne in 1921, Charles tried to make use of the latter proclamation as the legal basis for his claim to the Hungarian crown.

In the meantime, sensing the totally impotent actions of the Károlyi government (according to some signs intentional) – especially the disarmament of the Hungarian soldiers returning from the front – the German population living in western Hungary saw a surge in the movement to separate, whose roots stretch back a decade. In the heat of a 1905 Austrian parliamentary debate, it was suggested that Hungary cede its western, German-populated area, occupied by Austro-Hungarian troops as part of the terms of the 1878 Berlin Congress, in exchange for governing power over Bosnia-Herzegovina, under civilian public administration since 1882.

Shortly after, in the summer of 1906, Josef Patry, Austrian newspaper reporter, from the Czech Sudeten region, once again brought up in a Viennese paper[4] the detachment and annexation of Western Hungary. This time, in response to the fact that, in some Hungarian political circles, the possibility of annexation of Bosnia-Herzegovina to Hungary became a daily topic. In his writing, Patry predicted the collapse of the Austro-Hungarian Monarch, and its break-up. As a result, German-Austria must lay claim to the area between the Danube and Raba rivers and, furthermore, not only Pozsony [today Bratislava] and Győr but, for military reasons, the city of Komárom, too, as

[3] Wlassics, Gyula: Az eckartsaui nyilatkozat. A királykérdés. I–II. Rész [The Eckartsau declaration. Monarchic question, part I-II]. In: *Új Magyar Szemle,* year II, vol. I, issue 1, January 1921, pp. 21–26; A trónöröklés. III. Rész [The Succession, part III]. In: issue 2, February 1921, pp. 133–138; Nagy, József: IV. Károly. Az utolsó magyar király [Charles IV. The last Hungarian king]. Budapest, 1995.
[4] Patry, Josef: Westungarn zu Deutschösterreich. [Western Hungary to German-Austria.] In: *Alldeutsche Tagblatt,* June 17, 1906.

well as the territory along the Raba River, with Szentgotthárd as its center, all the way to the Styrian border. According to Patry's suggestion, essentially the western portion of Trans-Danubia, with a population of approx. 900,000 (of which only 38.3% or 345,000 were Germans), would have been transferred to German-Austrian rule. For this, Hungary would have received, in exchange, Bosnia-Herzegovina and the southern part of Dalmatia, with about 2.2 million South Slav subjects.[5]

Patry's article did not find wide support in Austria. The newspaper that originally ran Patry's piece in 1906, the Viennese *Altdeutsches Tagblatt,* also reprinted it in the form of a flyer, titled *Westungarn zu Deutschösterreich* [Western Hungary to German-Austria], and distributed it in Hungary. On its front page, it demanded the annexation of Western Hungary to a not-yet-existing German-Austria that was still a part of the German Empire. Around this time, the Croats petitioned to have Dalmatia annexed to Croatia. The flyer seized this opportunity to foment dissension with Hungary, which – as it stated – "the weak emperor allowed to grow in size at the expense of its loyal nations." It proclaimed that the non-Hungarian speaking people of Hungary awaited their liberation from a forcible Hungarian rule. It graciously allowed the annexation of Dalmatia to Croatia, under the aegis of the Hungarian Holy Crown but, in that case, Austria is entitled to compensation by the Hungarian territory between the Danube and Raba rivers, which was partially populated by Germans. The flyer also added demands over and above the original article and went on to lay claim to the cities of Pozsony for reason of it being partly German, Győr for economic reasons, Komárom for military reasons, then laid claim to the purely Hungarian island of Csallóköz (Žitný ostrov) and Szigetköz for its rich agricultural lands. This contagion was carefully planted in Austrian society, and it made its way to Western Hungary, as well. As but one minor example, Dr. János Wurditsch of Szentmargitbánya, who received his degree at the medical school of the University of Vienna, for years, infected the minds of his sick and healthy patients with this.[6] In the matter of the dissemination of the German-language flyer, at the February 22, 1908 meeting of the Hungarian Diet, Hugo Laehne, member for the Kőszeg riding, addressed a question to the prime minister, Sándor Wekerle (1848-1921). He suggested that Patry's flyer be officially confiscated and banning its dissemination in the country,[7] as well as curbing the Greater Germany

---

[5] The ideas of Josef Patry and similar ones by Austrian politicians are covered in more detail by Schlag, Gerald: Aus Trümmern geboren... Burgenland 1918-1921 [Born from the rubble... Burgenland 1918-1921]. Eisenstadt, 2001, pp. 38–48.
[6] Sopronyi-Thurner, Mihály: A magyar igazság kálváriája [The Calvary of Hungarian truth]. In: Sopron és Sopronvármegye ismertetője 1914–1934 [Sopron and Sopron County Review]. Összeáll. Horváth László, Madarász Gyula, Zsadányi Oszkár. Sopron, 1934, pp. 38–39. (Hereafter referred to as: Sopron and ..., 1934.)
[7] Nagy, Iván dr. vitéz: Nyugatmagyarország Ausztriában [Western Hungary in Austria]. Pécs, 1937, p. 23.

sympathies. (Patry's circular appeared again in 1918, in its second edition.[8])

Germans have been slowly settling in western Hungary for centuries. The suggestion that the area be annexed to Austria was proposed even more strongly two years later, during the 1908 so-called Bosnian Crisis, by the editorials of the Vienna newspaper, *Österreichische Rundschau*. At this time, the Hungarian press was demanding that Bosnia-Herzegovina be annexed to Hungary. In response, certain Austrian circles counter-proposed that, in exchange, Hungary cede to Austria the four western counties of Moson, Sopron, Vas and Pozsony, with special mention of the city of Pozsony. The situation was finally settled when, on November 6, 1908, Austrian Emperor (and Hungarian king) Franz Joseph (1848-1916), citing the prerogative of the Hungarian Holy Crown, announced the addition of Bosnia-Herzegovina into the Austro-Hungarian Monarchy.

The topic of ceding of the four mentioned counties to Austria – and the emphasized demand for Pozsony – continued to remain on the agenda. In fact, it made its way into Archduke Franz Ferdinand's (1863-1914) plans for the creation of *Gross-Österreich* [Greater Austria]. The question was also hotly debated in 1918 by the Austrian-German officers on the battlefields. The issue was tabled in the Austrian parliament in September.[9] This movement gained new momentum when, a day after Charles IV's Schönbrunn Manifesto, on November 12, 1918 the interim Austrian National Assembly proclaimed the country a republic. Next, it went on to declare that the new state is to be called German-Austria (*Deutschösterreich*) and it is joining (*Anschluss*) democratic Germany.

Here we must recount the fateful events that led up to the previous events. The last prime minister of (pre-Trianon) historic Hungary, Sándor Wekerle, who made numerous attempts to prevent the breakup of the Monarchy, stated "for the opinion of the Hungarian nation at large": "Unfortunately, now after the fact, I can say that ex-king Charles (Habsburg IV) was not honest. He asked István Tisza to go down and hold talks with the South Slavs and, behind our back, he also *empowered Korosetz to create against us the Yugoslav state*. This Korosetz had such great influence over the ex-king that he [the ex-king] immediately *passed on every understanding I had with him* [again the ex-king] to Korosetz so that he [Korosetz] could immediately begin countermeasures against me. It happened often that, if I reminded the king of his previous promises, he *claimed he could not remember them*. You have no

---

[8] Patry, Josef: Westungarn zu Deutschösterreich. Ein Vorschlag zur Lösung der deutsch-ungarischen Frage. [Western Hungary to German Austria. Proposal for the solution of the Western Hungarian question]. 2nd. ed. Wien, 1918.

[9] Gagyi, Jenő: A nyugatmagyarországi kérdés [The Western Hungary question]. Budapest, 1921, pp. 4–5; Angyal, Dávid: A boszniai válság története [History of the Bosnian crisis]. Budapest, 1932; Gulya, Károly: Az annexiós válság és az Osztrák–Magyar Monarchia balkáni politikája [The annexation crisis and the Balcan policies of the Austro-Hungarian Monarchy]. In: Acta Universitatis Szegediensis. *Acta Historica*, vol. 20, Szeged, 1965.

idea how often I resigned. Not three times, many more, but officially that number was published. Twice, he sent a messenger after me, just so I would stay. At the end, I could not stay under any circumstance. In any case, I told the king that he was running to his end. *"Majesty, you will even lose your throne, if you continue like this,"* I told him, and not just once, but he refused to listen. And yet, everything could have been saved, possibly only Bosnia would have to have been sacrificed. I know ... that even that will be counted as my fault that we did not bring home the Hungarian soldiers, and yet I appealed many times in this matter. *The former king made me a solemn promise, the last one on October 2, that he will order the Hungarian soldiers home to defend the threatened borders.* But that is not how it happened. The Czechs only came under Charles, obviously at the *covert encouragement of the Court, to demand the Hungarian counties. Their secret hope was not the Entente but Vienna.* I learned all these intrigues only later, after the fact. The secret reports are on file. I can prove how my honest efforts were frustrated by the Viennese hand."[10]

As is known, the former prime minister, Count Tisza (1861-1918), was sent by King Charles IV in September of 1918 on a southern circuit. The former government leader's two week tour of 3,451 kms. was in vain. The trip, on narrow gauge railway, by car and on the Italian submarine-threatened Adriatic, ran Zágráb/Zagreb – Zára/Zadar – Raguza/Dubrovnik – Cattaro/Kotor – Cetinje – Mostar – Sarajevo – Brod – Eszék/Osijek – Újvidék/Novi Sad. This last royal assignment of Tisza, to hold consultations with South Slav politicians eager to secede, brought little concrete results.[11]

In the meantime, on September 14, Count István Burián (1851-1922, the common Foreign Minister for the Austro-Hungarian Monarchy, [Under the terms of the 1867 Compromise, Austria maintained control over Foreign Affairs, Treasury and Defense. Hungary had its own ministers for all other ministries-*ed.*] approached the Allied countries with a diplomatic note in the name of the Central Powers. He suggested that the warring parties open a confidential and non-binding conference in a neutral place, regarding the fundamental premises of a peace treaty, while "acts of war carry on unabated." The tone of the note did not reflect the true military situation of the

---

[10] Gelsei Bíró, Zoltán: A Habsburg-ház bűnei. Magyarország négyszázéves szenvedésének története [The sins of the House of Habsburg. The history of 400 years of Hungarian suffering]. Budapest, 1918, p. 96. (Bolding mine–*J.B.*) For the views and policies of prime minister Wekerle (third time from Aug. 20, 1917 to Oct. 30, 1918) in the South Slav and Croat-Magyar question, see: Bajza, József: IV. Károly és a délszlávok [Charles IV and the South Slavs]. In: *Új Magyar Szemle,* year I, vol. III, issue 1, November 1920, pp 31–46. Korosetz (variants: Korosec,Korošec), Anton (1872–1940) Catholic priest, politician, member of Austria's parliament from 1906. From 1917, president of the South Slav Club, whose members are South Slav politicians.

[11] Palotás, Zoltán: Tisza István "délszláv missziója" [István Tisza's "South Slav mission"]. In: *Új Magyarország,* May 22, 1992, p. 10.

Austro-Hungarian Monarchy or Germany at the time, and did not suggest the adoption of President Woodrow Wilson's 14 Points, made public by the U.S. president on January 8, 1918. Burián's suggestion was rejected in a response note, in the name of the Entente Powers, by British Foreign Secretary Arthur Balfour on September 16th, by French Prime Minister Clemenceau on the 17th, and by US Secretary of State Robert Lansing on the 19th.

Ten days later, on the 29th, as a result of the Entente forces' Balkan offensive, Bulgaria sued for a cease fire. As a result, Germany and the Monarchy were forced to face up to defeat. On the same day, the German Imperial War Council decided to sue for truce and, taking into consideration the Wilsonian 14 Points, to open peace talks. On October 4, at the same time as Germany and Turkey, Foreign Minister Burián sent another note to Woodrow Wilson on behalf of the Monarchy, proposing a truce and, based on Wilson's 14 Points, the beginning of peace negotiations.[12] Wilson rejected the notes sent by the Central Powers on October 8. Austrian Emperor and Hungarian King, Charles, proclaimed the transformation of Austria into a federative state on October 16 and directed the provinces to form their own National Councils. This, however, did not extend to the countries under the Hungarian Holy Crown (historical Hungary, including Transylvania, and the associated countries of Croatia-Slavonia and the semi-autonomous territory of Fiume/Rijeka). Also, the common ministries of foreign affairs, finance and war remained. Two days later, on October 18, President Wilson wrote a reply to Foreign Minister Burián's second note in which he stated that the 14 Points did not form the basis of talks with the Monarchy, having been born of different military and political circumstances.[13] The answer to the American note came on October 27 from Count Gyula Andrássy (1860-1929), the new – and last – Foreign Minister of the Monarchy – Burián having been, in the interim, replaced – in which he accepted the Wilsonian settlement principles and the right of self-determination of the Czech-Slovak and South Slav peoples. During these weeks, the newspapers were full of the rabble-rousing and inflammatory speeches of parliamentary representatives Mihály Károlyi, László Fényes[14] (1871-1944) and their ilk. Moreover, "the Italians threw thousands of leaflets (into our trenches) containing the subversive parliamentary speeches of Count Mihály Károlyi and friends, informing us before the arrival of the newspapers to the front,"[15] wrote Colonel Ferenc

---

[12] Révai Mór, János: Magyarország integritása és a wilsoni elvek [Hungary's territorial integrity and the Wilsonian principles]. Magyarország Területi Épségének Védelmi Ligája. Budapest, 1920, pp. 14–42.

[13] For the documents of the texts of exchange of the so-called Burián notes, see addenda in Rubint, Dezső: Az összeomlás [The collapse]. Budapest, 1922.

[14] In 1918, László Fényes was Minister of State for War in the Károlyi government and commissar for Defence, organizing the disarmament of Hungarian and Szekler troops in Transylvania, which were self-organizing against a Romanian occupation.

[15] Nyékhegyi, Ferenc: A Diaz-féle fegyverszüneti szerződés. (A páduai fegyverszünet) [The Diaz ceasefire agreement. (The Padua ceasefire)]. Budapest,

Nyékhegyi, commander of the 9th Infantry Battalion of Kassa, on the northern Italian front.

And thus, we return to the forcible grabbing of power on October 31, 1918 by Mihály Károlyi and his 'circle,' actually, up to the day of his *coup d'état*, when Archduke Joseph August, *homo regius*,[16] named Károlyi as Prime Minister. On the same day, around 5:30pm, armed soldiers broke into the house of Count István Tisza, former Prime Minister, and killed him.[17] Earlier, one Otto Korvin (1894-1919), the leader of the revolutionary Socialists, personally prepared an assassination attempt on Count Tisza, carried out by János Lékai (1895-1925) on October 16. On top of all this, due to all the accusations spread by Károlyi and his circle, the majority of public opinion held Tisza responsible for Hungary's entry into the war. Yet, it was a fact little known by the public that, after the assassination of the heir to the throne, Franz Ferdinand (June 28, 1914), in opposition to the rest of the responsible decision makers of the Monarchy, the Hungarian Prime Minister opposed, for long weeks, military action against Serbia. Tisza only agreed to a declaration of war against Serbia after getting assurances that South Slav territories would not be annexed to the Monarchy, as that threatened, in his eyes, to unravel the Dualist system.

The past decades' Marxist-Communist historiography missed no opportunity to trumpet that István Tisza, precisely the day following the unsuccessful attempt on his life by Lékai, admitted in parliament that the war was lost. The truth is very different, as proven by the Parliamentary Record for 1918, unavailable for a long time. What did happen, among other things, in the parliamentary chamber on the day of the attempt on Tisza's life? On October 16, 1918, during the 823rd sitting of Parliament convened on June 21, 1910 [The election of 1914 was cancelled due to the outbreak of war-*ed.*], Prime Minister Sándor Wekerle described the political situation of the day, the peace offer made to President Wilson and the plans to alter Austria's

---

1922, p. 54. Colonel Ferenc Nyékhegyi describes it based on personal experiences and *bona fide* documents.

[16] *Homo regius*: the king's man. The ruler's confidante, charged with handling difficult situations. King Charles IV named Archduke Joseph August (1872-1962) *homo regius* on October 27, 1918, a position from which neither the democratic civil revolution nor the revolution of the proletariat could displace him. The so-called unionist government, led by Gyula Peidl (1873-1943), was in power from the first day after the fall of the Commune, August 1, 1919, until its removal by a *coup* on August 6. On that day, Archduke Joseph announced that he will temporarily assume the role of head of government as Governor. The following day, he named István Friedrich (1883-1951) and his government officials. At the request of the Entente Powers, who were afraid of a return of the Habsburgs to the Hungarian throne, he resigned his post on August 26.

[17] Szász, Károly: Tisza István. Élet- és jellemrajz [István Tisza. Biography and character portrait]. Budapest, 1921; Fogarassy, László: Kik ölték meg gróf Tisza Istvánt [Who killed Count István Tisza]? In: *Történelmi Szemle,* 1980, issie 2, pp. 338–341; Pölöskei, Ferenc: Tisza István [István Tisza]. Budapest, 1985.

make-up into a federative union. In the heated debate, Count Károlyi, too, got the floor and began with: "Honored House! We have lost the war. Now, it is important for us not to lose the peace. We have lost the war and the situation today must be assessed from this perspective."[18] It is thus unchallengeable that the first speaker of what was to become axiomatic was, in fact, Mihály Károlyi!

How, then, did the almost-legendary statement, ascribed to Tisza, actually get said on the following day, Thursday, October 17 on the 824th sitting of the Hungarian parliament? During the morning sitting, Count Tisza was first to take the floor and said the following with regard to political situation following the government announcement and the ending of hostilities: "Honored House! *I do not wish to play tricks with words. I agree with what the Hon. Rep. Mihály Károlyi said yesterday, that we lost the war ... We lost not in the sense that we could not carry on with exacting and heroic defense; that we could not but make the final victory for the enemy very costly. But yes, we lost in the sense that, due to the shift in the balance of strength, we have no more chance to win the war and, as a result, we must seek a peace on such terms as our enemies will accept under the situation. ... Hence, I am of the same opinion that, with our German allies, we offered peace to our enemies based on the Wilson 14 Points and their attached points.*"[19]

On the day after the *coup* carried out by the Károlyi government, November 1, King Charles IV released the government, at their request, from the oath (of allegiance) they swore to him. Later the same evening, the members of the government took an oath to "Hungary and the Hungarian people" before the president of the Hungarian National Council, János Hock (1859-1936), who was appointed to the position by the designated Prime Minister Károlyi, as his second-in-command. Also on this day, Minister of War, Béla Linder (1876-1962), ordered that Hungarian forces lay down their arms, while truce talks were going on in Padua between the Entente Powers and representatives of the Austro-Hungarian Monarchy.

Well before this time, beginning in early 1918, encouragement and agitation towards Austria from the "Greater Germany" circles could be noted among the Germans of western Hungary. This became particularly worrisome by the fall when, five days after the creation of the Austrian State Council led by Karl Renner, on November 17, 1918 it officially declared its claim to the – by this time independent – western areas of Hungary, made so by the

---

[18] Az 1910. évi június hó 21-ére hirdetett Országgyűlés Képviselőházának Naplója [Parliamentary Record of the National Assembly convened on June 21, 1910]. Vol. XLI. Budapest, 1918. Athenaeum Irodalmi és Nyomdai Részvénytársaság Könyvnyomdája, p. 277.

[19] Ibid, p. 292. (Bolding mine—*J.B.*) Count István Tisza was Prime Minister of Hungary for the second time between June 10, 1913 and June 15, 1917. After that, he was leader of the parliamentary opposition – the majority, by the way. During this time, as colonel in the 2nd Hussar Battalion of Debrecen, he also spent several months fighting on the Italian front.

Belgrade military treaty,[20] signed by the Károlyi government on November 13. The Austrian State Council stressed that it wished to achieve this not by military means but by a plebiscite, based on the principle of self-determination as stated in Wilson's 14 Points. Emphasizing that the German populated settlement of western Hungarian areas adjacent to Austria have the same right to self determination as all the other nationalities whose same right Hungary has already granted.

In the meanwhile, with the tacit approval of the Viennese government, a large propaganda campaign was begun to win over the western Hungarian Germans and create a *fait accompli* whereby the settlements will petition for their transfer to Austrian hegemony. As one of the first events in this campaign, in the smallest, by population, 'free royal city' in Hungary, Ruszt (Rust), on the western shore of Lake Fertő, placards appeared on the city streets on November 15, urging the population to join Austria.

Even before this, on November 5, at a session of the interim German-Austrian National Assembly, Rep. Heilinger demanded that the minority-German populated counties of Moson, Sopron and Vas, as well as part of Pozsony county, including the city of Pozsony, be annexed to German-Austria. The situation became more serious when a proposed law by the National Council, the November 14 "German-Austria's territorial extent, borders and conditions" and a Declaration of State (*Staatserklärung*) were introduced before the National Assembly. The fifth item of the latter clearly states: "The blocks of German populated settlements in the current counties under the Hungarian Crown that immediately border on German-Austria are to be annex to the state of German-Austria." Rep. Heilinger went on to demand immediate military occupation of the four mentioned counties.

The question was again on the agenda of the National Assembly's November 17 session. On the very same day, the National Council, reacting to media reports from the western Hungarian counties, passed the following resolution: "1. The National Council assert that the German populated areas of Pozsony, Moson, Sopron and Vas counties are part of German-Austria geographically, economically and ethnically, are in the most close economic and intellectual relationship with German-Austria for centuries past, and are indispensable for the feeding of Vienna. Hence, the German-Austria will do its utmost at the peace conference to be able to annex these territories. In this context, the National Council greets the vigorous national and economic annexation movement of the Germans of Western Hungary. 2. The Public Food Distribution Office is directed to send, as soon as possible, buying agents to western Hungarian counties, to ensure Vienna's food supply."[21]

---

[20] Gagyi, op. cit., p. 6.

[21] Harrer, Ferenc: Egy magyar polgár élete [The life of a Hungarian citizen]. Vol. I. Budapest, 1968, pp. 368–369. Ferenc Harrer (1874–1969) was the first ambassador of the Károlyi government to Austria (Nov.-Dec. 1918), then appointed as head of the newly constituted Hungarian Foreign Ministry and temporary Deputy Foreign Minister. In his memoirs, he analyzes the wester Hungary question and the

In his November 22 speech to the National Assembly, President of the National Council Karl Renner stressed that they are trying to establish good relations with the Hungarian government and are desirous of signing an agreement regarding the delivery of foods, an agreement signed on November 25. The tensions were somewhat eased, although the Hungarian government sensed that Vienna had not abandoned its plans for the acquisition of Westungarn, or Western Hungary.[22] This was confirmed by the beginning of Austrian military operations against the region.

Austrian propaganda, in the meanwhile, kept repeating that, instead of the 1000-year Austro-Hungarian border, the new "just" eastern border should run along the spine of Trans-Danubia from the Danube along the railway line from Pozsonyligetfalu – Rajka – Hegyeshalom – Mosonszentjános – Csorna – Szany – Celldömölk – Türje – Zalaegerszeg – Lenti – Alsólendva – Csáktornya. The movement demanding territorial expansion set its sights on appropriating the entirety of three western Trans-Danubian counties. The data of the 1910 census illustrates its magnitude (and greed).

Moson County: area: 1,937 km^2, settlements: 59, population: 94,479 (34.9% Hungarian, 55% German, 8.6% Croatian). County seat: *Magyaróvár* with 5,273 people (62.1% Hungarian, 34.8% German, 1.8% Slovak). The 3 administrative units: the districts of Magyaróvár, Nezsider and Rajka.

Sopron County: area: 3,256 km^2, settlements: 232, population: 283,510 (51% Hungarian, 36.1% German, 12.3% Croatian). County seat: *Sopron* (130 km^2) with 33,932 people (44.3% Hungarian, 51% German, 2.3% Croatian, 1.8% Czech, Vend(Slovenian)). Incorporated towns: *Kismarton* (17 km^2) with 3,073 people (27.1% Hungarian, 67.5% German, 3.3% Croatian) and *Ruszt*: (20 km^2) with 1,535 people (14.2% Hungarian, 84% German, 1.6% Croatian). The seven administrative units: Csepreg, Csorna, Felsőpulya, Kapuvár, Kismarton, Nagymarton and Sopron districts.

Vas County: area: 5,475 km^2, settlements: 611, population: 435,793 (53.9% Hungarian, 28.4% German, 13.5% Vend (Slovene), 4% Croatian). County seat: *Szombathely* (30 km^2) with 30,947 people (94% Hungarian, 4.4% German). Incorporated town: *Kőszeg* (46 km^2) with 8,423 people (61% Hungarian, 36.4% German, 1.6% Croatian). The ten administrative units: Celldömölk, Felsőőr, Körmend, Kőszeg, Muraszombat, Németújvár, Sárvár, Szentgotthárd, Szombathely and Vasvár districts.[23]

The Austrian irredentist movement and the country's leaders not only wanted all of Moson, Sopron and Vas counties but also a strip in northwestern Zala County, as well as laying a claim to Pozsony County, lying North of the Danube on its left bank, especially the city of Pozsony.

Hungarian-Austrian relations. (pp. 357–379)

[22] Soós, Katalin: Burgenland az európai politikában (1918–1921) [Burgenland in European politics (1918-1921)]. Budapest, 1971, pp. 11–12.

[23] Magyarország Közigazgatási Atlasza 1914. A Magyar Szent Korona országai [Hungarian public administrative atlas 1914. The countries under the Hungarian Holy Crown]. Szerk./Ed. Zentai, László. Baja–Pécs, 2000, pp. 73-74, 77, 132.

Pozsony County: area: 4,371 km², settlements: 295, population: 389,750 (44.3% Hungarian, 48.6% Slovak, 5.6% German). County seat: *Pozsony* (75 km²) with 78,223 people (40.5% Hungarian, 41.9% German, 14.9% Slovak, 2.1% Czech). Incorporated towns: *Bazin* (29 km²) with 4,809 people (12% Hungarian, 32.4% German, 54.9% Slovak); *Modor* (50 km²) with 5,009 people (6.9% Hungarian, 10.5% German, 82.3% Slovak); *Nagyszombat* (64 km²) with 15,163 people (30.3% Hungarian, 15% German, 53% Slovak, 1.3% Czech/Polish); and [Pozsony]*Szentgyörgy* (32 km²) with 3,458 people (18.5% Hungarian, 26.5% German, 54.9% Slovak). The seven administrative units: Pozsony, Dunaszerdahely, Galánta, Malacka, Nagyszombat, Somorja and Szenc districts.[24]

According to our calculations, the total area of the four counties Austria intended carve out of Hungary totaled 15,039 km², the number of settlements was 1,197, with two judicial seats (Pozsony, Sopron), as well as eight incorporated towns (Bazin, Modor, Nagyszombat, [Pozsony]Szentgyörgy; Kismarton, Ruszt, Kőszeg, Szombathely). The total population of the intended territory was 1,203,532. The average distribution in the four counties of the two most populous groups was 46.6% Hungarian and 31.2% German.

As well, the irredentist agitators also voiced a claim to a strip of about 1,000-1,200 km² part of Zala County, located in the southwest of Trans-Danubia, populated by ethnic Magyars. The claim covered, to a lesser or greater degree, the western parts of the Sümeg, Zalaszentgrót, Zalaegerszeg, Nova, Alsólendva and Csáktornya districts, citing their key importance. The claim extended up to the railway line running from Celldömölk – Türje – Zalaegerszeg – Lenti – Alsólendva – Csáktornya in Zala County. In its entirety, Hungary's former ally, Austria – both of who were on the losing side in WWI – strove to appropriate about 16,000 km² of western Hungarian territory.

The Austrian territorial claims set down in mid-November of 1918 appeared not only at the level of creating and influencing public opinion but was followed by action. *Before* the (previously mentioned) Declaration of State by the Austrian National Council made its official territorial claim, the *Westungarische Kanzlei* (Western Hungary Bureau) was created in Vienna.[25] The apparent goal of the Bureau was to organize, seemingly without the

---

[24] Ibid, p. 74.
[25] The political leadership of the *Westungarische Kanzlei* consisted of: Rep. Neunteufel, dr. Ernst Wallheim, teacher, as well as Adam Müller-Guttenbrunn (1852–1923), writer and theater manager. The last named person moved from the souther Hungarian Banate to Vienna. In his earlier endeavours, he tried to strengthen the consciousness of Germans living in the Carpathian Basin, while also proclaiming the ideals of a 'Greater Germany' and belonged to the confidential inner circle of the heir to the throne, Archduke Franz Ferdinand. In: Gagyi, op. cit., pp. 7–8; Világirodalmi lexikon [Encyclopedia of world literature] vol. 8. Editor-in-chief Király, István. Budapest, 1982, p. 701. The *Westungarische Kanzlei* later operated as the Burgenländer League.

knowledge of the National Council but, in reality, with its support, volunteer armed forces to occupy Hungarian territories marked for annexation. It can be supposed that this Bureau is identical with the *Westungarische Abteilung* (Western Hungary Department) set up around this time within the Austrian Interior Affairs Office, which also had a military branch. The Department's goal was to organize, in advance, the public administration of the to-be-occupied Hungarian territories. Its military head, a Captain Weigert, first launched an attack of armed volunteers from the direction of the Styrian town of Fürstenfeld[26], aiming to take Németújvár. Once there, to proclaim the *Heanzenland* (in some sources *Hienzenland*) *Republic*,[27] which would have later declared its union with Austria. The General Staff of the Department finally decided that a military attack must be aimed toward Sopron as that was chosen as the center for *Heanzenland*.

The name chosen for the short-lived state of Heanzenland came from the word 'heanc,' the name of a Germanic group. It meant 'the province of the Heanc.' The number of *Heanc* (or *Hienz*) living in western Hungary in the 19th-20th century was around 300,000, of whom about 125,000 lived in Vas County, in the districts of Felsőőr (now Oberwart), Németújvár (Güssing), Körmend, Kőszeg and Szentgotthárd, as well as in Sopron County's Felsőpulya (Oberpullendorf) district. On the other hand, not everybody called the inhabitants of the Kismarton and Nagymarton districts as Heanc. In Moson County's Nezsider district, lying on the North and East shores of Lake Fertő, its people were called Heidebauers.[28] According to different sources, after WWI, the *Heanc* or *Hienz* population of Sopron and Vas counties was 226,000, whose "language was distinctively different than the German-speaking Austrians of Styria and Lower Austria."[29] German farmers living in and around Sopron were referred to as poncichters, who made their living primary from viticulture.[30]

---

[26] Fürstenfeld is located immediately next to the millenial Austrian-Hungarian border in the Graz Basin of Styria, which was, for a period, part of Hungary in the Árpád era (XIII century).

[27] The Frankish and chiefly Bavarian-origin Germans (not Austrians) living in the western parts of Moson, Sopron and Vas counties have, for centuries, called themselves as Heidebauer, Poncichter and Hienc / Heanc. For more information, see: Schwartz, Elemér: A nyugatmagyarországi németek eredete [The origins of the western Hungarian Germans]. In: *Ethnographia,* vol. XXXII, 1921, pamph. 1-6, pp. 113–119; Thirring-Waisbecker, Irén: Néhány szó a heancok eredetéről [A few words on the origin of the Heanc]. In: *Ethnographia,* vol. XXXIII, 1922, pamph. 1-6, pp. 99–102; A magyarországi németek [The Germans of Hungary]. Ed. Manherz, Károly. In: *Változó Világ,* vol. 23. Budapest, 1998, p. 7.

[28] Brenner, Vilmos: A hiénc néptörzs egykor és ma [The Hienc tribe, once and today]. In: *Vasi Szemle,* vol. LII, 1998, issue 5, p. 611.

[29] Thirring-Waisbecker, Irén: A nyugatmagyarországi németek és a nemzetiségi kérdések [The Germans of western Hungary and the ethic questions]. Budapest, 1920, p. 4.

[30] In the Hungarian usage of German, *pohnzichter* came originally from

17

The naming of the Western Hungary Bureau, and Department, was not unintentional. The German-speaking population of Moson, Sopron and Vas counties have, for decades, used *Westungarn*, or Western Hungary to refer to it. In the Fall of 1918, there was still not a word of *Burgenland* as that, as Austria's ninth federated province, only came into being later, on January 1, 1922. Its boundaries were finalized in the same year by the Council of the League of Nations. Hence, Burgenland did not exist before 1922 in a historical, geographic, political or legal sense. This author does not refer to this political aggregation called today as Burgenland when looking back to the Trianon Treaty, the Sopron plebiscite and the border drawn after boundary adjustments, or previous centuries. The decades and centuries before 1922, Austrian politics (and ideology), historiography, ethnography and other sciences consistently refer to the former western Hungarian territory sharing the Austrian-Hungarian border as Burgenland. This is historically inaccurate, a twisting of the facts and a crude falsification.[31] It s important to note that, in recent decades, – and some even today – numerous Hungarian historians, ethnographers and other scientists slavishly use the term 'Burgenland' when talking about the pre-1922 events of Moson, Sopron and Vas counties, even going back to centuries ago.

To return to the events of the day: on December 2, 1918, Austrian army officers drove to Szentmargitbánya, a small community on the shore of Lake Fertő. There, they "hastily assembled the miners from the quarry, made all manner of rosy promises to them, and got them to exclaim their desire to separate from Hungary. Next, they fired up the mob to go to the next town of

---

bohnenzüchter, meaning 'bean grower.' (Bohne 'bean' / züchten 'grower'). Traditionally, the name stems from the fact that, to make better use of the land, grape growers planted a lot of beans between the rows.

[31] According to the leading figure of post-WWII Austrian ethnography, Leopold Schmidt (1912–1981), 'Burgenland' has been much more a part of Lower Austria's culture since the end of the Turkish period than of Hungary's. [Hungary was reconquered from Turkish occupation in 1686-*ed*.] A three-volume book published between the wars (fourth published in 1959), purporting to be the definitive bibliography of 'Burgenland,' traced the borders created in 1922 back to 1800. See, Litschauer, G. Franz: Bibliographie zur Geschichte, Landes- und Volkskunde des Burgenlandes 1800–1929. Vols. 1–3, Linz–Wels, 1933–1938. Vol. 4, Eisenstadt, 1959. It was in regard to the three-volume Litschauer bibliography that Károly Mollay (1913-1997), linguist, Germanophile wrote in 1939 that: "…I pointed out that purposeful work of the Germans, through which they wish to intellectually appropriate the history of not only 'Burgenland' but all of western Hungary. Since then, the expropriation of Hungarian intellectual achievements was begun with seemingly amazing planning. It is this direction that Litschauer's book serves. His title promises a book on Burgenland but his Burgenland includes Körmend, Vasvár, Szombathely, Sopron and Pozsony, too, with every Magyar element of our culture. In any case, it is strange to find such thesis shift in a scientific work but, beyond the political objective, we must also admit to Litschauer's great scientific achievement." In: *Soproni Szemle,* 1939, issues 1–2, p 91.

Ruszt, chase away the (Hungarian) authorities and declare there too their wish of joining with Austria. Some part of the mob started out but broke up at the edge of the village and turned back."[32]

Delighted by its seeming success, the *Westungarische Kanzlei* decided to distribute weapons among the German-speaking population of western Hungary for the purpose of an insurrection, to enable it to wrest, by force of arms, the marked-for-appropriation Hungarian territories. Each shipment of arms, accompanied by an Austrian military escort, was sent to the border crossing railway station of Wiener Neustadt, from there on to Lajtaújfalu and the county seat, Nagymarton. At the same time, it tried to fulfill another goal: to acquire (rob) foodstuffs for the starving capital, Vienna, and its surrounding Austrian population. The reason for this was that the people of Vienna and of the surrounding industrial zone have, for decades past, took it as natural that Hungarian agricultural produce would be available to them. They "visited the weekly farmers markets in Sopron and took home whatever struck their fancy. This now [due to the declaration of an independent Hungary] ceased, the [Hungarian] border guards ruthlessly confiscated all foods, contributing to the spread of anti-Hungarian hatred among Austrians, but especially among Hungarian citizens living in Vienna and their relatives in Hungary. Thus, the agitation found fertile soil on both sides of the border. They voiced nationalistic slogans but thought of their stomachs. Official circles viewed with dismay that the feeding of Austria was impossible without Hungary and, as an independent country – no longer an Austrian dependency – they tried to appropriate a portion [of western Hungary] to feed Vienna.[33]

On the morning of December 5, an Austrian military truck pulled into the Hungarian border settlement of Lajtaújfalu, beside the Sopron-Vienna railway tracks. On it were eight non-coms under the command of Lt. Franz Temmer, formerly a schoolteacher in Wiener Neustadt. The intruders cut the telephone wires, disarmed the border guards and surrounded the barracks of the gendarmerie. However, the Hungarian railway security detail attacked them and, after a short firefight, captured the Austrian unit and their equipment. This prevented them from handing out the 300 Mannlicher (5-shot) repeating rifles and large amount of ammunition on the truck earmarked for the Austrian workers who were hurrying on foot to Lajtaújfalu.[34] The lieutenant and his followers were arrested. At the Sopron police station, Temmer made a statement that Captain Mühlhofer, commander of the Wiener Neustadt Home Guard, ordered the occupation of Lajtaújfalu. The event stirred up a lot of dust. The Austrian authorities offered in their defense that the illegal incursion into Hungarian territory was the act of an overzealous army officer.

However, the fact is that, on the same December 5, messengers appeared

---

[32] Gagyi, op. cit., p. 6.

[33] Ibid.

[34] Fogarassy, László: A nyugat-magyarországi kérdés katonai története [The military history of the Western Hungary question]. Part I. 1918, December – 1921, August. In: *Soproni Szemle,* Year XXV, 1971, issue 4, p. 291.

in the German-speaking settlements of Sopron County, handing out the pamphlets of the Viennese *Westungarische Kanzlei*. The flyers informed the residents that on the same afternoon, the independent *Heanzenland Republic* will be proclaimed in Sopron to unite all the German populated areas of *Westungarn*. Although such an event did not occur, the evening editions of Viennese newspapers carried the official announcement of the *Westungarische Kanzlei*. It stated that the representatives of the German settlements of Western Hungary proclaimed their separation from Hungary in Sopron and declared an independent republic called *Heanzenland*.[35]

Also on December 5, an Austrian detachment sent to the Nagymarton district center reached its destination and handed over 300 rifles and about 50,000 rounds of ammunition to the local Austria-friendly home guard. The creation of the *Heanzenland Republic* was officially proclaimed in the town on the following day, whose armed units began the occupation of the surrounding area. Units were sent out to the neighboring settlements of Márcfalva and Borbolya. All communication with the county center, Sopron, was severed. However, residents of Nagymarton were able to notify the Sopron authorities of the armed attack. The *Heanzenland Republic* was in existence for only one day because an armored train arrived from Sopron the following day with a machine gun detachment. At their appearance, the local irregulars, made up of Austrian-leaning ethnic-German Hungarian citizens, put down their weapons without a fight.[36] The leaders of the Austrian detachment were arrested and criminal charges laid. However, *at the instruction of the Károlyi government, they soon received a general amnesty*. Their cautionary punishment would have had a dampening effect on the treasonous, Austria-friendly attempts.

With the elimination of *Heanzenland*, a company of soldiers was sent to each of Lajtaszentmiklós and Lajtaújfalu, the latter an important railway station next to the Austrian town of Ebenfurth. It was done because the Austrian lieutenant confessed that shortly an armored train was going to attack, supported by a *Volkswehr* (National Guard) battalion. The Austrian National Council, of course, officially denied that it had a hand in the Austrian incursion into Western Hungary, as well as the proclamation of *Heanzenland*, again attributing the military attacks to individual over-eagerness.

In this time period, from the Fall of 1918 to the middle of April, 1919, the 200 km. stretch of the Hungarian-Austrian border from the Danube to the Mura rivers was guarded by an insignificant Hungarian military force. Its security, as well as border inspection, was organized and manned by the 18th brigade of Vas-Sopron County, set up on March 31, 1919, whose strength on April 16 was a mere 1,622 men. The unit was headquartered in Szombathely and was organized into four battalions. Over and above, four machine gun

---

[35] Gagyi, op. cit., p. 7.
[36] Fogarassy, 1971. Op. cit., pp.291–292.

companies were also created. Company 3, with a mixed battalion, was stationed in the strategic Vas County settlement of Köpcsény, on the right bank of the Danube, across from Pozsony, which was then under Czechoslovak occupation. The Köpcsény defensive sector, from Dévény to Oroszvár and on to Rajka, was held by the following forces: 862 soldiers, 47 officers, 178 horses, 20 machineguns and 12 artillery pieces.[37]

The reasons for the minuscule military strength of Western Hungary go back six months. Of them, the most important: Károlyi and his government's restrained – and blind trust in the Entente Powers' promises – behavior, the unwise disarming of Hungarian military units returning from the eastern and Italian fronts, the blameworthy neglect to organize national self-defense, the deliberate obstruction of armed resistance. In other words, the imprudent and evil policy of voluntary surrender. On top of it, Károlyi fell for the siren song of Wilsonism, – which had no more effective meaning for Hungary – the fevered dreams of pacifism and the fruitless quagmire of the exchange of diplomatic notes of the Paris Peace Conference and the Entente Powers.

What was the number of Hungarian soldiers returning from the fronts in the Fall of 1918? With the authorization of the Károlyi government, Béla Linder (1876–1962), Minister for War, issued an order on November 1 – while the truce terms were being negotiated in Padua between the Monarchy and the Entente – to all the Hungarian forces on all the fronts to lay down their arms. He did this two days before the truce agreement was signed (Nov. 3), making the armed defense of Hungary impossible! With this order, Prime Minister (later president of the republic) Károlyi, his Minister for War, Linder, and after November 4, the Undersecretary responsible for disarmament, Vilmos Böhm (1880–1949) and their circle, are guilty of treason against the country and the nation for ignoring Hungarian national interests. They failed to organize defenses against the Czech-Slovak, Romanian and Serb forces that broke into the country. Serving foreign interests, they deliberately disarmed and demoralized the returning units from the fronts, from the beginning of November to the end of December 1918. The returning army was mostly in orderly units, under the command of officers, carrying their weapons and artillery. Böhm, in his biography, disclosed the following numbers: "By the end of November (1918), almost 700,000 soldiers were demobilized, by the middle of December, their number reached 1,200,000. Total demobilization was completed by the end of December."[38] In the second half of December, another source estimates

---

[37] Fogarassy, László: Sopron és az 1919-es hadszíntér [Sopron and the 1919 battlefield]. In: *Soproni Szemle*, 1961, issue 1, p. 75; Fogarassy, László: A Magyar Tanácsköztársaság vörös hadseregének köpcsényi védőszaka [The Köpcsény defensive sector of the Red Army of the Hungarian Soviet Republic]. In: *Soproni Szemle*, 1960, issue 3, p. 251.

[38] Böhm, Vilmos: Két forradalom tüzében. (Októberi forradalom. Proletárdiktatúra. Ellenforradalom.) [In the inferno of two revolutions. (October Revolution. Dictatorship of the Proletariat. Counter-revolution.)]. Published: *Verlag für*

another 300,000 soldiers returning from the battlefield and disarmed. Thus, in total, the Károlyi government disarmed a total of 1.5 million soldiers.[39] It is important to examine the ethnic composition of this huge force (never having been done by any Hungarian historian in the past 90 years) to ascertain the proportion of Magyars among the demobilized. Relying on them, it is felt that the Károlyi government could have organized a national armed resistance for the defense of the country, if it was their intention to do so. All the more so since the strength of the enemy armies were – as shown later – extremely modest, considering their military objectives.

The territory of the Kingdom of Hungary, including Transylvania – minus the previously departed allied country of Croatia-Slavonia and the territory of Fiume – was 282,870 km^2, with a population, according to the 1910 census, of 18,264,533. The ethnic distribution was: Hungarian 9,944,627 (54.45%), Romanian 2,948,186 (16.14%), Slovak 1,946,357 (10.66%), German 1,903,357 (10.42%), Ruthenian 464,270 (2.54%), Serb 461,516 (2.53%), and Croat 194,808 (1.07%). Thus, the proportion of non-Hungarians is 45.55%.[40] Drawing a conclusion from the census data and the national composition of the population – after the departure of the Slovak, Serb and Romanian soldiers to their mother countries – the number of Hungarian soldiers can be calculated accurately, which we will disclose in rounded numbers. In the two months, ending in December of 1918, of the returning 1.5 million soldiers – given the ethnic proportions – 816,000 were ethnic Hungarians. Of all the nationalities that have lived for centuries together in the Carpathian basin with Hungarians, only Prince Ferenc Rákóczi II's (1676-1735) most faithful people (*gens fidelissima*), the Ruthenians (Rusyns), could be given Hungarian weapons because they did not attack Hungarians in the back as the Slovaks, Serbs and Romanians have done for centuries. The Rusyns fought in the 1848-1849 Freedom Revolution – the "Kossutova vojna" (Kossuth War) as they called it – on the Hungarian side. By the end of 1918, 46,000 Rusyn soldiers returned from the fronts. By the way, the overwhelming proportion of the Germans of Hungary (Schwabians, Zipsers, Saxons) were not hostile toward Hungary, as proven by their voluntarily becoming Hungarians in great numbers and of whom about 190,000 soldiers saw active duty. In total then, 862,000 soldiers (816,000 Hungarian and 46,000 Rusyn) could have been fielded to face the intruding Czech-Slovak, Romanian and Serb forces. This

---

Kulturpolitik, München, 1923, p. 78.

[39] This fact of the period, forgotten for decades, was republished in the Kadar-era, after dressing it in appropriate ideological attire and twisting of facts. In: Az első világháború és a forradalmak képei [WWI and scenes of revolutions]. Szerk./ed.: Farkas,Márton – Józsa, Antal - Vajdáné Csizmarik, Irén – Varga, Éva. Budapest, 1977, Európa Könyvkiadó, p. 424.

[40] Lőkkös, János: Trianon számokban. Az 1910. évi magyar népszámlálás anyanyelvi adatainak elemzése a történelmi Magyarországon [Trianon in numbers. The analysis of the data of the 1910 census by mother tongue in historical Hungary]. Budapest, 2000, pp. 197, 236.

number would have to be, of necessity, lowered by several tens of thousands who were seriously injured and maimed but it still represented a sizeable force.

The former Marxist-Communist, and the current Left-Liberal, historiography has for decades spread the lie that the Hungarian-speaking soldiers returning from the fronts in November-December of 1918 were exhausted and did not want to fight on in defense of the country. The reality was that (as we wrote earlier) the overwhelming majority returned to the country in disciplined formations, with their weapons and artillery, under the command of their officers. What gives a lie to the Marxists' and Liberals' statements, among other things, is that, within six months of the disarmament of the returning armies, in three weeks in May of 1919, the Hungarian Soviet Republic was able to organize an army of 200,000 battle tested veterans, with a professional officer corps, under the slogan of territorial integrity and defense of the country. The Red Army of the Hungarian Soviet dictatorship was able to carry out a victorious Northern military campaign between May 30 and June 24, 1919 up to a line running along Komárom – Nyitra/Nitriansky –Besztercebánya/Banská Bystrica – Rozsnyó/Rožňava – Eperjes/Prešov – Bártfa/Bardejov. In fact, they beat back the invading Czech-Slovak forces to the proximity of the Polish border. The Hungarian forces were pulled back as a result of Clemenceau's mendacious promises – sent in notes on June 7 and 13 – that the Romanian forces would pull out of the Hungarian Plains South of the Tisza River. As it was, with Entente permission, the Romanian occupiers were allowed to remain in possession up the Great Plains up to the Tisza River.[41]

In the ranks of the Hungarian Red Army, there were, as young officers – colonels, brigadiers, division and corps commanders – twenty major- and lieutenant-generals of what was to become the Hungarian Royal Military in the 1920-1945 period in the Horthy (so-called counter-revolutionary) era. From their ranks came three minister of defense, four chief-of-staff and various high ranking officers, whose military career continued unbroken after being accepted into the new armed forces following a 1920 security check. Of special interest is the typical story of one Demeter Stojakovics (1883-1946), of Serb origins but he Hungarianized his name to Sztójay Döme in 1935. During the Hungarian Soviet Republic days, he was chief of military intelligence and counter-intelligence. He joined the Hungarian National Army in August of 1919, where he served from 1920 as the chief of military intelligence and counter-intelligence departments of the General Staff. Next, he was posted as military attaché in Berlin (1925-1933), promoted to full general in 1935, then served as Hungarian ambassador in Berlin (Dec. 1935-March 1944), finally rising to Prime Minister (and Foreign Minister) of Hungary between March and August, 1944. In the second half of the Horthy

---

[41] Bertényi, Iván – Gyapay, Gábor: Magyarország rövid története [Short history of Hungary]. Budapest, 1992, pp. 511–513.

era, fully two-thirds of the Hungarian military elite (112 officers or 65.12%) served in the Red Army of the Hungarian Soviet Republic.[42]

To return to the situation at the end of WWI, what was the size of the forces that attacked Hungary beginning on November 1, 1918?

Czech-Slovakia: "Armed Czech forces available in early November of 1918 for the occupation of Northern Hungary were made up of Sokolists,[43] volunteer units and Slovak recruits of soldiers and irregulars. Their number by the end of November did not exceed 4,000. (...) The situation of the Czech army improved considerably when units arrived from the Italian and French fronts, the Czechoslovak Legions made up of soldiers and deserters."[44] According to the Dec. 7, 1918 official data of the Czech-Slovak forces, according to Prague headquarters, the Slovak portion of the force which attacked Northern Hungary was, in total: 6,788 men, 317 officers, 41 cavalry, 158 engineers (7,304 in total), 75 machine guns, 4 cannons, 1 armored train, and three airplanes. For the occupation of Northern Hungary, North of the zone from the Czech/Moravian border, from Dévény along the Danube through Vác – Gyöngyös – Mezőkövesd – Miskolc – Tokaj – Sátoraljaújhely – Ungvár – along the Ung River to the Uzsok Pass and up to the Hungarian-Polish border, an area of approx. 60,000 km^2, the Czech-Slovak military order-of-battle counted on 8,300 men and 50 horses.[45]

Romania: According to the latest archival sources, the Romanian forces which made a surprise attack on Transylvania at the end of the first week of November, 1918 – without a declaration of war – were badly equipped, without logistical support (thus the starving forces robbed and looted daily)[46] was estimated at 4-5,000.[47] This datum is partially misleading as the size of the Royal Romanian forces that attacked Transylvania could, in the following week or two, swell to double or triple with the addition of disorganized, and of little military value, local Romanian guards and armed irregulars. The main objective, initially, was the conquest of about two-thirds of Transylvania

---

[42] Szakály, Sándor: A magyar katonai elit 1938–1954 [The Hungarian military elite 1938-1945]. Budapest, 1987, pp. 163–208.

[43] A Czech sporting movement. The Czech word 'Sokol' means 'hawk.' The association was Czechoslovakia's most popular athletic organization between the wars.

[44] Incze, Kálmán: Háborúk a nagy háború után. A béke háborúi [Wars after the Great War. The wars of the peace] Vol. I. Budapest, 1938, pp. 27–28.

[45] Hronský, Marián: Priebeh vojenského obsadzovania Slovenska československým vojskom od novembra 1918 do januára 1919 [The occupation of Slovakia by the Czech military from Nov. 1918 to Jan. 1919]. In: Historický časopis, 1984, iss. 5, pp. 734–755. Kiad. Honvéd Hagyományőrző Egyesület, Budapest, 1993, p. 21.

[46] Raffay, Ernő: Erdély 1918–1919-ben [Transylvania in 1918-1919]. Szeged, 1988, pp. 138, 141, 331, 336, 340, 352, 358–359.

[47] Fráter, Olivér: Erdély román megszállása 1918–1919 [Romanian occupation of Transylvania 1918-1919]. Logos Grafikai Műhely. Tóthfalu (Vajdaság), 1999, p. 47; Eördögh, István: Erdély román megszállása (1916–1920) [Romanian occupation of Transylvania (1916-1920). Szeged, 2000.

(about 38,500 km^2) up to the line of demarcation as detailed in the armistice document signed in Belgrade on Nov. 13, 1918. The line ran along the Maros River up to the headwaters of the Greater Szamos River. This meant that the Royal Romanian Army could, with no obstacles, take possession of areas South and East of the Maros River from Arad, from Marosvásárhely (Tirgu Mureş) North to the county seat of Beszterce (Bistriţa), from there to the headwaters of the Greater Szamos River, turning East to the eastern Carpathian Radnai Pass. The Belgrade agreement meant that Romanian forces were free to march into, and occupy all of, Krassó-Szörény, Szeben, Kis-Küküllő, Fogaras, Nagy-Küküllő, Brassó, Maros-Torda, Csík, Udvarhely, Háromszék counties, as well as lesser or greater portions of Hunyad, Alsó-Fehér, Beszterce-Naszód and Kolozs counties.

The Romanian Army advancing in Transylvania and the Banate did not encounter military resistance (end of November and early December) and, with insignificant forces (often units of only 20 or 30), occupied the cities and town of Transylvania, and the other named places.[48] The Bucharest military command's major objective, apart from seizing Transylvania, was to take possession of eastern Hungary up to the Tisza River, as well as two-thirds of Sub-Carpathia to the line of Csap (Čop) – Nagydobrony (Velika Dobrony) – Munkács (Mukačevo) – Szolyva (Свалява/Szvaljava) – Verecke Pass.

The three parts of Hungarian territory claimed by Romania covered an area of 135,000 km^2, an area the size of Greece or Alabama.

An eyewitness, the camp chaplain of the Szekler Division, Endre Koréh, wrote in his book: "...after French intercession, the Magyar (sic) government began negotiations regarding the handing over of Kolozsvár. The command, the officer corps, down to the youngest Szekler soldier, were convinced that this is treason and senseless, as were the Belgrade negotiations and agreement. The Szeklers, with commendable fighting spirit, wanted to crush the weak forces that broke into Transylvania that *did not even number 8,000*.[49]

István Apáthy[50] (1863-1922), Chief government Commissioner of eastern Hungary (Transylvania), well informed of the current situation, wrote the following regarding the loss of Transylvania: "Initially, some small [Romanian] units entered through the Tölgyes Pass, followed through the Borgó Pass and mostly through the Gyimes Pass, from where they shortly entered Csíkszereda (Miercuera Ciuc). Later, after the retreat of the German

[48] Mikes, Imre: Erdély útja. Nagymagyarországtól Nagyromániáig [The path of Transylvania. From Greater Hungary to Greater Romania]. Sepsiszentgyörgy, 1996, pp. 151–152.
[49] Koréh, Endre: „Erdélyért". A székely hadosztály és dandár története 1918–1919 ["For Transylvania." The history of the Szekler division and brigade]. II. ed., Budapest, 1929, p. 113. (Bolding mine–*J.B.*)
[50] István Apáthy, instructor at the Franz Joseph University of Sciences and world renowned scientist due to his research in histology, was named by the Hungarian government as Chief Government Commissioner on Dec. 7, 1918, after having been the president of the Kolozsvár, and later the Transylvanian, National Council.

forces (led by Field Marshal Mackensen), they also entered from Predeal [at the time, a border post South of the Tömös Pass–J.B.] *In total, their troop strength in Transylvania around Dec. 10 could only have been around 15,000, according to information reported to me.*[51]

According to Romanian (Bucharest) military archival documents made public at the end of the 1960s, *only at the end of December of 1918 did the Romanian army's strength that invaded Transylvania reach 39,000.*[52] It can be reasonably assumed that the military command in Bucharest added to the occupying forces the numbers of Transylvanian and local Romanian free forces and irregulars. As an aside, the arming of the latter was done from the supplies of the Hungarian army, by permission of the Károlyi government. Samuel Barabás, dean in Kolozsvár, noted in his diary for December 5, 1918: *"The Hungarian National Council supplies the Romanians with weapons, gives them ammunition and money from the state coffers. Perhaps it is also stipulated that they can only shoot at Hungarians with those rifles."*[53] The dean took part in the Dec. 5 session of the Szekler National Council, where he publicly disclosed the previous to the present István Apáthy, still president at the time of the Transylvanian Hungarian National Council, who "listened with a pale face."

Serbia: After being dealt a defeat by the armies of the Monarchy, the Serbian army withdrew to the island of Corfu. Between Nov. 7 and 19, the partly reorganized Serb force occupied – by simply marching in – huge Hungarian territories North of the border of the Kingdom of Hungary, up to the line of demarcation agreed upon on November 7 in the armistice document in Belgrade. Serbia, however, also laid claims to the Banate, portions of the Muraköz (Medimurje) and the Vend region – a total of about 45,000 km^2 of Hungarian territory. When Béla Linder, minister without portfolio, signed the Belgrade Convention on November 13 in the name of the Károlyi government[54] – with which Hungary negated the favorable truce negotiated in Padua, which did not disturb the historical borders of Hungary, leaving them unaltered(!) – Serb forces, with occupied Újvidék (Novi Sad) behind them, reached the line of Antalfalva – Pancsova – Versec in the Banate county of Torontál. The Belgrade agreement granted free hand to the achievement of the majority of Serbian military objectives, since one of the signatories was Vojvod Misic, chief of staff of the army. Szabadka (Subotica)

---

[51] Apáthy, István: Erdély az összeomlás után [Transylvania after the collapse]. In: *Új Magyar Szemle*, vol. III, issue 2, 1920, December, p. 168. (Bolding mine–J.B.)

[52] Magyarország története 1918–1919, 1919–1945 [History of Hungary 1918-1919, 1919-1945]. Ed.-in-chief: Ránki, György. Budapest, 1976, p. 117.

[53] Mikes, op. cit., p. 139.

[54] The full title of the Belgrade Convention, signed on November 13: *Military Convention Regulating the Conditions under which the Armistice, Signed between the Allies and Austria-Hungary, is to be applied in Hungary.* See Nyékhegyi, 1922, op. cit., pp. 58–61. Original in Hungarian National Archives (Hereafter MOL), K 28, bundle 1, item 2, 1918–II, number 103, pp. 1–4.

was occupied on Nov. 13 by Serb forces. The armistice pact detailed a line starting at Varasd along the Drava River, then along a line 5-20 km. North of the of the railway line of Barcs – Szigetvár – Pécs – Bátaszék – Baja – Szabadka (Subotica) – Szeged, then from the confluence of the Tisza and Maros Rivers, ending at the city of Arad, which was occupied on November 21. This realized two-thirds of Serbian territorial aims vis-à-vis Hungary because south of this line represented a successful occupation of approx. 30,000 km^2 of Hungarian territory. With this operation, the units of the Kingdom of Serbia took control of the entirety of Torontál County, almost the entirety of Temes, Bács-Bodrog and Baranya counties and the southeast corner of Somogy County.

The Serb armed forces advancing unopposed into southern Hungary in 1918 were made up of about 20,000 armed men. However, a good third of this strength were local irregulars, of negligible military value, newly released Orthodox Serb prisoners of war, forcibly recruited farmers, shepherds and "Bunyevci peasants [Roman Catholics of Croatian origins] who had a Serbian cap put on their heads." The Serb military command quickly armed them with weapons and ammunition left behind by the Austro-Hungarian armies and sent them across the Száva (Sava) River to occupy the Szerémség (Syrmia), part of Croatia-Slavonia, an associated country with Hungary. However, the forces available were not adequate to achieve the Serbian objectives. In early November, the Entente forces in the Balkans were far from Hungary's southern border and, in any case, were undergoing a process of replenishment of ranks.

The ranks of the Serbian army only reached a strength of 30,000 six months later. The following data were recounted by Vilmos Böhm, at the time one of the armed forces commissars of the Hungarian Soviet Republic and the commander of the Hungarian Red Army: During the second half of May, 1919, in the southern sector, under the high command in Eszék (Osijek), three divisions of the Serbian Army (Drina, Morava, Duna) were stationed (21,500 infantry, 1,300 cavalry and 54 artillery pieces), while in the Muraköz (Medimurje) sector, a further division with approx. 7,000–7,200 men.[55]

On the other side of the equation, the Károlyi government could have fielded a force of 200,000 to 300,000 men, mainly Hungarians and Rusyns, to oppose the attack on Hungary, which was comprised of about 4,000 Czech-Slovak, 4-5,000 Romanian and approx. 20,000 Serbian forces. A total of perhaps 28-29,000 in all. Since he failed to do so, Mihály Károlyi, the 'Red count' and his associates have – as we have already written – committed the crime of treason.

---

[55] Böhm, op. cit., pp. 280–281.

Chapter 2: The annexing of the western parts of Moson, Sopron and Vas counties to Austria

Saint-Germain-en-Laye, October, 1918 – September 10, 1919

The Austrian forces attacking Western Hungary, especially around Sopron, were defeated and the *Heanzenland Republic*, in existence for all of one day, was abolished in early December of 1918. The main reason was Austria's weak military position. In spite of it, aspirations for secession / detachment from Hungary continued to grow, primarily inflamed by Austrian circles embracing the idea of Greater Germany. Since October, the civic officials in the counties of Moson, Sopron and Vas saw its prevention as their most important task. It is a fact, though, that separation from Hungary was fuelled by serious economic difficulties. As an example, confidential reports sent to the High Constable of Vas County in the latter half of 1918 reported, among other things, that due to lack of food, the German-speaking population was becoming insolent towards the Hungarian authorities. For some time, it was impossible to obtain basic necessities in the villages, such as petroleum for lighting, along with salt and sugar. Hence, the people of some border villages threatened that, if the Hungarian government did not provide adequate supplies, then they would join Austria.

At the November 25, 1918 meeting of the Vas County Municipal Committee declared that "the Austrian annexation attempt was an attack fuelled by greed and categorically rejected it." The minutes of the same meeting went on to record: "The municipality is open to the populace of the named areas exercising their unique national culture. (…) It is not opposed to the idea that the population receives education and public administration in their language." The administrators of Vas County, in effect, laid out a third option as a solution to the German question: secession/annexation, or autonomy. The German demands could be satisfied by increasing their linguistic and cultural rights, within the framework of existing administrative constraints.[56]

---

[56] Soós, Katalin. A nyugat-magyarországi kérdés 1918–1919 [The question of Western Hungary]. Budapest, 1962, p. 10. Regarding sources: For two decades following the March 1938 annexation of Austria by Germany (*Anschluss*), no Hungarian-language publication was published treating the territorial change of Őrvidék / Burgenland. At the beginning of WWII, several pamphlets were published: Követeljük Burgenlandot [We demand Burgenland]. (Egyesült Magyar Nemzeti Szocialista Párt, Budapest, 1938.); Pálosy, I.: Nem sértjük a magyar–német barátságot. Követeljük Burgenlandot a magyar haza szent testéhez [We will not violate the Hungarian-German friendship. We demand Burgenland as part of the nation's sacred body.]. Budapest, around 1939.
After the 1956 Revolution and Freedom Fight, the quoted author was among the first to address the question under the name G. Soós, Katalin: Adalékok a Magyar Tanácsköztársaság és az Osztrák Köztársaság kapcsolatainak történetéhez. A nyugat-magyarországi kérdés 1919. március–augusztus [Addenda to the history of relations

The tacit support by the Austrian government for western Hungarian secessionist aspirations and the officially declared claims of the Vienna government for the territory of Western Hungary significantly contributed to the December 3 semi-official announcement of the Károlyi government: it supported the autonomy petition expressed by the Germans of Hungary. The idea of self-government found support primarily in the city of Sopron and its surroundings. A German National Council was organized in the city by Géza Zsombor, which claimed the right to represent the interests of all the Germans in Western Hungary. Géza Zsombor published a 70 page German-language pamphlet in the second half of the following year (Sopron, Corvina publishing) titled *Western-Hungary. With Hungary or Austria?*[57] The question, or territorial affiliation, would drag on until the end of 1921.

Initially, the German National Council only asked for ending the mandatory use of the Hungarian language in public administration and educational matters. However, shortly after, it proposed to the government the creation of a German autonomous region. Following this, adherents of autonomy held meeting after meeting until the representatives of the German-speaking population of Pozsony, Moson, Sopron and Vas counties formed, in Sopron on December 23, 1918, the Western-Hungary German People's Council (*Deutscher Volksrat für Westungarn*), which declared the autonomy of Western Hungary.[58] It is important to note that the emerging German national movement of Hungary wanted to remain within the borders of the country and did not wish to secede from Hungary, as opposed to the Slovaks, Romanians, Croatians, Vends (Slovenians) and Serbs. Two directions emerged: one, led by Jacob Bleyer (1874-1933), literary historian, linguist and politician, and two, led by Rudolph Brandsch. The difference between the two views consisted of the measure of minority rights Germans living in various parts of Hungary were to enjoy. The chief supporters of the creation of the self-administered municipality were those who did not want to join Austria. Among them were the sizeable strata of manufacturer and commercial middle class, possessing various amounts of influence, who would be shorn of their customers and markets. A sector of the press trumpeted in its articles that mainly Hungarian populated towns and county seats within the autonomous region would slowly become Germanized. At the turn of 1918-1919, the influencing of public opinion was in full swing in Western Hungary, the campaign to popularize Austria. The chief magistrates of the districts directed

---

between the Hungarian Soviet Republic and the Austrian Republic. The Western Hungarian question, March-August, 1919]. In: *Soproni Szemle*, 1959, issue 4, pp. 289–304. Also, Soós, Katalin, G.: Magyar–bajor–osztrák titkos tárgyalások és együttmüködés 1920–1921 [Hungarian-Bavarian-Austrian secret talks and collaboration]. In: *Acta Historica*, vol. XXVII. Szeged, 1967, pp. 3–43.

[57] Zsombor, Géza: Westungarn. Zu Ungarn oder zu Oesterreich [Western Hungary. In Hungary or Austria]? Corvina Verlag, Oedenburg [Sopron], 1919.

[58] Kővágó, László: A Magyarországi Tanácsköztársaság és a nemzeti kérdés [The Hungarian Soviet Republic and the national question]. Budapest, 1989, p. 78.

the notaries working in the villages to try their utmost and prevent the agitation among the populace for the secession of the territory.

It was not by accident that at the same time, the regular visits to the German populated border communities by the National Propaganda Commission increased, spreading the logic of staying with Hungary. Its Szentgotthárd office petitioned, on January 27, 1919, to ensure a supply of petroleum and a payment of 1,000 Kroner in an attempt to calm the German villages.[59] On top of all this, due to diminished public safety, robberies were frequent along the border, to the extent that armed gangs occasionally even confronted the police forces. It was for this that the border counties requested the strengthening of military units along the border. These difficulties were not only used by German propaganda, but further stirred up opinions against the country.

To address the situation, the Hungarian government publicized on January 29 the law passed the previous day, 1919:VI, titled *"On the practice of self-government of the German people of Hungary."*[60] Among other things, the statute stated that, in areas where Germans formed the majority, "autonomous self-governing zones" may be created – with the agreement of other ethnics living there. The law, within appropriate limitations, ensured complete self-governing rights for the Germans in judicial matters, governing, internal administration, the law, religious matters, public education and culture. A German Ministry was created in Budapest, with local administrators who can choose the location of their administrative centers, their areas of responsibility further subdivided into districts. Probably because Germans were living dispersed in Hungary that the new statute did not specify where their self-administrative areas were to be. This only came about during the time of the Hungarian Soviet Republic. In the days following the publication of the statute, on February 3, 1919, Mihály Károlyi, President of the Republic,[61] named János Junker, a judge on the Court of Appeals, as Minister responsible for German Affairs.

Two weeks after the passage of the 'German Ethnicity Law,' on February 14, the mayor of Sopron, Mihály Thurner,[62] also Government Commissioner,

---

[59] Kiss, Mária: Gazdasági-társadalmi és politikai viszonyok 1918 és 1945 között [Socio-economic and political matters between 1918 and 1945]. In: *Szentgotthárd*. Szerk/ed.: Kuntár, Lajos - Szabó, László. Szombathely, 1981, pp. 232–233.

[60] Collected statutes for 1919. Budapest, 1919, pp. 20–23; Bellér, Béla: Az ellenforradalom nemzetiségi politikájának kialakulása [The development of the ethnic policies of the counter-revolution]. Budapest, 1975, pp. 11–20.

[61] Károlyi earlier resigned his post as prime minister on January 11, 1919. Subsequently, Dénes Berinkey, the Minister of Justice, was named to the post on January 18, who also took the job of minister without a portfolio responsible for preparing the self-government of the minorities from Oszkár Jászi (1875-1957), who also resigned.

[62] Mihály Thurner (1878–1952) was born in Márcfalva (Sopron County), later annexed to Austria. In 1912, he assumed the job as head of Sopron's audit office.

addressed a memorandum[63] to Prime Minister Dénes Berinkey (1871-1944) regarding the "the fate of the Magyars and Germans" of the city. The head of Sopron's council first of all stated that "the German and Magyar portions of the city were equally happy" with the statute. *"there has never been an ethnic question* in our city. (...) Loud voices have only recently been heard, as a result of *Austrian agitation.* (...) The city's Hungarian National Council has always kept affairs of the county's Germans on the agenda; urged the settling of the issue, so that the movement would not deteriorate to the point which, after separation from Hungary, would lead to union with Austria." Thurner then drew attention to: *"the independence of Sopron must be maintained, even further developed.* This is what the city's economic interest requires, but the country's interests demand it, too, regardless whether we view it from the Hungarian or German point-of-view. (...) This fine goal can only be reached if the city of Sopron can remain in its present form, as chartered in 1277[64] and will not be forced to give up its rights and privileges acquired during the centuries by being forced by statute 1919:VI, § 2, to become part of the German administrative unit, or the Hungarian area governed by self-government laws."[65]

During this time, Sopron was mainly a center of trade and not industry, owing to a shortage of water, as well as an old center of learning, all of which would be lost if it melded into the German-administered portion. The mayor then went on to list the schools, some of which were founded several centuries earlier, and the number of their students.[66] At the same time, stressed Thurner, "Sopron has a need for the locating here of the German seat of administration because without it, the city would stop to grow, but it cannot give up its Hungarian institutions, either. *Sopron straddles the boundary* between the German and Hungarian populated areas. (...) Sopron cannot give

---

During WWI, he was a soldier for a while but the city recalled him citing his indispensability. Between 1918 and 1945, he was mayor of Sopron. It was during this period he performed his duties as Sopronyi-Thurner. Of his career, see Turbuly, Éva: Adatok Thurner Mihály polgármester személyének és szerepének jobb megismeréséhez a két háború közötti Sopron életében. [Details of the person and role of Mayor Thurner in the life of Sopron between the two wars] In: *Magyarok maradtunk, 1921–1996. Konferencia a soproni népszavazásról.* Sopron, 1996, December 12. [We remained Hungarians, 1921-1996. Conference of the Sopron plebiscite. Sopron, Dec. 12, 1996]. Szerk/ed.: Turbuly, Éva. Sopron, 1997, pp. 99–105; *„Tisztemben csak a város érdeke és az igazság fog vezetni"* [Only the city's interest and the truth will govern me in my post]. Szerk./ed.: Turbuly, Éva. Sopron, 1998.

[63] Thurner, Mihály: Emlékirat Sopron magyarságának és németségének sorsáról [Memorandum on the fate of the Hungarians and Germans of Sopron]. Sopron, 1919, Rábaközi Nyomda, pp. 1–11. (Sopron Archives, T 8 / 2287.)

[64] Ibid, p. 4. Sopron was made a free, royal city by King László IV (1272-1290) of the House of Árpád.

[65] MOL. K 26. 1240. csomó. 1920–XLII–2035. szám, 9. old.

[66] Ibid, pp. 10-11.

up either the Hungarian or German areas. The loss of either will cut off the circulation of a side of our city, *leading to the atrophy of our economic existence.* (…) Sopron's success can only be possible if both the Hungarians and Germans succeed, as a free, independent city, only subordinated to the national government."[67]

The statute was received with mixed feelings by the affected sides. Some groups felt that the self-government rights of the Hungarian Germans were too much; the leaders of the Western Hungary National Council, too little. They especially felt the German community lacked the right to elect a national assembly with legislative powers, and did not garner significant economic opportunities. It did not dissuade the intention of those wishing to unite with Austria. The development of an autonomous legal area completely faltered in the last weeks of the Károlyi regime, mostly due to various, often overriding, interests. One of the main reasons was that, with the planned creation of German autonomy, some villages, which have been county seats for centuries, were going to lose their position. Among them was Szentgotthárd, which had 36 German-speaking settlements in its district. The village's National Council petitioned the government in early 1919 to have Szentgotthárd be the district seat for the villages of the German autonomous area, with a German county court and office for the German county chief magistrate. The petition was taken by a delegation to the Minister of Nationalities in Budapest, to the head of the German National Council in Sopron, Géza Zsombor, and the High Constable of Vas County. The 500 copies of the appeal were printed in Szentgotthárd, in Hungarian and German, and sent to all the settlements in the district, even to all shopkeepers with the request to have it displayed in their place of business.[68] The stand of the Szentgotthárd council met with success. The delegation to Budapest reported on March 19 that they received assurance from the Minister that, within the German autonomous region, the village would remain the district center.

Mihály Károlyi handed over power to the Hungarian People's Proletariat on March 21, 1919 and the Hungarian Soviet Republic was born; the Communist-Social Democrat coalition Revolutionary Governing Council[69] assumed power. The new Nationalities Minister, Henrik Kalmar[70] (1870-1931), took over from János Junker and held the position at the German People's Commissariat as a People's Commissar, until his resignation on July

---

[67] Thurner, op. cit., pp. 9–10.

[68] Kiss, Mária, 1981, op. cit., p. 234.

[69] Revolutionary Governing Council: the highest executive body of the Hungarian Soviet Republic, which transcended governmental spheres of authority and held state and party powers. Members of the Council, on the Soviet model, were commissars, heading various commissariats that replaced the former ministries. Its president was a former bricklayer, the Social Democrat Sándor Garbai (1879-1947), but the real power was excercised by Foreign Affairs Commissar, Béla Kun.

[70] Biography of Henrik Kalmár. In: Révai Új Lexikona, vol. XI. Főszerk/ed-in-chief: Kollega, T. István. Szekszárd, 2003, p. 114.

25. Kalmar was originally a printer, was active in Pozsony as party secretary of the Social Democrats, and later became Undersecretary in the German Ministry in the Berinkey government. During the period of the Hungarian Soviet Republic, he continued on the development of autonomy of Western Hungary. The newly created county directorates published their decrees and directives in the language of the population in the German areas. The German Commissariat decreed on March 25 that for all German-language settlement, all official notification and records were to be written in German. At the same time, the instruction went on, district leaders and chief district magistrates were to announce this resolution in every German community and settlement. The April 4 decree of the Commissariat posted that local Soviets (councils) to be elected. The creation of the planned administrative arrangement of districts (*Bezirk*) and region (*Gau*) ran into a lot of difficulties – for various reasons and interests. As an example, at the April 23 meeting of the Workers' Council of Vas County, it was noted with consternation that the German-language paper, *Volksstimme*, reported that two districts of the county were to be transferred to Sopron County and a separate German district was to be formed. Many objected vehemently against the plan, especially since the Revolutionary Governing Council decided in the matter without consulting the Vas County directorate or the people.

The seven member board of the *Gaurat für Deutsch Westungarn* [German Regional Council for Western Hungary] was formed at the end of April in Sopron from the German representatives of Pozsony, Sopron, Moson and Vas counties. Sándor Kellner[71] was elected as the German Commissioner for Western Hungary. Sopron became the center for the German region. The first session of the *Gaurat Versammlung* [Regional Assembly] was on May 20 in

---

[71] Sándor Kellner (1887–1919), printer, worked in the Röttig printing shop in Sopron before WWI. He fought on the Eastern Front, fell into Russian captivity where he met Béla Kun. He returned home on Nov. 1, 1918 and was one of the founders of the Hungarian Communist Party. The Recolutionary Governing Council named him the council's commissioner for Sopron and Sopron County on March 26, 1919. As such, he also oversaw the activities of the county directorate. In the press of the day, and after 1945, the local papers often erroneously referred to his title as Commissar. Papp, István: Az első magyar proletárforradalom és a Sopronba került Bányászati és Erdészeti Főiskola 1919-ben [The first Hungarian proletarian revolution and the location of the Mining and Forestry Academy in Sopron in 1919]. In: *Soproni Szemle*, 1969, issue 1, p. 28. About the period, also see Környei, Attila: Adatok az 1919. évi Sopron vármegyei osztályharcokhoz. I. A tanácshatalom osztályjellege [Information pertaining to the class warfare of 1919 in Sopron. I. The class characteristics of the power of the Soviet]. In: *Soproni Szemle*, 1973, issue 1, pp. 24–38; II. Ellenforradalmi kísérletek [II. Counterrevolutionary attempts]. Issue 2, pp. 123–138; Koncsek, László: A bécsi és Sopron megyei ellenforradalom kapcsolatai 1919-ben. I. rész [The counterrevolutionary relationship of Vienna and Sopron County in 1919. Part I.]. In: *Soproni Szemle*, 1956, issue 2, pp. 97–115; II. rész. A bécsi és soproni ellenforradalom kapcsolatai 1919-ben [Part II. The counterrevolutionary relationship of Vienna and Sopron in 1919.]. Ibid, 1959, issue 1, pp. 73–90.

Sopron. It was attended by three representatives from each of the Western-Hungarian German districts, a total of 90.[72] Representing the majority Hungarian-populated Felsőőr[73] (Oberwart) was Comrade Wallner, from the Kőszeg district, József Halász. Béla Kun (1886-1938) spoke at the meeting. Although officially he was only one of five Foreign Affairs Commissars, but, as the actual head of the Soviet Republic, every weighty decision had to be introduced or approved by him. It was here that he made his famous/infamous call towards Austria: "We are ready at a minute's notice to create a unified, federative country with the proletarians of German-Austria."[74]

The appearance of the Foreign Affairs Commissar in Sopron was not accidental because it was important in the interest of the Hungarian Soviet Republic to maintain good relations with its western neighbor. Also, hostile powers ringed the country, while Hungary shipped foodstuffs to Austria.[75] The Workers Council of Western-Hungary immediately objected against unification of the region with German-Austria.[76] The *Gaurat* held the same view and, citing the self-determination of people, opposed the annexation of *Westungarn*. This was not by chance because it was aware of the top echelon of the Republic's, mainly Béla Kun's intention, to voluntarily cede the demanded western Hungarian territory to a socialist-structured Austria. It was also not by chance that Kun, a little more than two months later at the collapse of the Socialist Republic, fled to Austria, where he received political asylum.

The situation of the Germans was settled at the June 23 meeting of the national meeting of Soviets, where it was incorporated into the constitution that acknowledged the Germans living in Hungary as a nation.[77] The Governing Council decreed – by decree CXXIX, based on paragraph 86 of the constitution – the setting up of an ethnic German territory in western

---

[72] Gergely, Ernő: A proletárforradalom és a tanácshatalom Kárpátalján és Nyugat-Magyarországon [The proletarian revolution and Soviet power in Sub-Carpathia and Western-Hungary]. In: *Jogtudományi Közlöny*, 1963, Oct-Nov. issue, p. 548.

[73] According to the data of the 1910 census, the population of Felsőőr was 3,912. Of this, 3,039 were Hungarians (77.7%), 842 Germans (21.5%) and 17 Croatians. In: Magyarország Közigazgatási Atlasza 1914 [Hungarian public administrative atlas 1914.], op. cit., p. 109.

[74] Kővágó, op. cit., p. 58; Szinai, Miklós: A Magyar Tanácsköztársaság és Ausztria kapcsolataihoz. Otto Bauer levele Kun Bélához [The relations of the Hungarian Soviet Republic with Austria. The letter of Otto Bauer to Bela Kun]. In: *Századok*, year 103, 1969, issue 2–3, pp. 449–467; Flanner, Karl: Bécsújhely volt 1919-ben a „fordítókorong" a Magyar Tanácsköztársaság irányában [Wiener Neustadt was the 'turntable' that pointed towards the Hungarian Soviet Republic]. In: *Soproni Szemle*, 1988, issue 2, pp. 156–162.

[75] Gábor, Sándorné: Ausztria és a Magyarországi Tanácsköztársaság [Austria and the Hungarian Soviet Republic]. Budapest, 1969, p. 81.

[76] Nyugat-Magyarország proletársága az elszakadás ellen [The proletarians of Western-Hungary against secession]. In: *Népszava*, 1919, May 21.

[77] Tanácsköztársasági Törvénytár. Vol. V. Szerk/ed.: Pongrácz, Jenő. Budapest, 1919, pp. 20-21.

Hungary, to be an autonomous part of the Soviet Republic. The July 11 session endorsed the transfer of the towns of Moson, Magyaróvár,[78] Kőszeg and Szentgotthárd – all of them with a majority Hungarian population – to the German ethic region with its seat in Sopron. It brought forth much friction and sharp objections. The German region was to have consisted of the mainly German – but sometimes mixed – populated areas of Pozsony, Moson, Sopron and Vas counties (about 5,000 km^2) but Pozsony County, North of the Danube, was already under Czech-Slovak military occupation since the beginning of January 1919. The proposed plan for the German autonomous area was discussed at the June 11-14 meeting of the German Regional Council (*Deutscher Landesrat*) – introduced by Henrik Kalmár – and was forwarded to the constitutional committee with clarification of certain points. The *Landesrat* again discussed the proposal at its second meeting (July 28-29) but arrived at no decision.[79] The administration of the *Gau* that was organized in the territory – which was deemed to be an autonomous region of the Republic – was administer by the German Regional Council in Sopron and 'German-Western Hungarian Regional People's Office.' In parts of Western Hungary, especially around Felsőőr and Kőszeg but also in Moson and the western rim of Trans-Danubia, regions of Hungarian-majority settlements or islands projected into the German autonomous area. What it mean that, of the 10 districts of Vas County, four came under dual administration. The same affected 60 settlements of the Felsőőr district, 36 in Kőszeg, 51 in Szombathely, 5 in Körmend and 4 in the Muraszombat districts.[80] In the final weeks of the Hungarian Soviet Republic, a peculiar dual public administration functioned in the German autonomous region. The decrees of both the German Regional Council and the County Directorate were sent to every settlement. Unfortunately, disagreements between the two authorities were not able to be settled.

The creation of the Western-Hungarian German autonomous region came to an abrupt halt on August 1, 1919 because the Revolutionary Governing Council resigned [the communist Hungarian Soviet Republic experiment came to an end-*ed*.] and Gyula Peidl (1873-1943) formed a Unionist-Social Democrat government. Simultaneously, the leading Communist leaders and commissars, led by Béla Kun who took with him all the money in the government coffers, and their families fled by special train to Vienna. The Austrian government, with the knowledge of the Entente Powers, extended them refugee status. The Hungarian government requested their extradition already on September 5, which Austria denied. On appeal, it was also rejected in 1920 by a ruling of the Austrian Supreme Court.[81]

---

[78] The towns of Moson and Magyaróvár were later amalgamated in 1939 under the name of Mosonmagyaróvár.

[79] Kővágó, op. cit., pp. 62, 63-64, 77-82.

[80] *Tanácsköztársaság* (Hivatalos lap), 1919, July 17 (issue 94).

[81] G. Soós, Katalin: Menedékjog vagy kiszolgáltatás [Refugee status or extradition]? In: *Századok*, 1963, issue 2, pp. 369–381.

The president of the so-called 'behind the front committees' – in reality summary tribunals – Commissar Tibor Szamuely (1890-1919) fled separately by car. Near the border, in the village of Savanyúkút, he was recognized and the Austrian authorities did not permit him to enter Austria. They knew well his role in the most horrific series of commune massacres. He, his brother and their band travelled the country by trucks and trains, hanging and executing hundreds of Hungarians they accused of being 'counter-revolutionary.' They would arrive unexpectedly at various settlements and begin their killings at the train stations. Often, they would murder in unison with the other 'political terror group,' organized and led by József Cserny (1892-1919).[82] This notorious 200-man unit, wearing their 'uniform' black leather jackets and sailor hats, named the "Lenin boys," travelled the country in a special armored train that the people named the "death train." Assistant District Attorney Albert Váry published in 1922 the names of those butchered by the Red Terror. His book lists 587 names.[83] The number of brutal rapes committed is unidentified.

Szamuely, to escape arrest and the subsequent judgment, shot himself at the border with his pistol and died. They tried to bury him in the Jewish cemetery of Wiener Neustadt on the Austrian side but the congregation objected with indignation. His earthly remains were taken back to Savanyúkút in secrecy. On hearing of it, the villagers mobbed the cemetery and pelted the coffin with rocks, swearing and cursing the deceased. The local police then tried to bury Szamuely in the neighboring cemetery of Pecsenyéd, then Lajtaszentmiklós, but both villages also objected strenuously. Finally, the police buried him along a forested stretch of road between Savanyúkút and

---

[82] Vádbeszéd gyilkosság, rablás stb. bűntettével vádolt Cserny József és társai bűnügyében. Elmondotta Dr. Váry Albert főállamügyész, a B[uda]pesti Államügyészség vezetője 1919. december hó 6-án a Budapesti Törvényszék előtt [Jozsef Cserny and accomplices, charged with the crimes of murder, robbery, etc. Recounted by Dr. Albert Vary, head of the state attorney general's office of Budapest, on December 6, 1919, before the court in Budapest]. Kiadja Rákosi Jenő Budapesti Hírlap Ujságvállalata R.-T. Budapest, 1919, p. 48.

[83] A vörös uralom áldozatai Magyarországon. Hivatalos jelentések és bírói ítéletek alapján írta és kiadja Dr. Váry Albert koronaügyészhelyettes [The Hungarian victims of the Red regime. Based on official reports and judicial rulings, written and published by Dr. Albert Vary, assistandt District Attorney]. Budapest, 1922. Váci Kir. Országos Fegyintézet Könyvnyomdája, p. 172. Of the Karolyi Peoples Republic and the subsequent Hungarian Soviet Republic's everyday affairs, the dictatorship, the terror, the expropriations and ruthless confiscations in Western-Hungary, read: *A vörös dúlás nálunk.* Sopron és [a] vármegye a két forradalom alatt [Red devastation. Sopron and the county during the two revolutions]. Coll. by Mayer, Géza. Sopron, no date (1920?), p. 144; Bajzik, Zsolt: Vasi kastélyok a tanácsköztársaság idején. I. rész [Castles of Vas County during the Hungarian Soviet Republic. Part I]. In: *Vasi Szemle*, 2000, issue 5, pp. 636–660; Part II. Ibid, issue 6, pp.793–812; Feiszt, György: Ahogy az iskolákból látták. 1919 Vas megyében [As they saw it from the schools. 1919 in Vas County]. In: *Vasi Szemle*, 1994, issue 4, pp. 573–584.

Pecsenyéd, in an unmarked grave.[84]

The later name of 'Burgenland,' denoting the annexed western Hungarian territory, surfaced in on the front page of a newspaper in Sopron in June of 1919, a month after the acceptance of the Austrian truce terms. A bi-weekly literary and artistic journal, the *Vierburgenland*,[85] was begun for the German speaking population in the four counties marked for annexation by Austria. The publication's statement of purpose read: *Illustrierte Halbmonatschrift für Literatur, Kunst, Kritik und Humor. Offizielles Organ de Kulturbundes für Deutschwestungarn.* [Bi-weekly journal of literature, art, critique and humor. Official journal of the German-Western-Hungarian Cultural Association.] It was published by the *Gauamt Deutschwestungarn*, or German-Western-Hungary Regional Office. The journal, published until March of 1920, had Odo Röttig as its publisher and editor-in-chief. It was printed by the local Röttig-Romwalter Press.[86] The newspaper's name came from a common ending of the four counties to be annexed (Pozsony/Press*burg*, Moson/Wiesel*burg*, Sopron/Öden*burg*, Vas/Eisen*burg*), '*burg*' meaning 'castle' and '*land*' meaning country or province, and '*Vier*' meaning four in German. After the journal, the four counties were also referred to as 'Four-counties' or 'Vierburgenland.'

A rather pithy opinion was voiced by a Sopron-born contemporary, Lajos Krug, well informed of the local circumstances: "From the spineless soil of the Károlyi regime grew this literary magazine, *Vierburgenland*, drawing on unknown financial sources that gave effective support in an unusually attractive form to continue its destabilizing, almost decisive internal divisive work; filling its readers with news of its Vierburgenland, until the purloined land did, in fact, become Burgenland."[87]

After this previous section, we must comment on the birth of a previously non-existent, new administrative and geographic name: Burgenland. A month after the signing of the official Austrian peace treaty (officially: *Staatsvertrag* or State Treaty), on October 6, 1919, a group of Western Hungary citizens, living in Viennese and favoring annexation to Austria (*Anschluss*-supporters),

---

[84] Nemeskürty, István: Mi történt velünk [What happened to us]? Budapest, 2002, pp. 70–74. Later, in the spring of 1945, the Soviet Army occupying Austria did everything to find Szamuely's eartly remains, without success. After the fall of the Proletarian Dictatorship, József Cserny was arrested in Hungary, sentenced and executed on December 24, 1919.

[85] *Vierburgenland*, 1919, year I, issues 1-12; 1920, year II, issues 1-6. szám.The Hungarian press of the day objected against the German-Western-Hungary — Deutschwestungarn name, stressing instead the more legal Western Hungary — Westungarn. Schwartz, Elemér: A Burgenland név [The Burgenland name]. In: *Magyar Nyelv*, 1927, Sept.-Oct., p. 485.

[86] Győr-Moson-Sopron megye időszaki sajtójának bibliográfiája (1779–1995) [Bibliography of the periodicals of Győr-Moson-Sopron County]. Szerk/ed.: Horváth, József. Győr, 2000, p. 769.

[87] Krug, Lajos: Tüzek a végeken [Fires on the frontiers]. Sopron, 1930, p. 38.

went to see Chancellor Karl Renner. After paying their respects, they asked the head of the government to give instructions regarding the name of the newly created federated Austrian province (*Bundesland*). In his response, the chancellor said he was wary of the name *Heanzenland* and would hold *Dreiburgenland* (Three-county) more appropriate – as the Paris Peace conference did not award Pozsony County to Austria – only the western parts of Moson, Sopron and Vas counties. One member of the delegation, Sopron-born Alfred Waldheim, drew attention to the length of the name, thus making it unsuitable for public use. Instead, he suggested *Burgenland*. This suggestion appealed to the chancellor and he used the name in his reply.[88]

According to tradition, or to some, Waldheim gave the area the name Burgenland, which he himself also claimed in later years, saying he named the new Austrian province after the many western Hungarian castles annexed.[89] According to other sources, a person by the name of Gregor Meidlinger used the term 'Burgenland' a month before with Chancellor Renner.[90] The statements of the Viennese professor were later refuted by the real creator of the name, Karl Amon, who drew attention that *"Burgenland is an artificially created name, which has political significance."*[91] According to some, the name 'Burgenland' is an exact translation into German of the Hungarian term 'royal county,' which this author holds to be a artificial interpretation, since our administrative unit of *county* has an equivalent in German of *komitat*. Incidentally, it was from the Fall of 1919 that the expression took root among the Croats of the region, mirroring the translation of the German concept of 'Burgenland,' the name of *Gradišće* and *Gradiščansko* among the Slovenes.[92]

---

[88] Schwartz, Elemér: A Burgenland név [The name: Burgenland]. In: *Magyar Nyelv*, 1927, Sept.-Oct. issue, p. 486. Alfred Waldheim, fourth Governor of Burgenland between July 14, 1923 and January 4, 1924. About the name Burgenland, also see: Schwartz, Elemér, 1927, op. cit., pp. 484–487; Kubinyi, Elek: A burgenlandi németek [The Burgenland Germans]. In: *Magyar Szemle*, 1928, vol. III, issue 3, pp. 251–252; Schwartz, Elemér: A Burgenland magyar neve [The Hungarian name of Burgenland]. In: *Vasi Szemle*, year I, 1934, issue 3, pp. 226–231.

[89] Walheim, Alfred: Wie das Burgenland zu seinem Nanem gekommen ist [How Burgenland came by its name]. In: *Volkszeitung,* Vienna, 1924, January 27.

[90] Tóth, Imre: Elméleti és módszertani megjegyzések a regionalitás kérdéseinek kutatásához. Regionális identitások Burgenlandban és Nyugat-Magyarországon [Theoretical and methodological remarks in the research of questions of regionality. Regional identities in Burgenland and Western-Hungary]. In: *Arrabona* 45/1. Kiad. Győr-Moson-Sopron Megyei Múzeumok Igazgatósága. Győr, 2007, p. 305.

[91] Amon, Karl: Wer hat dem Burgenland den Nanem gegeben [How Burgenland got its name]? In: *Burgenländische Heimat* (Sauerbrunn), 1926, July 11.

[92] Schwartz, Elemér: A nyugatmagyarországi német helységnevek [German settlement names in Western-Hungary]. Budapest, 1932; Schwartz, 1934, op. cit., pp. 226–231; Kranzmayer, Eberhard: Die österreichischen Bundesländer und deren Hauptstädte in ihren Namen. Wien, 1956, p. 25; Kiss, Lajos: Földrajzi nevek etimológiai szótára [Etymological dictionary of geograpgical names]. Edition IV, vol.

Following the meeting between Chancellor Renner and a group of western Hungarian Germans living in Vienna, Austrian propaganda and the irredentist movement immediately picked up the newly created Burgenland name and began to clamor for the military occupation of the Western Hungary zone not granted them in the Treaty of Saint-Germain.

In the meantime, the Paris Peace Conference was officially begun on January 18, 1919 amid formal ceremonies. Three weeks later, on February 5, the representatives of Romania, Czechoslovakia and the Kingdom of Serbia-Croatia-Slovenia, announced on December 1 of the previous year, handed a joint memorandum to the Entente Powers, stating their territorial demands against Hungary. In it, they objected against any possible request(s) for a plebiscite from Hungary. [A plebiscite denied is a plebiscite taken-*ed*.] It is important to note here that in February-March of 1919, the idea of annexing Western Hungary to Austria had not even surfaced, although the Interim Austrian National Assembly representatives of the Great-Germany direction raised such claims in October of 1918. They were the ones who proposed the *Anschluss*, or union with Germany and the National Council proclaimed it on November 17. The peace treaty terms with Austria was handed to the Austrian representatives on June 2, 1919 in Paris *which defined the Hungarian-Austrian border along the 1867 line, from the time of the Dual Monarchy (the Lajta/Leitha River, peaks of the Rozália mountain range and the Lappincs River, a line that served as a border for the previous millennia).* This last was not by accident because the Entente Powers knew very well that *pre-1867, Austria did not exist as an independent country and post-1867 only as the other half of the Austro-Hungarian Monarchy with Hungary.*

In reaching what we today understand as statehood, Austria had taken a unique road. For a millennia, the current country was merely a province – albeit a central one – of the Habsburg Empire. Hence, Austria as a semi-independent country came into being in 1867 with the Austro-Hungarian Compromise (*Augsleich*). The Hungarian Kingdom, on the other hand, became an independent country with the crowning of King Saint Stephen in 1001, almost 900 years before. The facts of the unique historical 'statehood' of present day Austria are as follows: 976-1156 - estates of counts [frontier counts like those of the Welsh Marches-*ed*.], 1156-1453 - dukedoms, 1490 – archdukedoms, 1521-1522 – perpetual provinces, 1564 – after the Habsburg family division into three parts (Upper and Lower Austria; Tyrol; Styria and Carinthia), 1648 – center of the Habsburg dynasty, 1804 – center of Habsburg empire. From 1867-1918, a new state form in the Austro-Hungarian Empire, its western provinces organized as an empire,[93] while its eastern allied country, Hungary, is a kingdom. Its joint ruler at the time was Francis Joseph

I. Budapest, 1988, p. 266.

[93] Ausztria. In: Magyar Nagylexikon. Főszerk/ed-in-chief: Élesztős, László. Volume II. Budapest, 1994, pp. 659–665; Zöllner, Erich: Ausztria története [History of Austria]. Budapest, 1998.

(1830-1916) who was crowned Austrian emperor in 1848 and Hungarian king in 1867.

After the military collapse of the Dual Monarchy, the *Anschluss* movement gained strength in the Fall of 1918, which had made attempts at union with Germany in the 19th century. The aspiration was supported by most Austrian parties and associations because they had doubts about the viability of an independent Austria shrunk to its oldest provinces. After the proclamation on Nov. 12, 1918 of the German-Austrian Republic (*Deutschösterreich*) and the announced intent of union with democratic Germany shortly after, Austria was governed by a National Council made up of Under-Secretaries, presided over by the Social Democrat Karl Renner, also in favor of union. In the Austrian elections held in February 1920, the Social Democratic Party won, elevating Renner to the post of Chancellor, a post he filled until June 1920.

At the Paris Peace Conference, Austria – same as Hungary – was not able to state its case, could only outline its views. The Austrian government took a position strictly on ethnic grounds but soon had to realize that it had to give up all claim to the Sudetenland to the newly created Czechoslovakia. In part because the Entente Powers have promised it a long time ago to a future Czechoslovak state, partly because it had never been historically an Austrian province, and finally, it would be impossible to attach it to Austria due to its geographic location. The continued retention of South Tyrol was also a loss due to British-French pledges to Italy. Austria's territorial ambitions were only promising in two areas: the zone around Klagenfurt, and the Western Hungary strip, the former Borderland, populated mainly by Germans, it is true – but not Austrians.

How was Austria, on the same losing side in the war as Hungary, able to emerge from its defeat with territorial gains? The answer is surprising from several points of view. "For a long time, an attitude of empire was prevalent and it occurred to no one to identify the various provinces of the empire with Austria. This view of empire, however, allowed a latent sense of Austrian consciousness to lurk. No matter how much they spoke of 'German' imperialism on the Entente side when talking of Vienna, the reality was Vienna's dynastic imperialism, with little to do with Austrian nationalistic imperialism. At the collapse of the Empire, the dynastic stand-point was pushed aside and replaced by a country, mostly civil but in the long term, oriented towards nationalism. This orientation, however, was only latent, not realized. (…) Among the foreign policy moves of the Austrian Republic, these conditions are clearly evident."[94]

It follows from this then, that the newly created German-Austria Republic was, in some ways, more sheltered from the small but eager countries – Czech and Slovak, Romanian, Serb – who finished on the victorious side with the Entente Powers, than Hungary. Their hunger for territory and its attendant

---

[94] Ormos, Mária: Padovától Trianonig 1918–1920 [From Padua to Trianon 1918-1920]. Budapest, 1983, p. 150.

military , economic, trade and financial benefits knew no bounds. Their desire for an even more unfair border for Hungary is well documented, one that would have seen vast areas of purely Hungarian populated areas torn from the country. The Czechoslovak demand, as noted before, laid claim to Northern Hungary along the line from Dévény (Devin), along the Danube, then Vác – Gyöngyös – Miskolc – Tokaj – Sátoraljaújhely – Csap – Verecke Pass. It would have included the coal deposits of Salgótarján, the industries around Borsod and a large part of the Tokaj vineyards. It would have contained a part of Sub-Carpathia from Verecke along the Ung River to the upper Tisza River. The Romanians, in like manner, wanted the Great Hungarian Plains up to the Tisza River, East to the millennial border and along the eastern and southern Carpathians. Serb demands included a zone North of Szeged – Baja – Pécs (with the Mecsek coalfields), the area southwest of Lake Balaton, the area between the Zala and Rába Rivers up to Lake Fertő, where the South Slav country would have had a common border with Czechoslovakia. The so-called 'Slav corridor' presented by Eduard Beneš (1884-1948), Foreign Minister of Czechoslovakia, was meant to create a corridor through Western Hungary, giving Czechoslovakia contact with the South Slav country, and an outlet to the Adriatic Sea.

To remark briefly on the proposed 'corridor': this question was one of the most difficult matter at the peace conference, a faithful mirror of the state of affairs at the Congress. The decision makers went back and forth on the question of the Slav corridor, for weeks between January and March of 1919, with diligence and complete seriousness. This raised a new hope not only for Czechoslovakia but the Kingdom of Serbs-Croats-Slovenes (Yugoslavia only after 1929) of grabbing new Hungarian territories in the West or Southwest. For the proposed capital of the as-yet-nonexistent Slovakia, Pozsony, to be connected with the Croat capital of Zagreb (a Slav corridor or Western Hungarian Slav corridor) was proposed early during the war by the leading Czech politicians Tomáš Garrigue Masaryk,[95] Eduard Beneš and Karel Kramář. They also repeated the importance of its creation. Later, Beneš worked it out in detail while an émigré in France, presenting a series of lectures at Sorbonne University on the Slav question and the Austro-Hungarian Monarchy. He published his thesis in 1916 in Paris, in a French-language pamphlet.

According to the concept formulated by Beneš, Great Serbia, created from Serb, Croat and Slovene lands, was to be "joined to Czechoslovakia by a

---

[95] After his university studies in Vienna, he studied philosophy in Leipzig in the early 1870s. Here he met his future wife, the American Charlotte Garrigue, who was Woodrow Wilson's niece. The founder of Czechoslovakia even took his wife's name and became the well known Czech, later Czechoslovak, politician as Tomáš Garrigue Masaryk (1850–1937). In: Tomáš Garrigue Masaryk a Podkarpatská Rus / Т. Г. Масарик та Закарпаття [T. G. Masaryk and Sub-Carpathia]. Šéfredaktor Ivan Latko. Užhorod, 2000. Klub T. G. Masaryka v Užhorodě, p.6.

corridor running between the Lajta and Rába Rivers through Hungary."[96] This corridor, approx. 200-220 km. long and 150-200 km. wide, was to run between the Danube River in the North and the Mura River in the South. Its western boundary was to be the millennial Hungarian-Austrian border on the West (the Eastern Alps), while its eastern edge would have run between Győr and Nagykanizsa and the western tip of Lake Balaton. The zone was to be under the joint control of Czechoslovakia and the Kingdom of Serbs-Croats-Slovenes. It would have swallowed all of Moson, Sopron, Vas and Zala Counties (16,663 km^2), with their seven towns (Kismarton, Ruszt, Szombathely, Kőszeg, Zalaegerszeg, Nagykanizsa and Sopron) and 1,466 settlements. According to the 1910 census, the population of the four counties was 1,171,000 million people: 662,000 Hungarians (53.1%), 280,000 Germans (23.9%), and 190,000 Slavs (11.6% Croats and 4.7% Slovenes, a total of 16.3% Slavs).[97] The corridor would also consist of the western half of Győr County (approx. 800 km^2, the city of Győr and 45 settlements, with a population of 90,000, of which 88,000 were Hungarian, one thousand German and one thousand Slovak) and about 80% of Veszprém County (approx. 3,200 km^2, the cities of Veszprém and Pápa and 150 settlements, with a population of 191,000, of which 167,000 were Hungarian and 24,000 German).

The 1915 map of the Slav corridor that the later president of Czechoslovakia, Masaryk, envisioned ran from Pozsony along the Danube to the city of Győr, then in a straight line to the district center of Alsólendva, turning northwest along the Mura River, then North along the Hungarian-Austrian border to Pozsony. According to another Czech map drawn up during the war, the Slav corridor was significantly enlarged to the East: starting from the confluence of the Mura and Drava Rivers to Nagykanizsa, East to the southern tip of Lake Balaton, following its northern shore to its eastern end. From there, taking a western bend from Pápa to Győr, to continue along the left bank of the Danube taking two-thirds of the purely Hungarian populated island of Csallóköz (Žitný ostrov) and, after an easterly curve, ending at the town of Révkomárom (Komárno). According to a Serb plan, also drawn during the war, the territory to be annexed to Serbia was to consist of all of Baranya County, as well as lands South of the line of Barcs – Nagykanizsa - Szentgotthárd. The corridor's eastern boundary was to be the line of Pozsony–Győr–Nagykanizsa–Szentgotthárd, while the western boundary was the existing Hungarian-Austrian border.[98]

The openly stated goals of the Slav corridor were the following: a direct access to the Adriatic for Czechoslovakia; to allow the three successor states

---

[96] Beneš, Edvard: Détruisez l'Autriche–Hongrie. La martyre des tcheco–slovaques à travers l'histoire [Destroy Austria-Hungary. Czechoslovak sacrifices through history]. Paris, 1926. Libraire Delagrave. Nagy, Andrea: JATE Történész Diákkör. Szeged, 1992, p. 45. (The Beneš pamphlet was also published in 1917 in London, in English.)

[97] Magyarország Közigazgatási Atlasza 1914 [Hungarian public administration atlas 1914]. pp. 70, 73-74, 77, 114, 145, 167.

[98] Ibid.

of the Austro-Hungarian Monarchy (Czechoslovakia, Romania and South-Slav Kingdom) to get Hungary in a vise; to separate the German people from Central Europe and the East; and to seize Pozsony, as the capital of the 'ancient Slovak empire,'(!?) and build it into a large Danube port and capital of Slovakia. According to the plan of Beneš and Masaryk, in the four counties and two partial counties of the Slav corridor, with a total population of 1,413,000, *the 191,000 (13.5%) Slavs would have become the ruling nationality*. It would have meant that the other 85%, 917,000 Hungarians (64.9%) and 305,000 Germans (21.6%), would have come under Czechoslovak and South-Slav occupation and into minority status.

The need bring to life the plan was vociferously repeated by Beneš and the Czech-Slovak representatives at the Paris Peace Conference in January-February of 1919. On February 5, the Czechoslovak delegates were invited to state their claims before the Supreme Council. Beneš mentioned the Slav corridor, among other territorial claims, but by this time he had somewhat modified the memorandum with regard to the corridor. He claimed that, according to his calculations, there were now 200,000 Slavs living in Moson, Sopron, Vas and Zala counties, giving him a basis for claiming the northern part of the corridor, Moson and Sopron counties, while the South-Slav kingdom should have Vas and Zala counties.

Following the example of Beneš, Belgrade also put together a plan which was even more grasping, not being satisfied with the previously detailed territory but laying claim to a huge swath of southern Trans-Danubia for the South Slav state.[99] This southern Hungarian territory area, a zone 5-20 km. North of the demarcation line along the railway line from Barcs–Szigetvár–Pécs–Bátaszék–Baja–Bácsalmás–Szeged, then from the Maros River to Arad, Serbia intended to seize permanently. This vast swath was thoughtlessly and myopically signed away by the Károlyi government as part of the Belgrade Military Convention (truce treaty), with disastrous consequences. Between November 7 and 19, the Serb army was able to secure it by simply marching in.[100] According to the new Serb plan, areas to the West and South of the Barcs–Nagykanizsa–Szentgotthárd line was to come under the control of the South Slav country. North of it, anything West of the straight line linking Nagykanizsa and Győr, was to go to Czechoslovakia.

As a matter of interest, the claimed corridor's central and eastern thirds were inhabited by a substantial majority of Hungarians. Croatians lived in dispersed settlement in Moson, Sopron and Vas counties, but in the majority in Muraköz (Međimurje), in southwest Zala County. The Vends/Slovenes

---

[99] Ormos, Mária: Civitas fidelissima. Népszavazás Sopronban 1921 [Most loyal city. Plebiscite in Sopron 1921]. Győr, 1990, pp. 22–27; Romsics, Ignác: A trianoni békeszerződés [The peace treaty of Trianon]. Budapest, 2001, pp. 45, 124.

[100] Botlik, József – Csorba, Béla – Dudás, Károly: Eltévedt mezsgyekövek. Adalékok a délvidéki magyarság történetéhez 1918–1993 [Lost boundary markers. Addenda to the history of the Hungarians of the souther territory 1918-1993]. Budapest, 1994, p. 39.

lived in the southeast corner of Vas County and in neighboring Zala County along the Mura River. In the four counties intended for expropriation for the corridor, the only sizeable cities were Sopron, Szombathely and Nagykanizsa (with populations from 34,000 down to 27,000). Only in Sopron did the Germans-speakers have a minimal 51% majority, while the other two had Hungarian majorities of 94% and 95%.[101]

Based on the Czechoslovak's demands and the Beneš memorandum, the representatives of the Kingdom of Serbs-Croats-Slovenes immediately joined with the Western Hungary Slav corridor plan and without delay came forward with new territorial demands. Their plan would have seen the establishment of the corridor running through Trans-Danubia from the town of Baja, North of Pécs in a western direction to the southwestern corner of Lake Balaton, following the course of the Zala and Rába Rivers, to end at Lake Fertő. The hastily composed demand of the Belgrade government would have encompassed two-thirds of the Hungarian populated counties of Somogy and Zala, the eastern part of Vas County and even the eastern third of Sopron County. This additional new claim of approx. 7,000 km^2 brought Serbian claims of Hungarian territory to a total of 52,065 km^2. (approx. 1.25 million acres).

These unrealistic claims could only be justified by astonishing feats of logic. *The South Slav Kingdom always preferred to use two: spreading of fictitious data and military power.* Under this plan, Czechoslovakia would have received all of Moson County and the western portions of Sopron and Vas counties. On top of it all, the Serb military command demanded in a February 10 note the permanent annexation of the already occupied city of Pécs and its surrounding coalfields. Satisfying the new territorial claim would have meant that the entirety of the southern Trans-Danubia, including the Mecsek Mountains, and even a part of western Trans-Danubia, would have been attached to the Kingdom of Serbs-Croats-Slovenes.

Subsequently, a new Belgrade plan was formulated, this one far more modest in its demands. According to this one, the Hungarian territory to come under South Slav control would lie South of the Barcs–Nagykanizsa–Szentgotthárd line. North of this line and West of a straight line from Nagykanizsa to Győr would have become a part of Czechoslovakia. In the meantime, at the end of February, the Czech-Slovak representatives presented their final plan concerning the Slav corridor to the Peace Conference, which, naturally enough, was supported by the South Slav delegates. Compared to the plan presented during the war, the then 150-200 km. wide Western Hungary corridor had now shrunk to about 100km. with its eastern boundary now running between Magyaróvár to Nagykanizsa. This demand was based not on ethic principles but historical (claiming the area was Slav populated before the Hungarian conquest) and strategic ones (separating the Hungarians

---

[101] Magyarország Közigazgatási Atlasza 1914 [Hungarian public administration atlas 1914], pp. 74, 77.

and Germans). None of the Entente representatives were in support of the plan.

In the end, the proposed Slav corridor failed to materialize because the British authorities were sharply against annexing the Vend/Slovene populated area between Szentgotthárd and the Mura River to the South Slav state. Leaving this area with Hungary was beneficial for Hungary because it indirectly rejected the territorial claims of Czechoslovakia and the Serb-Croat-Slovene Kingdom against Western Hungary. Subsequently, the appropriate committee of the Peace Conference unanimously rejected, without any vocal debate, the Czechoslovak proposal regarding the Slav corridor on March 8. Thus, the Prague and Belgrade governments were unable to establish direct contact between their two countries[102] via the so-called Slav corridor, and Czechoslovakia also did not secure an outlet to the Adriatic Sea.

After long negotiations, the Belgrade government finally gave up its claim to the Rába and Zala River area but, as part of the Trianon treaty agreement, it received, in exchange, the valley of the Lendva River, today's Međimurje (Muravidék). As well, it was given the area South of the Mura and Rába Rivers, the southern part of the Vend region. We will treat the final Hungarian-South Slav border in greater detail in the next chapter.

Whose interests would the annexation of the western Hungarian Borderland serve? Consider that it was part of the country for a thousand years and to which it had always been loyally devoted. "Not the West Hungarians, not German-Austria – beset as it was by enemies – but solely in the interest of the Czech and Serb imperialists, as well as the Greater Germany faction in Austria. Initially, the voracious Czech and Serb predators wanted to claim this valuable territory for themselves, to create a corridor between northern and southern Slavs. Then, when this seemed an impossibility due to the heated opposition of Italy, they had the servile French friends arrange to annex it to Austria, obviously with the clever aim of driving a wedge between two countries thrown on each other, Austria and Hungary. (…) In the calculations of the Pan-German Austrians, Western Hungary obviously had another role. They saw it as an ace-in-the-hole in a European-level movement begun with the intention of uniting Austria to the German empire – a movement going ahead towards its own goal, without regard to any casualties."[103]

The new Austria-Hungary border, defined later in the Treaty of Trianon, cannot be separated from the Treaty of Saint-Germain signed by Austria on September 10, 1919, from France's Central European policies (or attempts at influence) and the American delegates' pro-Austrian behavior. During the

---

[102] Romsics, 2001, op.cit., pp. 124–125.

[103] Ajtay, József: Külpolitikai helyzet – Nyugat-Magyarország [Foreign policy situation in Western Hungary]. In: *Új Magyar Szemle*, year II, vol. II, issue 3, June, p. 359; also Romsics, Ignác: Szláv korridor, Burgenland, Lajtabánság: koncepciók Nyugat-Magyarországról [Slav corridor, Burgenland, Lajta-Banat: models of Western Hungary]. In: *Regio*, 1992, issue 1, pp. 90–99.

Paris conference, the consideration of the Austria question underwent significant change after the Entente Powers decided against the union of Austria with Germany. Thus, they began to search for a possibility of Austrian independence, a shift that Vienna quickly realized. In the meantime, *Anschluss* faded by degrees into the background – seen by the French as Germanization – and the idea of an autonomous and independent Austria gained ground. One of the main reasons was that – although German-Austria signed an agreement with Germany of the terms of a union in February 1919 – Berlin could less and less accept, could afford be seen to accept, a union openly. Austria's situation was further improved when the Austrian National Assembly passed a law banishing the Habsburg family from the country. Shortly after, the ex-emperor, Charles IV, left Austria on March 25, 1919 and settled in Switzerland. However, in the first months of 1919, Austrian politics were defined by *Anschluss* tactics. Vienna cleverly continued to raise the possibility of a union with Germany in the hope of receiving economic benefits and a reduced territorial loss from the Entente.

In light of the previous circumstances, Austria's position improved in the eyes of the Entente Powers. Exploiting it – but also encouraged by the unrestrained territorial claims by the Czechoslovak, Romanian and South Slav against Hungary – the Austrian government continued to raise the Western Hungary question ever more vigorously. Naturally, not as hard demands but on a wish, based on ethnic grounds, which primarily found support among the American circles of the Peace Conference. This meant that the Austria-South Slav and Hungary-South Slav new borders were linked with the question of the reassignment of the Klagenfurt zone, Szentgotthárd and area, the Baranya triangle, and Bácska (Bačka). The South Slav armed forces tried to occupy the area around Klagenfurt in January (1919) but local Austrian units were successful in repelling them. Austria's economic situation, in the meantime, became worse, having lost its sources of raw materials – the population of Vienna was starving due to a trade embargo. As a consequence, the populace tended to shift toward the 'Red' or Left-wing, even to Communism.[104] Because of the revolutionary atmosphere in Vienna, the Austrian countryside distanced itself from the capital, some provinces even wanted to secede from Austria. In a plebiscite held in May (1919) in Vorarlberg Province, 80% of voters wanted a union with Switzerland, the 1921 referendum in Tyrol showed a 98.8% wish to join Germany, 99.2% in the Salzburg area. However, the victorious Entente Powers refused to accept the provincial plebiscite results and, under their pressure, the Austrian government did not authorize further expressions of the people's wish in the other regions.[105]

The Austrian government was able to avoid the outbreak of a revolution in

[104] Ormos, 1983, op. cit., pp. 258–270.
[105] Paál, Vince: Ausztria identitásai [Austria's identities]. In: Nemzeti és regionális identitás Közép-Európában. Szerk/ed.: Ábrahám, Barna – Gereben, Ferenc – Stekovics, Rita. Piliscsaba–Budapest, 1999, pp. 76–77.

Vienna in April (1919), easing the threat of a Communist takeover. The Hungarian Communists were expelled from the country and border controls were stepped up along the Austria-Hungary sector in an attempt to crack down on arms smuggling into Hungary. The 'masters' of the Paris Peace Conference were satisfied, the upper leadership of the Hungarian Soviet Republic, however, was disappointed. Relations between Vienna and Budapest cooled and by June were almost adversarial, since Austria again officially raised its territorial 'claim' to *Westungarn* or Western Hungary on May 11. The claim was linked to a rejection of the *Anschluss* (union) option. Days before this announcement, the staff officers of the Austrian Military Office (*Staatsamt für Heerwesen*) worked out the plan for the military occupation of Western Hungary. The secret plan consisted of seven irregular columns advancing into Western Hungary under the guise of providing assistance to a population revolting against Hungarian authorities. The headquarters staff was instructed to forbid accepting Communists, monarchists, Jews and Crown Council members as volunteers into the seven bands.[106]

Chancellor Karl Renner and Foreign Minister Otto Bauer notified Colonel Thomas Cunningham, the head of the Entente mission in Vienna, on May 11 of the plan. The colonel had previously linked the territorial gain in Western Hungary with the repudiation of the *Anschluss* plan and specifically urged the Austrian government to state its territorial claims. This the highest level of the government officially registered on the same date. Colonel Cunningham urged the Austrian government on May 16 to militarily occupy the *Westungarn* territory, stressing that "the Entente will not object." At the same time, he repeatedly urged that German-Austria join in the war against the Hungarian Soviet Republic on the side of the Czechoslovak, Romanian and South Slav armies.[107] It was not, then, by chance that the other leading politicians of the Entente Powers drew the attention of the Austrian government, confidentially but not officially, that: *because they cannot gain border adjustments for Austria in the Italian and South Slav areas, it should lay a claim in western Hungary as compensation.* It thus became clear to Chancellor Renner, in Paris at the time, that the right decision was made with regard to Austria's standpoint: to seek compensation in western Hungary in lieu of South Tyrol, given to Italy. For Vienna, the Hungarian Proletarian Dictatorship came as an opportune event. The Austrian delegates to the Peace Conference wasted no opportunity to raise alarm over the dangers of Bolshevism – presenting the annexation of Western Hungary as a defensive move. On top of it all, they did it with great skill, raising the specter before the Entente decision makers, in turn, the dual possibilities of *Anschluss* and Hungarian Bolshevism. Of the latter, they were fully aware of its usefulness as an argument only as long as the Hungarian Commune was in existence.

---

[106] Fogarassy, 1971, op.cit., p. 293.

[107] Ibid, pp. 293–294; Ormos, 1983, op.cit., pp. 194, 275.

The fate of *Westungarn*, or Western Hungary, was decided at the Peace Conference between May 27 and 31, 1919, although few notes remain in the minutes of the discussions. We can only deduce from various sources the loathsome and distasteful negotiations. The Hungarian Soviet Republic began its northern campaign at this particular time (May 30-June 24) to recapture the Hungarian populated areas of Northern Hungary and Sub-Carpathia, which again favored Austria's stand. The essence was that the annexation of Western Hungary was ultimately linked with the South Slav country's failure to make gains of Austrian territory (Klagenfurt and area) and Belgrade was instead recompensed by Hungarian territory (Baranya County and the Vend region/ Medžimurje). This was confirmed when *the Supreme Council of the Peace Conference decided to consider Austria as a new country on May 28-29, whose current official name of German-Austria (Deutschösterreich) was changed to the Republic of Austria.* The official documents of the Supreme Council refer to it in French and English as République d'Autriche or Republic of Austria. The heads of the Peace Conference also decided henceforth to treat Austria differently from Germany. The terms of the peace treaty were handed to the Austrian delegation on June 2, 1919, which was sharply protested by the Austrian National Assembly at its extraordinary meeting of June 7.[108] Next, numerous notes, submissions and memoranda were written by Austria regarding the matter of *Westungarn* – not yet called by its new name, Burgenland. Most pointed out the dangers threatening the Austrian capital, Vienna, from "Bolshevik Hungary." Austria's position was further improved by the resignation of the most *Anschluss*-leaning Austrian politician, Foreign Minister Otto Bauer. The Chancellor, Renner, then announced a new, Entente friendly, foreign policy. Austria's image was further enhanced when a large demonstration was put down in Vienna on June 15, preventing an attempted revolt by the Communists.[109]

By the date of the Peace Conference, the demands of the representatives of the transitional Austrian National Assembly who sided with the Greater Germany concepts have substantially modified their territorial demands first introduced in October of 1918, i.e.- all of Pozsony, Sopron, Moson and Vas counties and a western strip of Zala County. By the Spring of 1919, the official land claim shrank to 5,055 km^2 with a population of 392,000. This claim was, by now, only one-third of the unofficially claimed 16,000 km^2 with 1,300 settlements and a population of 1.2 million. The Austrian government demanded to have, first of all, Sopron, as well as the district around Hegyeshalom–Moson–Magyaróvár, and Kőszeg and Szentgotthárd

---

[108] Pozsonyi, Márta: A saint-germaini osztrák békedelegáció és a területi kérdés [The Austrian peace delegation at Saint-Germain and the territorial question]. In: Történelem és nemzet. Tanulmánykötet Galántai József professzor tiszteletére. Szerk/ed.: Kiss, Károly – Lovas, Krisztina. Budapest, 1996, pp. 295–332; Romhányi, Zsófia: A saint-germaini békekötés és az osztrák sajtó [The peace treaty of Saint-Germain and the Austrian press]. Ibid, pp. 277–293.

[109] Ormos, 1983, op. cit., pp. 286–287.

awarded to it, on top of the actual award that later became Burgenland. The one-time ally of Hungary, co-founder of the Dual Monarchy and equal loser of the war, turned out not to be any less predatory than the Czechs, Romanians or Serbs.[110] Some Austrian sources mentioned a slightly larger claim of 5,379 km².[111] Due to changes in the foreign policy environment, Austria later gave up any claim to Pozsony County and, in the Paris Peace Conference, in 1920, only asked for a plebiscite in the city of Pozsony, with the reasoning that if it was not Hungarian, then it is more German than Slovak.[112] The Entente Powers rejected Austria's request.

What justification did Austria, also a loser of the war with Hungary, have to claim Western Hungary? In their memorandum, the Austrian delegation to Paris presented arguments based on historic 'rights,' the food supply of Vienna, military-defensive reasons and the wish of the local population to separate as the basis for the annexation of Western Hungary. The Hungarian delegation replied to the Austrian demands, which we will cover next. The extract below, from an undated Hungarian submission,[113] is in response to the points raised in the June 16, 1919 Austrian memorandum.[114] *"Historical rights are claimed, based on the ancient Germanic settlers of the area and certain pledges, which Austrian princes were granted on certain castles or estates in later centuries by the Hungarian kings. The majority of ancient settlers of the area were Slavs, the sparse Germanics among them being Goths, and in the same manner, Avars too, but the population was sparse and there was no country-like formation in this region. No one laid claim to it, as there were not even border clashes here for three hundred years after the Conquest, only in the 13ᵗʰ c. with the buildup of population. Beginning then, Austrian princes and nobles began to grasp for the Hungarian border castles and large estates. This ambition strengthened with the ascension to the throne by the Habsburgs but their aspiration was not specifically toward Western Hungary but focused on the Hungarian throne. The collateral rights the Habsburgs acquired through their pledges, the largest among them from the eternally fiscally pinched King Sigismund, covering many castles and large*

---

[110] Lőkkös, op. cit., pp. 123, 124. (map)

[111] Zsiga, Tibor: *Communitas Fidelissima* Szentpéterfa. A magyar–osztrák határmegállapítás 1922–23 [Most loyal town, Szentpéterfa. The Hungarian-Austrian border settlement 1922-1923]. Szombathely, 1993, p. 10.

[112] Halmosy, Dénes: Nemzetközi szerződések 1918–1945 [International agreements 1918-1945]. Budapest, 1983, p. 95.

[113] Title: Ad XV. jegyzék. A Nyugat-Magyarországról szóló jegyzék kivonata [Note XV. Synopsis of the note regarding Western Hungary]. In: A magyar béketárgyalások. Jelentés a magyar békeküldöttség működéséről Neuilly ˢ/S.-ben [-sur-Seineben] 1920. januárius–március havában. I. köt. Kiadja a Magyar Kir. Külügyminisztérium. Budapest, 1920, p. 458.

[114] The historical background, from a legal history perspective that is still noteworthy today, is suitably analyzed by Nagy, Iván: Nyugatmagyarország Ausztriában [Western Hungary in Austria]. Pécs, 1937, pp. 12-17.

lands, were always of a personal nature. The peace treaty of 1463 codified the matter of rights over estate collateral given in exchange for a loan in which Frederick III agreed, verbatim, that he enters into possession of the collateral-held properties as a Hungarian nobleman, and that they lie within the boundary of Hungary. The peace treaty also clarified Frederick's claim to the Hungarian throne. Hence, Austria cannot create a historical right from the collateral nature of these estates, as they were granted to the Habsburgs as rulers-in-waiting of the Hungarian throne, or from the non-repayment of the loan underlying the collateral because that was nullified when the Habsburgs ascended to the Hungarian throne. In fact, Hungary could lay a claim, partly monetary, in the matter of the 400,000 Florins, which the 1478 Treaty of Olomouc guaranteed it as compensation for the possible loss of the fringe provinces of the Czech crown after the death of King Mathias. Also, territories, if any remain on the right bank of the Lajta River, which the 1491 peace was returned to Hungary after Maximilian's campaign and which are now under Austrian administration. As well, smaller areas on the Styrian(-Hungarian) border, where border adjustments have been prevented by Austria to this day."[115]

The economic justification of the Austrians for the annexation of the territory was that Western Hungary was Vienna's larder and vegetable garden. It is a fact that this area has significantly contributed for centuries to the feeding of the Austrian capital. For Budapest, early vegetables came from the Banate, later vegetables from the southern valley of the Vag River, eggs from Transylvania and meat from eastern Hungary – all now torn from the country. How can the peace treaty give Vienna what it took away from Budapest? With regard to food supply, Western Hungary was a transit point to Vienna: milk was taken there from the western counties (not the German but Hungarian populated ones), meat from other parts of Trans-Danubia and the Great Plains through the city of Győr for centuries past. *"If indeed, the feeding of Vienna, within Austria, is to be ensured through moving the current border, then it should be moved far in, almost to the center of Hungary. If, however, we look at geographic standpoints and assess territorial cohesion from an economic point-of-view, then the borders should be moved not as a detriment to Hungary but pushed toward the West to Austria's disadvantage. The Graz Basin is, as a matter of course, a part of Hungary. Politically it was a part of Hungary at one time, under kings of the House of Árpád. It was not only Hungarian settlements that wanted union with Austria, but only during the Bolshevik period, but Austrian settlements wished to join Hungary, such as Aspang Markt, clearly denoting the direction of economic gravitation. It is true that the industrial centers were fed by Hungary but Hungary shares no blame in their industrial centers growing big and not its own, and that its dependence on Austria and the whole of Austrian economical policies suppressed Hungarian industry."*

---

[115] Ibid, pp. 458–459.

The Austrian government hoped that the three annexed sugar factories (Nagycenk, Cinfalva and Félszerfalva) will cover the sugar needs of Vienna, which Austrian factories could only supply with 10% of its need. The three factories were located in areas two-thirds populated by Hungarians, processing sugar beet grown mainly on the flat lands of northwestern Hungary. After border adjustment, they would be unable to supply Austria's sugar needs and would go bankrupt. Especially the factory in Nagycenk "which is in a purely Hungarian populated village, right next to the border, and it is probably the reason why this purely Hungarian village was added to territories claimed by Austria." The treaties of Saint-Germain and Trianon gave the estate of Count István Széchenyi (1791-1860) and the Hungarian populated Nagycenk[116] to Austria. In the crypt under the Széchenyi chapel, the count – the "greatest Hungarian," according to Lajos Kossuth (1802-1894) – rests. Nagycenk only returned to Hungary later, after the Sopron plebiscite.

After stating the previous points, the submission of the Hungarian delegation emphasized that the territorial demand would not represent an easing of the situation for Austria but rather a large burden. First of all, in the "German Western Hungary area" there was a large shortfall of produce, especially grains, potatoes and feed grains. The situation is reflected in the buying permits issued for seed grains for 1918, when, for example, the two German-populated districts of Vas County had more seeds allocated by the Hungarian government than the rest of the county. *"The allocated grains for the past year in the Hungarian districts, per capita, was 1/20 of a metric centner* [a metric centner = 100kg. or 220 lbs.-ed.], *while in the German districts it was 1/3 m/c. The Hungarian districts showed a greater surplus vs. the German districts (the Hungarian districts of Vas County showed a surplus of 389,000 m/c of wheat, 15,800 m/c of feed grains, 160,000 m/c of potatoes). This surplus, which goes to Austria, in particular Vienna. The situation is the same in Sopron and Moson counties, too. The German [populated] parts do not live off the growing of these products and foodstuffs but from their trans-shipment. The result of annexation to Austria will have the result that Austria will gain nothing but these areas, especially the city of Sopron and the villages along the southerly railway line – acting as agents between the producing Hungarian areas and the consuming Austrian market for grains, fruits, beef and meats – will go bankrupt."*[117]

Why did Austria lay claim to the annexation of Western Hungary with such easily refutable historical claims and economic reasoning, when they failed to stand up to scrutiny? The answer is simple: because the issue was a question for the Austrian parties and their ability to mobilize support, especially for the German National Party, *"which strove to unite all Germans.*

---

[116] According to the 1910 census, Nagycenk had a population of 1,740. Of that 1,625 were Hungarian (93.4%), 97 Germans (5.6%) and 7 Croats. In: Magyarország Közigazgatási Atlasza 1914. P. 138.

[117] A magyar béketárgyalások [The Hungarian peace talks]. Vol. I, p 459. (Bolding mine–*J.B.*)

The ethnic argument they raised did not stand up, because the Western Hungary Germans were neither Hienc, nor Styrians; in their songs, traditions and language, we find traces of a mix of French (Frankish) and Flemish. They differ from their immediate neighbors, in fact, we can find elements of Hungarian in their language and traditions. These people were always loyal to their Hungarian country, never exhibiting irredentist tendencies until the outbreak of Bolshevism in Hungary. It was then that the deeply Catholic people wanted to secede and the annexation to Austria became a strong plank in the program of the Austrian socialist party. When Hungarian Bolshevism ceased, the secessionist intent of these people also ceased until today village after village states their intention to remain as part of Hungary. Lastly, the Social-Democratic Party joined those demanding annexation, whereas the delegation to the Peace Conference only asked for plebiscites. Austria was awarded the area without one. This was the most visible and greatest achievement of the Austrian delegation, and why the Austrian government and ruling party are so staunchly behind it."[118] The Austrian delegation to Paris had prepared plans for the plebiscite it wanted to conduct in Western Hungary.[119]

The more serious Austrian politicians were worried because this gift of a territory carried a heavy economic burden. As well, it caused growing anti-Austrian sentiment in Hungary, which sacrificed a lot during the centuries for the territory about to be annexed. Kings and nobles heaped rights and privileges on this area, where even Ruszt, pop. 1,000, could rise to be a free royal town. The submission finally pointed out: "Should Hungary suffer this fate because, in 1848, the western powers turned their back on the Freedom Revolt and She, falling, was forced after a decade and a half of absolutism and slavery to come to terms with Austria and Tsarism, to save as much of its freedom as possible? But, in essence, it remained dependent on Austria, which restricted its industries and fed its own industries from Hungarian agricultural products, until those industries were highly developed and, in this relationship of dependency, was forced to follow Austria into the world war. /The loss of Western Hungary would be an historical injustice toward Hungary. The claims of German Austria cannot be established either historically, or geographically, or economically. Austria itself realizes this and the question for it is one of prestige, while for Hungary, the loss of its most developed industrial and commercial zone would be catastrophic./ Based on these arguments, we ask the Supreme Council to alter its decision in the Austrian treaty and leave this area for Hungary or, if it wishes to do so, order and execute a fair plebiscite in the region."[120]

The population of the Western Hungary area claimed by Austria sent an

---

[118] Ibid. (Bolding mine–*J.B.*)

[119] Nagy, Iván, 1937, op. cit., pp. 57-77.

[120] A magyar béketárgyalások, op. cit., vol. I, p.459.

undated memorandum[121] to the Hungarian delegation to the Peace Conference, which it also handed to the Supreme Council. The signatories claimed to be "the official representatives of the Hungarian, German and Slav-language population," first and foremost, because "it is our duty to protest against that in all the decisions up to now, no opportunity has been given to nearly half a million people, who worked in brotherly agreement for centuries, to express their will in this question. This is a fact, which, in our opinion, is in opposition to the well-known principles of President Wilson and the right of self-determination and is not in harmony with the Entente's intentions, which tries to consider the question of political and linguistic borders with the cooperation and consultation of the affected population."[122] The reality was that, in opposition to the memorandum, *the Entente Powers at the Paris Peace Conference only supported the unencumbered right to self-determination of the Czechs, Slovaks, Romanians, Serbs, Croats and Slovenes and others, but not the Hungarians.* That is why plebiscites were not held in areas with significant majority Hungarian populations (Csallóköz/Žitný ostrov, Mátyusföld/ Mat'úšové žemé, Bodrogköz/between the Bodrog and Tisza Rivers, Tiszahát/upper reach of the Tisza River, Partium/North and West of Transylvania, Székelyföld/Szeklerland, Bácska/Bačka and other places).

The memorandum goes on to state that Western Hungary "has been part of Hungary for a thousand years," which "the Hungarians often protected and defended with their blood." The German settlers were never subordinated to the Hungarians, rather, they received protection and privileges. "The border zone of Western Hungary is the richest, most advanced in industry and culture, factories located here are among the most significant in the country ([Lajta]Újfalu, [Pozsony]Ligetfalu, etc.)." Of these, the most important were: in Sopron – metallurgy, carpet weaving, plastics, food processing, brewery, two tobacco factories and several brick works; in Királyhida – meat canning, grain husking; in Lajtaújfalú – jute and weaving works, two chemical plants; in Szarvkő and Vimpác – one each of ribbon factory; in Pinkafő – carpet and blanket manufacture; in Nagycenk, Cinfalva and Félszerfalva – sugar and sugar refineries. Losing these factories "means the decline of trade and manufacturing."[123] Of these, let us look at the expected future of the sugar refineries: with their loss, these factories lose access to the Hungarian raw materials, meaning the sugar beet growing areas of eastern Sopron and Vas counties. The factory in Nagycenk, as an example, has 18 beet growing estates, of which only three would be transferred.

It is, however, important to note that the majority of the factories on the territory earmarked for annexation were branch plants of Austrian companies,

---

[121] Az Ausztria által igényelt terület magyar lakosságának emlékirata. XV. jegyzék, 4. melléklet. 470–472. old.

[122] Ibid, p. 470.

[123] Ibid, pp. 470–471.

opened in the second half of the 19th c., with sizable Hungarian government assistance, to produce for the Hungarian market. As but one example, Ede Kühne (1839–1903), opened a factory in the village of Moson in 1869, which became one of the largest farm implement factories, making 90 different machines by 1885. There was also a significant arms and ammunition factory in the village. In the village of Szentgotthárd, also on Austria's wish list, there was a Europe-wide known scythe works, clock making manufacture, silk weaving and tobacco factories, as well as smaller workshops.[124] At the end of the 1910s, of the 365,000 population of Western Hungary, 102,000 made their living in manufacturing and trade, or 28%, while the country's average, including Budapest, was only 20%. In the affected territory, there existed at the time 84 plants employing between 10 and 20 employees, and a further 61 that provided jobs for over 20. At the time of the 1910 census, there were 8,138 independent tradesmen enumerated in the territory.[125] *The previous list of the more significant factories of Western Hungary stands as proof of the falsehood trumpeted by Austrian historians, and their Hungarian followers, when they state that, on January 1, 1922, an impoverished and backward Western Hungarian territory was annexed to Austria, under the name of Burgenland.*

The extent of the railway network in the intended zone of annexation was somewhat more developed and denser than the overall average in Hungary. Hungary's stock of railway lines around WWI was similar to that of the rest of the Monarchy, meaning Austria and Czech Bohemia and Moravia but significantly ahead of Romania and Serbia. The distribution within the country was, by and large, even, with the exception of northeastern Transylvania and Sub-Carpathia, due to their sparse population and mountainous terrain. In Trans-Danubia – the Austrian claimed zone is on its western edge – there were 8.9 kms. of rails per 100 km^2 in 1914 (this lagged only marginally behind the area between the Danube and Tisza Rivers, with 9.2 kms. per 100 km^2, railway track per population was 12.8km / 10,000). This latter number was the highest in all the various geographic areas of the Kingdom of Hungary.[126]

We have not yet mentioned the advanced culture of the area, the first class schools in Sopron, Szombathely, Kőszeg, Felsőőr and elsewhere. "It is unarguable and statistically provable that Western Hungary is the part of the country with the least number of illiterates. Several outstanding personages in the sciences and arts were born in Western Hungary. The German population always appreciated this privileged situation. Here, there never was any Pan-Germanism, or other similar trend, but most of all, never any anti-Hungarian movement. The population of this region with a German background has

---

[124] Kiss, Mária, 1981, op. cit., pp. 241–248.

[125] A magyar béketárgyalások. Vol. II, 1921, p. 62.

[126] Horváth, Ferenc: Magyarország vasútépítések 1900 és 1914 között [Hungarian railway construction between 1900 and 1914]. In: Magyar vasúttörténet. Vol. 4, 1900 to 1914. Főszerk/ed.-in-chief: Kovács, László. Budapest, 1996, pp. 121–123.

always identified through the centuries with the ethnic Hungarians and in times of danger, stood shoulder to shoulder risking life, fortune and blood for the common homeland. Not to go back too far in time but during the 1848 Freedom Uprising, not only did the Germans of Western Hungary but all the Germans of the country, without exception, took up arms and fought against Austria alongside the Hungarians in the fight for independence and freedom. Also, in a political respect, this population identified with the Hungarians. In elections, the majority of these districts elected representatives who were of Hungarian national character."[127]

Subsequent to the collapse of the industries – wrote the authors of the memorandum – the expected loss would be borne by commerce. The city of Sopron and the Hungarian villages along the Southern Railway Corp. line all lived almost entirely off the freight trade of grains, fruits and cattle to Austria. Also significant was the trade in poultry and eggs, collected by wagons all over Trans-Danubia, to be forwarded to the neighboring Austrian market. As well, the German populated areas of Western Hungary are mountainous, able to produce much wine but little grain. For this reason, the local Germans obtained their wheat, potatoes and other foodstuffs from their overwhelmingly Hungarian neighbors, along the Raba River, now smuggling these to the Vienna markets and selling them at great profit.[128] The markets of Western Hungary and Sopron are well supplied with grains and cattle, shipped from the neighboring Hungarian-populated areas. The annexation is not expected to improve Austria's and Vienna's food supplies, while separation from the

---

[127] A magyar béketárgyalások. Vol. I, p. 470.

[128] After the creation of the Western Hungary government commissioner's office, trade began once more along the border. Contrary to the intent of the authorities, the counter trade with Austria in livestock, in barter trade and in food distribution opened opportunities for abuses and smuggling. In this regard, representative Albin Lingauer addressed an urgent submission on March 22, 190 to the National Assembly to the Agricultural, the Finance and the Food Distribution Ministers. After his question in parliament, the National Assembly decreed that the heads of the three portfolios will meet the following day to consider the question. In: Az 1920. évi február hó 16-ára hirdetett Nemzetgyűlés Naplója [Minutes of the National Assembly session begun Februrary 16, 1920]. Vol. I, Budapest, 1920. Athenaeum press, pp. 149–175. The next day's ministerial response: ibid, pp. 176–198. On the basis of Lingauer's submission, a fact finding committee of representatives was sent out. The group tabled their report on July 8, 1920 (Report 94) which determined that representative Lingauer "was led by complete well-meaning towards the public good. However, it can be determined beyond the shadow of a doubt that the objectionable events can not be attributed to the responsible ministers, as the responsible departments of the National Assembly, can not be charged with ommissions because the problems can, on the one hand, be attributed to the special circumstances in effect, and on the other, are attributable to lapses of the local supervising branch." In: Az 1920. évi február hó 16-ára hirdetett Nemzetgyűlés Irományai [Notes of the National Assembly session begun Februrary 16, 1920]. Vol. III, Budapest, 1920. Pesti Könyvnyomda, p. 328.(The entire report: pp. 319–329.)

fertile Hungarian regions will, in all likelihood, be detrimental to the Austrian side. At the writing of the memorandum, the mainly German-populated districts of Sopron, Felsőpulya and Nagymarton districts of Sopron County, but also the city of Sopron, requested the government to allocate for the first half of 1919 grains totaling 1,476 freight cars for the annual needs of the population, some of which has already been received. Earlier, the three districts were allocated wheat by the Hungarian government in the amounts of: 1916-1917, 515 freight cars, 1917-1918, 360 freight cars, or 93% of the allocated amount to all of Sopron County. The German-populated districts of Vas County (Kőszeg, Felsőőr, Németújvár and Szentgotthárd) were treated in similar fashion: for 1917-1918, they received 97 freight cars of grains, over and above the food vouchers given to a large number of the populace. In early 1919, the Germans of the Felsőőr and Németújvár districts requested wheat from the Hungarian government, citing a poor grain harvest. The mainly German-populated Moson County took so much grain from the neighboring, Hungarian-populated Csorna district that, it is likely, there was not enough left for the district's needs. The preceding facts can be verified locally, or in the local food distribution offices, noted the memorandum.[129] Finally, the memorandum asked for a plebiscite in the areas intended for annexation by Austria, under the supervision of a neutral power.

The fate of Western Hungary, or *Westungarn*, was soon decided. Austria was awarded the swath of the Borderland – if not to the extent it wished – on the July 11, 1919 session of the Paris Peace Conference. The reason was that the Entente Powers had, in the meantime, fulfilled the request of the Czechoslovak government. There were two railway lines running to the Adriatic, to the port of Fiume. One of them (Pozsony – Zagreb – Fiume), the section running through Trans-Danubia (from the new Hungarian-Austrian-Czechoslovak border) from Hegyeshalom – Mosonszentjános – Csorna – Szombathely – Nagykanizsa – Zákány was to be retained by Hungary,[130] from where it continued along Kapronca – Körös– Zagreb – Karlovac to Fiume. About half of the other railway track to Fiume (Pozsony – Vienna – Semmering – Graz – (Marburg/Maribor – Laibach/Ljubljana – Fiume) ran through Austria. Thus, Eduard Beneš urged at the Peace Conference not to allow the majority of the two railway lines in the possession of one country. In the event of the closing of one line (due to economic or military reasons), Czechoslovakia should be allowed free access for trans-shipment to the South Slav country using the railway line through the other country. Paris, of course, satisfied this wish to the detriment of Hungary: an American initiative with tacit – later effective – French support and loud Italian opposition.[131] *In the end, the Peace Conference awarded Western Hungary to Austria mainly for*

---

[129] A magyar béketárgyalások, op. cit., vol. I, p. 472.
[130] Soós, Katalin. Burgenland az európai politikában (1918–1921) [Burgenland in European politics (1918-1921)]. Budapest, 1971, pp. 24–25.
[131] Ormos, 1983, op. cit., p. 288.

*the loss of South Tyrol and a smaller area along the Austrian-Czech border –
Gmünd, or Feldberg district – handed to Czechoslovakia.*

The Austrian-Czech border districts were awarded to Czechoslovakia, instead of the bridgehead demanded by Eduard Beneš on the right bank of the Danube across from Pozsony, which Prague did not get from the Moson County areas given to Austria. This also meant that the Entente Powers completely dropped idea of the Western Hungary corridor, the so-called Slav corridor, advocated from the beginning by the Czechoslovak delegation. With the materialization of the Austrian peace treaty, the previously marshaled facts fundamentally refutes the arguments of those Austria-friendly Hungarian historians, ethnographers and other researchers who claimed that ethnic boundaries were taken into consideration when the new boundary was drawn in the annexation Western Hungary. Two examples of them are: László Fogarassy, "In truth, it must be stated that the Peace Conference, with regard to the Hungarian peace treaty, was most respectful of ethnic boundaries relating to Austria," and Zoltán Palotás, "The Austrian-Hungarian border drawn in Trianon – we repeat – is ethnically correct. It is the only correct and impartial border sector of Trianon."[132]

The previous positions simply do not cover the reality. In fact, it represents the continuation of the earlier Habsburg-friendly, Austrian-leaning, as well as the worker movement / communist, point of view. Contrary to the above, historiography in the spirit and cause of Hungary – of whatever medium: newspaper articles, monographs or published statistics – must rest on historic truths and facts, not nationalism! The names and concepts of Burgenland, Slovakia, etc. should all be used in the times they existed, not applied centuries back, slavishly accepting the Austrian, Slovak, Romanian, and Serb view-points.

Finally, we must reiterate: there was no hint of the application of the ethnic principle with regard to Western Hungary. *Austria, as we have stated, received what was to become Burgenland in exchange for the loss of South Tyrol!* One of the territorial conditions of Italy entering the war in 1915 was the annexation of South Tyrol (as well as Trient, Trieste, Gorizia, Gradisca, Istria and Dalmatia) up to the strategic Brenner Pass, the most important crossing point as far back as the Roman legions and Germanic tribes. The Italian government received assurance from the Entente Powers in a secret treaty, signed in London on April 26, 1915. Having received an official pledge, Italy declared war on the Austro-Hungarian Monarchy on May 23. As previously noted, following the November 3, 1918 armistice of Padua, Italian troops marched unopposed into the promised southern part of Tyrol Province

---

[132] Fogarassy, László: A nyugat-magyarországi kérdés katonai története. II. rész. 1921. augusztus – szeptember [The military history of the Western Hungarian question. Part II, Aug.-Sept., 1921]. In: *Soproni Szemle*, 1972, issue 1, p. 23; Marosi, Endre: Magyarok Burgenlandban [Hungarians in Burgenland]. In: *Unio*. 1989, August, pp. 68-69; Palotás, Zoltán: A trianoni határok [The Trianon borders]. Budapest, 1990, p. 51.

(area: 13,613 km^2, population at the time: 215,000 Germans, 16,000 Italians). The reason was that in the 24-hours preceding the November 4 effective date of the armistice, the Austrian forces were to suspend military activities, i.e.-they could offer no resistance against the Italian army, while the Italians could use their weapons.

Thus, Austria, using clever behind-the-scenes diplomacy, was able to attain it territorial ambitions at the Peace Conference to the detriment of the Hungarian Kingdom, its ally and partner-country. It was awarded a strip of Western Hungary, a part of the claimed *Westungarn*. It only remained to occupy it militarily, as detailed in the final treaty terms handed over on July 20, 1919 at Saint-Germain. As it soon became apparent, this was the most difficult task for the Vienna government. In the last days of July, the population of Western Hungary in the areas assigned for transfer to Austria held numerous demonstrations against the territorial decision by the Entente Powers. The Austrian delegation, led by Chancellor Renner, handed back their written reply to the peace treaty in Paris on August 6. In it, *they expressed their thanks for Westungarn*, but continued to ask for a plebiscite among the population, directed by the Entente Powers, to decide if the people wanted to belong to Austria or Hungary. Renner's advisors brought up that the deciding point of the peace treaty's decision, to increase the viability of Austria, becomes totally irrelevant if Moson County is divided into two. Austria would be deprived of exactly the part of the county that plays a deciding role in feeding Vienna. Moreover, they asked for a plebiscite in the Kőszeg and Szentgotthárd districts, with its large German population. The previous action may seem generous but, in reality, it was not for Hungary's benefit. They were trying to create a precedent for a future plebiscite in Styria, where Austria lost significant territories.[133] A few days later, Chancellor Renner modified his previous position and sent a note to President Clemenceau offering to send Austrian military units to liquidate remaining pockets of Hungarian communists.

During these weeks, especially in August of 1919, the Western Hungary situation was very murky. Grabbing the opportunity, the Czech-Slovak and Serb armies began a concerted campaign for the creation of the Western Hungarian Slav corridor, in spite of the fact that this plan of Beneš was rejected by the Peace Conference on March 8. After the occupation of the Muraköz/Međimurje region in the previous year, between August 12 and 17, Serb forces advanced and took the part of Zala and Vas Counties today called Muravidék (the portion of the former Alsólendva, Muraszombat, Szentgotthárd, Letenye and Nagykanizsa districts, totaling 894 km^2, 155 villages with a population of 67,800.[134] (The events between the end of 1918 and August of 1919 in southern Vas County, the Vend area and the Mura

[133] Soós, 1971, op. cit., pp. 30–31.
[134] Zsiga, Tibor: Horthy ellen, a királyért [Against Horthy, for the King]. Budapest, 1989, p. 32.

River region will be treated in the next chapter.)

In the meantime, the Czech-Slovak armies were not idle in the North. On August 14, they crossed the line of demarcation on August 14 at the village of Pozsonyligetfalu on the Danube's right bank and disarmed the local 50-man Hungarian outpost, the so-called Danube sentries. On hearing this, the district military commander in Szombathely ordered the local command headquarters of Moson County to ask, through a peace negotiator, for the withdrawal of Czech-Slovak forces. The invaders refused. In fact, they stated that they crossed the line of demarcation to secure the bridgehead South of Pozsony, that their aim was not to occupy Moson County. Later, they pressed South of the bridgehead but soon returned to their former positions.[135] The reason was that the Entente Powers prohibited fresh military action by the Serb and Czech-Slovak armies for the creation of the Slav corridor.

Meanwhile, the Austrian government became emboldened and sent irregular units into Vas County on August8, which the Hungarian forces quickly repelled. The Hungarian government sent a diplomatic note to Vienna on August 16, stating that every armed incursion before the Entente's decision will be met with armed force. German Austria was not, at this time, prepared for an armed confrontation with Hungary, which is why it made the decision to send 'free irregular' troops to occupy *Westungarn*, seemingly independent of the Vienna government, as they already planned to do in May. The territory of the Borderland earmarked for annexation soon saw Austrian units cross the border. A public meeting was called in Némettújvár on August 17 with the pretext that the use of the Hungarian Socialist Republic's currency, the so-called white money, still in circulation had to be discussed. In the second half of the meeting, they announced that 251 Western Hungarian settlements intend to join Styria and petitioned the Austrian government to assume public administration of the area. The Hungarian border guards and gendarmes broke up the meeting. Colonel Baron Antal Lehár[136] (1876-1962), commander of the Szombathely military command, dispatched an armored train and an armed company of officers to Némettújvár to restore order. Hungarian authorities also broke up an Austria-friendly meeting in Rábafüzes, which had passed a resolution that those in attendance will no longer pay taxes to Hungary.

Colonel Lehár notified the War Ministry by telegram that the Austrians intend to occupy Western Hungary with four armored trains and volunteer irregular battalions, even though they officially proposed a plebiscite. Hence, he suggested that Austria be held responsible for the actions of the irregulars, recall the Hungarian ambassador from Vienna and put the prospect of beginning military action on the table. Colonel Lehár also indicated his intention to gather all available forces (the Szekler Brigade, the battalion brought back by him from Feldbach in Styria, the reserves in the county and

---

[135] Ibid, p. 33.

[136] Baron Antal Lehár, younger brother of the world famous composer and conductor Franz Lehár (1870–1948).

the 106th battalion) on the right bank of the Danube along the line of Petronell – Királyhida/Bruckneudorf, southwest of Hainburg, and possibly attack towards Vienna.[137] The colonel also sent a note to Pozsony, to the commander of the Czech-Slovak forces in western Czechoslovakia, French General Eugene Mittelhauser, requesting that, in case of a possible action with Austrian troops, his forces remain neutral. Lehár's plan was not approved by the Hungarian government since Budapest was already under Romanian occupation. The Romanian military command now threatened the Hungarian government: if it does not sign a separate armistice with it, hostilities will resume. This agreement was only finalized on August 27.

Austria, in the meantime, sent notes to the Paris Peace Conference, without avail, regarding its goal of occupying the Borderlands. The Entente Powers remained mute, or at least were in no hurry to hand the territory over to Austria. In fact, the Supreme Council of the Peace Conference decided on August 18 not to answer the notes of the Austrian delegation regarding the handing over of *Westungarn*. Georges Clemenceau, in his last note of September 2 commenting on the final Austrian peace terms, wrote: the borders drawn for Austria we cannot change; in any case, the line follows very closely the ethnic boundaries. That is why they did not consider a plebiscite necessary.

After an insignificant debate in the Austrian National Assembly, Chancellor Karl Renner signed the peace treaty for Austria on September 10, 1919 in the Paris suburb of Saint-Germain-en-Laye. It was ratified by the Austrian parliament on October 17. The peace – which prohibited *Anschluss* – trimmed Austria back to the core provinces. It lost the South Tyrol, Trieste, Istria, Dalmatia, Krajina, and a part of Carinthia. It did, however, manage to gain a strip of Western Hungary that was part of Hungary for a thousand years, which later, from January 1, 1922, was called Burgenland.

With the result of the subsequent plebiscite in Sopron, and later minor border adjustments, the peace treaty of Saint-Germain ordered 4,364 km^2 of Western Hungary, with 345 settlements, to be transferred to Austria. Among them, three cities (Sopron, Kismarton and Ruszt) were carved from the country. According to the data of the 1910 census, it represented 345,082 people, of whom 44,191 (12.5%) were of Hungarian mother tongue, 245,714 (77.2%) German and 49,374 (14.3%) Croatian. [**Nota bene**: German mother-tongue is not the same as Austrian ethnicity-*ed*.] Of the total population, almost twice as many as those recorded as having Hungarian as the mother tongue – another 80,632 (23.4%) – spoke Hungarian.[138]

The Austrian government did not want to accept some of the terms of the

---

[137] Fogarassy, 1971, op. cit., pp. 295–296.

[138] Lőkkös, op. cit., pp. 143, 288–289, 292. Regarding the size and population of the annexed territory, numerous imprecise numbers appear in historical literature. The reason is that Hungarian authorities ordered a census on December 30, 1920 on the Western Hungary region ceded to Austria. As a result, the data from the 1910 and 1920 census appear intermingled or erroneously attributed.

treaty it felt were unjust, either. Shortly, at the end of 1919, it requested plebiscites in all the German speaking areas along the Austrian border, to have the population decide to which country they want to belong. The Peace Conference only ordered one referendum – in Carinthia. In the meantime, Austria continued to push for plebiscites in western Hungary. In fact, it suggested that it be expanded to the eastern portion of Moson County, as well as in Kőszeg and Szentgotthárd. As a result of the January 1920 Austria-Czechoslovakia friendship agreement, Austria dropped the idea of plebiscites in Western Hungary.[139] (The referendum in Carinthia was held on October 10, 1920, as a result of which Austria was able to keep Klagenfurt and its surrounding area.)

Finally, and once more, we must firmly establish: *Austria did not gain a strip of Western Hungary as a result of the existence of the Hungarian Socialist Republic or due to respect of ethic principles but as compensation for the loss of South Tyrol.* This fundamentally refutes official statements of Austrian history, and of some Austria-friendly Hungarian researchers, that the Hungarian-Austrian border was determined on ethnic grounds as opposed to the millennial, historical border.

---

[139] Fogarassy, László: Nyugat-Magyarországi bandaharcok. (1921. augusztus–november 4.) [Western Hungary gang wars (August – November 4, 1921)] In: *Soproni Szemle*, 1961, vol. I, p. 40. Fogarassy's treatise appeared on the 40th anniversary of the creation of Burgenland. The sole Hungarian language treatment of its time. According to the expectations of the era, the title '*gang wars*' gives away its orientation. It reflects a servile acceptance of the period's Austrian media's and technical literature's direction, which brands the Western Hungarian revolutionaries, to this day, as 'bandits.'

Chapter 3: The occupation of the Vend (Slovenian) region of Vas County by Serbs – the Mura Republic
December 1918 – August 1919

We have already noted that the Serb army has completely occupied all the villages up to the line of demarcation, from the Trans-Danubian sector along the Barcs and Maros Rivers to Arad by November 21, 1918. Now, it was just a matter of time when the occupation of the southern end of Zala and Vas Counties would begin by the crossing of the Drava River. The district center of Muraköz, bounded by the Drava and Mura Rivers, Csáktornya,[140] was taken on December 24, 1918 by a Croatian unit of only 200, bolstered by some Serb elements. With this action, the Serb government and military command aggressively broke the terms of the November 13 Belgrade Convention when its forces crossed the demarcation line, the Drava River, and illegally pushed into the Muraköz. Here "they took over public administration, all the posts and offices, courts and schools were taken over with all their equipment. Civil servants, judges, teachers were let go and expelled [from the region], their places filled by their own men. (…) …people complaining about the arbitrary actions (i.e., individuals—*J.B.*) were jailed, beaten. The people of Muraköz also raised objections against this aggression because the Serbs and Croats had no right to do it."[141]

The occupying Serb and Croat soldiers closed not only the railways leading into Hungary (the Alsólendva–Lenti–Zalaegerszeg–Vasvár–Szombathely and Murakeresztúr–Nagykanizsa lines) but also blockaded the main public roads, as well. Contact with the Hungarian side was completely cut off. Thus, the Muraköz region was lost to the country. The region was completely dependent on Hungary: countless farmers had fields, vineyards on the far side of the Mura River and sold their produce there, too.

On hearing the news of the hostile occupation of Muraköz, the Hungarian border defense forces that entered the other district seat, Alsólendva, 20 kms. North of Csáktornya, in the middle of December, received the inexplicable order from Nagykanizsa – from the Communist Commissar of Somogy County, Jenő Hamburger (1883-1936) – to immediately withdraw from the village. The order was carried out and the village remained without protection. The Serb units immediately exploited this and, on the following day, entered the mainly Hungarian-populated Alsólendva with a meager force of about 20 soldiers on December 25 (according to some sources December 26).[142]

---

[140] According to the 1910 census, the population of Csáktornya was 5,213 of which 2,433 were Hungarian (46.7%), 2,404 Croatian (45.5%), and 251 Germans. In: Magyarország Közigazgatási Atlasza 1914, p. 100.

[141] A magyar béketárgyalások. Vol. II, 1921, p. 63.

[142] Göncz, László: A muravidéki magyarság 1918–1941 [The Hungarians of the Mura region 1918-1941]. Lendva, 2001, pp. 36–37.

The center of the Vend region,[143] the half-Hungarian populated seat of the Muraszombat district[144] was captured without any resistance by another hostile unit of the South Slav army. The Hungarian government handed a note of protest to French General Franchet d'Espèrey regarding the advance of the Serb-Croat forces past the line of demarcation but, before an answer was received, the 'capital' of Muraköz, Csáktornya, as well as being the most important village of the Lendva area and mainly Hungarian populated, the seat of the Alsólendva district, was in foreign hands.

The Hungarian War Ministry finally acted and issued orders for the recapture of the area down to the Mura River. To expel the Serb-Croat forces, significant forces were concentrated around Szombathely. During the night of January 2-3, 1919, a 250 or so unit of 'Vend volunteers' arrived by train, as well as a unit composed of irregulars, border guards and gendarmes under the command of Captain Jenő Perneczky. They recaptured the county seat in the so-called 'Muraszombat battle.' The Hungarian unit attacked the Serb sentries, first taking the train station, then the center of the village, where the enemy set up, and made use of, its cannons. The engagement resulted with four Hungarian wounded and two dead. One was a sailor, Lajos Matisz, who his mates considered as a hero. During WWI, he served on the battleship *SMS Saint Stephen*, which was torpedoed on June 10, 1918 by an Italian torpedo boat and sunk. Although he was in the icy water for several hours, he survived. During the action around the train station, he was shot through the heart. The other Hungarian casualty was Vince Bednyák, a local volunteer with the 83rd Infantry Battalion of Szombathely. The Serb defenders lost 20 dead and 8 wounded, and a further 7 officers and 21 privates were captured. The Hungarians also captured 2 cannons, 2 machine guns, 100 rifles and a large quantity of ammunition.[145]

After the victorious engagement, the territory northeast of the Mura River was again under Hungarian control, after the South Slav units gave up Alsólendva without a fight. To forestall another possible South Slav incursion, a special force of 500-600 Hungarian soldiers was posted in Alsólendva, complemented by units of machine guns, artillery and one

---

[143] The Međimurje (Slovene: Medžimurje) region, essentially the area between the Mura and Raba Rivers, has been called the Vend-region since the middle of the 19th century. It lies in the southwestern corner of Trans-Danubia and was part of the Kingdom of Hungary from 900 AD to 1919, and of Hungary between 1941 and 1945. Annexed in 1919 to the Kingdom of Serbs-Croats-Slovenes, then to Yugoslavia, it was called Prekmurje. In recent decades, it has been called *Mura mente*, or along the Mura. See Kocsis, Károly: A Muravidék mai területének etnikai térképe [Today's ethnic atlas of the Mura region]. Scale: 1: 200 000. Budapest, 2005.

[144] According to the 1910 census, the population of Muraszombat was 2,748 people. Of that 1,305 were Hungarian (47.5%), 1,310 Vend/Slovenes (47.5%), and 122 Germans. In: Magyarország Közigazgatási Atlasza. 1914, p. 137.

[145] Zsiga, Tibor: Muravidéktől Trianonig [From the Mura region to Trianon]. Lendva, 1996, pp. 52–54.

63

company of the 9th Nádasdy Battalion of hussars of Sopron. As well, southeast of the village, a telephone-eavesdropping / tapping device, the invention of Elek Schrantz, cinema owner of Alsólendva, was set up on top of one of the hills. Through it, important information was collected from the Serb forces' calls, mainly in French.[146]

As these events were happening, the Károlyi government, at its December 12, 1918 session, named Béla Obál[147] as Commissioner for Vend Affairs, who was also the High Constable of Vas County. In early January, Obál brought forth his plan to create a separate Vend county, as part of the autonomy to be granted to the minorities of Hungary. The Vends (Slovenes) were to be part of a new administrative department. The new county was to be made up of the southern Vas County districts of Felsőlendva and Muraszombat, plus a new one in Zala County, to be called Belatinci [Slovene: Beltici] district. The proposal did not gain favor because a portion of the Slovenes wished to be joined to the new South Slav country.

At the same time, József (Jožef) Klekl, retired parish priest of Cserencsóci (Črenšovci), with the assistance of four of his Vend-leaning Catholic priest associates, worked out their own proposed autonomy, aimed at uniting all the Slovenes living along the Mura and Raba Rivers. It was to be an independent administrative unit called *Slovenska krajina* (Slovene region), centered on Muraszombat (Murska Sobota). This independent territory was to be under the administrative control of Hungary, or, as dictated by events, the Kingdom of Serbs-Croats-Slovenes. The proposal included in the *krajina* villages lying on the Slovene-Hungarian language border and decisively Hungarian populated, the Slovene population making up only a few percent, among them the two district seats of Alsólendva and Szentgotthárd (these two with a Slovene population of 283 and 85, respectively).

Beside the Obál and Klekl proposals, there was another one, created by Vilmos Tkálecz, assistant ethnic commissioner and former choir-master of Cserencsóci, and his associates regarding autonomy of the Vend region. At Obál's request, prime minister Dénes Berinkey invited the representatives of the three proposals dealing with the Vend region autonomy to a conference in Budapest on February 12, 1919.[148] The plans for the autonomous region, received with unexpected indifference by the public, were swept away by the events of the following weeks and months.

In the first week of February, János Mikes,[149] Roman Catholic bishop of

---

[146] Göncz, op. cit., pp. 39, 51.

[147] Béla Obál (1881–1952), born in Vashidegkút, novelist, newspaper reporter, taught Church history in Eperjes (Prešov) between 1907-1918 at the Evangelical Theological Academy. After the change of governments, he returned to Vas County. Of the activities of 'Comrade Obál' in the Hungarian Socialist Republic, see the forgotten memoir by Éhen, Gyula: A felfordult ország [Country in turmoil]. In: *Vasi Szemle*, 1995, issue 1, pp. 128–129.

[148] Göncz, op. cit., pp. 43–49.

[149] Count János Mikes, born in the Transylvanian village of Zabola in 1876. He was

Szombathely travelled to the Vend region at the request of Commissioner and High Constable Obál, to restore public order. Obál did not accompany him but, using trumped up charges – Mikes favored a Pan-Slav policy and had begun organizing armed forces – reported him to the Ministry of Religious Affairs[150] while the prelate visited several settlements, urging all to stay in Hungary. He avoided confrontation by not visiting some Vend-populated settlements where Sloveneophile priests roused the people against him. The subsequent reports and false accusations played a crucial role in the Interior Ministry's February 26 decision to take the bishop into custody and to restrict him to house arrest in the Benedictine abbey of Celldömölk.

After the proclamation of the Hungarian Soviet Republic on March 21, 1919, the local organs of it came into existence in Vas County. Béla Obál, government commissioner and High Constable under the Károlyi government, continued to retain his position and became the president of the Vas County Directorate, as well as the people's commissar of minorities. Similarly, Vilmos Tkálecz, deputy commissioner for minorities, became deputy people's commissar for the Vend region and headed the nationality department in Muraszombat, while also filling the post of president of the Vend Region Directorate. The so-called 'Vend Region Government Committee' had responsibility for 114 settlements in the Muraszombat district, 14 in the Szentgotthárd district and 28 in the newly created Belatinci district.[151]

Tkálecz was often arbitrary in many of his decisions and one of the members of the Directorate reported him to the higher authorities, which made him somewhat more guarded. But, sensing the trust of the officers and soldiers he met, he decided to proclaim the Mura Republic, citing the self-determination of people. His plan was nothing less than a pre-emptive move. Making use of the vicinity of the Hungarian-Styrian border, the increasing

---

ordained a priest in 1899, elevated to bishop on December 16, 1911 by Pope Pius X and became bishop of Szombathely on January 6, 1912. During his time, his diocese opened 7 new poor-houses and 22 new parishes. He was a supporter of Count László Almásy (1895–1951) in his explorations of Africa. [Think the film *The English Patient*-ed.] During the period of the Hungarian Soviet Republic, bishop Mikes spent March to July, 1919 in a Budapest jail. Later, he played a key role in Charles IV's first attempt in 1921 to regain the throne. The bishop was an inveterate monarchist, which played a part in his forcible resignation on December 31, 1935. The following year, Pope Pius XI made him designated archbishop of Selimbria. He was a member of the House of Lords from 1911-1918, of the Upper House from 1927-1935 and a Hungarian royal privy counsellor from 1936 onwards [similar to *Queen's Counsel* (QC)-*ed.*]. He died in 1945. For more, see Székely, László: Emlékezés Mikes János gróf szombathelyi megyéspüspökről [Recollections of Count János Mikes, bishop of Szombathely]. Vasszilvágy, 2009, p. 286.

[150] Bakó, Balázs: Az ellenforradalmár püspök. Eljárás gróf Mikes János szombathelyi püspök ellen 1918–19-ben [The counter-revolutionary bishop. Case against Count János Mikes, Bishop of Szombathely, in 1918-1919]. In: *Vasi Szemle*, 2007. 1. szám, 75. old.

[151] Göncz, op. cit., p. 50.

traffic of goods acquired from Austria, mainly smuggled, has taken greater proportion in easing of necessities lacking in the Vend region. The individual enterprises, initially illegal, soon gained official status because the autocratic Tkálecz drew the Communist Directorate of Muraszombat into the Styrian 'trade,' even the lucrative smuggling. This eventually became known to the Budapest authorities, which wanted to call him to account. Tkálecz then began a double game. He contacted the politician Count László Szapáry (1864–1939), former governor of Fiume and Dalmatia, who had been in cooperation for a while with the neighboring Styrian (Austrian) political and military authorities. He asked the count for help in organizing armed resistance, or to obtain money and arms for the realization of his plans.

When Tkálecz sensed the unavoidable conflict with the upper tier of the Hungarian Soviet, and had won the support of the authorities of many of the settlements for his plan, he unilaterally announced the secession of the Vend region from Hungary. On May 29, 1919, he proclaimed the Mura Republic (Murska Republika) from the balcony of the Dobray Hotel. Its territory consisted of the Vend populated areas of Vas and Zala Counties, in all about 150 settlements. The president of the 'new country' was, naturally enough, Vilmos Tkálecz, former choir-master and first lieutenant, who notified the government organs in Budapest by telegram of the events, among them the Foreign Commissariat of the Hungarian Soviet Republic. The telegram sent to Foreign Commissar Béla Kun informed him that the Vend region became an independent republic because the people were not sympathetic to the communist principles and ask for, and expect, aid from Austria. As well, he disclosed to Béla Kun that the Mura Republic wished to live in a peaceful, good neighborly relation with Hungary. He asked the Revolutionary Governing Council not to take military action against the new republic.[152]

The last statement clearly points to Tkálecz and his personal gains from the smuggling operation, and the interests of the Directorate led by him and its members, individually and as a group, their activities and gains hiding behind the statement. Apart from some vague concepts, the deputy commissar responsible for the Vend region or the president of the Vend Region Directorate and President of the Mura Republic – all combined in the person of Vilmos Tkálecz – had no clear plan regarding the ethnic continuity, development and future of the Vend people living along the Mura River. With his circle of perhaps a dozen, he did not link with the previously mentioned goals formulated by the Slovenian Catholic priests for autonomy. It was also not coincidental that the head of the South Slav delegation at the Paris Peace Conference, Matija Slavič, attributed little merit to Tkálecz for any growth in Slovene consciousness, or the secession from Hungary by the Vend region.

It is a fair conclusion that, in spite of his Slovene background, the goals of the president of the Directorate had no Slovene national foundation but merely happened to be active in this unsettled period in the area mostly

---

[152] Zsiga, 1996, op. cit., p. 65.

populated by his co-nationals in the Vend region. Tkálecz proclaimed the Vend region country to make use of it for his personal ends and to avoid the looming reckoning with the leadership of the Hungarian Soviet Republic. Thus, *there can be no doubt that the Mura Republic did not, in fact, reflect a yearning for independence by the Vends living along the Mura River or express their wish to join the Kingdom of Serbs-Croats-Slovenes*, as some Slovenian historians and other researchers fondly suggest.

Regarding the assistance expected from Austria mentioned in his telegram to Béla Kun, Tkálecz got in touch with Austrian circles the following day, May 30. He told them that he was expecting the promised aid. With it, he prepared his escape route because he was barely involved with subsequent events. He sent his wife and easily portable valuables to Graz.[153] He simply abandoned the Mura Republic to its fate.

The main armed force of this new 'country' was a unit that consisted of about 300 men, with a few machine guns, stationed in Muraszombat and commanded by Captain Jenő Perneczky. The captain was known for leading the 'Battle of Muraszombat' five months earlier, on January 3, 1919 when his soldiers expelled the Serb forces from the center of the Vend region. Perneczky also assumed command of the armed forces stationed in the region. Tkálecz was able to secure the loyalty of the Muraszombat garrison, officers and men, by his promise that, through the mediation of Count Szapáry, he would obtain significant monies from the anti-revolutionary *Anti-Bolshevista Comité* of Vienna, and military support from the Graz arm of the Austrian Christian Democratic Party.[154] However, due to the expected overwhelming force, the army of the Mura Republic was expected to hold out for only two days. Tkálecz attempted to obtain the good-will of the commanders of the Serb-Croat military forces camped on the far side of the Mura River but was turned away.

The Revolutionary Governing Council of Budapest and the Military Commissariat ordered Red Army units to the Vend region from Zalaegerszeg and Győr to, as they called it, restore order. The clashes began on May 31 at the settlement of Mátyásdomb, approx. 15 kms. North of Muraszombat. Another Red unit advanced from Alsólendva toward the center of the Vend region, while the third unit of the *commune* forces started moving against the Mura Republic from the Gyanafalva/Jennersdorf area, close to the border. The forces under Captain Perneczky were, by this time, retreating toward the Hungarian-Styrian border. Not long afterwards, they merged into the Hungarian unit being organized under Colonel Lehár in the Styrian town of Feldbach.

The units of the Proletarian Dictatorship entered Muraszombat on the

---

[153] Göncz, op. cit., p. 59.

[154] Fogarassy, László: A magyar–délszláv kapcsolatok katonai története 1918–1921 [The military history of Hungarian-South Slav relations]. In: *Baranyai Helytörténetírás 1985–1986*. Pécs, 1986, pp. 537–574. (Baranyai Levéltári Füzetek 71. Szám / Baranya Archives pamphlet #71)

morning of June 3, where they met no opposition. Thus, the existence of the Mura Republic ceased, without it having been able to exert any kind of control. Although the population watched the entry of the Red soldiers with trepidation, there were no reprisals. The president of the Mura Republic, Vilmos Tkálecz, and several other leaders of the 'country' managed to escape to Styria. The surrounding population soon calmed down and the only resistance that we know of came from a Mura-side village where several soldiers attacked the Reds with machineguns. In retaliation, the Red command ordered four villages (Barkóc, Korong, Muraszentes and Csendlak) to be bombarded by artillery for four hours on June 3 and 4 – but in such a way as to avoid killing anyone or damaging any property – merely to frighten the population.[155]

The new president of the Muraszombat Directorate, Sándor Révész, quickly sized up the situation and concluded that the population of the county seat could not be charged with anti-revolutionary offenses. As his first order, he announced on wall posters that, in the name of the government of the Hungarian Soviet Republic, a general amnesty is proclaimed for all who were involved in any way in the 'Muraszombat anti-revolt.' The soldiers were not harmed, either, except they were urged to seize their officers, especially First Lieutenant Vilmos Tkálecz. Soon after, Révész had to travel to Budapest, so he left a three-member board in charge of affairs. This board selected hostages from among the important citizens, who had to report daily to the Directorate and the Red Army high command. This irregular situation lasted for only ten days, until Révész returned to Muraszombat and immediately cancelled the unwarranted order.[156] Apart from this episode, the following weeks in Muraszombat were characterized by general public calm, until the fall of the Commune on August 1. Vilmos Tkálecz reappeared in the Vend region in August and was immediately arrested by the Serb occupiers, jailed in Alsólendva, from where he escaped shortly and fled to Hungary.

In the weeks after the seemingly unnoticed end of the Mura Republic, in existence between May 29 and June 3, 1919, nothing notable happened in Muraszombat or the wider Vend region. Sándor Révész, taking over from Vilmos Tkálecz as president of the Directorate, behaved honorably and did not commit illegal acts. For his (lack of) actions, he was reported to higher authorities many times for lacking drive, and was instigated against. However, it was primarily thanks to Révész that, given the circumstances, relative calm reigned in the southern region of Vas County, in Muraszombat and environs, during the Hungarian Soviet Republic.

Two weeks after the fall of the dictatorship of the proletariat, on August 12, 1919, before the announcement of the decision of the Paris Peace

---

[155] Göncz, László: Muravidék, 1919. A proletárdiktatúra időszaka a Mura mentén és a vidék elcsatolása [Mura Region, 1919. The period of the dictatorship of the proletariat along the Mura and the annexation of the area]. In: *Vasi Szemle,* 2001, issue 2, pp. 155–156.
[156] Ibid, p. 156.

Conference, the royal South Slav forces arrived in the Lendva-region (Prekmurje) in such force – 7 battalions, 8 mounted companies and 5 artillery pieces – that the local population could not even consider resistance.[157] In spite of that, three months later, on November 29, half a company of Hungarian border guards crossed the demarcation line from the village of Rédics and attacked the Serb soldiers in Lendvahosszúfalu and Alsólendva. In the hopeless engagement against superior forces, five Hungarians were killed. In retribution, the Serb occupiers selected 40 hostages from the local population, who they tortured terribly.

In drawing up the final Hungarian-South Slav frontier on August 25, 1919, the Paris Peace Conference (of course) did not take note, here either, of the language border. As a result, three Hungarian-populated villages of the Szentgotthárd district (Domonkosfa, Kapornak, Őrihódos) and five from the Muraszombat district (Cserefa, Kisfalu, Kisszerdahely, Pártosfalva, Rátkalak) were annexed to the South Slav state. These eight villages were joined by 20 purely, or mostly, Hungarian-populated villages of Zala County in the Alsólendva district, which were similarly transferred. Finally, a totally Hungarian-populated village (Pince) of the Letenye district of Zala County was also ordered to the South Slav state. According to the data of the 1910 census, the population of these 29 villages was 18,330 people, of which 16,552 (90.3%) were Hungarians. These 29 Hungarian-populated villages represented a surface area of approx. 750 km², running about 60 kms. from North to South and 10-15 kms. wide. A further six villages had Hungarian populations between 25% and 50%, and others with smaller minorities.

When the peace decree of Trianon awarded the Lendva region and Hetés area to the South Slav country, the entire Vend Region had a population, according to the 1910 census, of 90,359 people, of which 20,889 (23.1%) were Hungarians.[158] The center of the annexed – and majority Hungarian-populated – Lendva region remained Alsólendva, a centuries-old market town. Its population in 1910 was 2,729, of which 2,375 (87.0%) were Hungarians, 283 (10.4%) were Slovenes and 51 Croats. The proportion of Hungarians in Lendvavásárhely was 99.2%, in Kebeleszentmárton 95.3% and in Bántornya 78.3% but even in the most populous Muraszombat, an island of Hungarians, it was 47.5%.[159] A large part of the small region between the Lendva River and Kebele Creek, with its 11 Hungarian villages, was also ordered to be handed over to the Muravidék/Prekmurje. The villages torn from the mother country were: Alsólendva, Bánuta, Lendvahídvég, Radamos, Zsitkóc, Göntérháza and Kámaháza, while Hungary retained Bödeháza, Gáborjánháza, Szíjártóháza és Zalaszombatfa.

The neighboring region, the 750 km² triangle bound by the Drava and

---

[157] Fogarassy, 1960, op. cit., p. 253.

[158] Pogány, Béla: A magyarság települési viszonyai a megszállt Délvidéken [The relationships of the Hungarian settlements in the occupied Southern Hungary]. Budapest, 1941, pp. 34–35.

[159] Magyarország Közigazgatási Atlasza 1914, op. cit., pp. 91, 94, 121, 130, 137.

Mura Rivers, has been a part of Hungary since the day of the Árpád-era, and only part of Croatia for a fleetingly short period. The Drava River has always been the natural border between Hungary and Slavonia, an associate country under the Hungarian Crown for 800 years. The exception was after the suppression of the 1848-49 Hungarian revolution and fight for freedom, when, as punishment, the Habsburg emperor temporarily separated the Muraköz, and other areas, from Hungary between 1850 and 1861.[160] The ancient Croats living here had, centuries before, a strong local identity and called/call themselves *Medjimurec* or *Muraközi*. On January 17, 1861, Emperor Franz Joseph ordered the re-annexation of Muraköz to Zala County, at the urging of the Croat and Hungarian population. It was done on March 11. Hence, the emperor admitted that the temporary Croat tenure had no legal basis.[161] Thus, from a historical-legal perspective, the tearing away of the Muraköz from Zala County, through the Croatian unilateral announcement of separation on October 29, 1918 (and its becoming part of the South Slav Kingdom through the amalgamation of Croatia), is but one of the many unjust decisions of the Trianon peace decree.

The current Muraköz region was formed in 1919 from the Csáktornya (72 villages) and Perlak (33) districts of Zala County and a tiny part (6,164 cad. hectares) of the Nagykanizsa district. Thus, the historical size of the Muraköz grew by a tiny amount to 785 km^2. According to the 1910 census, the 105 villages in the region were populated by 93,283 people, of whom the overwhelming majority were Croats and only 7,706 Hungarians (8.3%). The Hungarians lived in more significant numbers in the seven villages of the Csáktornya district, in the county seat of Csáktornya (2,433 Hungarians (46.7%)). The size of the seven villages varied between 165 and 788 people and their proportion of Hungarians also varied, between 21.1% and 45.4%. Of their total population of 2,564, there were 744 Hungarians (29.1%). Only one village in the Csáktornya district had a significant Hungarian majority (93.2%), Hétház with a population of 59. From a Hungarian perspective, the second most Hungarian populated place was the village of Légrád, at the confluence of the Mura and Drava Rivers but part of the Nagykanizsa district, where a third of the 2,896 population were Hungarians (940 persons, 32.5%).[162] With its inclusion in the territorial transfer, the number of Hungarians in the Muraköz rose to 8,646.

In historical literature, it became a widely accepted view by the 1980s that the Paris Peace Conference awarded the Muraköz and the Vend region of Zala and Vas counties to the Kingdom of Serbs-Croats-Slovenes as compensation for two cities and their surrounding areas. *It is an undeniable fact that the South Slav country received the Muraköz in compensation for the zealously*

---

[160] A magyar béketárgyalások. II. köt. 1921. 63. old.
[161] Botlik – Csorba – Dudás, op. cit., p. 65; Fára, József: Muraköz történetének rövid foglalata [Short recap of the history of Muraköz]. In: *Vasi Szemle*, 1942, issues 3–4, pp. 101–119.
[162] Pogány, op. cit., pp. 34–35.

demanded Banate city of Temesvár (Timişoara)*, which was, in the end, given to Romania*. Incidentally, to bolster their claim for the majority Hungarian-populated Temesvár, Otto Roth, government commissioner, ordered a plebiscite on December 21, 1918, as the urging of the local occupying Serb authorities.[163] The population of Temesvár at the time was 72,55: 56.6% Hungarian, 27.5% German, 8.1% Romanian, 3.6% Serb, 2.9% Jewish (for a total of 98.7%), the rest being a mix of others.

The other 'South Slav' settlement lost by the Kingdom of Serbs-Croats-Slovenes was the provincial capital of Carinthia, Klagenfurt. Increasing territories were being occupied after the end of the war by the invading Serb-Slovene forces. So, in early December, 1918, the provincial commandant decided on armed resistance. After the clashes, they declared a truce in January of 1919, which was broken by the Serbs on April 29. They launched an attack and captured Klagenfurt. However, at the order of the Paris Peace Conference, they were told to withdraw.[164] Afterwards, *the victors ordered the transfer of the Lendva region and the southern parts of the Vend region to the South Slav Kingdom in exchange for Klagenfurt.*

[163] Geml, József: Emlékiratok polgármesteri működésem idejéből. 1914 VI. 15.–1919. IX. 4 [Memoirs from my time as mayor, June 15, 1914 – October 4, 1919]. Timişoara, 1924. Helicon Könyvnyomdai Műintézet, pp. 108–109.
[164] Zöllner, op. cit., pp. 373–374.

Chapter 4: From the Treaty of Saint-Germain to the Peace Decree of Trianon

September 10, 1919 – June 4, 1920

After the collapse of the Hungarian Soviet Republic on August 1, 1919, during the period of the short-lived Peidl and Friedrich governments, Romanian troops occupied the northeast portion of Trans-Danubia to the line of Győr – Pápateszér – Nemesvámos – Peremarton – Úrhida – Adony. They did not press on because Colonel Antal Lehár,[165] who had just assumed control of western Trans-Danubia, took effective military action. Earlier, after the military disintegration of October 1918, he moved his command center to the Styrian town of Feldbach, approx. 40 kms. from the Hungarian border, where he collected Hungarian soldiers in Austria, at loose and looking for their units. He kept his units outside Hungary's border to avoid the well-known but irrational disarmament program of the Károlyi government.[166] He kept his battalion together, which later grew into a sizeable force. He and his forces crossed the Hungarian border near Szentgotthárd on August 6, a week after the collapse of the Hungarian Soviet, and returned home. The firm stand of the colonel played a part in the Romanian command asking Austrian Chancellor Renner on August 27 for co-operation in military actions. The chancellor's reply: his forces have no taste for fighting.

As it happened, on the following day, a battalion-sized Austrian irregular unit, with a cannon and six machine guns, attempted to take the important trade and railway center of Lajtaújfalu. They were recruited primarily from among the Hungarian Communists who escaped to Austria. The place was defended by only 58 Hungarian border guards. An armored train and a special unit, made up of Szekler soldiers and artillery, were sent to their aid from Sopron. The forceful response prompted the Austrian government immediately to cease military action against Western Hungary.

At the same time, a Romanian unit started from Győr along the Győr-Sopron-Ebenfurt railway to occupy Sopron and disarm the Szekler brigade's officers and men garrisoned there. The commander, Lt.Col. Gaáli dispatched

---

[165] Brenner, Vilmos: Koronás uránan hű szolgája volt csupán. Lehár Antal ezredes élete és szombathelyi működése 1918–1921 között [Merely the faithful servant of his crowned master. Life and actions of Colonel Antal Lehár between 1910-1921]. In: *Vasi Szemle*, 2001, issue 2, pp. 131-146; his memoirs, Lehár, Anton: Erinnerungen. Gegenrevolution und Restaurationsversuche in Ungarn 1918–1921. Herausgegeben von Peter Broucek. Verlag für Geschichte und Politik. Wien, 1973, p. 280; Lehár, Antal: Egy katonatiszt naplója, 1919–1921 [Diary of an officer 1919-1921]. In: *História plusz*, XV, 1993, issue 11, pp. 7–48; Zsiga, Tibor: A Nyugatmagyarországi Katonai Körlet Parancsnokság az ellenforradalmi rendszer újjászervezésében. A katonai szervezet létrejötte [The restructuring of the command structure of the Western Hungary theater in the anti-revolutionary period. The creation of a military organization]. In: *Vasi Szemle*, 1978, issue 3, pp. 385–395.

[166] Nemeskürty, op. cit., p. 49.

two Szekler battalions and an artillery unit to stop the attackers. The Romanians, reaching the village of Vitnyéd, retreated on August 29 and withdrew from occupied Kapuvár, then Csorna, all the way back to Győr.[167]

In the meantime, on August 12, the temporary head-of-state, archduke Joseph, appointed Miklós Horthy as commander-in-chief of the Hungarian National Army. Horthy's hands were tied in the collection of military forces by the enemy occupation of Szeged. Thus, the next day, he relocated his command center and units to Siófok, to bolster his forces with units in Trans-Danubia. Horthy named the monarchist Col. Lehár as commander of the Szombathely sector on August 22, whose unit was nominally entered into the order of battle of the National Army, while actually retaining its independence. The C-in-C was able to draw under his command units being (re)formed in Szombathely, Sopron, Győr, Veszprém, Székesfehérvár, Kaposvár and other places and add them to his forces. While bolstering his military forces, he reviewed his numerically growing Trans-Danubian forces through parades and city-wide events. The C-in-C review took place on the main square of Szombathely on September 21, 1919, attended by General Károly Soós (1869-1953), chief of staff of the National Army, and Col. Antal Lehár. The review scheduled for the following day in Kőszeg was cancelled due to weather. Horthy combined his Szombathely review with meeting of the regions leaders (government commissioner, county Vice-Constable, mayor, Catholic bishop).[168]

By the end of October, Horthy was able to reorganize the Hungarian National Army into an effective force made up of the units around Szeged, Siófok and the western Trans-Danubian Szombathely. This was an adequate force with which to enter Budapest and restore order, assume control and take

---

[167] Koréh, op. cit., pp. 193–194. The 2nd Szekler Brigade escaped Romanian capture through the brave actions of Captain Kálmán Verbőczy after the collapse of the Red Army in eastern Hungary. A smaller portion of the unit and their officers reached Budapest by train. Verbőczy assumed command of the 4-5 battalions and artillery left behind in the area of Kál-Kápolna. Since the Romanians ripped up the railway tracks, the brigade began to march toward Vác and annihilated, by artillery barrage, the Romanian forces blocking their route at Eger. They crossed the Danube on August 6 near Vác, having successfully evaded Romanian encirclement. They marched on toward Esztergom, then Komárom, from where the brigade continued by rail. They regrouped in Csorna on August 15. The approx. 3,500-strong Szekler unit was finally garrisoned on August 25 in the villages of Nagycenk and Sopronnyék. In: Fogarassy, László: Háború hadüzenet nélkül. Hadműveletek Magyarország területén a páduai fegyverszüneti egyezménytől a soproni népszavazásig. II rész. [Undeclared war. Military actions in Hungary from the Padua truce to the Sopron plebiscite. Part II]. In: Soproni Szemle, 1990, issue 4, p. 295.

[168] Simola, Ferenc: Horthy Miklós csapatszemléje Szombathelyen, 1919-ben [Armed forces review in Szombathely by Miklós Horthy in 1919]. In: Vasi Szemle, 2002, issue 6, p. 831. The work fundamentally refutes the popular opinion that Horthy's first visit to Szombathely was on September 1, 1929 when he cut the ribbon on a new hospital in the city, the predecessor of the current Markusovszky hospital.

command of the Trans-Danubian sector occupied by the Romanians.

At this time, the Romanian High Command began to withdraw its forces on September 23 from Trans-Danubia, on orders of the Entente Mission in Budapest. Their positions were assumed by units of the National Army. With the tacit approval of the Entente, the Vas County-Szombathely units led by Col. Lehár began their slow infiltration of Budapest and its environs in the first days of October. The main force, the Szombathely division, began its movement toward the capital by rail on November 8. After the creation of security and other concerns, the National Army officially marched into Budapest on November 16, led by C-in-C Miklós Horthy, later to be governor of Hungary. The entry of Horthy and the Vas-Szombathely units into the capital made all the papers and a newsreel clip was also made. It was ceremoniously shown in the cinema on the main square of Szombathely on December 5-7 to the city's and county's worthies. The important role of the units was lauded by the Western Hungarian counties' Government Commissioner, Count Antal Sigray (1879–1947), who later acclaimed them on December 15, 1919 at his official inauguration as High Constable.

Initially, after the fall of the Commune – principally because of the occupation of Budapest by Romanian forces – strong Hungarian central authority was lacking. Hence, three-four counties were organized into government commissions, whose appointed head, the commissioner, wielded almost unlimited authority. The Hungarian Government Committee for Moson, Sopron, Vas and Zala Counties, including the city of Sopron, of Western Hungary was set up on August 12, 1919.[169] Archduke Joseph, Hungary's temporary head of state, named Count Antal Sigray as head of the public administration.[170] Sigray received authority over all civil public

---

[169] Soós, Katalin. A Nyugat-Magyarországi Kormánybiztosság megszervezése [The organization of the Western Hungary government commission]. In: *Acta Historica*, vol. XXXIII. Szeged, 1969, pp. 21–39; Zsiga, Tibor: Az ellenforradalmi rendszer hatalomra jutásának eszközei és sajátosságai Vas megyében (1919-1920) [The methods and features of the anti-revolutionary regime coming to power in Vas County (191901920)]. In: *Vasi Szemle*, 1977, issue 3, pp. 394–403; Zsiga, Tibor: A Nyugatmagyarországi Kerületi és Vasvármegyei Kormánybiztosságok, mint az ellenforradalmi állam első decentralizált szervei [The district and Cas County government commissions of Western Hungary as the first de-centralized organs of the anti-revolutionary state]. In: *Vasi Szemle*, 1978, issue 1, pp. 105–114.

[170] Count Antal Sigray headed the government committee until January 1920, until elected as representative of the Christian National Unity Party. The post was then filled until August 1920 – the position was then suspended – by Count József Cziráky (1883-1960), former High Constable of Sopron County, monarchist politician and manager of the Habsburg estates in Hungary. The position was re-activated on November 13 and Sigray was again appointed to it. The actual reorganization only took place in January, 1921. Békés, Márton: A becsület politikája. Gróf Sigray Antal élete és kora [The politics of honor. Life and times of Count Antal Sigray]. Magyar Nyugat Könyvkiadó, Vasszilvágy, 2007, pp. 67–79; Békés, Márton: Sigray Antal Nyugat-Magyarország 1919-es szerepéről [The role of Antal Sigray in Western

74

administrative bodies and contact with foreign entities, all the while having to try and neutralize the threatened occupying attempts from all sides by Austrian, Czech, Romanian and Serb forces. He also had to address the calling to account the local henchmen of the Communist terror and the neutralization of the extremist, anti-Semitic elements appearing in the county.[171] Two days later, on August 14, German autonomy in Western Hungary was suspended, along with the activities of every local governing body.

The Western Hungary Government Committee, headed by commissioner Antal Sigray, cooperated closely with the II. Division headquarters, also in Szombathely, under Col. Antal Lehár, whose sphere also extended over the previously named four counties. The already mentioned March 22, 1920 parliamentary question of National Assembly representative Albin Lingauer[172] also posed that the government commission initiate contact not with the government in Vienna but the Styrian provincial government (*Landesregierung*) operating in Graz and co-operate closely with it. The reason for it was that "the Landesregierung of Graz was the one that gave sanctuary to the Hungarian counter-revolutionaries of the time, benevolently closing its eyes to us, permitting to bring in our weapons, men and equipment. The Landesregierung only asked that, if we should have a surplus of animals and food, we should let them have some of the surplus. In return, it assumed the responsibility that, for the to-be organized Lehár battalion of the National Army, and indeed the entire division, will permit us to ship equipment, boots, overcoats, etc. through their territory. This has, in fact, happened."[173]

With the active work of the Government Committee[174] and the aid of the

---

Hungary in 1919]. In: *Vasi Szemle*, 2006, issue 6, pp. 757–766.

[171] Békés, 2006, op. cit., p. 758.

[172] Albin Lingauer (Lékay-Lingauer), born in 1877 in the village of Gönyű. He studied law in the University of Sciences in Budapest. He was editor, editor-in-chief and owner of the publication, *Vasvármegye*, of Szombathely. In WWI, he fought in the front lines and was wounded three times. During the era of the Hungarian Soviet Republic, he was ordered arrested for anti-revolutionary actions but managed to escape to Serb territory, where he was briefly jailed under suspicion of spying. In 1921, he took an active part in both attempts by Charles IV to regain the throne, while being one of the main organizers of the Western Hungary revolt. He was the city of Kőszeg national (1920-1926) then parliamentary (1926-1935) representative. He died in Linz in 1962. See Békés, Márton: Egy vidéki „újságkirály sorsa. I. rész [The fate of a provincial "newspaper baron." Part I]. In: *Vasi Szemle*, 2006, issue 1, pp 15–34; part II, issue 2, pp. 171–185.

[173] Nemzetgyűlési Napló [Parliamentary Minutes], Vol. I, 1920, p. 150.

[174] The reinstatement of public administration could only be done by citing pre-October 31, 1918 statutes. Basing its actions on special Law LXIII of 1912 that the government passed in the event of a war, it created government committees on the territory of what remained to Hungary, first of all in Western Hungary. The statute – among other things – authorizes the government to take extraordinary actions even under the (mere-*ed.*) threat of war, gave instructions on the use of the police and

units of Col. Lehár, the control of the government slowly solidified in Western Hungary.[175] According to Count Sigray, all these came to be under difficult circumstances. "While threatened from the East by Romanian occupation (meaning Romanian troops wanted to capture Sopron and Szombathely—*J.B.*), we had to be continually alert on the western border in case the Austrians wanted to wanted to make use of the unreadiness resulting from the change in government to take possession by arms of the German-populated areas of the western counties. (…) We attributed great importance here to the question of Western Hungary not only from a local perspective but from the perspective of Hungary's future, which the upper circles – with the exception of a few – did not perhaps consider in its entire gravity. While those territorial areas which our adversarial neighbors have simply taken, under various pretexts and without opposition following the revolution, have *de facto* been under different governments for long periods but Western Hungary, whose ownership is demanded by our loyal ally in arms during the war, has never had Hungarian rule interrupted, not even during the revolutionary period and not today – it remains under Hungarian sovereignty."[176] After the Saint-Germain treaty that the Vienna government was forced to sign on September 10, 1919, the strip of western Hungary awarded to Austria continued to be under Hungarian administration because Austrian troops were still unable to occupy the territory.

The Supreme Council of the Paris Peace Conference notified Hungary on December 1, almost three months after the signing of the Saint-Germain treaty, to send representatives to receive and sign the peace treaty. The uninhibitedness and contemptuousness of the Entente politicians was shown by the fact that Hungary's borders were decided and drawn by February – March of 1919, while the summons to appear at the Peace Conference was only forwarded to the Hungarian government nine months later. The Hungarian delegation, led by Count Albert Apponyi (1846-1933), arrived in Paris on January 7, 1920. They were quartered in the suburb of Neuilly. In a humiliating fashion – similar to the other losers: Germany, Austria, Bulgaria – no direct negotiations were made with Hungary. Apponyi was only able to make one address to the Council of Five on January 16. He was even unable to contact the Entente representatives in writing; mail was forwarded through Lt.Col. Henry, the head of the military mission assigned to the Hungarian delegates to the peace 'conference.' Contact with Budapest was through the French telephone and radio service (the French naturally listened in) and couriers.[177]

After their arrival, the members of the Hungarian delegation were "immediately housed in a building, the Chateau de Madrid, under police

---

gendarmerie, the suspension of trials by jury.
[175] Sigray, Antal: Nyugatmagyarország az ellenforradalomban [Western Hungary in the counter-revolution]. In: *Új Magyar Szemle*, vol. II, 1920, issue 2, pp. 147–154.
[176] Ibid, p. 151.
[177] A magyar béketárgyalások [Hungarian peace negotiations]. Vol. I, pp 20-21.

guard. The Hungarian delegates were forbidden to contact other members of the conference, except by writing. As they were cut off from all personal contact, the delegation members sent one memorandum after another and dispatched large volumes of maps and statistical facts to the other delegates. However, all their work was in vain, since all had been decided in advance and the counter-arguments of the Hungarians were dispensed with. While the Hungarian delegates were essentially under house arrest, their opponents [the Czech-Slovak, Romanian and Serb delegates—J.B.] had free access to the delegates of the Peace Conference and did everything possible to promote their own interests.[178]

The Entente Powers handed the terms of the peace treaty to the Hungarian delegates on January 15, 1920, which was in harmony with the terms signed by Austria on September 10, 1919, in Saint-Germain. Austria was awarded a strip of western Hungary approx. 170 kms. long, 60 kms. wide at its widest and a mere 4 kms. wide at its narrowest (West of Sopron, at the village of Szikra). In his speech on the following day, January 16, Count Apponyi deemed the decision objectionable, if it is not amended. In memorandum XV that the Hungarian delegates delivered, with three appendices, they attempted to refute Austria's western Hungary claims. Here we quote the closing thought of appendix three: "We ask the Supreme Council to alter its decision made in the Austrian peace treaty and leave to us – if it so wishes, after an impartial plebiscite – this territory, which, based on the reality, the tug of the heart, and the fundamental interests of its people, has been, for over 1000 years, Hungarian."[179]

The circumstances around the discussions and affirmation of the new Austria-Hungary border reflect the state of affairs that held sway in Paris at the peace conference. István Czakó[180] reported it, based on the published stenographic record made by David Hunter Miller (1875-1961), special legal adviser to the American commission.[181] It becomes apparent from it that the

---

[178] Sisa, István: Magyarságtükör. Nemzet határok nélkül [Nation without borders]. Budapest, 2001, pp. 236–237; Kelecsényi, Ferenc: Párisban a békekonferencia idején [In Paris at the Peace Conference]. Budapest, 1920.

[179] A magyar béketárgyalások. Vol. I, op. cit., pp. 455- 469. The quote, p. 469.

[180] Czakó, István: Gyorsírói feljegyzések a trianoni béke létrejöttéről. Egy amerikai memoár leleplezései. I. rész [Stenographic notes to the creation of the Trianon peace. The revelations of an American account. Part I.]. In: Magyar Szemle, vol. VIII, 1930, issue 3, pp.301–308; part II, issue 4, 1930, pp. 391–400; Czakó, István: A trianoni „békekötés" felelőssége [The responsibility of the Trianon "peacemaking."]. Budapest, 1933, p. 54.

[181] Miller, David Hunter: My Diary at the Conference of Paris with Documents, Vol. I-XXII. Published by author, 1929, USA, no city given. Miller was a well known figure of the Paris peace treaties. Secretary of State Robert Lansing named him a special assistant of the State Department on June 9, 1917, for a nominal $1 a month salary (the USA only paid for his transatlintic and official travels). Miller arrived in Paris on November 19, 1918 and afterwards kept a diary, based on stenographic records, of the preliminary and key debates of the peace conference, the meetings of

Council of Foreign Ministers, and the Supreme Council of Four, usually accepted, without alteration, the suggestions of the committees for border determination, which operated very superficially and without regard for facts, or actual ethnic realities – except when those decisions would have been favorable to Hungary. Decisions to carve up a 1000 year-old country were made in such crude fashion.

As we noted earlier, the idea of annexing Western Hungary to Austria had not even surfaced in February-March of 1919, although claims to it were raised in October of 1918 by the representatives to the interim Austrian National Council who championed the idea of a Greater Germany and *Anschluss*. The terms of the Austrian treaty were handed to the Austrian representatives on June 2, 1919, *in which the Austria-Hungary border remained as that determined in the year of the Dualism, 1867* (the traditional, millennial border). This was not accidental because the Entente Powers were clearly aware that *pre-1867, Austria did not exist as an independent country. Even afterward, it was only as the other founding country of the Austro-Hungarian Monarchy – with Hungary.*

One of the most astonishing chapters of David Miller's stenographic notes deals with the question of the Austria-Hungary border. The revealing series of facts shocks even those with only a rudimentary knowledge of the proceedings of the Trianon peace treaty. *It is unique in the history of the world that, at an international peace conference, a boundary dispute is settled without any official consultation of the affected parties.* According to Miller's notes, the chief delegates were the most surprised when the topic was tabled. Miller recorded this interesting committee debate thusly:

Sonnino (Baron Sidney, Italian Foreign Minister): "I do not see the need to discuss this border question without preliminaries."

Pichon (Stephen Jean Marie, French Foreign Minister): " I think I am clear that we appointed no sub-committee to deal with this border question."

Lansing (Robert, American Secretary of State): "If that is the case, for myself, I fully agree with Mr. Sonnino's opinion and see no need to make any amendments to the present border."

Balfour (Arthur James, British Foreign Minister): "I consider a border amendment possible because, allegedly, a large number of Germans live in this territory and they allegedly wish to join Austria. If this is a fact, then it would be desirable to make preparations to discuss this matter."

Sonnino: "To the best of my knowledge, a request in this direction has not surfaced either from Austria or Hungary."

Balfour: "In my view, the Great Powers are not very interested in this question. But, in light of the ongoing difficulties between Austria and Hungary, it would be good to dispose of this question because it can still

---

the committees and sub-committees, almost minute by minute. The invaluable source material (with countless maps) was organized into 40 series and published in 22 volumes (approx. 500 pages each) and published in 1929.

create great difficulty if left disorganized.

Sonnino: "I do not understand and can give no reason for why difficulties would arise in the relations between these two countries."

Pichon: "In my opinion, it is unnecessary to put this question on the agenda."

Lansing: "Perhaps it would be best to assign this for a sub-committee to study, which would later report to the conference if there is a need or not for any alteration of the present border between these two countries? This committee could evaluate all suggestions that would be put forward by either Austria or Hungary."

Sonnino: "I see no need to send out a special group, since neither side raised the problem of a new border settlement. If they raise it, we can discuss it. Italy, for its part, completely agrees with the current border and we have no reason to alter it."

Lansing: "I only wish to prepare the problem, in case the border question should arise and the council should not be unprepared for the problem."

Sonnino: "I see no reason to forcibly raise the question. The Hungarians, although they were not present at the drawing of the Romanian border, still presented sharp objections. This matter would only create needless chaos. In any case, the two countries have never disagreed for fifty years over their mutual border. Their current governments are very uncertain and the time is not right to give rise to opposition over it between the two countries."

Lansing: "It is also my opinion that any work be undertaken by a committee if the matter does not create special problems."

Sonnino: "If it would be possible to do this, without the affected parties knowing of the preparations in the matter, then I have no opinion against the special committee."[182]

The peace arbitrators – after the French Foreign Minister's comment – finally agreed that the question of the Hungarian-Austrian question will be 'objectively' prepared for the time if this topic should ever arise in the future between Austria and Hungary. They also decided that, with regard to a potential border adjustment, fact finding was to begin as soon as possible and without attracting attention. However, until the two countries raised the issue, all future decisions were to be suspended. In spite of the decision of the committee, at one of the next meetings of the Supreme Council, *Woodrow Wilson again brought up the question of altering the border between Austria and Hungary*. It can be justifiably supposed that the Austrians and the Czechs (especially Beneš and Masaryk, related to the US president by marriage, through his wife) pushed to realize their dream of the Slav corridor. Having won the confidence and support of Balfour and Lansing, they must also have reached Wilson, too – and with momentous result. Miller recorded the following about the unexpected comment of the American president, which

---

[182] Czakó, 1933, op. cit., pp. 32–34.

caught the Italian Sonnino completely by surprise:

Wilson: "I have received some information that the 'Austrian side' raised the problem of border adjustment between Austria and Hungary and so a decision should be made in this question."

Sonnino: "I cannot understand why it would not be sufficient if Hungary recognized Austria's independence and Austria Hungary's without raising the border issue at all?"

Wilson: "I repeat, I have been informed that the problem has been raised by the Austrian side."

A long debate started after the president's final comment, at the end of which they finally agreed to the following: "Austria is urged to recognize the border in existence since 1869 (actually 1867—*J.B.*) between it and Hungary and, if any disagreement arises over it between the two countries, then the Allied and Associated Powers will address the question, as needed."[183]

As is now known, the "any disagreement arising" was eventually raised to such a level that border "adjustment" was required in the western area of Hungary. Davis Hunter Miller did not record how all this came to pass or later, how the victors were forced to redress somewhat the injustices performed by the Sopron plebiscite. He only recorded that the recommendation of the four border adjustment committees (The Czechs, Romanians, South Slavs and Austrians) was unanimously accepted by the Council of Foreign Ministers. In the end, *the notes and memoranda submitted by the Hungarian peace delegation, which rebutted with facts and figures the deluge of border claims based on false and skewed facts, the decision makers did not even deign to read.* Hungary's new borders were submitted to a full session of the highest body of the peace conference as the decision of the Entente's foreign ministers for the purpose of entering the terms into the future treaty with Hungary. Before it was done, however, perhaps to assuage their consciences, British Prime Minister David Lloyd George expressed an interest at the last minute how Austria and Hungary may be ensured free access to the seas, which their artificial borders precluded. The suggestion was supported by Italian prime Minister Orlando and US President Wilson, who wished to 'guarantee' for both countries possibilities and protection in this regard. A four-member subcommittee was formed (the 179th of the peace conference) which, in cooperation with the sub-committee of ports, waterways and railway matters, attempted to create, *on paper*, sea access for the two countries. After amicable discussion, they were unable to ensure 'guaranteed' access to a sea for either Hungary or Austria.

Hungarian public opinion and the highest levels of government were deeply disturbed by the unrestrained behavior of their former ally and partner country. Sensing this, the Austrian government – while the Hungarian delegation continued to dispute Austria's claims to Western Hungary – looked for support to strengthen its foreign policy subsequent to the Saint-Germain

---

[183] Ibid, pp. 35-36.

treaty. Chancellor Renner and Foreign Minister Beneš signed a secret agreement on January 12, 1920 in Prague. The agreement stipulated that, in the case of an attack on either country, mutual assistance – including military – was to be extended to the other. The agreement also offered assurances to Austria in recognizing its right to *Westungarn*. The Hungarian paper, *Az Újság*, printed the subject matter and content of the agreement on the day of its signing.[184] Diplomatically, politically and even militarily, the Renner-Beneš agreement was clearly aimed against Hungary, no matter how vehemently the Chancellor denied it, while only claiming good relations between Czechoslovakia and Austria. Beneš simply stated that a treaty of friendship and defense was signed. The agreement made possible, in the case of a potential Hungarian-Austrian war, for Czechoslovakia to use Austria's roads and rails to marshal its forces against Hungary.

The Czechoslovak-Austria agreement threatened Hungary with complete military encirclement and political isolation, which was the main goal of Beneš, since cooperation between Czechoslovakia, Romania and the South Slav country had essentially been finalized. Even if the series of agreements between the Little Entente countries was only finalized six months later, on August 23, 1920, between the South Slavs and Czechoslovakia. With regard to the Renner- Beneš pact, the Entente Powers, through the so-called Inter-Allied Military Mission, were forced to assert that they would not permit transit rights to Czechoslovak troops through Austria to occupy Western Hungary as that falls exclusively under Entente jurisdiction.[185] In the meantime, Austria also achieved for the Council of Ambassadors to send an Inter-Allied Military Mission to Sopron, to oversee the western Hungarian authorities. The presiding president of the Inter-Allied Military Mission in Budapest, British General George Gorton, notified, and at the same time asked, Hungarian Prime Minister Károly Huszár (1882–1941) on January 13, 1920: "… you would please inform the civil and military authorities of Moson, Sopron and Vas Counties of the arrival of this Mission and its purpose, and please instruct them to offer all assistance to the Mission."[186] The Peace Conference continued to favor Austria, more and more obviously. Austrian diplomacy achieved that Vienna could send two delegates to the Entente Mission to Sopron, based on a decision by the Council of Ambassadors on February 17. The president of the Council sent a note the following day to the Hungarian delegation in which the Council, "…led by thoughts of impartiality (…) has decided to authorize the Austrian government to send two representatives to the Mission active in the western counties of Hungary."[187]

The Hungarian government sent a diplomatic note on February 14, 1920 to

---

[184] Ormos, 1990, op. cit., p. 44.
[185] Soós, 1971, op. cit., pp. 59–60.
[186] MOL. K 26. 1234. csomó. 1920–XXII–525. szám, 6. old.
[187] Ibid, 1920–XXII–1703. szám, 1. old.

Chancellor Renner in which it expressed that Austrian territorial claims have upset the traditional good relations and cooperation between the two countries. It asked for a reinstatement of cordial relations, as well as approval of the setting of a plebiscite since – according to all his public statements – that was the method Austria meant to use to obtain Western Hungary. The Hungarian government – attempting to improve its position at the peace talks – offered a favorable trade agreement in return. Renner quickly replied to the Hungarian note in the negative. He replied that he does not consent to a plebiscite because the Treaty of Saint-Germain, signed on September 10, 1919, considered it as *res judicata*, i.e. a closed matter and a final decision. The territory in question, in his view, is legally an integral part of Austria, notwithstanding that it is still under Hungarian control. Subsequently, the Austrian delegates arrived in Sopron on March 4, 1920 where Hungarians demonstrated against them in front of the railway station and pelted them with rotten eggs. The Entente Mission in Budapest reported to the Council of Ambassadors in Paris that the population of Western Hungary is opposed to the annexation and demands a plebiscite regarding it.[188] Later, at the request of Count Albert Apponyi, the head of the Hungarian peace delegation, the Budapest government was able to name two delegates alongside the Austrians, in the persons of Baron Frigyes Villani, Foreign Ministry counsel and the mayor of Sopron, Mihály Thurner.[189]

Meantime, Albert Apponyi handed his comments on the peace terms to Paris on February 12, 1920, in which he suggested amendments to section II, article 27, and asked for plebiscites in every territory marked for annexation.[190] On the same day, he filed his response memorandum regarding the new borders of Hungary, in which he briefly summarized the Hungarian counter-arguments of the new Austria-Hungary border. In it, he pointed out that the Hungarian peace delegation has earlier handed over a separate, detailed memorandum on the topic. He again drew attention to the following: "The Austrians themselves have not demanded the annexation of this territory without a plebiscite, the population also wishes a plebiscite in which it wishes to verify that it wants to stay with Hungary of its own volition. The Supreme Peace Conference, if it wishes to retain the belief of the world which it set for itself, and remains true to those principles, cannot act without arranging a plebiscite for this territory, too."[191] All the more so because the territory of western Hungary marked for separation from Hungary cannot have only the ethnographic principle taken into consideration, which would seem to give German Austria the benefit of legitimacy – repeated Apponyi in the appendix to his memorandum on the new borders, the geographic units of Hungary. "The people's feelings must also be consulted, not only language. *The*

---

[188] Fogarassy, 1971, op. cit., p. 298.
[189] MOL. K 26. 1240. csomó. 1920–XLII–1945. szám, 6. old.
[190] XXII. jegyzék. Magyarország határairól [Of Hungary's borders]. In: A magyar béketárgyalások. Vol. II, 1921, p. 26.
[191] Ibid, p. 24.

German-speaking people along the western border do not consider themselves as Austrians in the same manner that the Swiss Germans do not consider themselves as belonging to Germany. Kindly ask them, the Germans of western Hungary. There already have been several manifestations of their feelings."[192]

The planned new Austrian-Hungarian border did not take into any consideration the existing western boundary, formed over centuries and in existence for a thousand years – stressed the appendix. This border came into being naturally, as it separated the hilly existence from the mountainous. The mountains of the eastern Alps are gradually transformed into hills, then into plains. The latter was completely part of the ancient Hungarian settlement area, with which the hilly terrain was economically tightly bound, with gradual transition. To the North, the new boundary would run in the middle of the Moson flatlands, without any geographic justification. South of Lake Fertő runs a line of hills and it would separate villages from each other that have had centuries old, clear-cut relationships. The separation would bring an especially devastating blow to those villages in the area surrounding of Szombathely because the Pinka, Gyöngyös and their feeder rivers all flow toward the city, and all their trade is destined there.

The new border would sever, among other things, and make unusable the Szombathely-Pinkafő (Pinkafeld) and Körmend–Németújvár (Güssing) rail lines. Also, the flood control levees of the Raba and Szigetköz would be affected and possibly cause unforeseeable damages. The flood control measures along the northern part of the western border, the marsh draining activities, the state constructed canals and the entire system of flood dams would be thrown into chaos in the event of annexation. The dam controlling the level of Lake Fertő and the Hanság marshes would also be in foreign hands, which would put the economic life along the marshes at the good-will or spite of a foreign country. The Moson branch of the Danube, the Hanság canal and Raba waterway are well coordinated and unified, which a ruthlessly drawn language boundary would wreck completely and expose a well-cultivated, densely populated area to the greatest peril. Perhaps the geographic harmony cannot be expressed any better than in the water control works.[193]

In early 1920, many Hungarian Cabinet meetings were devoted to vacating the western Hungary territory demanded by Austria, and its hand-over, but no official instructions were given for it. At the same time, getting ready for every eventuality, orders were given for the prompt removal of all national and public assets – without drawing undue attention – which Commissioner Sigray also urged in his telegram of January 19 to Prime Minister Huszár. On this point, there was no unanimity within the government: the Interior Minister and the Trade and Agriculture Minister supported the move, while

---

[192] XXII. jegyzék. 1. melléklet. Magyarország földrajzi egysége. Ibid, p. 61. (Bolding mine–*J.B.*)
[193] Ibid, pp. 61–62.

Finance did not give its assent, in the short term, wanting to take the matter before the Cabinet,[194] where it was shortly put on the agenda.

The various diplomatic efforts of the Hungarian government in early 1920, for the retention of the entire Borderland region, bore no fruit. The Hungarian ambassador to Vienna, Gusztáv Gratz (1875-1946), reported on January 27 that he had a long conversation with Chancellor Renner the previous evening whose "statements raised the most painful reactions in Hungary and are only useful, in the end, to exacerbate relations between Austria and Hungary. (…) I offered the calling for a plebiscite, which he deemed unacceptable, alluding to our exerted pressure. (…) Finally, he asserted that Austria has utter need of this area (meaning Western Hungary—*J.B.*) for strategic and economic reasons. (…) the reluctance to hold a plebiscite proves that Austria was an eager student of the annexation methods against which it rightfully complained in Saint-Germain – learned much and forgot everything."[195]

On February 11, 1920, the government commissioner for Sopron County, Jenő Fertsák,[196] reported, among other things, the following in a telegram to the prime minister's office on the activities of the Entente Mission: "It is more and more certain by the hour that the Mission is preparing for the handover: today they were asking outright questions regarding the methods of the handover, whereas, up to now, they tried to make it seem their aim is only information gathering. (…) the comments made yesterday and today by members of the Mission lead me to conclude that there is faint hope for a favorable turn in the matter of Western Hungary." Fertsák urgently asked for instructions from the government on what to do if the territory awarded to Austria had to be begun to be evacuated and handed over to Austria. At the same time, he drew attention to "if, as originally planned, all national and military assets are to be shipped out from here, that will have an adverse impression on the population here, which could be positively catastrophic on the outcome of a possible plebiscite."[197] The March 17 memorandum of Jakab Bleyer, minister without portfolio for minorities, also added to the previous report. "I am powerless," he reported to the prime minister that, against the decision of the Cabinet, the dismantling and evacuation of Western Hungary was continuing, especially by the army. He asked the Ministry of War, without success, "to suspend the action due to the negative effect on the mood of the population" but by no avail. Finally, Bleyer urged that: local authorities be given instructions regarding "the type of conduct to be shown and actions to be performed which would support the Hungarian government and activities of the peace delegation in their effort to save Western Hungary."[198]

The Hungarian government received frequent updates of the political mood of the mainly German-populated Western Hungary from the reports of

---

[194] MOL. K 26. 1234. csomó. 1920–XXII–524. szám, 1–3. old.

[195] Ibid, 1920–XXII–1166. szám, 1., 3. old.

[196] Fertsák Jenő korábban Sopron törvényhatósági jogú város főispánja volt.

[197] MOL. K 26. 1234. csomó. 1920–XXII–1331. szám, 2., 4. old.

[198] Ibid, 1920–XXII–3691. szám, 1–2. old.

the Hungarian Territorial Integrity Protection League [Magyarország Területi Épségének Védelmi Ligájától / TEVÉL, rövidítve Területvédő Liga]. The league was formed in November of 1918 as a civil organization, electing as its president Lajos Lóczy (1849-1920), geologist, geographer, at its general meeting in Budapest on December 14. The goal was to try and retain the borders of King Saint Stephen (ruled 1000-1038), with the exception of Croatia, using social and scientific means. It meant to make use of internal and external political education, raising the level of Hungarian nationalistic feelings, as well as to try and win over the former ethnic minorities. Numerous bodies, associations, benevolent societies joined the League, until it had a membership of 1 million. Expert committees were created, publications were distributed in the Entente countries (in French and English) supporting the political, economic and cultural single entity of Hungary. For a while in 1919, the League operated illegally, then, after the publication of the terms of the peace treaty and its signing at Trianon, the League's activities increased and became an umbrella organization for several irredentist movements.[199]

The delegates of the League from Szombathely, Mosonmagyaróvár and Sopron sent reports, drawing attention to the increasing Austrian influence toward secession, the living conditions of the population and the results of the loyalty oaths being taken for Hungary. As an example, the February 27 report noted that: the February 15 public meeting in the village of Borostyánkő, "at which the villages of Edeháza, Háromsátor, Mencsér and Újvörösvágás were represented in large numbers, a four-point resolution was accepted amidst great enthusiasm." The second point read: "We protest against any means of forcible annexation to Austria and demand a plebiscite to allow everyone to freely express their opinion to decide which country they want to be a part of." A public meeting the same day in Rohonc, attended by 2,500 men, unanimously announced that they wished to add their names "to the list, part of a memorandum handed to the head of the Entente Mission visiting Western Hungary, supporting the plebiscite, as they are not willing to separate from Hungary because they are Germans loyal to Hungary."[200] [**N.B.:** Germans, not

---

[199] As part of the obligations in the peace decree, the Hungarian government, *pro forma*, abolished the irredentist associations. After the Interior Ministry's directive took effect on July 5, 1921, the League merged into the Hungarian National Association, which assumed the assets of the League, its associates and its considerable amount of publicity materials. Zeidler, Miklós: A revíziós gondolat [The idea of revision]. Budapest, 2001.

[200] MOL. K 26. 1920. csomó. 1920–XLII–2035. szám, p. 33. Alongside the League, the Western Hungary League (WHL), formed in Budapest on December 7, 1919, set as its goal the retention of the to-be annexed parts of Moson, Sopron and Vas counties. It elected Gusztáv Thirring (1861-1941), statistician, demographer, as its president. The three counties each had a head representative, as well as district ones, who began regular in January 1920, monthly local summary reports. The WHL worked closely with the League, taking active part in all its activities. Later, it merged

Austrians—*J.B.*]

Over the next two days, February 16 and 17, meetings held in the villages of Alsószénégető, Felsőszénégető, Gyöngyösfő, Vágod, Barátmajor, Hármasfalu, Kulcsárfalva, Rumpód, Léka, Hosszúszeghuta, Hámortó, Hosszúszeg, Szabar, Óhodász, Csajta, Incéd and Németgyirót unanimously declared that "under no condition would they allow themselves to be transferred to Austria and protest every attempt aimed at forcibly splitting them from Hungary."[201]

Meanwhile, the Austrian military preparations for the occupation of the Borderland continued. Also on February 17, the Hungarian National Army's High Command notified the Prime minister and other affected ministries in a report (11 593 / I. a.) that, according to information received from the Chief District Magistrate of the Németújvár district, 2,000 well-armed soldiers were transported by rail from the Styrian town of Feldbach, close to the Austrian-Hungarian border.[202]

The *Soproni Hírlap* (Sopron Gazette) published a special edition at the end of March in which it addressed – in French, German and Hungarian – a *Proclamation* to the members of the Entente Military Mission in Sopron. The proclamation drew the Mission's attention to the fact that, during the time of the Hungarian Red Terror, "the Austrian socialist government (…) showed scant regard for the troubles of their 'German brothers' [of Western Hungary] but rather showed at every turn their sympathy towards the Bolsheviks. (…) With the end of Bolshevism, Austria suddenly changed into the guardian angel of Western Hungary, to free our people from Christian terror and persecution of Germans, which do not exist. Nobody here knows anything about German persecution. The punishment of Bolshevik misdeeds can only be interpreted as persecution of Germans through malicious slander. The cultural and political rights of Germans are guaranteed by Hungarian minority laws, which have been broadened recently in the most liberal spirit." The *Proclamation* then points out that, through almost four centuries, Austria "has done everything to destroy Hungary's ancient constitution and force German language and German law on the Hungarians. Vienna was not particular in its methods when it came to crushing national resistance."[203]

The leaders of the Hungarian freedom fights died in exile (Ferenc Rákóczi II, prince of Hungary and Transylvania, Governor and President Lajos Kossuth), 13 Hungarian generals were executed on October 6, 1849 in Arad, and hundreds more executed. "Our lands make a perfect historical, cultural and economic unit with the mother country, the breaking of which is pointless

---

into the League, quietly ceasing independent operation in September of 1922. Sarkady, Sándor, ifj./jr: A Nyugat-Magyarországi Liga. Egy területvédő szervezet tevékenysége 1919–1922 között [The Western Hungary League.]In: *Soproni Szemle*, 2001, issue 1, pp. 34-57.

[201] MOL. K 26. 1920. csomó. 1920 – XLII–2035. szám, 33. old.

[202] Ibid, 1920 – XXII–1511. szám, 1. old.

[203] *Soproni Hírlap*, (year VII, issue 73) March 30, 1920, p. 3.

for Austria, ignominious for Hungary, and would be ominous for our little rural area. (…) No, gentlemen, the people of Western Hungary are not willing to sacrifice themselves for a sick neighbor. (…) You will not shove us around on a map like chess pieces, hither and yon, we demand our right to self determination, a plebiscite. (…) Your mission, gentlemen, is to enlighten the powerful of the world and draw the attention of the peace conference to a small but determined people who demand that their voice be heard before decisions are made of their fate. Do this, gentlemen, without prejudgment and the thanks of three hundred thousand people will follow you back to your country."

The editors added the following comment, in bold typeface, to the *Proclamation*: "Our historical issue, expressing Western Hungary's people's loyalty to the thousand-year Hungary, condemned to be torn from the country, and their protest against separation, has been handed to the members of the Entente Mission in Sopron and forwarded to the appropriate places in Paris."[204] It is interesting to note that the prime minister's office annotated with regard to the *Proclamation*: "Without doubt, it fulfills our needs very well, but too bad that the author included his initials at the end, which could lead to identification of the author."[205] According to the document, the author of the piece was A. Ullein, a Foreign Ministry official of German background.[206]

The following situation report was attached to the previous proclamation to the Budapest management of the League on April 23, 1920: "As regards to the general situation, happily I can finally report that the atmosphere in the border villages is improving by the day, especially due to the more open manifestation of Austrian bolshevism. We have included the improvements into the present mapping after mutual agreement, i.e., whether this is of temporary or permanent character?! The Austrian workers threaten us with a May 1 raid, hence the border settlements are begging for soldiers at the county military headquarters. All of a sudden, they are happy to see

---

[204] Ibid, pp. 3–4.

[205] MOL. K 26. 1240. csomó. 1920–XLII–2939. szám, 1. old.

[206] A. Ullein, later known as Antal Ullein-Reviczky (Ullein until 1934, 1894–1955). Sopron born lawyer and diplomat, served in the shared Foreign Ministry of the Austro-Hungarian Monarchy (1913-1918), afterwards in the Hungarian Foreign Ministry. He served in various capacities in Vienna, Paris, Ankara and Zagreb (1923-1938). He led the Press and Propaganda department of the Foreign Ministry (1938-1943). As ambassador to Sweden (Sep. 1943-March 1944), he was part of the Kallay government's peace feelers towards the western allies. After the German occupation of Hungary, he resigned on March 21, 1944 and criticized the Sztóyai government in an official statement. After WWII, he lived as an émigré in several countries, finally settling in London in 1950. From June of that year, he was the London representative of the Hungarian National Committee, headquartered in New York. His memoirs: German war – Russian peace. Hungary's Drama, was publishe in French (Neuchàtel, 1947) and later in Hungarian (Budapest, 1993, p. 324).

Hungarian soldiers, which is a great achievement."[207]

While these events were unfolding, the final text of the Trianon peace treaty was being finalized in Paris.[208] The 'circumspection,' and often cynical behavior of the decision-making gentlemen, was reflected in the borders of the 'new' Hungary. It soon became clear that the decisions of the border defining committees, which consistently ignored ethic realities, facts and operated perfunctorily, were essentially accepted without alterations by the Council of Foreign Ministers and the Council of Four. Their decisions resulted in the pitiless breakup of the thousand-year-old Hungary. The documents of the peace conference contain numerous, flagrant instances of partisan treatment. Such as one general of the Entente not recognizing the November 3, 1918 Padua truce agreement signed by another Entente general, Armando, Diaz. Or some foreign ministers vetoing their prime minister's suggestions, see later the case of David Lloyd George. Some Hungarian historians see the existence of the Hungarian Soviet Republic as playing a key role in the annexation of Western Hungary. This does not stand up to scrutiny because, as we have already stated, *this territory was given as compensation to Austria for South Tyrol, annexed to Italy. In this decision, a key role was played by President Wilson, who supported Austria, in opposition to the French, in its unrestrained and odious claims against Hungary.*

The Hungarian memoranda handed to the peace conference, especially the French-language speech of Albert Apponyi (and its English and Italian summary) did not go totally without effect. Italian PM Nitti and British PM Lloyd George suggested at the Supreme Council meeting of February 25, and again on March 3, that the question of Hungary's borders be sent back for reconsideration, based on available materials and "without bias." The British PM, citing relatively accurate numbers, pointed out that the peace agreement will place 2,750,000 Hungarians, meaning "a third of the Hungarian population," under foreign rule, which "will not be easy to defend." (The reality was closer to 3,500,000, most of whom lived immediately alongside the newly drawn borders, now in a foreign country, and what was (or used to be) an integral part of the Hungarian ethnic bloc.) There will be no peace in Europe, Lloyd George predicted, "if later it becomes known that Hungary's claims are justified and entire Hungarian communities were given to Czechoslovakia or Transylvania [sic! meaning Romania—*J.B.*] like a herd of cattle, just because the conference refused to discuss the Hungarian issue."[209]

Subsequently, a French language memorandum was prepared, which was

---

[207] MOL. K 26. 1240. csomó. 1920–XLII–3459. szám, 7. old.
[208] Count Albert Apponyi, Albert Berzeviczy et al: Igazságot Magyarországnak. A trianoni békeszerződés következményeinek ismertetése és bírálata [Justice for Hungary]. Magyar Külügyi Társaság. Budapest, 1928, p. 175.
[209] Documents on British Foreign Policy 1919-1939. Ed. by P. T. Bury & R. Butler. First Series. Vol. VII. London, 1958, pp. 384-388. Cited by Romsics, Ignác: Magyarország története a 20. században [Hungarian history in the 20th century]. Budapest, 1999, p. 140.

discovered among the papers of Vittorio Cerruti, the chief Italian representative in Budapest. The author suggested plebiscites in some of the Hungarian-populated areas earmarked for annexation, including Western Hungary. "The dismemberment of Hungary will happen – reads one of the documents – without taking into the least consideration the will of the affected people. They are herded from one country into another like reluctant flocks in a barn." It then continued: "More than half of these people are Hungarian or German and nothing entitles us to the conclusion that the other half totally wishes to separate from its old country." And finally, a conclusion: "Only a plebiscite would be able to conclusively determine the will of the population, and it seems impossible for us to deem this demand as a *quantié négligeable* (negligible amount)."[210]

French Prime Minister and Foreign Minister Alexandre Millerand rejected the reexamination of the Hungarian borders. Yet, the Ambassadors and Foreign Ministers meeting in London on March 8, 1920 returned to the question of Hungary's borders. In the discussions, the Italians suggested investigation of the Hungarians' counter-arguments, while the French deemed reconsideration as superfluous and out-of-date. The British diplomats – among them Foreign Minister George Curzon – tipped the scales by not lining up behind their own prime minister, Lloyd George, but behind the French position. In Curzon's proposal, they finally reached a symbolic agreement: the reopening of the Hungarian border question was rejected before the signing of the peace treaty but made it possible for the border settlement committees to make suggestions for minor alterations if local visits to certain sectors find actual unfairness. It was also decided here that the possibility of later modifications would not be included in the text of the peace treaty but would be made known to the Hungarians through a separate accompanying letter. This became the so-called *lettre d'envoi* of Millerand, which was later attached to the Trianon decree. The attached letter was, thus, not of French but of British origin but signed by the French President as president of the Peace Conference.[211] It was also he who handed the final text of the Trianon Treaty to the Hungarian delegation on May 6, 1920.

The so-called Millerand letter[212] affixed that: Hungary's wishes could not be taken into consideration but – as it soon became cynically evident – that the League of Nations would 'discuss' minor border adjustment requests. But only, naturally, if the determined border "perhaps does is not completely adequate for the ethnographic or economic requirements." The failings will be remedied by the border committees. The Supreme Council sent its reply to the comments of the Hungarian peace delegation on May 20, 1920, along with the final text of the peace treaty. The Entente Powers deemed as irrelevant the

---

[210] Archivio Storico [Roma], AP, B. 1740 (Ungheria), Cerruti, Feb. 3, 1920. Cited by Ormos, 1990. op. cit., p. 43.

[211] Romsics, 1999, op. cit., p. 141.

[212] A magyar béketárgyalások. II. köt. 479–480. old.

Hungarian suggestions regarding territorial solutions and plebiscites.

The border adjustment promises of the Entente Powers remained just that, high-sounding promises, because the Council of Ambassadors sent secret instructions to the border adjustment committees on July 22, 1920 to ignore the Millerand letter and to post the borders according to the terms of the peace treaty. In the meanwhile, the letter raised unfounded optimism in official Hungarian circles, which was further fed by the non-ratification of the peace treaties by the United States, although for reasons independent of the Hungarian question, and even signing a separate peace with Hungary on August 29, 1921.

Chapter 5: Austrian efforts and the failure of territorial transfer
June 1920 – August 1921

The obligatory signing of the Trianon peace decree – as already noted – took place on June 4, 1920 in Paris. The decision – in harmony with the Austrian treaty of Saint-Germain signed on September 10, 1919 – cut off 4,364 km^2 of western Hungarian territory. The last census, in 1910, enumerated a population of 345,082, of which 245,714 were of German mother-tongue, 49,374 of Croatian and 44,191 of Hungarian. Of the total population, including the ethnic Hungarians, 80,632 (23.4%) spoke Hungarian.[213] It is important to point out once again that, *the majority of the population given to Austria were of German extraction and mother-tongue and not of Austrian extraction and mother-tongue, as the latter did not yet exist!* [In fact, the majority of the German speaking population traced their ancestry not to what was to become Austria but to other German provinces or states-*ed*.]

Hungarian public opinion could not come to grips with and accept the obviously unjust and cynical decision that gave Austria, an equally defeated country in the war, territory from its also defeated ally, Hungary. "It is doubly painful – wrote Foreign Minister Miklós Bánffy (1873–1950) in his memoirs – that we had to hand over Sopron and its surrounding area not to one of the victorious countries but to Austria. There was something terribly humiliating in it, and hellishly ironic. Hungarians fought for centuries to protect their country against Austria. And now that the Entente breaks up the Austrian empire, they wish us to hand over lands, to what remains of Austria, that have always been ours; wishes it at a time when Austria is as much a defeated country as we are. What is more, our affiliation with Austria is what drew us into the war, into a war that nobody in Hungary wanted. A war started over the assassination of an Austrian archduke."[214]

Due to the ongoing humbling of Hungary, some nationalist radical circles began to organize. It is a unspoken fact that, beginning in early 1920, large amounts of arms and ammunition were shipped from Austria to Hungary for the Hungarian National Army. It was partly official, partly as smuggled supplies but of which the Viennese Ministry of War was aware, as were some officials of the Austrian disarmament committee. The country had a burning need for this materiel since it was totally vulnerable and unprotected at this time. Romanian forces had only withdrawn from Trans-Danubia between October 4 and November 15, 1919, from Budapest on the latter date, from the areas between the Danube and Tisza Rivers on November 23, retreating to the

---

[213] Lőkkös, 143, op. cit., pp. 288–289, 292.

[214] Major, Zoltán: Bánffy Miklós: Huszonöt év (1945) [Miklós Bánffy: Twenty-five years (1945)]. Budapest, 1993, pp. 65-66. Bánffy was Foreign Minister during this most active period (April 14, 1921 – December 29, 1922). The pinnacle of his ministerial career was as a participant at the Venice talks (October 11-13, 1921).

left bank of the Tisza River by November 23, which they vacated only on March 31, 1920.[215] French forces pulled out of Szeged on March 1.

A unique situation formed on the western edge of the country. Although the Saint-Germain Treaty accorded a narrow strip of western Hungary to Austria, lacking adequate military forces, the Vienna government was not able to take effective possession for a long time. Thus, it remained under Hungarian administration after the Trianon treaty of June 4, 1920, and even a large part of the following year. With keen perception, the nationalistic government of Count Pál Teleki (1879-1941), elected on July 19, 1920, set conditions for the evacuation of the western territory ordered for handover. He would be willing to comply with the Paris Peace Conference order only if the South Slav army withdrew from Baranya County and its center, Pécs, and the areas surrounding the nearby towns of Baja and Barcs, which were left to Hungary by the Trianon decision.

In the rest of the truncated country, Miklós Horthy and the Hungarian National Army gradually assumed control. However, concurrently, irregular free units, similar to the 'Ragged Guard' [Rongyos Gárda] were being formed. Their creation is primarily linked to Lt.Col. Pál Prónay[216] and the

---

[215] Breit, József: A magyarországi 1918-19. évi forradalmi mozgalmak és a vörös háború története [Hungarian revolutionary movements and the history of the Red war of 1918-1919]. Budapest, 1925; Laky, Dezső: Csonka-Magyarország megszállásának közgazdasági kárai [Economic losses of the occupation of truncated Hungary]. Budapest, 1923. The book deals exclusively with the damages caused by the forces of the successor states. Also, Bandholtz, Maj.Gen. Harry Hill: An Undiplomatic Diary. Budapest, 1993.
The Romanian forces took everything movable with them that they could. From the Royal Hungarian Railways: 1,292 engines, 2,006 coaches, 32,154 boxcars (and not empty, either); the entire equipment of the Hungarian Cannon Foundry of Győr; 37,756 truckloads of goods. It was the personal intervention of Maj. Gen. Bandholtz on October 5, 1919 that prevented the organized looting of the treasures of the Hungarian National Museum in Budapest. The damages inflicted by the Romanian occupation exclusively on the truncated territory left to Hungary after the Trianon Treaty amounted to $29.65 billion (in US dollars as on August 15, 1919 valuation).
[216] Baron Prónay, born in 1874. After a probationary year, as a professional soldier he was promoted to lieutenant. He fought in WWI, was promoted to captain, then major. He began to organize counter-revolutionary activities in Western Hungary in May of 1919 and joined the *Anti-Bolshevik Comité* in Vienna. From June, he served in the headquarters of the Hungarian National Army, being organized under the command of Miklós Horthy. As commander of a special unit raised by him, and bearing his name, he was one of the chief leaders of the White Terror, in answer to the Red Terror after the fall of the Hungarian Socialist Republic. His unit was active in Trans-Danubia, in the region between the Danube and Tisza Rivers and, after the withdrawal of Romanian troops, in the southeast of Hungary. In 1920, he was promoted to lieutenant colonel. He became the leader of the Western Hungary insurrection after leaving the armed forces. Between the two wars, he was a member, and occasionally head, of several secret societies. During the 1944 period of the Iron Cross, he organized a new troop, several of whose units separated and joined the

Transylvanian Lt. Iván Héjjas.[217] Prónay passed several times through Graz, about 50 kms. from the Hungarian border in Styria, at the end of 1919. Here he was notified that the Austrian border police had a large stockpile of weapons and equipment in the village of Fürstenfeld, a mere 4 kms. from the Austrian-Hungarian border. The depot was later commandeered by the Social Democrat-Socialist armed workers' unit, the *Wehrmacht*[218] (better known as the Reds) and, in mid-July, prevented it falling into the hands of the

---

resistance movement. Prónay, at the age of 71, fought for weeks against the Russian forces trying to capture Castle Hill in Budapest. Soviet troops captured him in Budapest on March 20, 1945 and took him away. The Soviets sentenced him, on June 10, 1946, to 20 years of hard labor, on suspicion of spying and sabotage, and sent him to a camp in Siberia. The date of his death is unknown. He was rehabilitated on June 27, 2001 (based on "The rehabilitation of the victims of political persecution" law, Russian Federation, dated 1991, October 18, 3. § b). In: Vallomások a holtak házából [Confessions from the house of the dead]. Ujszászy István vezérőrnagynak, a 2. vkf. osztály és az Államvédelmi Központ vezetőjének az ÁVH fogságában írott feljegyzései. Ed.: Haraszti, György. Állambiztonsági Szolgálatok Történeti Levéltára, Corvina Kiadó, Budapest, 2007, p. 425.

[217] v. Iván Héjjas, born in 1890. During WWI, he fought on various fronts and demobilized as a reserve airforce first lieutenant. He was a founding member in November of 1918 of the Awakening Hungarians Association [Ébredő Magyarok Egyesülete], later its co-president. During the Hungarian Soviet Republic, he was active in counter-revolutionary organizing among the rural population, for which he had to escape. He joined the Hungarian National Army in Szeged. After the fall of the Commune, his company, later battalion (the so-called Héjjas detachment), settled scores with Communists and Communist-suspects in the area between the Danube and Tisza Rivers. He supported Regent Horthy during the two attemps by Charles Habsburg IV to regain the throne. He was the other leading figure, beside Prónay, of the 1921 insurrection in Western Hungary. Between 1921 and 1922, he was the deputy military commander of the Double Cross Blood Alliance [Kettőskereszt Vérszövetség]. From 1927 to 1931, he was the National Assembly representative of the riding of Kunszentmiklós, in the Hungarian National Independence Party [Magyar Nemzeti Függetlenségi Párt]. From 1937 to 1940, he was department counsel of the Trade and Transportation Ministry, head of the Trasnportation Department (1940-1943), finally head of the Aeronatical Section of the Transport Ministry (1943-1944). From 1938, he was president of the National Race-protection Alliance of Hungary [Magyar Fajvédők Országos Szövetsége]. After the First Vienna Award of November 2, 1938 (when the Hungarian-populated parts of Northern Hungary, annexed to Czechoslovakia by the Trianon Treaty, were reunited with Hungary), he fought as detachment commander (in the Ragged Guard [Rongyos Gárda]) against the Czechs in Sub-Carpathia (1938-1939). In 1944, he fled to Germany ahead of the Soviet Army, moving on to Spain. For his actions in 1919, the People's Court in Budapest sentenced him to death in 1947-1948. However, he could not be extradited. He died in Vigo, Spain, in 1950.

[218] *Wehrmacht* [Defense Force]. This unit is only related by name to the National Socialist (Nazi) armed force of Germany, whose official name was the same, in existence between 1935-1945.

Heimwehr,[219] supported by the Styrian government. The Reds of Austria intended to occupy the southern part of Western Hungary, making use of the contents of this armory.

Previous to that, Héjjas – according to a report handed by the Austrian embassy in Budapest to the Hungarian Defense Ministry – crossed the border on the night of July 30, 1920[220] with an independent force 63 men (other sources 117) in 8 trucks and trailers and carried out a raid on the Fürstenfeld armory. They disarmed the guards and kept the village's 400-500 Austrian garrison in check. In the meantime, they loaded 3,000 rifles, 30 machine guns and a vast amount of ammunition on the vehicles. They headed out with the spoils and crossed the Austrian-Hungarian border without incident. Prónay hid the munitions and used it later during the Western Hungary insurrection. The raid on Fürstenfeld lasted barely an hour and was accomplished with no loss of life.[221]

During these weeks, the constant and resolute Austrian propaganda became more intense in Western Hungary, especially in Sopron County. The main organizers were the delegates of the Austrian government to the Inter-Allied Military Mission in Sopron. The Austrian representatives – whose presence was sanctioned by the Hungarian government – were met at the Sopron train station on March 4, 1920 by a crowd of several thousand who noisily protested and pelted them with rotten eggs and vegetables. Only police intervention saved them from physical harm. The Austrian delegates did not

---

[219] Soós, 1971, op. cit., p. 86. *Heimwehr:* armed volunteer independent unit made up of army officers of the former Monarchy (K.u.K.) forces, the first units of which were organized in 1918 in Carinthia, Tyrol and Styria against the 'un-nationalist' forces, and the defense of the borders of Austria. They were linked to the Greater Germany parties and the Social-Democratic Party. Some units held Austro-Fascist views. The influence of the *Heimwehr* grew in the second half of the '20s, some of its leaders holding government posts. *Heimwehr* detachments took part in the putting down of the armed revolt of the *Republikanischer Schutzbund* [Republican Defense Alliance, the military arm of the Social-Democratic Party] of February 1934. The *Heimwehr* was dissolved in October of 1936 by the Schuschnigg government.

[220] The date of the raid in other sources: in Jenő Héjjas as June 20, in István T. Ádám as August 5. Both are incorrect.

[221] Ádám, T. István: Soprontól Munkácsig [From Sopron to Munkács]. Budapest, 1939, pp. 15–16; Héjjas, Jenő: A nyugatmagyarországi felkelés [The Western Hungary insurrection]. Kecskemétiek az 1921. évi nyugatmagyarországi harcokban. Kecskemét, 1929, pp. 7–10. Jenő Héjjas took part in the Western Hungary fighting as a highschool student. His work only recounts those actions in which his brother, Iván, and members of his IV. Rebel Army took part. For that, critics of his book accuse him of bias. The book 'A Rongyos Gárda harcai 1919–1939' [The battles of the Ragged Guard 1919-1939], published in 1940 and written by 'one of the Ragged' is almost certainly the work of Héjjas as part 2 is essentially identical to his book. Part 1 covers the guerilla fighting, led by Iván Héjjas against the Romanian occupiers around Kecskemét in 1919. Part 3 covers the fighting against the Czech-Slovak forces in Sub-Carpathia (1938-1939) by the independent detachments.

understand, or misunderstood, the behavior of the Sopron population because, at their urging, the Austrian government again petitioned the Council of Ambassadors at the end of March 1920 for the handing over of Sopron and the territories marked for annexation.[222]

In the matter of the propaganda promoted by the Austrian delegates, representative Sigray addressed a question in Parliament on August 7, 1920 to Prime Minister and Foreign Minister Pál Teleki. According to Sigray, the Viennese delegates "are now trying to win the population to the idea of splitting from Hungary and are spreading word that the union of the Austrian Republic to the German Empire is a foregone conclusion and that the German-speaking region of Western Hungary will not be part of an unviable Austria but a revived and territorially enlarged, again mighty, Germany through *Anschluss*."[223] Sigray finally asked what steps the Hungarian government is taking to counter the Austrian propaganda?

In his reply, the prime minister stated that "I have no immediate and official knowledge" that Western Hungary is to be annexed to Germany and not Austria. With regard to the Austrian agitation, he would order an inquiry and asked the aid of the representative posing the question. "Insofar as there is agitation – said Teleki – I must, at the least, bring it up with the Austrian government because the representatives of German Austria are not there with the goal of agitation but are delegated to the Mission for other reason. In any case, the question itself with which they agitate is perhaps of interest not so much for us as for the Entente, which gave this territory to Austria in the Saint-Germain peace and over which Austria intends to hold a plebiscite. (…) I will take steps if necessity demands it."[224]

Count Sigray acknowledged the prime minister's response and noted that he would attempt to provide as much information as possible to the Hungarian government regarding the opinion-influencing activities in Sopron County by the Austrian delegates. "It is certain that they are taking advantage of the situation and are creating agitation. In fact, we will prove that they are maintaining an entire office where they receive all the malcontents and grant some jobs and positions. In other words, behave as if the territory was already not under Hungarian sovereignty. (…) They overstep the Austrian government signed (…) Saint-Germain treaty's point 88, which precisely forbids Austria's union with Germany, [yet] they agitate with it. It is essentially not our problem (…) it is the Entente's because it would interest them more that a Germany, which they certainly do not wish to strengthen, would extend to the line of the Raba [River] through this union."[225] Sigray

---

[222] Träger, Ernő: A soproni népszavazás [The Sopron plebiscite]. A szomorúság, bizakodás és hűség napjairól. In: Sopron. *Civitas Fidelissima*. Szerk/ed.: Thirring, Gusztáv, Sopron, 1925, p. 76. (The work also appeared in German as Träger, Ernst: Die Volksabstimmung in Sopron. Dezember 1921. Ödenburg, pp. 14–16.)

[223] Nemzetgyűlési Napló, IV. kötet. Budapest, 1920. 304. old.

[224] Ibid.

[225] Ibid, pp. 304–305.

again drew attention to the fact that, in spite of the Entente matter, the Hungarian government "should not tolerate" the Austrian agitation in Sopron.

Although Austria did not possess adequate military forces, it took an ever stronger stance with regard to Western Hungary. This was indicated by the first paragraph of the constitution, newly accepted by the National Assembly on October 1, 1920, which stated that the country is a democratic republic with nine provinces – among them Burgenland, allowed to send three representatives – in a federative union.

A unique manifestation of the territorial claim was the emergency currency printed in October of 1920, which was used for propaganda purposes.[226] Copies of the paper currency found in 1981 in the Ferenc Móra Museum of Szeged shows: 93x66 mm. vertical rectangle, whitish-yellow, without watermark, on the top of the front is written: *Ödenburg*, that is to say Sopron. Below it, in the upper half, in the middle of an oak leaf border, is a picture of its well-known main square, in the center of which is shown the equally well-known Fire Tower, flying the German flag (not Austrian!!). The denomination is shown in the lower corners by 2K (2 Crown or Kroner).

The bottom half of the rectangle shows a poem:

„*Südmarkspende.*
Über Ödenburg die deutschen Farben.
Deutscher Herzen Trost in trüber Nacht!
Reife Zukunft, in der Zeiten Schacht!
Bald stehst prangend du in vollen Sorben.
Dr. A. Walheim".[227]

The rough translation of the poem is: Southern border voucher. German colors above Sopron. / Solace of German heart in a blustery night! / Ripe future in the depth of time! / Soon to stand proud over all the Sorbs.[228] The poem's title alluded to the western Hungarian strip granted to Austria (in Pan-German usage called the Southern Borderland) by the Treaty of Saint-Germain, including Sopron, over which the German flag (again, not Austrian–J.B.) was flying. The poet Walheim, one of the later provincial governors of Burgenland, suggests that the so-far unmerged Slavic group, the Sorbs, will become German, too.

---

[226] After the collapse of the Austro-Hungarian Monarch, the successor states (Czechoslovakia, Romania, Kingdom of Serbs-Croats-Slovenes) issued some emergency currency to address shortage of small denominations.

[227] Barbalics, Imre János: Sopron egy 1920. évi osztrák szükségpénzen [Sopron on a 1920 Austrian interim currency]. In: *Soproni Szemle*, 1983, issue 1, p. 54.

[228] The poet, dr. Alfred Walheim, refers to the Sorbs, a western Slav tribe along the upper flow of the Spree River. The Sorbs, living is southeastern Germany around the towns of Cottbus and Bautzen NE of Dresden (calling themselves Sorbski, Ger.: Sorbe), founded their umbrella organization, Domovina, in 1912. After WWI, the Sorbs enjoyed relative freedom; from 1933, their national organizations and intellectuals were persecuted by the authorities; from 1937, the use of the Sorb language was banned.

On the obverse of the bill – and this was the propaganda use – two lines were printed on the upper half thusly:

Südmark.

Bund der Deutschen zur Erhaltung ihres Volkstums im In- und Ausslande.

Which translates roughly to: Southern Borderland. / Union of Germans for the Preservation of their Culture, in the country and outside.

The translation of the text on the lower half of the back[229] is as follows: "German Western Hungary – Hienz or Burgenland – is a border province and, as with all border provinces, owners changed frequently; it was so with Austria and so with Hungary. Finally, a Habsburg emperor, Ferdinand III (1647) gave it to Hungary, unlawfully and forcibly. Now it is returned to Austria by the peace treaty of Saint-Germain. Ancient Germanic heritage, birthplace of Dietrich von Bern, province of Charlemagne, once again became German; 300,000 Germans, Hienzen and Heidebauers, as they call themselves, will raise the black-red-gold flag [meaning the German flag— *J.B.*] It is possible that the return of the land of the Hienz is an encouraging omen for the return to the homeland of all that we were forced to lose in the surrounding German provinces. / Vienna, October 1920 / Dr. Alfred Walheim."

The author of text popularizing the emergency money, Walheim, was simply lying in his historical arguments when he wrote that emperor Ferdinand III gave German Western Hungary [Hienzenland or Burgenland did not exist at the time—*J.B.*], "unlawfully and forcibly, to Hungary" in 1647. He could not have done it because the territory was an integral part of the greater principality, later the Kingdom, of Hungary a few years after Trans-Danubia was occupied (in the year 900) after the Conquest of 895 until the Treaty of Saint-Germain of 1919. Emperor Ferdinand III simply could not have given away the mentioned territory because, between 1637 and 1657, not only was he Emperor but also King of Hungary, at the same time. Austrian historical and other writing stated, and continues to state today, without any historical basis – even entering international scientific works and encyclopedia – that, after the 1490 death of King Mathias (ruled 1458-1490), Burgenland (sic!), meaning Western Hungary, was, between 1491 and 1647,

---

[229] The original text on the lower half of the back is: „Deutschwestungarn – das Heinzen- oder Burgenland – ist ein Grenzland und hat wie alle Grenzländer öfter den Besitzer gewechselt: bald war es bei Österreich, bald bei Ungarn. Zuletzt hat ein habsburgischer Kaiser, Ferdinand 3:, das Land willkürlich und widerrechtlich an die Ungarn verschenkt (1647). Durch den Friedensvertrag von St. Germain kommt Deutschwestungarn nun zu Österreich zurück. Uraltes Germanenerbe, die Heimat Dietrichs von Bern, die Mark Karls des Grossen, ist wieder deutsch geworden: 300 000 Deutsche, die Heinzen und Heidebauern, wie sie sich selber nennen, pflanzen die schwartzrotgoldene Fahne auf. Möge die Wiederkehr des Heizenlandes und eine frohe Vorbedeutung sein für die Heimholung aller derer, die wir, jetzt rundum an den deutschen Marken verloren geben mussten! / Wien, im Oktober 1920. / Dr. Alfred Walheim". (Barbalics, 1983, p. 54–55.)

"for a century and a half under Austria's custody."[230]

Shortly after the issuing of the emergency currency, Michael Mayr again filled the post of Chancellor on November 20, 1920 and he was willing to continue talks with Hungary. However, the talks at ambassadorial and foreign ministerial levels during the following weeks brought no results because, clinging to the Saint-Germain treaty, the Viennese government insisted on the immediate transfer of Western Hungary to Austria. The strengthening movement to popularize Austria on the territory to be transferred added further weight. As an example, the Viennese company 'Kosmos' offered to ship, free of charge, German-language schoolbooks to schools in the Borderland. The school superintendent of the Sopron district instructed the educational institutions in a circular dated June 19 not to accept the sent texts as they "intend to infect the young."[231]

Meantime, the Hungarian government and military command continued to bolster the defense of Western Hungary. In an order issued on October 26, 1920, the headquarters of the Hussar Battalion of Trans-Danubia and logistic units, as well as the men of the I. Detachment (two mounted companies and a machine gun company) were ordered to a new garrison in Sopron, while IV. detachment (a mounted company) was ordered to the Nezsider district by November 5. The units arrived at their destinations by rail. The Sopron Barracks of Sopron County, built in 1884, were adequate for the needs of the battalion offices and the supporting units. There were roomy barracks for the men, as well as two indoor and several outdoor riding rings, and a large house for the officers. Apart from the two years before WWI, the barracks always served as the base for the 9th (Nádasdy) Hussar Battalion. The barracks in Nezsider offered less comfort for the soldiers, as the ancient building was waiting for renovation / rebuilding. It has always served the needs of the Trans-Danubian mounted battalions. Only after construction was completed could it accept the command unit of the II. Detachment (and 3rd mounted and 2nd machine gun companies), until then left behind in Kalocsa.[232]

According to the January 1921 Order of Battle, the Western Hungary military region, headquartered in Szombathely, consisted of 659 full-time and 184 reserve officers, 666 professional NCOs, 14,624 infantry and 373 mounted men. Their equipment consisted of 13,706 rifles, 123 standard and 114 light machine guns, 16 guns and one infantry cannon, 2,478 horses, 438 vehicles (horse drawn carriages and wagons), 35 automobiles but no airplanes. The commander of the region was Lt.Gen. *chevalier* Sándor Szívó, who also exercised direct command over the units in his region. These were: the infantry battalion of Csurgó, the Trans-Danubian mounted brigade with

---

[230] Dabas, Rezső: „Burgenland" álarc nélkül ["Burgenland" unmasked]. Történeti-földrajzitanulmány az elrabolt nyugati végekről. Montréal, 1984, p. 213.

[231] MOL. K 26. 1920–XLII–1653. szám, 208. old.

[232] Kubinszky, Jenő: A „M. kir. Nádasdy Ferenc 3. honvéd huszárezred" Sopronban 1921–1939 [The Royal Hungarian 3rd Nádasdy Hussar Battalion in Sopron 1921-1939]. In: *Soproni Szemle*, 1995, issue 3, pp. 219–220.

the Hussar battalion of Szombathely, the command units of Moson, Sopron, Vas and Zala counties and the border-guard battalions of the counties. The 3rd Infantry Division of Szombathely, commanded by Col. Antal Lehár, also came under the command of Lt.Gen. Szívó. The units under his command were enlarged by the infantry regiments of Zala, Sopron and Vas counties (the latter of 2 battalions), the Guard Battalion of Szombathely, the Hussars and an artillery regiment.[233]

On December 23, 1920, the Council of Ambassadors in Paris sent an unexpected note to the Hungarian government in which it demanded handing over *Westungarn*, or Western Hungary, into the control of the Entente Military Mission in Sopron at the time. The body was to assume control over the area in question. The gist of the note was that the Hungarian territory to be annexed to Austria was first symbolically to be handed over to the Entente countries, who immediately would then hand it over to the Vienna government. This turn of events was discussed by the Hungarian Cabinet at its January 4 session, where Prime Minister Teleki raised that the note was only received by the Hungarian *chargé d'affaires* in Paris, Iván Praznovszky – still without an official text – but the new responsibilities of the Hungarian government are to be recognized from it. After that, Foreign Minister Kálmán Kánya (1869-1945) spoke at the session, analyzing the newest turn of the Western Hungary question, followed again by PM Teleki. He deemed that Western Hungary was not to be handed over to Austria under any circumstance. In the worst case, have the Entente occupy the area militarily. In the meantime, the matter of the territorial handover can be tied to matters of extracting warranties for the rights of the Hungarian minority handed over to Austria, and the withdrawal of Serb troops occupying Baranya County and the city of Pécs. Also, to point out that the border adjudication committees have not yet arrived and the parliaments of the Great Powers have not ratified the Trianon Treaty. Thus, it is clear that the government was not about to hand over Western Hungary to the Allies. Teleki closed the session with the statement that they must only yield to armed force. At the same time, he said, if the area's population resisted by armed force, it would be a mistake to prevent it.[234]

In its counter-memorandum of January 13, 1921, the government of Hungary protested against the December 23 decision by Paris. In fact, it stated that it would not follow the instructions because, according to the May 6, 1920 Millerand letter,[235] the noted *lettre d'envoi*, the borders of Hungary have not been finally settled. The task of the border determination committees is to resolve it, to post the final borders, as well as remedy the injustices

---

[233] Fogarassy, László: Védelmi előkészületek Ausztriával szemben gróf Bethlen István kormányának hivatalba lépése után [Defensive preparations against Austria after the government of Count István Bethlen took office]. In: *Soproni Szemle*, 1994, issue 3, p. 307.

[234] MOL. K 27. Minisztertanácsi jegyzőkönyvek. 1921. január 4.

[235] The Millerand letter has been covered in detail in the previous chapter.

committed. Through the note, the Hungarian government fundamentally shook the legality of Paris' December note, since it was the Peace Conference that appended the Millerand letter to the Trianon decree. In any case, the Council of Ambassadors notified the Austrian government on January 2, 1921, two days before the Hungarian Cabinet meeting, that under the terms of the Saint-Germain and Trianon treaties, it was to be the recipient of Western Hungary. Chancellor Michael Mayr informed the Foreign Committee of the Austrian government of it and added: the Czechoslovak and South Slav governments offered military assistance to help take control over the area, and rejected the plebiscite once again suggested by Hungary.[236]

The January 13 note of Hungary – authoritatively worded, legally based on the Millerand letter and extensively reasoned – was answered on January 27 when the president of the Council of Ambassadors, Jules Cambon, handed Hungarian *chargé d'affaires* in Paris, Iván Praznovszky, its reply. The tone of the note made it clear that the Peace Conference retreated because it fell into a trap of its own making by the promises contained in the Millerand letter, its own creation. It no longer demanded the Hungarian government's immediate handover of Western Hungary to the Entente Mission in Sopron. In fact, it stated the Great Powers wished direct discussions between the Hungarian and Austrian governments regarding the Western Hungary question. Thus, official Hungarian-Austrian talks were held in Vienna on February 23 and 24. The Hungarian delegation tried to convince the Austrian party that the Hungarian solution to the question, i.e.- retaining the current millennial border, was in the interest of Vienna. East of it, no better natural geographic line could be found. The Hungarian government alluded to the already noted Millerand letter; the Austrian government alluded to the complete harmonization of the Saint-Germain and Trianon treaties.

The fourth Hungarian-Austrian meeting took place in Budapest on March 19, where the Hungarian government – reviewing its earlier position – came forward with a suggestion which, "given Austria's understandable and economically justified claims is, at the same time, acceptable to the local population." The Austrian delegation rejected the proposal. In April, their proposition was to annex the economically 'active' Moson County to Austria, leaving the 'passive' Vas County with Hungary and that the two countries split Sopron County, lying between the two.[237]

This was also the time of the first royal *coup d'état*[238] attempt. Charles IV of the House of Habsburg[239] crossed the Austrian-Hungarian border on March 26, 1921 at Pinkafő. Around midnight, he reached the bishop's palace in Szombathely, to meet the Catholic prelate, Count János Mikes. His goal was

---

[236] Fogarassy, 1971, op. cit., p. 299.

[237] Soós, 1971, op. cit., pp. 125-126.

[238] IV. Károly visszatérési kísérletei [Charles IV's return attempts]. I. füzet. Kiadja a Magyar Kir. Minisztérium. Budapest. 1921, pp. 8-29.

[239] As noted earlier, Charles IV announced the suspension of his regal rights as ruler of Hungary in Eckartsau on November 13, 1918.

to regain the Hungarian throne, based on his Eckartsau proclamation. At the time of his arrival, József Vass (1877-1930), prelate and Minister of Education, 'happened' to be in the city. Prime Minister Pál Teleki and the American High Commissioner Ulysses Grant-Smith were also nearby on the estate of Antal Sigray, Western Hungary's Chief Government Commissioner. In these weeks, certain Hungarian aristocrats and Catholic prelates put their faith only in the restoration of Charles IV, which is why they organized his return. Many supported it in the hope that the king would prevent their western Hungary estates being annexed to Austria. The change of border would have a detrimental effect – especially on profitability and taxation – on the estates of the families of the Esterházy of Fertőd, the Széchényi of Nagycenk, the Erdődy of Vép, the Batthyány-Strattmann of Körmend and the Graskovics of Németújvár.

The former monarch travelled to Budapest in an army officer's uniform on March 27, 1921 to confer with Regent Horthy about assuming authority. Hungary remained a monarchy after the March 1, 1920 election by the National Assembly of Horthy as Regent. The Entente Powers protested to the king in a note on April 3, stating they would not recognize him nor would they tolerate, in any form, the renewed reign of a Habsburg in Hungary. After the fruitless task, Charles IV left Szombathely on April 5.[240] The presence of the former monarch caused serious damages to the country because subsequently Czechoslovak Foreign Minister Beneš was able to isolate Hungary completely by mid-1921, while demonstrating the political unity of the Little Entente. As a result of the attempted return, the Czechoslovak-Romanian defensive agreement was signed on April 23, 1921 and the South Slav-Romanian on June 7, bringing to completion the triumvirate of the Little Entente brought into existence with a specifically anti-Hungarian aim.[241]

---

[240] Speidl, Zoltán: IV. Károly két restaurációs kísérletének nyugat-magyarországi vonatkozásai (1921) [Two restoration attempts by Charles IV and their impacts in Western Hungary]. In: *Vasi Szemle*, 1971, issue 1, pp. 107–119; Zsiga, Tibor: Az első királypuccs és Vas megye (1921) [The first royal *coup* and Vas County (1921)]. In: *Vasi Szemle*, 1979, issue 2, pp. 269–286; Zsiga, Tibor: Szombathely az utolsó királyi székhely. IV. Károly első visszatérési kísérlete [Szombathely, the final royal seat. The first return attempt of Charles IV]. In: *Vasi Szemle*, 1991, issue 4, pp. 549–560; Simola, Ferenc: Elfeledett fénykép IV. Károly Vas megyei tartózkodásáról [Forgotten photograph of Charles IV's stay in Vas County]. In: *Vasi Szemle*, 2005, issue 6, pp. 785–789; Ormos, Mária: „Soha, amíg élek!" Az utolsó koronás Habsburg puccskísérletei 1921-ben [„Never, as long as I live!" The *coup* attempts of the last crowned Habsburg in 1921]. Pécs, p. 157.

[241] The basis for the Little Entente was the Czechoslovak-South Slav alliance signed on August 23, 1920, followed on April 23, 1921 by the Czechoslovak-Romanian, and finally on June 7 by the Romanian-South Slav agreement. All three ensured military assistance for the other in case of an attack by a third country. The signatories also agreed to harmonize their foreign policies in regard to Hungary. See Tóth, Endre: IV. Károly első magyarországi restaurációs kísérletének következménye: a csehszlovák–román szövetségi egyezmény [The consequences of the first restoration attempt of

In the meantime, Prime Minister Teleki handed in his resignation due to his involvement in the royal *coup* attempt. The following day, April 15, Count István Bethlen (1874–1946) formed a government and led the country for a decade and stabilized its situation. A week after taking office, the new PM called a meeting to seek a solution to the Western Hungary problem. It was attended by: Miklós Bánffy from the Foreign Ministry, General Sándor Belitska (1872–1939) from Defense, Count Gedeon Ráday (1872–1937) from Interior, Gusztáv Gratz, former Foreign Minister, as well as Count Antal Sigray, Chief Government Commissioner and István Zsembery, High Constable of Sopron County. The first option they considered was: co-operation with Austria, while counting on the fall of the Mayr government. Option two: The population of the territory earmarked for annexation declares its independence and offers armed resistance to the incoming Austrian forces. Option three: the territories to be handed over calls a provincial meeting according to valid Austrian law, legally refuses union with Austria and declares its intention to reunite with Hungary. As a possible new plan, it was suggested that the country ask for the mediation of a third country in this disputed question. In the interim, the country would offer economic concessions to Austria and autonomy to the German minority of the country.[242] The meeting eventually decided to continue talks with Austria, both official and unofficial.

The meetings continued until April 28. While they were going on, a partial plan of action was born for the retention of Western Hungary, earmarked for annexation, complete with political and military directives. The basic principle was that, as a last resort after the Trianon Treaty comes into effect, the area – now part of Austria – proclaims its independence. Its governing body will be the *provisorischer Landesausschuss* (Interim Provincial Committee), whose members will be the area's parliamentary representatives, the district's chief magistrate and the mayors of the larger towns. The committee will also name an also temporary *Landeshauptmann* (Provincial Chief / Head), probably in the person of Jakab Bleyer, the former Hungarian minister without portfolio for minorities, who will be advised by Gusztáv Gratz, Hungary's former ambassador to Vienna and later Foreign Minister. At the same time as the ratification of the Trianon Treaty, the Hungarian government intends to create a link between the handing over of Western Hungary and the evacuation of Serb troops occupying Baranya County, and the cities of Pécs and Baja. That is to say, Hungarian units will remain in the western zone until the Serb forces remain in southern Trans-Danubia. After the withdrawal of Hungarian forces from Western Hungary / Burgenland, elections will be held in the annexed territory, while preparations will be made for the return to Hungary of the contested territory.

Charles IV: the Czechoslovak-Romanian alliance agreement]. In: *Kisebbségkutatás*, year 16, 2007, issue 1, pp. 51–70.
[242] Fogarassy, 1994, op. cit., pp. 307–308.

The action plan detailed that, on the authorization of the Interim Provincial Committee, Col. Lehár, commander of the division garrisoned in Szombathely, will begin local recruitment and create a defensive force for the autonomous area. This organizing is to be supported by the Hungarian government through all possible means but not officially as that would have adverse diplomatic ramifications. The withdrawal of civil administration is, thus, to be suspended for the interim. The Szombathely headquarters and all military commands in the region were ordered to offer any and all assistance to Col. Lehár in his attempt to organize the Western Hungary force. The colonel was deemed to be independent and not part of the command of the regional command structure. Forty officers of the National Army were selected to form Lehár's staff and command structure who were from the annexed territory. These officers were officially retired by the Defense Ministry but would later be reactivated into the armed forces without any hindrance. On proclamation of independence, all public security (gendarmerie, police, customs, revenue and border security) would come under the jurisdiction of Col. Lehár. Cooperation with the organization and operation of the new defense force would take the form of relocating two infantry companies of the Vas County infantry regiment, and a company of machine guns, to the areas of Vas County intended for annexation (Felsőőr, [Nagy]Szentmihály és Németújvár) on the same day the Trianon Treaty was ratified. These would remain stationed there until the disputed areas were vacated, meaning the linkage with Trans-Danubia was satisfied. According to the action plan, the following material was made available to Col. Lehár: 5,000 rifles, 3,000 officers and men with all their gear, 1,000 grenades, 18 heavy and 18 light machine guns, a fully equipped mounted company, 2 field cannons and 2 mortars (from equipment hidden from the Entente supervising committee), 3 cars, 4 trucks and 3 ambulances, which was to be bought.[243] At the April 28 session, the artillery complement of the autonomous area was raised to two batteries.

The secret action plan and directives were acknowledged by the then-commander of the Szombathely military region, Lt.Gen. Pál Hegedüs, and Col. Antal Lehár. Lehár, most probably intentionally, left Lt.Col. Pál Prónay, who he met in the capital, out of the plans. The later leader of the insurrection recounted it as: "I noted in my journal of my meeting in the spring of 1921 in Budapest with Col. Baron Antal Lehár, commander of the Szombathely region,[244] when I reproached him on why he does not make all of Burgenland, including Sopron and Szombathely, independent based on the self-determination of people and why he does not order a draft and organize the necessary armed force in the territory to be handed over when its detachment from the mother country to Austria is already impending. (…) However, Lehár answered evasively and opined confidently regarding the loyalty of

---

[243] Ibid, p. 309.

[244] More accurately: division commander.

Burgenland to the mother country, which was so covered by his propaganda organs that it would never be Austrian. (…) My surprise was all the greater when, during the same summer, young Ivan Töpler, along with several Sopron citizens, led by mayor [Mihály] Thurner looked me up in Budapest, in the Nádor Barracks, as their last refuge. – Help us, Sir! Western Hungary must be handed over – It is a closed case – Please do something, at least let us save Sopron. (…) On hearing the above, I immediately issued the necessary instructions within the battalion, as well as to the associated irredentist organizations."[245]

The then-Foreign Minister, Miklós Bánffy, wrote in his memoirs that the previously mentioned action plan regarding the situation of Western Hungary was worked out in June of 1921 (in actual fact, the first half of April) during meetings chaired by Prime Minister Bethlen. Bánffy sensed exactly that: "The Hungarian public (i.e., the nation) felt the handing over as the greatest humiliation. The two of us (i.e., with Bethlen—J.B.) also saw it that way. Hence, we had to do something to prevent it. (…) We were certain that not only the mostly German-speaking population of Sopron but also the local Hungarian and Croat communities and also the German villages want to stay with us. It is only the Germans of the Pinka [River] valley and along the Lajta [River] that are drawn to Vienna, and they only because they sell their [fruit and vegetable] produce in the Austrian capital and Graz." It is not by accident that Bánffy notes that organizing the population of Western Hungary posted to be handed over was not his task, and hence he knew very little of the preparations. On the other hand, he did mention that Interior Minister Gedeon Ráday "very carefully hid his role, giving the impression that it was the people who were getting ready to act in response."[246] Also that neither former prime minister Friedrich, nor Prónay (according to his cited memoirs) knew that the Hungarian government was behind the movement.

In the end, armed resistance in Western Hungary was not organized by Col. Lehár because he sided with Charles IV in his March 1921 attempt to regain the throne, for which the new PM, Bethlen, in the weeks after assuming the post on April 14, forced him into the background and relieved him of his command with the Szombathely division. The armed resistance of the Borderland was begun by the Etelköz Association [Etelköz was the first known Hungarian principality, established circa 830AD. The territory was located around the rivers Dnieper, southern Bug, Dniester, Prut and Siret-ed.] in May, whose leadership PM Bethlen entrusted to one of his trustworthy men, a professional soldier, staff captain Gyula Gömbös[247] because we know

---

245 Prónay Pál emlékezései az 1921. évi nyugat-magyarországi eseményekről. Első rész [Memoirs of Pál Prónay of the Western Hungary events of 1921. Part One]. In: *Soproni Szemle*, 1986, issue 1, p. 27.

246 Bánffy, 1993, op. cit., pp. 66, 70.

247 Gyula Gömbös, born in 1886. During WWI, he served as a staff officer with the XIII. Corps in occupied Serbia, then fought in East Galicia as a captain. He was wounded in June, 1916. After his recovery, he was posted to the Defense Ministry.

from historical sources that Gömbös and Lehár did not get along, hence their collaboration was out of the question. Thus, resistance in Western Hungary took a totally different route, not relying on Col. Lehár who, as noted, was active in other political-military action plans in late April. Those, it seems, were completely discarded. The Etelköz Association began to organize between May and June but we have no known details of it. The reason for it is the documents of the Association have not turned up and also that it was such a secretive organization that public perception knew almost nothing of it. Thus, it was not by accident that, in the summer of 1921, as noted earlier, the Sopron delegation led by Mihály Thurner did not seek out the Association but went to Prónay to, at least, try to save the city [Sopron] from Austrian occupation. Nor that, after the outbreak of Western Hungary resistance, Gömbös, as president of the Magyar Országos Véderő Egyesület /MOVE/ [Alliance of Hungarian National Defense Force] sent an "urgent written message" to Prónay asking him to come to Budapest. In front of his headquarter staff, he offered Prónay command of the southern forces of the insurrection.[248]

To return to the events of May: after the dust settled following the attempted royal *coup*, Hungarian-Austrian dialogue resumed regarding the matter of Western Hungary. Both parties continued to refer to the so-called Millerand letter and its vague promises. At the May 25 session, led by Chancellor Mayr who announced that, until the clarification of his new position, the dialogue is suspended. After the fall of the Vienna government, a new chancellor assumed the post on June 1 in the person of Johannes Schober, former chief of police of Vienna, who later showed a willingness to continue the dialogue.

The following day, on June 2, the Hungarian government received the May 31 memorandum of the Council of Ambassadors, which advised the Hungarian leadership that, in accordance with the terms of Part II, article 27 of the Trianon Treaty – containing the detailed description of the new borders

---

After the armistice, he served as military attache in the Defense Ministry (Nov.-Dec. 1918), then head of operations for the Balkan theater (Dec. 1918-Jan. 1919). He became the first president (Jan. 1919-Jan. 1925) of the Right-wing officers' alliance, MOVE, and took a forceful stand against the Leftward shifting Károlyi government. He was ordered to Nagykanizsa as a staff officer, at which he had himself placed on inactive status (Feb. 21, 1919). Four days later, ahead of his expected arrest and incarceration, he left for Vienna, where he took part in organizing the Anti-Bolshevik Committee /ABC/. In April, he travelled to Szeged and served as the Secretary of State for War in the first and second counter-revolutionary government (May 30-Aug. 12), alongside Miklós Horthy and became part of his inner circle. He had a significant role in the organization of the Hungarian National Army. With Count Bethlen, he was a founder of the strong governing party, Egységes Párt (Unified Party); from 1920, national, then parliamentary, representative, and eventually prime minister (1932-1936). Died in Munich in 1936.

[248] Prónay, 1986, op. cit., pp. 29–31.

of Hungary – Western Hungary is to be ceded to Austria.[249]

The Pan-German agitation in Western Hungary, tied to the annexation to Austria and propaganda of *Anschluss*, gained steam in June of 1921. The movement was active in Moson County, where the area between Lake Fertő and the Danube was publicized as the 'Austrian-German' bridgehead. Linked to it was a secret report by Lt.Col. Ottrubay of July 1, 1921 to the Royal Hungarian Ministry of Defense. With regard to the situation, he reported the opinion of the French member of the Inter-Allied Military Mission, Gen. Hamelin, who: "Pointed out the Greater Germany propaganda in Western Hungary, working everywhere with ample money and agitation, noted with shock that the Germans, in some German-populated villages, fly German flags. He finds it strange of the Hungarian press that it does not raise its voice to protest against Germany but remains silent in the face of this scandalous propaganda, while taking every opportunity to protest against the Entente, especially France."[250]

In the meantime, the Austrian Ministry of War ordered on June 2 that the command of the six mixed brigades of the *Bundesheer*[251] prepare for a 'foreign engagement,' meaning the occupation of 'Burgenland.' Thus, every large unit was to make ready two infantry battalions, for a total of twelve. Nine days later, Col. Rudolf Vidossich, commander of the 1st Brigade was appointed to execute the military operation, and to prepare the entry of the *Bundesheer* in conjunction with Robert von Davy, ministerial department head and selected head of Burgenland province.[252]

The diplomatic channel for the Hungarian-Austrian dialogue opened once more at the end of June, 1921. On July 2, Chancellor Schober declared that, according to the decision of the Austrian Cabinet, units of the *Volkswehr* would not be dispatched to occupy Western Hungary.[253] Over the following days, the negotiating position of Hungary got worse because the Council of Ambassadors on July 5 handed a memorandum to Ivan Praznovszky, the *chargé d'affaires* in Paris. In it, the Council demanded the handover of Western Hungary to Austria in accordance with Article 71 of the Trianon peace treaty, which stated: "Hungary renounces in favor of Austria all rights and title over the territories of the former Kingdom of Hungary situated outside the frontiers of Hungary as laid down in Article 27 (I), Part II

---

[249] MOL. K 26. 1388. csomó. 1922–„H" tétel, p. 49-52. See also, Gagyi, Jenő: Nyugat-Magyarország átadása [The handing over of Western Hungary]. In: *Új Magyar Szemle*, September 1921, vol. III, issue 3, pp. 280–283. old.

[250] Fogarassy, László: Hamelin táborok egy titkos jelentés tükrében [General Hamelin as reflected in a secret report]. In: *Soproni Szemle*, 1981, issue 1, p. 49.

[251] *Bundesheer* = allied armed force: the new name of the earlier *Volkswehr* (Nation Defense Force), as dictated by the Austrian defensive force law of 1920.

[252] Fogarassy, 1971, op. cit., p. 301. Robert von Davy was appointed as provincial head on March 10, 1921, a post he held until March 5, 1922.

[253] Soós, 1971, op. cit., p. 130.

(Frontiers of Hungary)." The Council of Ambassadors attached two proposed territorial transfer agendas to the memorandum.[254]

The Hungarian side responded with a territorial counter-proposal to the previous step of the Peace Conference during the July 11-13 Austrian-Hungarian session, whose gist was: in the interest of good neighborliness, Hungary should retain Sopron and its surrounding area, whose loss was felt to be most painful. The new Hungarian-Austrian border should now run: from the Moson County village of Féltorony, Lake Fertő would be more-or-less divided into two to the village of Fertőmeggyes on the far bank, from where the boundary would skirt Sopron in a semicircle. From there, it is to run in a southern direction, parallel about 5-6 km. West of the indicated Trianon line, from the hill of the Keresztúr forest near Sopronkeresztúr to meet the line at the village of Pinkamindszent near Körmend. The Hungarian side also indicated that it is willing to discuss the affiliation of the Hungarian-populated settlements along the upper Pinka River – Felsőőr/Oberwart, Alsóőr/Unterwart, Őrisziget/Siget in der Wart, etc. – based on ethnography and some manner of territorial trade-off.[255] If accepted, about one third of the Borderland area proposed to be annexed to Austria would have remained with Hungary. This new development was debated at the August 1 session of the Hungarian Cabinet.[256] The only agreement reached by the two parties was that new, official meetings regarding Western Hungary would commence in three weeks. The "Sopron semi-circle," proposed in July, was finally decided by the plebiscite held six months later as a result of the Western Hungary insurrection. It finally remained with Hungary.

The Hungarian National Assembly ratified the Trianon Peace Decree (Law XXXIII) on July 26, 1921, which went into effect at 6PM on the same day. Also on the same day, Jules Cambon, president of the Council of Ambassadors, notified Hungary in a strongly worded memorandum that Hungary is to hand over officially by August 27 territories awarded to Austria. Still on the same day, South Slav forces vacated the occupied southern Hungarian regions, primarily the city of Pécs and Baranya County. The rotating president-of-the-day of the Entente Mission in Budapest, French General Jules Hamelin, also called on PM Bethlen on July 28 for the vacating of Western Hungary, citing the Paris memorandum of two days previous.[257] In Graz, also on the same day, the first meeting of a commission convened to determine the new Austrian-Hungarian border, comprised of a British, a French, an Italian and a Japanese military officer, plus an Austrian and a Hungarian delegate. Hungary was represented by Col. Artur Keresztes.

On the following day, on July 29, Deputy Foreign Minister Kálmán Kánya sent a "Strictly Confidential" report to the prime minister, advising him that

---

[254] MOL. K 26. 1388. csomó. 1922–„H"-tétel, 90–94. old.

[255] Soós, 1971, op. cit., p. 131.

[256] MOL. K 27. Minisztertanácsi jegyzőkönyvek, 1921. augusztus 1.

[257] Ibid, K 26. 1388. csomó. 1922–„H"-tétel, p. 70.

the Council of Ambassadors have assigned the task of the handing over to Austria of Western Hungary to the Inter-Allied Military Mission in Budapest, based on their earlier memorandum of June 29. In the interest of issuing all necessary Hungarian instructions "without attracting undue attention," he also informed the PM that the Entente Mission has prepared a hand-over plan. The meeting to deal with its execution is slated to take place on August 6 in Sopron and that 30 Entente officers are due to arrive there on the 17th. Hungarian forces are to withdraw between the 21st and the 26th from the Western Hungary territory to be ceded to Austria. The area is to be officially handed over on August 27 in accordance with diplomatic protocols.[258]

For the negotiations and resolutions regarding the matter, the Hungarian government appointed Chief Government Commissioner Antal Sigray with the authority that, during the time of the handover and evacuation, he is to be in charge of all the military and civil authorities. Following the Paris memorandum of July 26, an Inter-Allied Military Mission was formed in Sopron. The mission, comprised of an Italian, British and French general, was soon joined by the mentioned 30 Entente officers to oversee the handover of the annexed area. In their plan, they defined two zones, "A" and "B", which essentially corresponded with the new border proposed by the Hungarian government in July, and the partitioned area. The exception was in Moson County, where it diverged significantly. Zone "A" lay west of the North-South line of the historical Austria-Hungary border from Köpcsény – Féltorony – Fertőrákos – Sopron – Léka – Pusztaszentmihály – Németújvár. East of this sector lay zone "B" to the Köpcsény – Pomogy – Nagycenk – Füles – Rohonc – Pornóapáti sector. Zone "C" ran about 5kms. wide East of that.[259]

The information received by Deputy Foreign Minister Kánya was reliable. The Entente Mission's Italian, French and British officers in Sopron had worked out a nine page handover plan of 39 points, covering the three counties and their settlements (*Plan de Transfert à l'Autriche du territoire de la Deutsch-West-Ungarn*). It was published on August 1, 1921. The last page of the prime ministerial copy bears a hand written note (acknowledging Count Sigray and *chevalier* Davy as the Hungarian and Austrian delegates) and is signed by the heads of the Sopron Military Mission: British General George Gorton, French General Camille Hamelin and Italian General Carlo Ferrario. The note is dated August 6.[260] It was an accidental event that a one page

---

[258] Ibid, p. 72.

[259] Zsiga, 1989. p. 114. Map of the three zones defined in the handover of Western Hungary.

[260] MOL. K 26. 1388. csomó. 1922–„H"-tétel, pp. 80-85. The French member of the Mission, Gen. Hamelin, was deemed by Count Sigray as an unambiguous Austrian supporter. General Árpád Guilleaume did not consider him as such. Hamelin's siding with Austria is refuted by the already cited confidential military report of July 1 in which Hamelin "sees the Entente's behavior as ultimately in error, which, in all likelihood, will annex 'Burgenland' to Austria at the same time as returning Baranya

Hungarian-language version of the Inter-Allied Military Mission's (in some sources Inter-Allied Generals' Mission) August 1 plan appeared on bulletin boards and wall posters in the form of a notice – titled *To the people of Western Hungary!* – only after the national holiday honoring King Saint Stephen (August 20).

In conjunction with the August 1 plan (*Plan de Transfert…*), the Military Mission also issued a six-page French-language pamphlet, which separately detailed the duties and responsibilities of the assigned Entente officers. The secret instructions specified the distribution of the officers by districts and named the highest ranking or oldest as head. Under the supervision of the group of generals in Sopron, they had two main tasks to complete: supervise and control the handover process, with the cooperation of the Hungarian and Austrian officials sent to the scene. As well, thirdly, to prevent any abuses toward the population. They were to remedy any possible grievances in collaboration with the representatives of both Hungary and Austria. At the time of the handover, set for August 26-28, the Entente officers were expected to send reports every six hours to the generals of the Military Mission in Sopron. The gendarmerie, working alongside the local authorities, was asked to provide courier services. The Entente officers were empowered to requisition local cars and other means of transportation, typewriters, etc., over and above any resources provided to them. They were also to have free use of the railways, mail and telegraph services, and official and private telephones, day or night on a priority basis.[261]

The Hungarian-Austrian negotiations continued in August. The first discussion at the highest level took place in Vienna on the 3rd, attended by, among others, former Foreign Minister Gustav Gratz and Chancellor Schober. Here, they came to an agreement that about one-third of Western Hungary will remain as part of Hungary. The affected parts were: the part of Moson County stretching to Lake Fertő, Sopron County to Vulka Creek, the city of Sopron, as well as a strip of Vas County. The agreement was strongly supported by prelate Ignaz Seipel, the most influential member of the Christian-Socialist Party and later chancellor. Schober also stressed that this territorial agreement would have to be ratified by the Foreign Affairs committee of the Austrian parliament.[262] The committee, however, did not ratify the agreement at either its 13th or 27th meetings. In fact, it declared that any possible territorial concession will be contingent on the prior handing over of Burgenland. The committee was only willing to consider renouncing

---

County. (…) in its entirety, he deems it a foolish, senseless step to weaken Hungary for the sake of the Entente strengthening Germany – through Austria." Fogarassy, 1981, op. cit., pp. 48-49.

[261] Mollay, Károly: A Szövetségközi Katonai Bizottság bizalmas utasítása a hozzá beosztott antanttisztekhez. 1921. augusztus 1 [Confidential instructions to the officers delegated to the Inter-Allied Military Mission. Aug. 21, 1921]. In: *Soproni Szemle*, 1991, issue 4, pp. 316–317; unabridged French-language instructions, pp. 317–319.

[262] Fogarassy, 1971, op. cit., p. 302.

its claim to the almost entirely Hungarian-populated village of Nagycenk because the body of the "greatest Hungarian," Count István Széchenyi, was resting there in the family crypt. This, in spite of Foreign Minister Miklós Bánffy coming to terms with the handing over of the territory if Sopron and its surrounding area remain in Hungarian hands until the conclusion of the negotiations.[263]

In the meantime, the Hungarian government submitted another territorial proposition in which it laid claim to Sopron, a portion of the Lake Fertő area and about a 5 km. wide strip of Vas County. It, however, made no offer of any trade concessions. This was justified by reasoning that its original claims were already reduced to a quarter, while the Austrian leadership consistently rejected every one of its counter-proposals. The Hungarian government sought assurances in its final (August 18) proposal: 1. Austria agrees that the claimed areas – at least Sopron and its surroundings – remain a part of Hungary until the conclusion of the dialogue. 2. This fact to be conveyed to the Council of Ambassadors in Paris. 3. That public administration officials in the ceded area remain in their jobs.[264]

The Hungarian government also stated that, in the matter of the affiliation of contested areas, as a final solution, it will agree to a decision by plebiscite, with the proviso that the affected areas do not first come under Austrian administration. If the Austrian government is not willing to accept this, then Hungary requested agreement primarily to the following issues: exchange of currency, assurance on tax arrears, settlement of the government's debts and war bonds resulting from the war, as well as various guarantees for the Hungarian state assets in Western Hungary. The Bethlen government estimated that the common Austrian-Hungarian assets on the to-be-annexed territory ran to 3.971 billion Kroner. Of that, Hungary tried to tie the recovery of its proportion to the handover of Western Hungary, as well as the withdrawal of South Slav troops from southern Hungary. In fact, it stated that, if it was unable to come to an agreement with the Vienna government, Budapest would only cede Western Hungary if it was forced to do so by an ultimatum from the Entente.

From the above negotiations, it can clearly be seen that the earlier Teleki government, and from the middle of April, 1921, the Bethlen government, strongly defended Western Hungary, and indeed generally Hungarian, interests to the last possible moment. We will later show numerous examples of it. The very fixed stance of the Bethlen government finally forced the Austrian Foreign Affairs committee to make concessions to Hungary's demands at their August 27 session. The committee authorized the Vienna government, with the agreement of the signatories of the Saint-Germain treaty, to solve the border dispute one year after the handover of Western Hungary by the expressed wish of the people. Although they did not use the

---

[263] Fogarassy, 1982, op. cit., p. 16.
[264] Soós, 1971, op. cit., pp. 132–133.

term 'plebiscite,' the Austrian decision was clearly a political victory for the Hungarian government.

The giving up of the millennial western border region caused great mental anguish in the population remaining in a Hungary dismembered after the Trianon Peace Decree. Popular opinion was most upset by the fact that its ally and co-loser in the war, Austria, also grew in territory torn from Hungary. The events greatly influenced the population of Sopron, mainly German-speaking but of Hungarian-sentiment, who were especially dispirited and embittered on August 20, 1921 [Hungary's national day-ed.]. This was the day that posters appeared all around the city whereby the Entente Mission announced the handover plan of Western Hungary. The time and date of the official handover was fixed by the Council of Ambassadors – possibly in a cynical move – as August 29 at 4PM, the day of the fateful 1526 loss by Hungary in the Battle of Mohács to the Turks. The local citizenry felt that this year's Day of King Saint Stephen (Aug. 20) was to be their last Hungarian holiday. The Church of St. Michael was full to capacity for the memorial mass to Hungary's first crowned king (ruled 1000-1038). Afterwards, the multitude headed to the Dominican's church on Széchenyi Square, where thousands were already assembled, attending the farewell Mass of the departing Sopron garrison.

An eye witness, Ernő Träger, border adjustment delegate of the Hungarian government, wrote four years later: "Széchenyi Square filled up in minutes. The people in front of the postal central offices stood in two rows along the road the Hungarian soldiers of the garrison were marching along. The earth shook under their measured, heavy military tread... the Hungarian soil, for which they fought so much and which was now to be taken away. And they, who bled for Austria in the sands of Galicia, on the banks of the Isonzo [River], among the crags of South Tyrol and Doberdo, unable now to defend their own land from Austria! It was as if the crowd of thousands understood the thoughts of the soldiers, as if the pounding steps of the soldiers and the horses of the hussars awoke the people's consciousness from a lethargic dream; fists rose as one and the air shook with wild curses abusing Austria. Gábor Tauffer sprang up on the pedestal of the Széchenyi statue and whipped up passions by his fiery speech. The delegates of the Entente Powers watched this marvelous demonstration with baited breath and, although they did not understand our language, they were still touched by this patriotic show of loyalty and devotion."[265]

Chief Government Commissioner Sigray told the Military Mission in Sopron on August 21 that the appropriate Hungarian authorities have made all the necessary steps so that the evacuation of the affected territory could take place on time and without incident. On the following day, after a wait of one year, Hungarian forces were finally able to march into the southern Hungarian

---

[265] Träger, 1925, op. cit., pp. 79–80.

city of Pécs.[266] They were commanded by Lt.Gen. Károly Soós and were met with a "blizzard of flowers" and a "deafening cheers." After the long delay, the Belgrade government was forced to hand back to Hungary most of Baranya County, with the valuable coal deposits of the Mecsek basin, and the city of Baja and its surroundings.[267]

The site of the official signing of the handover protocol covering Western Hungary was designated by the Entente representatives in Sopron as the Széchenyi family's in-town palace. The family raised protests loudly and retained lawyer József Östör to ask that the memory of the greatest Hungarian not be tarnished by having "the death sentence of western Hungary" signed in one of his favorite residence. The Entente generals relented and the site of the signing was relocated to the military academy's building on Rákóczi Street.[268]

The turbulent parliamentary session of August 23, which was followed by a long recess due to the "grave times" – a move objected by many – opened with one question and three motions regarding the approaching date for the handing over of Western Hungary before opening the day's agenda. Among other things, Count Kunó Klebelsberg[269] said: "I was forced to ask for time before the agenda, as representative for the free royal city of Sopron, to raise my objections against placing the city under the Austrian yoke. (...) I protest with my entire being, in front of the Entente, Europe and the entire world, because what is happening in Western Hungary and the city of Sopron is the trampling underfoot of the self-determination of people. (...) Western Hungary, and especially the city of Sopron, has repeatedly expressed its wish, in official events, public assemblies and legal committee decisions, not to be separated from the country. (...) But we especially protest against Austria because we deny that Austria has any moral justification to take Western

---

[266] Bánffy, 1993, op. cit., p. 71.

[267] The occupying Serb military caused great damage to the local population (requisition agricultural produce, military levy on the towns and villages, etc.). A question was raised on August 23, 1921 regarding the losses in Parliament, to which Foreign Minister Bánffy replied the same day. In: *Nemzetgyűlési Napló,* vol. XII, 1921, pp. 623–625; Botlik–Csorba–Dudás, pp. 42-49.

[268] Träger, 1925, op. cit., p. 81.

[269] Kunó (Konrad) Klebelsberg (1875-1932). He was Minister of State for Education (January 1914-March 1917) in the second government of Count Tisza. With Count István Bethlen, he was a founder in February of 1919 of the counter-revolutionary Right-wing National Unity Party (Nemzeti Egyesülés Párt). During the months of the Hungarian Soviet Republic, he hid in the countryside. He was a parliamentary representative from 1920 to 1931, and from June 1921 to August 1931, he was minister responsible for the religious and educational portfolio in the Bethlen government. He instituted wide-ranging school reforms, building 5,784 modern public educational schoolrooms, 2,278 teacher accomodations, created 1,555 public and 1,500 school libraries, and 500 kindergartens. He built the science and technology universities of Szeged and Pécs, and completed that of Debrecen, suspended due to the outbreak of WWI, and laid the foundations for three academies and 21 public health clinics.

Hungary from us. The Hungarian nation fully shouldered its share in this world war and ample Hungarian blood was spilt in the sands of Galicia and the limestone rocks of the Karst Mountains[270] for Austria's territorial integrity. And when Austria and Hungary collapsed after fighting together, the defeated slinks among the victors and asks for his share of the body of the Hungarian nation. *(Loud noise. Shouts of 'Shame' from the right side.)* (…) It is my duty, as one who also has Austrian blood in his veins, to say – and Austria should well note – that there will not be one man among us who will not look upon it as a sacred duty to nurture in our souls despair against Austria if it snatches Western Hungary away from us. *(Vigorous agreement and applause.)* As representative of the royal free city of Sopron, I officially protest, in the name of the city, against letting the city and Western Hungary be allowed to slip into the Austrian yoke."[271]

The author of the first of three motions, József Barla Szabó (delegate from Szigetvár) stated: "On behalf of our party, we can state with astonishment and justifiable indignation that the Austria with which we lived for four centuries, in a union always disadvantageous to us, now wishes to take Western Hungary. An Austria whose politicians and military leaders are so guilty of starting the war that none of our greatest men were able to achieve anything against them to prevent the war."[272]

The next speaker, Albin Lingauer, expounded that, in the territorial annexation, the affected population "essentially knows nothing concrete." Opposing official, semi-official and private views come to light, of which the people only learn from the newspapers. The majority of the mass of papers coming from Germany to Western Hungary write that the settlements of Sopron, Felsőpulya, Rohonc and Felsőőr, as well as their surroundings, will remain Hungary's. "The town of Kőszeg looks forward to its future with the greatest trepidation because, to date it was living in the hope that negotiations were so favorable that we would be able to retain Western Hungary. The town of Kőszeg will be separated from its food supply so that the town, called the Hungarian Graz because it is full of retired bureaucrats, retired soldiers and, due to its nature, a typical school town, will be without an agricultural hinterland and this town, who could thank its existence to date for being cheap, now (…) will develop into a terribly expensive town. (…) For a year and a half, we, the representatives of Western Hungary always received the same answer to our queries from official sources: Have faith, have faith, there is hope for an agreement, and we will not lose Western Hungary. (…) We, honored Assembly, the representatives of Western Hungary can state here, in front of the National Assembly, if we knew that all those assurance were without solid basis and merely empty promises, then we ourselves would have

---

[270] The Karst Mountains lie North of Trieste. During WWI, particularly bitter fighting took place between the forces of Italy and the Monarchy along the Isonzo River and on the Doberdo plateau. Between 1915 and 1917, there were a total of 12 battles.
[271] *Nemzetgyűlési Napló,* XII. kötet. 1921. 616–617. old.
[272] Ibid, p. 623.

organized the population of Western Hungary and would have shown that this population id solidly loyal to Hungary and would have taken up arms against annexation. (…) Unfortunately, now it is too late. The people who would have been willing had the threat of annexation dropped on their shoulders so suddenly that it is impossible to think of organizing resistance now."[273]

Lingauer finally concluded: "Now, when (…) they are taking this part of the country, I must painfully conclude that today, on the last day of the session, we have heard some statements quavering with nationalistic bitterness in the matter of Western Hungary. Over the past three weeks, when these people awoke to the bitter truth of the fact of annexation, have wailed and cried, waiting for any manifestation, any encouraging word from the National Assembly, while we, from there in Western Hungary, saw with bitterness that here, the honored Assembly calmly debated the asset crisis proposal and for weeks nobody had a word to say on behalf of Western Hungary when a people, a quite large part of Hungary, looked towards Budapest, crying and sobbing, wondering if it was going to receive any help or not."[274]

The representative finally addressed the following three questions to the Assembly: "Is the government willing to make public the information regarding the negotiations in the matter of Western Hungary? Is the government willing, in the case Austria insists upon the handing over of Western Hungary, to resort to retaliation against Austria and break off diplomatic relations? Is the government willing to keep parliament in session until the question is resolved?" The president of the House passed the three questions to the Prime Minister. Next, Foreign Minister Bánffy took the floor and in his answer alluded to the meeting of the Foreign Committee and communicated developments with regard to the issue. The gist was that the Austrian Foreign Committee did not enter into direct talks with Hungary on the question after August 13. At the end, Bánffy noted: "I am confined to be able to say that this direction that the Western Hungary question has taken is extremely painful for Hungary." Albin Lingauer did not accept the essentially evasive answer of the Foreign Minister but, with the majority vote of the governing party, the National Assembly officially took note of it.[275]

The third motion was raised by Gábor Benkő, representative of the Tiszalök riding, who analyzed at length, linked to the approaching annexation of Western Hungary, the centuries of Austrian wrongdoings against Hungarians. Among them, that in 1848, it was the Austrian government that provoked the minorities (Serbs, Romanians, Slovaks) against the Hungarian revolt, that in 1919, it gave refuge to Béla Kun and his associates. "There is

---

[273] The last statement of Lingauer's was addressed to the public. In the meanwhile, he was one of the organizers of the Western Hungary insurrection that broke out a few day later on August 28, which struggle led to the eventually imposed Sopron plebiscite.
[274] *Nemzetgyűlési Napló,* XII. kötet. 1921. 625–626. old
[275] Ibid, pp. 626–627.

the historical file of József Diener-Dénes, in which Renner admits that they were ready to proclaim Communism at any minute but that they wanted to try it out first with us, to see if it does not turn out badly."[276]

In the following days, the streets of Sopron were crowded with wagons. We again quote Ernő Träger: "Offices and schools were being moved. The Vice-Constable's offices were relocated to Kapuvár, the county orphanage bureau to Csorna, with it the audit bureau and the pay office. The Sopron district reeve was moved to Pinnye; the gendarmerie headquarters, the Royal Courts, the county courts and finance bureau went to Győr. The Evangelical Theological Academy of Sopron was relocated to Kőszeg, the Evangelical Academy to Győr, and the Evangelical teacher's college to Bonyhád. The Trade and Manufacturing Chamber of Commerce was busy relocating its offices to Szombathely. Even the police received their withdrawal order, which began the exodus of the officers and functionaries. People were afraid to go out on the street, so they would not have to see the death of the city, so they would not hear the painful rumble of the wagons, so much like hearses. The Vice-Constable, Lajos Gévay-Wolff, wandered among the empty walls of the county seat, crying. He could cry but could not say farewell."[277]

Now it was the turn of another ancient, historical Hungarian city to play its part in the national tragedy series begun in 1918-1919. Then, it was as a result of the treason primarily of Mihály Károlyi, Béla Linder, Vilmos Böhm and others that purely Hungarian or majority Hungarian populated towns (e.g.- Rév-Komárom, Érsekújvár, Léva, Losonc, Rimaszombat, Rozsnyó, Kassa, Ungvár, Munkács, Beregszász, Sepsiszentgyörgy, Csíkszereda, Székelyudvarhely, Marosvásárhely, Nagybánya, Kolozsvár, Szatmárnémeti, Nagyvárad, Arad, Szabadka, Zenta, Magyarkanizsa) and huge areas of Hungarian-populated Northern Hungary, Sub-Carpathia, Transylvania and the Vojvodina from where 350,000 – 400,000 Hungarians were forced to flee.[278] To move to a truncated Hungary that remained after the Trianon Decree, a plundered Hungary, ahead of the conquering, robbing Czechoslovak, Romanian and South Slav forces. Many tens of thousands of them – without home or shelter – lived for long months, andr even years, in thousands of box cars in the railway yards of Budapest or improvised barracks. It was due to this that the Hungarian government was forced to restrict several times in 1920 and 1921 the influx of refugees from the severed parts. Because of the difficult economic situation, it was unable to assure accommodations or work opportunities.[279]

Naturally enough, a flood of refugees began from the territory to be handed to Austria; in fact, Hungarian authorities expected another wave ahead

---

[276] Ibid, pp. 639–644. The quote on page 639.

[277] Träger, 1925, op. cit., pp. 81–82.

[278] Of Trianon and its aftermath, see: Mórocz, Zsolt: Vereségek rejtett hálózata [Hidden network of defeats]. In: *Vasi Szemle*, 2000, issue 3, pp 295–301.

[279] MOL. K 26. 1299. csomó. 1922–XLIII–61. szám, pp. 114-125., 160-161., 183–186.

of the entry of the Austrian military. The executive of the Royal Hungarian Railways sent an extensive reports on June 30, 1921 to the Minister of Trades, stating, among other things: "There is a danger that when the eventual occupation of Western Hungary comes to pass, the 40 families housed in barracks in Bruck-Királyhida and Császárkőbánya will have to be moved. In fact, it can be expected that large numbers of loyal employees from the affected area will be forced to flee. In all probability, we will be forced to make available railway cars for their housing needs."[280]

Many citizens of Sopron left, out of fear, ahead of the anticipated entry of Austrian troops. The Rector's Office of the Royal Hungarian Mining and Forestry Academy, fleeing a mere two years previously ahead of the Czech-Slovak army from Selmecbánya [today Banská Štiavnica] in Northern Hungary, took no notice of the warning and took no steps to relocate, saying they have already moved two years before. It is important to briefly cover some of the background of this institution because its students – in continuous meetings during these days – would soon play an important role in the events of Western Hungary, in the anti-Austrian insurrection. The last lectures in Selmecbánya began on October 6, 1918. The vast majority of the 400 enrolled students (with the exception of 30 younger ones) fought in the war and almost all demobilized with the rank of second or first lieutenant. The students selected from among themselves, on November 2, 1918, a military commander in the person of Zoltán Szikorszky, a mining engineer student and former first lieutenant of the artillery. Afterwards, they marched to the building of the local military-mine security and demanded the handing over of arms and ammunition.

The students soon came up against the senseless pacifist, impotent policies of the Károlyi government, which gave up, without military resistance (in fact, prevented such initiatives), the 60,000 km^2 of Northern Hungary. The Mining and Forestry students disarmed the 38th Czech Artillery Regiment, a unit of the Monarchy and garrisoned in Selmecbánya, and took over the security of its barracks, armories and other buildings in the town.[281] The students thus provided, until the middle of December 1918, Hungarian public order in Selmecbánya, which the Károlyi government was unable to do, here as in many other places. When Czech forces advance in strength, the last group of approx. 300 students was forced to abandon the town. In the meantime, the head of the Academy looked for a new location inside the mutilated mother country to relocate the school, as it was their wish to continue to lead a Hungarian institution. The Hungarian government – bowing to the insistence of Mayor Mihály Thurner – designated Sopron (in directive 52,935) and the first group arrived on March 4, 1919, headed by Rector Géza Réz (1865–1936). The group consisted of four delegates from two ministries, the rector, five assistant professors and 22 students with the task of making

[280] Ibid, p. 114.
[281] Krug, 1930, op. cit., pp. 10, 14–15.

preparations for the relocation.[282] The rest of the teaching staff, now under Czech occupation in Selmecbánya, was only able to make their move starting April 26, 1919. A larger group of students, lacking the means, was only able to travel to Sopron in July. In the meanwhile, the salvaged equipment, collections, schoolrooms were temporarily housed by the end of April in the buildings of the King Charles Barracks, where instructions according to the former curriculum carried on. In fact, the cafeteria for the feeding for about 300 students was also arranged.[283]

Later, in 1921, a large proportion of the students did not go home for their summer break. They did not want to leave in case they would be unable to return. They stayed in Sopron to protect their school and city, if necessary. They met continuously, preparing for something. They established contact with the students of the Theological Academy, picking trusted students from among the middle schoolers. They included in their organizing the Boy Scouts under the leadership of Benedictine teacher, Detre Horváth, but kept their activities a secret in the city. The only thing that seeped out was that they swore an oath to each other that, whatever may happen, they would take care of traitors.[284]

When the Western Hungary insurrection broke out in August of 1921, the disarmament and reorganization of the Hungarian army to the 35,000 permitted under the Trianon treaty was under way for months. This, of course, touched the Szombathely district command, whose strength shrank to 423 officers, 221 civilian staff, 269 NCOs, and 3,913 men (from January's 846 officers, 666 NCOs and 14,624 men). As seen, the number of privates shrank to about a quarter of its former strength. As a result, the former Szombathely division shrank to become only a mixed brigade under the command of Gen. László Horváth, the district commander appointed was Gen. Árpád Guilleaume (1868-1951). The district gendarmerie consisted of 39 gendarme and 60 army officers, 881 professional gendarmes and a further 2,431 NCOs and men.[285] This does not include the two national gendarme reserve battalions, under Gyula Ostenburg[286] and Viktor Ranzenberger, which arrived

---

[282] Hiller, István: Sopron harca a hajdani selmecbányai főiskola idetelepítésért 1919-ben [Sopron's battle for the relocation of the former academy of Selmecbánya in 1919]. In: *Soproni Szemle*, 1969, issue 2, pp. 99, 102; Hiller, István: A soproni egyetemi hallgatók mozgalmai a két világháború között. Fejezetek a Soproni Egyetem történetéből. 1919–1945 [The movements of the Sopron University students between the two wars. Chapters from the history of Sopron University 1919-1945]. Sopron, 1975. The entire academy, students and professors, relocated to Vancouver, Canada in the aftermath of the 1956 Revolt, to become part of the University of British Columbia.

[283] Papp, 1969, op. cit., pp. 29–31.

[284] Träger, 1925, op. cit., p. 82.

[285] Fogarassy, 1994, op. cit., pp. 311-312.

[286] Gyula Ostenburg-Moravek (1884-1944), politician, army officer. Served in WWI, reaching the rank of major. During the era of the Hungarian Soviet Republic, he

in Western Hungary in the middle of August (142 officers and 2,291 gendarmes). Also, the district had an 800-strong unit (officers and men) of customs and revenue officers.

As a result of the terms of the Trianon Decree, Hungary was forced to close all military training institutions, with the exception of the Ludovika Academy in Budapest. After twenty-three years of existence, the Royal Hungarian Military Middle School of Sopron was forced to close its doors at the end of the 1920-1921 school year (closed by Law XLIV of 1921). "What happened next is the saddest event in the life of a military institution. They collected the rifles from the students; they took away all their military gear, even their belts."[287] The students were amalgamated into the commercial middle school of Sopron, along with the institution's equipment and assets.

---

joined the Hungarian National Army organized in Szeged. He sided with Charles IV in his October 1921 second attempt to reclaim the throne and was arrested on October 23 after the losing battle of Budaörs. He was sent into retirement after his release in 1922.

[287] Péterfy, Károly: A soproni M. Kir. Honvéd Főreáliskola története 1898–1921 [The history of the Royal Hungarian Military Middle School of Sopron 1898-1921]. Sopron, 1934, p. 106.

Chapter 6: The Western Hungary insurrection
August 28 – October 4, 1921

To direct the Western Hungary insurrection, an 11-member Military Committee[288] was organized in the second half of August, under Baron Zsigmond Perényi (1870-1946), national president of the Hungarian National Alliance. Its members, among others: former prime minister István Friedrich,[289] National Assembly representative and staff captain Gyula Gömbös, NA representative Albin Lingauer, politician and former NA representative Nándor Urmánczy,[290] one of the leaders of the Etelköz Association Captain Doctor Dezső Wein, NA representative Prince Lajos Windisgräetz (1882-1968), and military bishop István Zadravecz.[291] The task of the Military Committee was to exercise full power over the command of the Western Hungary insurrection with the knowledge of the Hungarian government and even, if necessary, without it. Gyula Gömbös requested unlimited power from the government to assure uniform leadership. To filter out undesirable elements, he encouraged the surveillance of train stations, allowing only those travelers to proceed to the western border zone who possessed a "Feltámadás" (Resurrection) identity card. It was the aim of the Bethlen government to gather the leadership of already-begun clandestine organizations and oversee them under the "Resurrection" cover name of the Etelköz Association. As a result, after August 21, the police picked up, or interrogated as witnesses, numerous people with intention to travel to Western Hungary.

According to the summarized situation report of the Royal Hungarian Defense Ministry for August 25-26: "the atmosphere in Sopron and its surroundings is calm, almost depressed."[292] On August 27, PM Bethlen instructed Chief Government Commissioner Sigray that if subsequent to the

---

[288] Páter Zadravecz titkos naplója [Secret diary of Father Zadravecz]. Szerk/ed: Borsányi, György. Magyar Történelmi Társulat, Budapest, 1967, p. 161.

[289] István Friedrich, one of the Secretaries of State for War in the Károlyi government between Nov. 1, 1918 and Feb. 8, 1919, then prime minister from Aug. 7 to Nov. 24, 1919.

[290] Nándor Urmánczy (1868-1940), politician, newspaper reporter, representative of the city of Szászrégen (1902-1918). After the dissolution of the Austro-Hungarian Monarchy, he organized a volunteer unit in Transylvania in the Fall of 1918 to hold up the advancing Romanian units. Between the wars, he lived in Budapest and dedicated himself to the revision of the Trianon Decree. From 1920 to 1940, he was the leading publicist for the Budapest publication, *Pesti Hírlap*.

[291] Fr. István Zadravecz OFM (1884-1965). Entered the Franciscan order and was ordained in 1907, founding member of the Etelköz Association (March 1919), then military chaplain of the Prónay detachment. Elevated by Pope Benedict XV to a bishop in 1920, ordained on Aug. 24. Organized and led the Royal Hungarian Army's Roman Catholic chaplaincy. Retired from the army in 1927 with the rank of Major General.

[292] MOL. K 26. 1264. csomó. 1921–XLII–6959. szám, p. 29.

withdrawal of the Hungarian soldiers "it may be possible that during the night some sort of local uprising or a *coup* will occur to take over the command post. I order Your Excellency to prevent it by all means at your disposal, maintain order in all eventuality and, if anyone tries in the least to break the peace, immediately arrest them and send them under guard to Budapest."[293]

Kedves Szabolcs! Ide kellene betenni az eredeti, 2008-as könyvemből (162. old.) a „Nyugat-Magyarország vázlatos térképe" aláírású térképet.

The Hungarian government had only two units to enforce law and order in the western Hungarian zone intended for annexation, both requested earlier by Chief Government Commissioner Sigray. One, the 1st Gendarme Reserve Battalion commanded by Lt.Col. Prónay, who had to remain behind in Budapest for grave reasons, arrived on August 15 in Felsőőr (Oberwart). Prónay had personal problems for his actions during the period of the White Terror. As well, he took some unorthodox action against a Jewish renter of his brother's who refused to pay and also swindled the local peasants. Prónay put him behind bars in the Nádor Barracks in Buda Castle. For his action, National Assembly representative Vilmos Vázsonyi (1868-1926) raised a complaint with the PM, Bethlen, who summoned him to the PM's office and personally demanded an explanation.[294] The lieutenant-colonel made the bad situation worse by sending a coarsely worded letter, full of insults, to István Rakovszky (1858-1931), President of the National Assembly, which caused an outrage in parliament.[295] On top of it all, Prónay accused the Minister of Defense, Sándor Belitska, with an auto swindle, committing a serious disciplinary offense.[296]

Commenting on the events, Army Bishop István Zadravecz said: "To me and other insiders, it was fairly clear why Bethlen executed (sic!) Prónay at just this time, and why Rakovszky's group assisted so strongly. Bethlen wanted to rid himself of Prónay because his battalion was sent to assist in the evacuation of the western parts and he was afraid that Prónay was going to prevent exactly that, as the local commander. Rakovszky knew Prónay as an anti-monarchist and was worried that the Ostenburg Battalion would find itself up against the fearsome Prónay in the King's *coup* planned in conjunction with the Western Hungary disturbances. In any case, the liberal Jewish press was glad for the fall of anti-Jewish Prónay."[297]

Due to the previous events, the 1st Gendarme Reserve Battalion left on

[293] Ibid, 1388. csomó. 1922–„H"-tétel. p. 135.
[294] Fogarassy, László: A Prónay–Ranzenberger pör (1930–1932) [The Prónay–Ranzenberger case (1930-1932)]. In: *Soproni Szemle*, 1978, issue 1, p. 23.
[295] *Nemzetgyűlési Napló*, XII. kötet. 1920. pp. 282–283.
[296] Prónay, Pál: A határban a Halál kaszál... Fejezetek Prónay Pál naplójából [Death is mowing in the fields... Chapters from the diary of Pál Prónay]. Szerk./ed.: Szabó, Ágnes and Pamlényi, Ervin. Magyar Történelmi Társulat. Budapest, 1963, p. 253.
[297] Zadravecz, 1967, op. cit., p. 154.

August 11 under Prónay's deputy, militia captain Viktor Ranzenberger,[298] to its destination of Felsőőr, the district seat. Although officially Ranzenberger was in command of the battalion, however, the unit considered Prónay as its real leader, and shortly as the commander of the Western Hungary insurrection, too.

The other unit in the field was the 2nd Gendarme Reserve Battalion, commanded by Gyula Ostenburg, which also arrived on August 15 at its base of Kismarton (now Eisenstadt).[299] The two gendarme units were, in every way, identical with the earlier Szeged and Székesfehérvár infantry battalions, which were withdrawn from the Army's Order of Battle on February 10, 1921 and transferred to the gendarmerie. The reality was that they were concealed military units, hidden from the eyes of the Entente. Hence, it is natural that Count Sigray did not notify the Entente generals in Sopron before the relocation of the two battalions to Western Hungary. Italian General Carlo Ferrario vehemently objected but the Chief Government Commissioner refused to withdraw them, thus staying in Felsőőr and Kismarton.

The third significant force in the Borderland in August was the so-called Héjjas free-militia unit, recruited from volunteers between the Danube and Tisza Rivers, commanded by Iván Héjjas.[300] The fourth, also a free unit of volunteers, was the militia led by District Reeve László Endre (1895-1946),[301] (whose complement soon grew to 200) and who were volunteers mostly from the towns of Gödöllő, Aszód, Vác and their surrounding villages. He started to Szombathely by train on August 28, arriving the following day in Nagyszentmihály and Felsőőr, with the intention to of equipping his men and occupying the village of Pinkafő. The unit was marching towards its goal, unarmed, when four trucks, filled with Entente soldiers and machine guns, caught up to them. They were all taken prisoners and escorted to the courtyard of the County Court of Felsőőr, where they were handed over to British Captain Trotter and French African-colonial soldiers. Count Tamás Erdődy, landowner in Vasvörösvár and chief of the local fire brigade, hurried to their aid. That evening, alarm bells were rung and agitated men collected in the street and broke down the court's front gate; with women and children, they surged inside for the fire hoses stored in the courtyard. It became apparent that it was a false alarm and that the count ordered the alarm to free the soldiers. In the chaos, the militia unit managed to escape, after hitting the few

---

[298] Prónay, 1963, op. cit., pp. 267, 274, 300, 303.

[299] The Ranzenberger battalion arrived on the western frontier with 1,610 men, of whom 150 deserted to the insurrection; other sources hold it to be possibly 300 or 400. The size of the Ostenburg battalion was 1,539 men, which was joined by 50 rebels in Sopron. Later, 105 deserted to the insurrection side, perhaps more. In: Fogarassy, 1994, op. cit., p. 312.

[300] Héjjas, 1929, op. cit., pp. 13–15.

[301] Endre László served as a reserve officer in WWI and was wounded on the Russian front. Served as reeve in a Temes County town (October 1918), later reeve and chief reeve in the Gödöllő district (1923-1938).

frightened black colonial soldiers over the head. The assembled during the night outside the village and, with the help of a local militiaman, sneaked into the Catholic school where they were provided with arms and equipment. In the evening hours of the following day, August 30, László Endre and his men marched into the border settlement of Pinkafő and set up camp pickets for the night. The rest of the unit retired for the night when they were attacked by a *Volkswehr* unit from Sinnersdorf on the Austrian side. After a fierce firefight, the attack was repelled.[302]

During the period of the insurrection, László Endre and his unit fought in the villages around Pinkafő against several incursions made by overwhelming superior forces from Austria. "Of these, the Austrian gendarmes were fairly disciplined, while the *Volkswehr* and the Social-Democratic defense force, made up mainly of Viennese unemployed loafers, presented little of military value."[303] Insurrectionist patrols – since the best defense is a good offence, and to retain the advantage of freedom of action – struck deep into Austrian territory, mainly at night, to spread fear and unease. A member of the unit was the commander's father, Zsigmond Endre, who refused to be left out of any action due to his age. Later, the Endre-militia was based in southern Vas County, around Szentelek, defending a stretch of the Hungarian-Austrian border. An equally important role was played in the insurrection by an armed unit of the students of the Mining and Forestry Academy.[304]

Col. Lehár was, by this time, an officer not on active duty for his action of having sided with former-King Charles IV in his March 26-April 5, 1921 attempt to regain the throne. Before being retired from the Army, he was sent on vacation starting July 1, and then officially retired on September 1.

In the midst of all these events, former prime minister István Friedrich was also actively organizing, having set up his headquarters in the spa-town of Balf, near Sopron, on August 26. On the following evening, he convened a military summit in the Pannonia Hotel in Sopron. His plan was to proclaim a separate and independent state of Lajta-Banate [Lajtabánság], covering the area earmarked for annexation and evacuated by Hungarian forces but not yet occupied by Austrian forces.[305] Subsequently – citing the self-determination of nations – his band of militiamen put up armed opposition to the Austrian forces marching in. He had the independence proclamation printed up in 8,000 copies, in Hungarian, German and Croat, and sent copies to Sopron and Szombathely for distribution. He directed his unit, known as the Friedrich rebels, to the vicinity of Savanyúkút and Lajtaújfalu close to the Hungarian-Austrian border on the night of Aug. 27-28, saying arms will be sent after

---

[302] Endre, László: Képek a nyugatmagyarországi fölkelésből [Scenes from the Western Hungary insurrection]. In: *A Cél*, year XVIII, 1928, Jan-Feb. issue, p. 25.

[303] Ádám, István: A nyugat-magyarországi felkelés története [The history of the Western Hungary insurrection]. Budapest, 1935, p. 75.

[304] Missuray-Krúg, Lajos: A nyugatmagyarországi felkelés [The Western Hungary insurrection]. Sopron, 1935, pp. 63-64. old.

[305] Lajtabánság: in German Leitha-Banat, for our purpose Lajta-Banate.

them by trucks. The lack of equipment, three boxcars at the Győr train station were pushed to a side spur – as it later turned out at the direction of PM Bethlen – forced the rebels to return to Sopron. The arms and equipment intended for them were soon in motion from Győr and was delivered to Iván Héjjas' unit, who made use of it in the first clash of Ágfalva. This was the reason that the proclamation of Lajta-Banate was delayed, although Viennese papers reported it as an event that had happened.[306] Friedrich was, at this time, a parliamentary representative in the opposition and it was not in the interest of the Bethlen government that he gain notable political success and popularity through possible successful resistance and proclamation of Lajta-Banate. Hence, he was soon removed from the scene of the insurrection, which was also demanded by the Entente Mission. The Mission had divided the territory earmarked for handover to Austria into two zones which indicated its intention regarding the allocation between the two countries. The definition of zones "A", "B" and "C" have been noted earlier.

The customs and revenue units operating in the villages of Köpcsény, Királyhida, Szarvkő, Savanyúkút, Sopron, Kabold, Pinkafő, Szentelek and Gyanafalva were the first to be withdrawn on August 26 from the intended handover area. On the following day, on the 27th, it was the turn of the infantry units and regimental command staff to vacate the Nezsider, Kismarton and Sopron barracks and relocate to their new districts behind the Trianon border. The garrison of Sopron left the city with a black shroud tied to their flag. The gendarmes began their withdrawal on the 28th and were to reach the line of the mentioned zone "A" by the same noon. This order also covered the local gendarme posts, the 1st and 2nd Gendarme Reserve Battalions and the Moson and Sopron counties' reserve gendarme companies, as well. Also forced to comply were the police detachments in Köpcsény, Királyhida, Lajtaújfalu, Savanyúkút, Lakompak, Pinkafő and Radafalva, the local garrison in Ruszt, as well as the staff of the police command centers in Sopron and Kismarton.[307]

On the morning of the same day, August 28, the Cabinet was in session in which Foreign Minister Miklós Bánffy, also minister without portfolio for the national minorities, made known the official communiqué of the Austrian Foreign Committee. According to its August 13 decision, Austria is only willing to resume negotiations after the handover of Western Hungary. At the same time, the Kingdom of Serbs-Croats-Slovenes had not yet signed the agreement covering its withdrawal from southern Trans-Danubia, forcing the Hungarian government to form a new position in the matter. Prime Minister Bethlen immediately remarked: "…the conditions for the handover of Western Hungary do not exist." The PM then went on to suggest that until

---

[306] Fogarassy, László: A nyugat-magyarországi kérdés katonai története. II. rész: 1921. augusztus – szeptember [The military history of the Western Hungary question. Part II: 1921 Aug.-Sept.]. In: *Soproni Szemle*, year XXVII, 1972, issue 1, pp. 26, 28.
[307] Ibid, pp. 28–29.

assurances are received from Vienna regarding financial and other interests, as well as ownership of assets, zone "B", including Sopron, will not be evacuated. It is possible, he went on, that the Entente will send an ultimatum, which prevents further resistance, but he saw hope that Paris would not reach for this option. The Belgrade government can comply in short order with the evacuation of southern Trans-Danubia but to satisfy Austrian demands would take much time. The Cabinet finally decided to suspend temporarily the evacuation of Western Hungary areas East of zone "A".[308] A Hungarian memorandum to this effect was handed to the Budapest and Sopron Entente Missions later the same day.

At noon, after the Cabinet meeting, PM Bethlen sent instructions by telegram to Chief Government Commissioner Sigray in Sopron. "Since the Cabinet decided this morning to temporarily suspend evacuation of the area East of line 'A' mentioned in paragraph 10 of the handover plan, I ask that the Entente military Mission in Sopron be officially notified at 4pm of this decision of the Royal Hungarian Government and, after said notification has been done, all necessary orders be issued to have the government's decision carried out. Furthermore, I ask that this order be kept confidential until 4pm, except for the appropriate officers on a need to know basis. Until that time, it is to be treated as strictly confidential. I again ask that every possible step be taken to end immediately the so-called Friedrich actions, and make their continuation impossible. This I ask all the more because this decision would undermine the government's diplomatic prospects."[309] After the Cabinet's decision, evacuation along the 'A' line was stopped by the gendarmes and army units, begun the previous day. Around this time, noonish on the 28th, the 2nd Gendarme Reserve Battalion arrived from Kismarton in Sopron. The city streets were soon covered by the posters of Maj. Gyula Ostenburg, proclaiming that he, by the order of Antal Sigray, has assumed command of the city. He also gave notice: "By my order, every non-Sopron resident male staying here is to report to barrack 48 between 18:00 hours today and 18:00 hours of Aug. 29. Anyone found not to have done so will be expelled from the city."[310] At the same time, a part of the battalion took up positions not in the city but at the junction of the 'A' and 'B' lines, west of the Ágfalva – Sopron – Fertőrákos sector.

Still on August 28, at 7:30pm, Foreign Minister Bánffy notified Count Sigray by telegram of his instruction: "I expect the strictest measures for maintaining order, especially since we have pushed to the utmost extent with the government's broadcast decisions."[311] Sigray then reported that the units of Maj. Ostenburg will rid not only Sopron but its surrounding area of all "undesirable outsiders" by the evening of the following day. He also reported

---

[308] MOL. K 27. Minisztertanácsi jegyzőkönyvek, 1921. augusztus 28.

[309] MOL. K 26. 1388. csomó. 1920–„H"-tétel, p. 224.

[310] Ibid, large poster without page number.

[311] Ibid, p. 225.

that during the afternoon, northwest of Sopron on the far side of line 'A', a unit of alleged rebels attacked the Austrian gendarmes and a firefight of several hours ensued. While it was going on, the future provincial head of Burgenland province, Robert Davy, drove by in an automobile, accompanied by a British and an Italian officer and was detained by the rebels. "As soon as I received word, despite the incident taking place past our front line, I ordered Ostenburg to free them immediately, which was done. The rebels dispersed and the car was able to continue on its way. I immediately reported it to the generals and they expressed their thanks for our forceful action."[312]

While these events were unfolding, units of the Héjjas rebels ripped up sections of railway tracks in several places around Sopron so that traffic between Sopron-Wiener Neustadt, Sopron-Kismarton (Eisenstadt) and Sopron-Ebenfurth was halted. These events did not surprise either the Entente generals or the Austrian government, since intelligence agencies and the press have both been reporting it as an expected action.

The Austrian government only mobilized smaller gendarme units and a somewhat larger number of government clerks and functionaries to assume control of the area. The majority of the latter group belonged to a unique ethnic group, the *Wiener Tscheche* or Viennese Czechs, who worked earlier as central administrators in the former Austro-Hungarian Monarchy and who did not return to their homeland, the newly formed Czechoslovakia. The Viennese government justified the dispatch of the slight occupation force by saying it did not wish to alarm the Christian-spirited peasants of Western Hungary, clinging to the old state of affairs, by sending in units of the *Volkswehr*, with its reputation for being "Red." The Austrian gendarmerie began their march into Western Hungary on the morning of August 28 – in eleven columns of 200 men each, accompanied by [Austrian] revenue officers – from the district headquarters barracks of Wiener Neustadt, Fürstenfeld and Graz. The Hungarian rebels pasted mild-toned posters in the border villages, on which they warned the foreign armed forces not to step on Hungarian soil "because they were playing with their lives (...) the reception could not be called enthusiastic anywhere," with the exception of four mountain communities around Gyanafalva. "To the great surprise of the Austrians, they were received not only with indifference but with frosty welcomes."[313] The Austrian military crossed the millennial border near Kismarton in the north, Felsőőr in the center and Szentelek in the south, to establish the administrative Németújvár administrative district in the latter two areas.

The Western Hungary insurrection broke out on August 28 when about one-third of Héjjas' force of 120, or about 40 rebels, gave battle at Ágfalva to the Austrian forces marching in.[314] The first casualty of the fire fight was a

[312] Ibid, pp. 255–256.

[313] Ibid, 1264. csomó. 1921–XLII–6959. szám, p. 4.

[314] Fogarassy, László: Lajtabánság [Lajta-Banate]. In: *Legújabbkori Múzeumi Közlemények*, 1967, issue 1–2, pp. 66–77; Zsiga, Tibor: A nyugat-magyarországi felkelés és Vas megye 1921 [The Western Hungary insurrection and Vas County

young man from Kecskemét, László Baracsi.[315] Units of Gyula Ostenburg disarmed the rebels taking part in this action and then the major called on them to join his battalion. The majority of the rebels refused, leading to their expulsion from Sopron by Ostenburg's men. "The increase in the unit's strength by the rebels had a less than wonderful result. Of the couple of hundred individuals arrested by Ostenburg in Sopron, and who wished to fight in the free force, only about fifty volunteered for regular military service at Ostenburg's appeal. Among them, a few reservist officers, Captain Madersbach (correctly Viktor Maderspach[316]) with 12 men, and a few Szeklers."[317] In the evening of the same day, the 28th, PM Bethlen contacted Sigray in Sopron by telegraph at 23:00 hours and gave detailed instructions, which he asked to be "executed with the greatest vigor." To wit, the removal from the territory still under the control of the Hungarian government of the command staff of István Friedrich, Iván Héjjas, non-Sopron residents and persons with no business in Western Hungary. If armed, they are to be disarmed and expelled by force. The interruption of train service and the ripping up of railway tracks must be prevented.[318] Earlier in the day, in the afternoon hours, an Austrian force (202 gendarmes and 22 revenue officers) was making its way from the Austrian village of Friedberg in the valley of the Pinka River when it ran into a small force of 50 near Pinkafő, led by 1st Lt. László Kuthy. After a sharp fire fight, the Austrian force, even though outnumbering the Hungarians 9:2, withdrew before darkness fell and retreated back to Austrian territory.[319]

At 11:00 in the morning of August 29, PM Bethlen again instructed Sigray by telegram that "irresponsible elements are to be disarmed and held in check, as well as Friedrich and Héjjas are to be rendered harmless." The situation report of the Chief Government Constable then recounted that there was total peace and quiet during the night in Sopron; Friedrich was no longer in the city and the whereabouts of Héjjas was not known. At 10:00, he had held a review of the Ostenburg battalion, which was greeted with great enthusiasm by the

---

1921]. In: *Savaria*. A Vas megyei Múzeumok Értesítője. Vol. 15. 1981. Szombathely, 1985, pp. 409–448.

[315] Héjjas J., op. cit., pp. 15–17.

[316] Maderspach, Viktor: Élményeim a nyugatmagyarországi szabadságharcból [My adventures in the Western Hungary freedom fight]. In: *Magyarság,* 1926, issues 1–5 and 7–38. Viktor Maderspach (1875-1941), volunteered for service in WWI and organized a mounted free-force after Romania's 1916 entry into the war, with which he reached the Black Sea. He demobilized as a Hussar captain at the end of the war. He was charged with suspicion of anti-Romanian activities in the summer of 1921, escaped from Transylvania and joined the Western Hungary insurrection. He commanded the 5th Rebel Army until September 24, then served in the Ostenburg battalion in Sopron. Promoted to major by King Charles IV.

[317] MOL. K 26. 1388. csomó. 1922–„H" tétel, p. 327.

[318] Ibid, pp. 246–247.

[319] A Rongyos Gárda harcai 1919–1939 [The battles of the Ragged Guard 1919-1939]. Budapest, 1940, pp. 102–107.

population. "Irresponsible elements were shown that a large, disciplined force was standing ready for our disposition." There were no reports of disturbances from Sopron and Moson Counties. Austrian gendarmes were unable to march into Pinkafő in Vas County, however, Szentelek was occupied by them the previous evening. The population of the village of Németszentgrót chased away the Austrian forces; in Rábakeresztúr, 17 Austrian gendarmes and revenue officers crossed the Trianon border, who were then disarmed by the Hungarian customs force and sent to Szentgotthárd. There were no reports from the village of Borostyánkő or the vicinity of Írott-kő mountain. It was noted that rebel forces were moving in the forest near Városszalónak.[320]

In the exchange between the PM and the Chief Government Constable that took place at 17:00 on the same day, Bethlen informed Sigray that "I sent Gyula Gömbös by special train to Sopron with the goal of persuading Iván Héjjas to return," as well as those who are on territory to be ceded to Austria by his orders. This "only escalating tensions, useful for increasing disorder and presenting to the Entente with the idea that resistance in the Hungarian territory is prepared with the knowledge or cooperation of the government, or that these people passing though the Hungarian and Austrian cordon are creating resistance in the areas occupied by the Austrians and from where they return to Hungarian territory, where they feel safe, once their stay becomes impossible."[321] In his report to Bethlen of the evening before, Count Sigray noted: "In my opinion, the mission of Gyula Gömbös here is pointless, since Ostenburg will remove Héjjas and the other elements. The clean-up has already begun and will be completed by noon tomorrow." Sigray then reported on the "fairly large sized" confrontation at Pinkafő, which "allegedly had 50 Austrian casualties." The Austrians had not, to this time, marched into either Pinkafő or Borostyánkő.[322] Finally, the Chief Commissioner suggested to the PM: "I would deem it extremely advisable if Gömbös, as well as every other person not living here, returned to Budapest as soon as possible because politicians, we know, only cause confusion. I can report that Friedrich will not come to Sopron again. He had announced that he was completely stepping aside from the conflict. This I did. However, the Urmánczy group will be harder to remove, as they are stealthier. I will look after them, too."[323]

The clash that took place in the village of Pinkafő on August 29 was also reported by telephone that evening at 17:30 by the head of the Sopron branch of the Interior Ministry's central investigation department. According to him, there were 60 casualties on the Austrian side, with a higher number of wounded but as yet unascertainable. Austrian units withdrew from the village. There were also clashes around the village of Nagyszentmihály, with 18 dead and many wounded but "on which side is not yet clear." The captain making

---

[320] MOL. K 26. 1388. csomó 1922–„H" tétel, pp. 298-301.
[321] Ibid, p. 290.
[322] Ibid, p. 292.
[323] Ibid, p. 293.

the report remarked that he had no knowledge of the whereabouts of Pál Prónay. He also reported that Robert Davy, the provincial chief named to head Burgenland by the Vienna government, resigned today. In Sopron, the band of the Ostenburg battalion gave a concert on Széchenyi Square at 4pm -- the time when the city was supposed to have been handed over.

Baron Frigyes Villani, deputy to Chief Government Commissioner Sigray, included in his noon report of August 30 to PM Bethlen that, according to his latest information, Robert Davy did not resign. He had installed his offices in Nagymarton but his authority extended over very little territory, only those settlements which the Austrian gendarmes already occupy.[324] Due to the previously mentioned clashes, Davy was forced to instruct that the staff of the Austrian provincial government for Western Hungary should remain in Wiener Neustadt. And the special train, standing by to take them to Sopron on the 29th should, instead, transport 200 gendarmes to Ágfalva.

Count Sigray also made a report to the PM by telegraph at 10:30 on the same day regarding the events of the previous day, adding new information. Firstly, regarding the Entente's report "whose passage that armed men continue to arrive does not square with reality because the volunteers are already prevented in Budapest from travelling any further." Ostenburg has already arrested a number of people in Sopron, cleansed the city "of dubious person who came here. (…) …as much as our force permits, we will also begin to clear the immediate neighborhood of Sopron from armed irresponsible elements. (…) The arrival of Gömbös was very good from the perspective that he was able to clear up the situation in large strokes. (…) Héjjas did not travel with him but, afraid of being arrested, he left the city during the night." Sigray also reported that he received telegrams from numerous Sopron and Vas county settlements with the request to provide safeguard against Austrian forces flooding in and "the Hungarian gendarmes return to the evacuated western [meaning 'A'-*J.B.*] zone. This I will inform the Entente Mission but the names of the settlements I can not reveal for fear of reprisals because, in many places, the Austrians are brutally collecting hostages, which clearly proves that they also know that the population is taking an active part in the resistance."[325] The Entente Mission's information that yesterday two boxcars of arms arrived at the Sopron station turned out to be false, which a British and an Italian officer verified. According to a telegraph report sent to the PM at 18:00 on August 31 from Sopron, Maj. Ostenburg expelled more than 500 people from the city.[326]

Gyula Gömbös, sent by the prime minister to Sopron on August 29, was able, after numerous meetings, to clarify part of the situation. The two leading members of the already mentioned Military Committee, István Friedrich and Nándor Urmánczy, issued a three-point proclamation on August 31at Balf.

---

[324] Ibid, p. 314.

[325] Ibid, pp. 307, 309.

[326] Ibid, p. 328.

"Since the Royal Hungarian Government has assumed the defense of Western Hungary, we, who only began our action in defense of the territorial unity of our thousand-year country, declare that we disband our free-troops and cease further engagements."[327] This, however, they were only willing to do if the government fulfills certain conditions. They were to receive 1.8 million Kroners to cover the costs of demobilization and travel home of the volunteers, as well as the value of the military equipment handed over to the army. As well, free telephone and telegraph usage to notify their organizations to stop arming and not to start to travel towards Western Hungary.

The most crucial point in the disbanding of the volunteer force was number three, which stated: "The leaders and participants of the action receive complete assurance that they will not be held accountable for their actions, except for any crimes and offences arising from greed." István Friedrich and Nándor Urmánczy were asking for amnesty from the government. Finally, they stated that they would not take any responsibility[328] in the future, as they had not in the past, for the volunteer units of Iván Héjjas and György Hir.[329] (György Hir was, at this time, a National Assembly representative and, with Nándor Urmánczy, Viktor Maderspach and Dr. Dezső Wein, a reserve medical captain, were part of the inner staff of István Friedrich.)

In the central portion of the Borderland, clashes continued between the volunteer rebel forces and the inward bound Austrian units. Beside the already mentioned clashes of Aug. 28-29 at Ágfalva, Pinkafő and Nagyszentmihály, there were also firefights at Felsőőr – where Árpád Taby and eight rebels, with only one machine gun and their rifles, put to flight 200 Austrians – Alhó, Frakno, Borostyánkő and Németgyirót, resulting in the rebels successfully pushing the Austrian invaders across the border into Austria.[330] Columns 11 and 12 of the Austrian gendarmes, advancing in the South, were attacked by the rebels on August 29. In the village of Nagyfalva near Szentgotthárd, a 35-strong unit, led by György Endresz,[331] successfully

---

[327] Ibid, p. 321.

[328] MOL. K 26. 1388. csomó 1922–„H" tétel, p. 321.

[329] György Hir (1888-1926), fought on the Eastern Front beginning in 1914. Transferred to the Western Front near Verdun in 1916 with the 69th Infantry Regiment of Székesfehérvár. Making use of his combat experience, he helped set up the first close order combat units of the Austro-Hungarian Monarchy.

[330] Missuray-Krúg, 1935, op. cit., pp. 74–83; Ádám T., 1939, op. cit., pp. 29–30.

[331] György Endresz (1893-1932), served as pilot in WWI, then commander of a "Red" airforce company in Győr during the Hungarian Soviet Republic. In 1931, he set a world record of 26 hours and 20 minutes by flying across the Atlantic in his plane, *Justice for Hungary*, taking off from Grace Harbour in Newfoundland, crossing the Atlantic and western Europe to land near Budapest. For their feat, he and his navigator received Lord Rothermere's grand prize for cross-ocean flight. In 1927, Lord Rothermere had run an article in his paper, "Hungary's Place in the Sun" (*Daily Mail*, June 21), in which he drew attention to the unjust borders dictated by the Trianon Treaty.

dislodged the Austrians from the village. After getting a few reinforcements, he beat back the Austrian gendarmes, along with a *Volkswehr* company come to reinforce them, to the Austrian side of the border.[332] By August 31, not only the area around Gyanafalva and Rábakeresztúr but the entire zone East of the pre-Trianon border up to Pinkafő was under the control of the rebels. In the last days of August and early September "our rebel units, marching day and night, appearing here and there, are being unbelievably overestimated, and over reported and these preposterous numbers are further swollen by the fantasies of the units we scattered. The Viennese of the day report the strength of our rebel forces at 20-30,000, when, in fact, it was merely several hundred."[333]

During these days, the unit of Iván Héjjas took control of the area around Királyhida on the Hungarian side – and Bruck on the Austrian side – in Moson County, along the Hungarian-Czechoslovak border. The rebels, led by Pál Gebhardt and Viktor Maderspach, initially joined by the Friedrich group, were waiting for the Austrian incursion in Ágfalva, west of Sopron. South of them, around Felsőőr (Oberwart) and Pörgölény (Pilgersdorf), were the units of Árpád Taby. The fifth rebel unit claimed as its battle zone in the South, around Gyanafalva. The patriots who took to the field were armed by Héjjas and Prónay with the arms and ammunition that Héjjas and company acquired through the daring raid of July 1920 from the armory of the Austrian garrison of Fürstenfeld.

By this time, the unit organized from the students of the Sopron mining and forestry academy had joined the uprising. A meeting was held in the morning of August 29, where it was decided that the academy was joining the Ostenburg battalion as a company comprised of [former] officers. The meeting sent a three-man delegation to Major, and city commander, Ostenburg and after an agreement was made, the students joined the battalion as the 5th Officer Company. The Major assigned the 5th Company, led by Elemér Székely, to the sector running northwest of Sopron along the line of Kelénpatak – Szentmargitbánya – Kismarton – Kishőflány – Lajtaújfalu. Ostenburg was not disappointed in the young men as they took their share in the struggles and played a large role in the plebiscite and Sopron remaining in Hungary. In their sector, they carried out nighttime raids on the villages and harried the gendarmes billeted in the houses with barrages of rifle fire. "During the day in uniform, weapons drill and various duties; then almost every night, in civilian coat and hat, armed with a rifle and grenades, one rebel raiding party after another. A little 'worrying' of the occupying 'Austrian cousins' and by morning another 'delicacy' for the Entente committees, preferably from an Austrian perspective."[334]

The majority of Sopron citizens could not accept that their city was to be

---

[332] A Rongyos Gárda…, op. cit., pp. 148–154.

[333] Héjjas J., 1929, op. cit., p. 31.

[334] Krug, 1930, op. cit., pp. 54–55.

torn from Hungary. They delegated former mayor Dr. Károly Töpler, the lawyer Dr. István Pinezich and the principal of the technical institute, Ernő Lauringer, who visited Deputy Chief Government Commissioner Frigyes Villani in his room in the Pannonia Hotel on August 29. They stated that they would not stand idly by and watch the occupation of their city but will support the Héjjas rebels. The baron took note of the decision with dismay and repeated that this move by the citizens harmed the country. It was in these circumstances that the 83-strong Sopron detachment of the Ragged Guard was born, which swore allegiance and joined the force of Iván Héjjas. The list of signatories contained many local notable families – such as Imre and Pál Storno – and doctors, and, based on purely their names, were not Hungarians but of German origins.[335]

In his report of September 1, Sigray telegrammed the following to PM Bethlen: "The Austrians have reached the 'A' line everywhere in Moson and Sopron Counties" but are loath to enter into certain villages, being afraid of the armed rebels. "In Kismarton, every night they move into the Esterhazy castle and set up machine guns, leaving the rest of the town undefended, saying that the town should look after itself as best as it can. The situation in Vas County is, for the moment, unchanged. [The] Austrian gendarmes could not penetrate but [the] Entente officers have received new orders to introduce new gendarmes – which will supposedly act braver. (...) [The] Austrians have released the hostages in Kismarton. (...) Telegrams and delegations from the villages attest to their loyalty and devotion to Hungary."[336]

The rebels fought an extended pitched battle with the Austrian gendarmes on September 1 and 2, in the outskirts of Cinfalva, between Sopron and Kismarton. The attack began at night, as reported by Sigray to the PM's office at 13:50 on September 1. In the next village, Darázsfalva, the occupying Austrian gendarmes forbade the local population from going out to work in the fields, saying they wanted to clear the area of rebels. "In Ágfalva, [the] Austrians arrested National Assembly representative Ödön Scholtz, postmistress Szabó and notary-intern István Bősze and sent them to Wiener Neustadt. The population is on edge."[337] On September 1, Deputy Commissioner Villani reported at 19:30 to the PM that the Croat population of the village of Kópháza, near Sopron, asked the Commissariat to forward a petition to the Entente Mission. Its text: "We do not wish to separate from Hungary and reach the fate of our formerly separated Croat brethren who have been stripped of their language and culture in Austria. Today, they are not Croats but ethnicityless Germans. We want to remain Croats and see it ensured with our brother Magyars."[338]

The Cabinet met the next day, September 2, where PM Bethlen honestly

---

[335] Ádám, 1939, op. cit., pp. 19–20.
[336] MOL. K 26. 1388. csomó. 1922–„H" tétel, pp. 331–332.
[337] Ibid, p. 334.
[338] Ibid, p. 335.

stated: "Generally, the Western Hungary situation is perhaps better today than a week or two ago because it seems certain that we will gain some time for negotiations. And it is not impossible that at least a part of this territory may be retained, perhaps all of zone 'B'." Then he discussed that he had talks with Sir Thomas Hohler, Britain's ambassador, from whom he learned that the Entente Powers will shortly hand a memorandum to Hungary. But no need to be frightened, assured the prime minister, because it does not contain an ultimatum, not even a deadline to complete the demands. Bethlen added to the previous that there was no need to worry about political or military intervention by the Little Entente countries, either.[339] Shortly after the Cabinet meeting, Imre Nádossy, national chief of police, issued instructions, to take effect immediately, to all the counties' vice-constables, districts and Budapest police chiefs of police and gendarme headquarters, that he was altering his instructions of August 29 regarding travel to Western Hungary. Henceforth, only the named offices can issue the necessary travel documents, which they are permitted to issue "only in very exceptional circumstances."[340]

On September 2 at 11:00, Sigray reported by telegram to the PM: "It is certain that revolts are happening in many places we did not know to date. In Vas County, for example, infantry and mounted bands of [count] Tamás Erdődy and landowner Egan [Imre, 1881-1944] are wandering around the Írott-kő peak, all the way to the Styrian border." Bethlen's reply: "I have been informed that the officers of Captain Ranzenberg [correctly Viktor Ranzenberger] took part in the Pinkafő events (…) [who] still organize raids even today, but only in the Austrian occupied 'A' zone. I ask that Ratzenberger (sic!) be called on during the course of today and he be strictly instructed in my name to immediately cease this (…) not to suffer any persons not belonging there, and with all means at his disposal make it impossible that they or their company officers create havoc in the 'A' zone."[341] Bethlen finally disclosed to Sigray that he will travel to Western Hungary the following day, or the day after, to assure himself personally that his instructions are obeyed. This took place on the following day. The prime minister held a review on the 3rd in Sopron, on the 4th in Szombathely and along the line of zone 'A'. He also came to the conclusion that the future border should run along the line separating zones 'A' and 'B', along Köpcsény – Zurány – Féltorony – Boldogasszony – Fertőmeggyes – Ágfalva – Doborján – Felsőpulya – Léka – Városszalónak – Pusztaszentmihály – Rábakeresztúr.

At 18:00 on the same day, Sigray reported the following to the prime minister: the Austrian gendarmes and communists retreating from Királyfalva (Szentgotthárd district) carried off with them the Roman Catholic parish priest, József Horváth. "They assaulted him most brutally, beating him

---

[339] MOL. K 27. Minisztertanácsi jegyzőkönyv, 1921. szeptember 2.
[340] MOL. K 26. 1388. csomó. 1920–„H" tétel, p. 339.
[341] Ibid, pp. 340-341.

bloody. (…) The Entente military mission in Szentgotthárd notified [the] chief district magistrate that, through their intervention, the parish priest has been freed 5 hours after his capture [but] is still in Fölöstöm [Fürstenfeld] today."[342] Count Sigray also reported to PM Bethlen late that night at 22:50 that a firefight took place between the rebels and the Austrian gendarmes in the outskirts of Pörgölény (Pilgersdorf) – in the northernmost part of Vas County, in the Kőszeg district. Its outcome was "losses on both sides, among them the capture of the landowner Imre Egan by the Austrian gendarmes."[343] Egan was wounded in the skirmish and the gendarmes took him in a horse-drawn wagon, tied up, to a hospital on the other side of the border. Along the way, the defenseless wounded man was set upon and beaten by the populace, almost being lynched in Kirschlag but for the intervention of an Austrian regimental doctor.[344]

The following day, September 3, PM Bethlen informed Deputy Commissioner Villani at 11:00 that he intends to take the afternoon express train to Sopron. The following day, he would "like to drive the length of the front by car" and return to Budapest from Szombathely.

Baron Villani: "Nothing to report, complete silence reigns."

They had not received an official report yet of the previous day's clash at Pörgölény, neither did they know whether Imre Egan died or was captured by Austrians.

Bethlen: "The Austrians have not committed other atrocities? Because we want to take diplomatic steps in this matter and it is desirable that we know about all similar events to be able to start the counter-offensive. Naturally, we want well founded, true news."
Villani: "I have spoken to the chief magistrate of Felsőőr who said that the rebels are keeping exemplary order, not committed any crimes. The population likes them very much and provides them with cheap foodstuffs. A number of the population has joined [the rebels]. A part of the rebel force is without arms. General Ferrario [the Italian general of the Sopron Entente Mission-*J.B.*] met with them the day before yesterday in Felsőőr and now he is also in agreement, having seen how the population of Vas County do not want the Austrians. The generals are calmed down, that Ostenburg has restored order so forcefully. The Croat speaking villages ask us, through delegations, to arm them against the Austrians."

---

[342] Ibid, p. 349.
[343] Ibid, p. 355.
[344] Krug, Lajos, ifj.: 1921. A nyugatmagyarországi szabadságharc története [1921. The history of the Western Hungary freedom fight]. In: *Emlékezés*. (1921-1931). Szerk/ed.: Tóth, Alajos. Magyar Kir. Bányamérnöki és Erdőmérnöki Főiskolai Ifjúsági Kör. Sopron, 1932, pp. 92-93.

Baron Villani seemed to know that "according to reliable information representative Scholtz has been freed. However, the parish priest of Királyfalva from Vas County, the one I reported by telegram, they don't want to release and are treating him very badly. (…) The rebels have most recently issued [postal] stamps with the overprinting 'The part of Hungary occupied by free forces'." The prime minister finally revealed to Villani: "We are expecting the Entente note today which, according to our information, will not contain an ultimatum."[345]

In his 19:00 report to the PM's office, Baron Villani reported that the Austrian gendarmes had released the Hungarian hostages, with the exception of the priest, József Horváth, and that there is no word of the whereabouts of the notary from Ágfalva, István Bősze. There was gunfire during the night in Darázsfalva, Cinfalva and Kismarton. A delegation arrived to the Commissariat from Répcesarud, a Croat-populated village, and stated "on behalf of the village, they protest in the strongest terms against the annexation of Western Hungary."[346] The carrying off and attack on the Királyfalva priest, József Horváth, had become an international incident to which not only the Entente Mission but Chancellor Schober devoted their attention. The Hungarian ambassador in Vienna, Szilárd Masirevich, telegrammed the following to the Foreign Ministry in Budapest at 20:00 hours on September 3: according to a report made to the chancellor, "the Hungarian rebels sent a message to the Austrians that, for every day Horváth is kept a prisoner, an Austrian gendarme will be hung." Schober asked for immediate action to prevent this. Masirevich saw a connection between the capture of 12 gendarmes and four customs officers in Rábakeresztúr and the priest's situation. The Hungarian ambassador urged the release of the parish priest, to which the chancellor replied: he cannot arrange it in his jurisdiction as the issue belongs in the Justice Ministry's sphere. It seems Horváth is being charged with posting a reward on the heads of the Austrian gendarmes. At that, Masirevich commented that "the charge is clearly without foundation, at first glance." The chancellor finally made it known to the ambassador that the National Assembly representative and Evangelical Dean, Ödön Scholz, has been freed and is presently in Agendorf (Ágfalva), where he has met with Robert Davy, appointed head of the Burgenland province.[347]

The next day, September 4, the Austrian embassy in Budapest interceded at the Hungarian Foreign Ministry, of which Minister Bánffy notified Baron Villani in Sopron and Count Sigray in Szombathely in identical telegrams. They were instructed to "do everything in their power that the captured gendarmes come to no harm." Baron Villani's telegram report of 13:00 refuted Chancellor Schober's information of the previous day: the 16 gendarmes and customs officers were captured not in Rábakeresztúr but

---

[345] MOL. K 26. 1388. csomó. 1920–„H" tétel, pp. 360–361, 364.
[346] Ibid, p. 362.
[347] Ibid, pp. 356–357.

Rábafüzes, on territory the Trianon Treaty left as part of Hungary. Baron Villani also disclosed that an agreement has been reached with the Entente generals in Sopron. Hungarian authorities will hand over their 16 captives to Austria in exchange for József Horváth in Gyanafalva, in the presence of the Entente sub-mission stationed there. This was supposed to take place in two days' time, on September 6, but was prevented when a 200-man volunteer rebel group showed up at the appointed time and demanded that, until the Austrians hand over the body of one of their fallen comrades, they will prevent the exchange. Finally, the prisoner exchange took place on the 7th without a hitch and the parish priest could return to his flock – reported Count Sigray to the PM's office the same evening.[348]

Still back on the 4th, it was the day that an 18-man patrol of the student Officer Company that joined Ostenburg's battalion saw action. During the night, they rained gunfire on the settlements of Kismarton and Kishőflány. On the following evening, another unit carried out a raid up to the former, historic border, to Lajtaújfalu. On their return, they exchanged fire with the Austrian gendarmes near the village of Kelénpatak.[349]

The chief of the Szombathely district investigation group, Sándor Swoboda, sent a report to the Interior Ministry at 9:00 on September 5, in which he reported heavy fighting in the dawn hours around Gyanafalva, where Austrian losses amounted to 30 dead, the rebels 7; the number of wounded was unknown. During the fighting, the Hungarians captured an Austrian machinegun, which they immediately turned against the occupiers. In the firefight at Kelen-patak [more accurately the village of Kelénpatak near Sopron-J.B.] between Austrian Communist elements and rebels, several people were killed or were wounded. Similarly, in neighboring Cinfalva, where the rebels threw bombs on the houses where Austrians were billeted. The Austrians fled.[350] Villani also reported on September 5 from Sopron to the PM, in which he stated that Robert Davy, Austrian governor of Burgenland, spent several hours today in Sopron, accompanied by an Austrian colonel. The colonel stayed behind with the task of acting as liaison between the generals' Entente Mission [Inter-Allied Military Mission-J.B.] and the Austrian governing committee now in Nagymarton (Mattersburg). Deputy Chief Government Commissioner Villani signed this report as "Foreign Ministerial Adviser."[351]

The reasons for this go back a week. As we have written, the Hungarian Cabinet suspended the evacuation of areas of Western Hungary East of the 'A' zone line at their session held on August 28. At the instruction of Prime Minister Bethlen, Chief Government Commissioner Sigray reported this to the Entente generals at 16:00, who replied that they will report this turn of

---

[348] Ibid, pp. 365–366, 376, 264, 390.

[349] Krug, 1930, op. cit., pp. 55–56.

[350] MOL. K 26. 1264. csomó. 1921–XLII. tétel, p. 10.

[351] Ibid, 1388. csomó. 1922–„H" tétel, p. 370.

events to the Council of Ambassadors in Paris. Next, they issued instructions to order a halt to Austria's advance at the 'A' line. Finally, they took the position that Sigray and his deputy, Villani, were primarily responsible for the eruption of the rebellion. Hence, they were not willing to hold talks with either. In fact, the committee of generals officially broke off contact with Count Sigray, with whom British general George Gorton maintained repeated contact – as a private person. In fact, he made it known to Sigray not to be concerned of a united Czechoslovak and Serb military intervention due to the Western Hungary events because the Entente Powers will not give their consent to Prague and Belgrade.[352]

Also on September 5, Kálmán Kánya, Minister of State for Foreign Affairs sent a memorandum to the Office of the Prime Minister regarding "the handover of Western Hungary and Colonel Cunningham." "Our Vienna foreign representation reports, from several reliable sources, that Colonel Cunningham was in Western Hungary in recent days and, while there, gained the confidence of Hungarian military and other sectors. He brought numerous facts to Schober, which bring to light the government's compromising connections to the Western Hungary insurrection. The chancellor seems not to want to use this information, not wishing to make the situation worse. At the same time, I was asked to ensure that I am to treat Col. Cunningham, whose duplicity we have known for a long time, and generally all Entente people coming from Vienna to Western Hungary, with the utmost caution by our side. I have immediately informed Baron Villani in Sopron, to immediately pass these to Count Sigray."[353]

The battle at Gyanafalva, with its many casualties, signified that the rebels were firm in their resolve. In the early morning hours of September 5, Austrian gendarmes based in the border villages of Létér (Lebenbrunn) and Németgyirót (Deutsch Gerisdorf) reported to the headquarters on the other side of the border in Kirchschlag, that they were attacked by rebels. Reinforcements were sent to their aid, while the rebel unit of Árpád Taby (and a part of Miklós Budaházy's unit) took the village of Németgyirót, then Lantosfalva (Bubendorf). Afterwards, they attacked Pörgölény (Pilgersdorf) and pushed on towards Kirchschlag, where the rumors of the fleeing Austrian gendarmes reported that a 2,500-strong Hungarian military unit was on its way. Some of the rebels were, indeed, wearing military uniforms, or parts of it. Panic broke out in Kirchschlag, the alarm bells were rung. The entire Austrian garrison marched out to the infantry trenches and an acute battle broke out in front of the village.

The battle of Kirchschlag was the largest fight in the history of the Western Hungary insurrection: on the Hungarian side were 290 rebels; on the Austrian, 270 soldiers, joined by 250 gendarmes and revenue officers. On the

---

[352] Fogarassy, 1972, op. cit., p. 32.
[353] MOL. K 26. 1388. csomó. 1922–„H" tétel, p. 367. The colonel's actual name was Col. Sir Thomas Cuninghame.

rebel side, there were seven casualties; the number of wounded and captured: unknown. The Austrians lost 10 dead, 17 wounded and 36 captured.[354] When the rebels reached the first houses of Kirchschlag, Taby ordered a retreat back to Hungarian territory. Austrian military command immediately sent army units from Wiener Neustadt to reinforce Kirchschlag, and defend the border sector. Chancellor Joannes Schober protested sharply about the attack to the Entente Powers.[355] The Inter-Allied Military Mission in Sopron, however, did not comply with the chancellor's request to order two Austrian battalions to Kismarton (Eisenstadt), and one to Nezsider (Neusiedl am See).

The news of the pitched battle at Kirchschlag was picked up by the international news media and focused attention on the unresolved western Hungarian situation. Naturally, the Hungarian government took immediate steps to shed light on the events. Prime Minister Bethlen instructed Sigray by telegram on September 6 to ask the Entente generals in Sopron to: please send immediately an Entente officer to the scene, accompanied by one or two Hungarian officers. "The Kirchschlag event was blown up by the Austrians, trumpeted to the world that, from the Hungarian side, a regular [army] unit of 2,000 men took part, it is in our great interest to have the Entente commission carry out a determination on-site. (…) I ask to have it definitely pointed out that, after the population looked on the Austrians as unwelcome foreigners, they defend themselves, meaning they side with Hungary and attack the Austrians. The Austrians are doing everything to give the world the impression of the event, as if it was not the population, as if it was not people from the population who organized the defense, as it happened, but that the Hungarian army and the Hungarian government are directing the armed resistance. Thus, as a result, we demand that the impartial commission of the Entente determine and investigate these events. I also ask you to draw their attention to the fact that, along the entire line from the Danube down to the Mura, we do not have 2,000 gendarmes, never mind that so many men would be available in the evacuated area. Even the rebels, according to the officers themselves in Felsőőr, cannot field more than 400 – 500."[356]

Italian General Carlo Ferrario of the Entente Mission in Sopron immediately left for Kirchschlag by car to assess the events, where he forbade the Austrian forces to cross the border. In fact, he ordered them to break off hostilities and pull back. He also did not agree to let the Austrian Republic's forces, the *Bundesheer*, occupy the militarily important high grounds in Western Hungary. Then, he turned to exploring the reasons for the clash. He determined that the firefight was carried out, on one side, by rebels in civilian clothes, numbering perhaps a few hundred, reports of 2,000 men are an Austrian exaggeration – reported Sigray to PM Bethlen in his 19:45 telegram. The previous facts he got from Gen. Ferrario, who authorized him to share

---

[354] Missuray-Krúg, op. cit., pp. 100-109; Fogarassy, 1972, op. cit., p. 38.
[355] MOL. K 26. 1388. csomó. 1922–„H" tétel, pp. 369, 379.
[356] Ibid, pp. 377–378.

them with Bethlen. After the assessment, on his way back to Sopron, Gen. Ferrario stopped in Hungarian-populated Felsőpulya (Oberpullendorf), where the Austrian gendarmes were in the process of withdrawing. They had received word that rebels were approaching from the North. The Italian general gave orders to the Austrian commander, a major, not to get into a pitched battle, but rather to avoid confrontations.[357] Subsequently, the Austrian gendarmes voluntarily gave up the villages of Felsőpulya, Csáva (Stoob) and Lakompak (Lackenbach), as well as the surrounding area.

Count Sigray's relationship with the Entente Mission, due to his previously mentioned negative behavior, also needed to be clarified. Also noted before that his deputy, Baron Villani, signed the previous day's report as 'foreign ministerial adviser.' The battle at Kirchschlag again brought the subject of Sigray to the forefront, in the memorandum written by the Entente generals and handed to the Hungarian government, in connection with the clash. Bethlen communicated this to Sigray during their conversation at 21:00 on September 6. In fact, he instructed the count to: compile from the journals of his commissariat the warnings and memoranda of the Entente generals and his actions in response. The need for this is that, in his response note, the government wishes to reference them. Bethlen also commented to Sigray: French Gen. Jules Hamelin complained to him in Budapest that he is not satisfied with the activities of the chief government commissioner. As well, the current Entente note is making hints at the activities of István Friedrich, too. Finally, the PM instructed Sigray to: inform the Entente generals in Sopron that Hungarian officers will go to the rebels, who will try to convince them not to make incursions into Austrian territory and return to Hungarian parts. Otherwise, if they delay the latter, they will face courts martial."[358]

During their conversation the following morning, September 7, Bethlen communicated to Sigray that: today the Szombathely district military commander informed the Minister of Defense that 70 Hungarian gendarmes also took part in the Kirchschlag action. That they withdrew when informed that Austrian gendarmes were in their rear. At that point, they met with some Entente officers who allowed them to proceed on condition that they give their word to disarm when they reached the Hungarian gendarme cordon and return home. On reaching their base, the gendarmes laughed at the Entente officers and exchanged their civilian clothes for gendarme uniforms. The prime minister stated: "I have instructed the district military command, through the Defense Ministry, that insofar if this is true, the 70 men are to be immediately discharged and brought up in front of a court martial. The officer, too, who made this possible, is to be held responsible. (…) The government will have to take the most serious retaliation." He then instructed Sigray to carry out immediate appraisal of the event and to make a report. The chief government commissioner reported by the same evening: he reviewed

---

[357] Ibid, p. 381.
[358] Ibid, p. 385.

the events at Gyanafalva and concluded that "the information received by the prime minister is not in agreement with the reality." According to "vague rumors," the events took place on August 28, or perhaps 29, but "the Entente Mission has not commented in writing, or verbally, yet had ample time to do so since the 28th."

Another event also happened on the 7th, of which Sigray informed the PM in his above mentioned report, that the Henrik Marschall-led rebel unit attacked the 35-strong Austrian gendarme outpost at night in the village of Zárány (Zagersdorf), halfway between Sopron and Kismarton. According to the Austrian report to the Entente generals in Sopron, three gendarmes were killed. The rest were forced by the rebels to strip to their underwear and released on the following condition: they march to Wiener Neustadt and never again venture across the Lajta River into Hungarian territory. The parish priest of Zárány was taken into custody by a new unit of gendarmes arriving in the village and taken away with the charge of having been in collusion with the rebels.[359]

Still on September 7, an officer of the Entente Mission, British Captain Trother, met with delegates of two German-speaking villages in the border zone in Felsőőr (Oberwart). We learn from Lt.Col. Ferenczy's report of the following day that: "Their spokesman, the parish priest of Árokszállás, said, more or less, in his enthusiastic speech that they are appealing to the victors' chivalry and sense of fair play. They ask that a sick Hungary not be driven into the arms of a dead Austria. They would rather die than be part of 'Red' Austria. They ask that the Entente Powers take note of this, all the more so because they are the representatives of purely German villages." The lieutenant-colonel also reported: "The Entente officers are searching for the rebels, whom they would like to convince to retreat." During the negotiations, they accepted that "the rebels act in the role of home guard" and that "the Entente officers deem it rightful that the population wants to defend itself by way of [its] home guard against 'Red' Austria."[360]

As we have already written, the staff of Robert Davy, the appointed governor of Burgenland province, have moved from the Austian town of Wiener Neustadt to Nagymarton in Sopron County. The governor travelled from here daily by car to the Entente Mission in Sopron. A public meeting was organized in Ágfalva, occupied by Austrian gendarmes, for September 7, where Davy also spoke and announced: "Morgen wird der Vormarsch nach Ödenburg vorgenommen!" [In the morning, we must press on to Sopron!] The mob – in which the leading shouters were people who arrived from Vienna and Wiener Neustadt – took up the chant: "Einmarsch! Einmarsch nach Ödenburg!" [Entry! Entry into Sopron!] at this time, the garrison of Ágfalva

---

[359] Ibid, pp. 386–388. The former Marxist-Communist historiography treated the 70 gendarme report as truth, ignoring the fact that Count Sigray had ascertained by that evening that it was a lie. See, Soós, 1971, op. cit., p. 145.
[360] MOL. K 26. 1388. csomó. 1922–„H" tétel, p. 394.

consisted of 400 Austrian gendarmes, with six machine guns, which had a good chance of taking over the waterworks of Sopron, thus forcing the city to its knees.[361]

The Officer Company that joined the Ostenburg battalion had made preparations in the morning of September 6 to take and occupy Ágfalva. In preparation, Captain Viktor Maderspach and Elemér Székely, commander of the company, set out on a scouting mission. Lajos Krug, intimately familiar with the neighborhood, got the assignment to obtain military maps of the village and its surroundings and mark any forest trails. On the following evening, about 100 rebels set out from Sopron towards Ágfalva, about six kilometers away. On the orders of Elemér Székely, the attack was begun at dawn on the 8th but the Austrians put up a stronger than expected defense. In the heated exchange of fire, cadet Gyula Machatsek forestry engineer, reservist sub-lieutenant Elemér Szechányi and Ferenc Pehm, volunteer with the Ostenburg battalion, lost their lives; two were critically wounded: Károly Held, forestry engineering student and Lajos Zorkóczy, student from Budapest. The unit of Captain Pál Gebhardt and 1[st]Lt. Varga hurried to the aid of the student company and managed to attack the flank of the Austrians, who began to flee. More reinforcements arrived with Maj. Ostenburg and the occupiers were finally routed.

Austrian eyewitnesses, among them Johann Müllner, superintendent of the Graz district gendarmerie, admitted in his diary (Der Kampf bei Agendorf / Battle at Ágfalva): their good fortune while escaping was that the rebels intentionally aimed high above their heads.[362] Lajos Krug, who took part in the Ágfalva mêlée, himself noted: if they wanted, they could have picked off the occupiers one by one, of whom only one gendarme was killed and two seriously wounded. The latter both died of their wounds, in the hospitals in Sopron and Wiener Neustadt. The first reports in the Vienna papers, true to their habit of overstating the facts, told of 60 Austrian dead and more than a hundred wounded, in an attack by a 2,000-strong Hungarian unit, reinforced by artillery. All the while, the goal of the rebels was to frighten and put to flight the Austrians, not to massacre them; to drive out the intruding enemy from the ancient Hungarian lands, which was completely successful. One of the means used at Ágfalva was the so-called 'spare cannon,' which was nothing more than a water-filled barrel. Firing into the barrel gave off the sound of a medium caliber cannon. The Austrian gendarmes, retreating in a hail of bullets, fled in the direction of Lépesfalva (Loipersbach im Burgenland) and, reaching the railway tracks, climbed aboard a slow-moving train that took them into Nagymarton. Shortly after the encounter, Entente officers from Sopron arrived on the scene, along with Commissioner Sigray, and Gyula Ostenburg reported to him the events of the combat. Next, the gendarmes of his battalion disarmed the rebels and Ostenburg sent them

---

[361] Krug, 1930, op. cit., p. 74.
[362] Hiller, op. cit., p. 88.

marching under guard towards Sopron. However, when they reached the edge of the forest, they were let go. Lajos Krug and others attest to this.[363] Sopron was saved for Hungary by the second, and equally victorious, battle of Ágfalva because Austria could not present the Paris Peace Conference with a *fait accompli* by marching in and militarily taking over the city. In the following three days, the rebels ejected the Austrian gendarmes from Western Hungary, leaving only Királyhida (Bruckneudorf), Lajtaújfalu (Neufeld an der Leitha) and Lajtaszentmiklós (Neudörfl an der Leitha) in Austrian hands. Subsequently, there were only local clashes against enemy incursion into Hungarian territory.

The Entente officers – as well as the Austrians – knew that the battle at Ágfalva was a coordinated operation between the rebels and the Ostenburg battalion. This became evident from the telephone conversation of the following day, September 9, which was tapped by the Sopron detachment of army intelligence. The following dialogue took place between two generals, the Italian in Sopron and the French in Kismarton.

Gauthier: "I have finished my investigation into the matter of Ágfalva. I will also put my report in writing. What I know, I mostly know from the retreating Austrian gendarmes (…) [who] have the feeling that the rebels and Hungarian gendarmes were in collusion, in other words, the appearance of Ostenburg was mere comedy. They took the rebels captive, disarmed them and released [them] toward the rear, and probably gave their weapons back, too."
Ivaldi (laughing): "Of course, of course."[364]

The Sopron Entente Mission managed, among other things, to ascertain: the rebels began their attack at 4am but Maj. Ostenburg reached the outskirts of Ágfalva from Sopron with a part of his unit at 5am. This route of march, with reveille, assembly and an approx. 6 km. march, would take at least 2 hours. The Entente generals shared the result of the assessment with Lt.Gen. Pál Hegedűs, who visited them on September 11.[365] The Austrian gendarmes who fled to Nagymarton, the seat of Robert Davy's Burgenland administrative center, stated: they have no desire to stay and fight in Western Hungary because they are civil servant. Let the Viennese government order in the army to take possession of the territory.

A few hours after the battle of Ágfalva of September 8, at 11:00 o'clock,

---

[363] Krug, 1930, op. cit., pp. 59-80; Missuray-Krug, op. cit., pp. 110-127; Tóth, Alajos, 1932, op. cit., p. 95-103; Maderspach, 1926. In. *Magyarság*, year VII, January 21, p, 4; January 22, p. 4; January 23, p. 6; Stelczer, István: Kik vívták meg az ágfalvai ütközetet [Who fought in the battle of Ágfalva]? In: *Magyarság*, year X, 1929, September 19, p. 6; Héjjas J., 1929, op. cit., pp. 24-28. More recently, Károlyfalvi, József: A nyugat-magyarországi felkelés és Kecskemét [The Western Hungary insurrection and Kecskemét]. In: *Kapu*, 2001, issue 10, pp. 24-25.
[364] MOL. K 26. 1388. csomó. 1922–„H" tétel, p. 261.
[365] Ibid, pp. 414–415.

Hungarian military counter-intelligence listened in on the telephone conversation between British General George Gorton and Chancellor Schober, between Sopron and Vienna. The Chancellor complained: "Our gendarmes were again beaten out of Ágfalva. The situation is impossible for us. (…) I ask that Entente forces support our gendarmes or allow us to send our army."

Gorton: "Austria cannot send army units under any circumstances because that would break the agreed accord [i.e., the Trianon dictate-*J.B.*]."
Schober: "But our gendarmerie is too weak."
Gorton: "Then let them retreat."
Schober: "The Austrian gendarme is used to working in an honest country unlike the Hungarian gendarmes, in a savage country."[366]

We know from the detailed report that Commissioner Sigray sent to PM Bethlen on the afternoon of September 8 that Austrian Inspector General Hueber expressed his special thanks to Maj. Ostenburg for the Austrian wounded being taken to the Sopron hospital. The Austrian gendarmes were "using dum-dum bullets in the battle of Ágfalva so that the three Hungarian dead have terribly traumatized wounds." [Bullets with a hollow tip or with an X shaped incision in the tip have a greater destructive effect on the target than regular bullets. The use of mushrooming bullets have been forbidden since the II. Hague Agreement of 1899, yet the Austrian units made use of them against the rebels.] Count Sigray also informed the PM that Ostenburg collected the equipment of the fleeing Austrian gendarmes and revenue officers, rifles and machine guns, and handed them over to the Austrian authorities, including the unit's cash box. He had personal effects left behind taken to the judge in Ágfalva for safekeeping.[367] This certainly brings into question Joannes Schober's recent opinion about a 'savage country'; the chivalry of Maj. Ostenburg towards the Austrian wounded and their hospitalization, as well as the return, or safekeeping, of the fleeing gendarmes. It is important to remember that it was the Austrian gendarmerie who used the internationally banned dum-dum bullets and not the Hungarian rebels. To top it off, Gyula Ostenburg had not only the three Hungarians who fell in the battle but also the Austrian gendarme buried with military pomp. In his evening report on September 8, Sigray disclosed: "I wish to report to His Excellency that Iván Héjjas has not left [Western Hungary] (…) his decision he has allegedly reported in writing directly to a higher authority."[368]

On the next day shortly before noon, the Italian ambassador in Budapest, Prince Gaetano Castagneto, phoned the Entente Mission in Sopron. The ambassador informed the Mission that French General Jules Hamelin just

---

[366] Ibid, pp. 411–412.
[367] Ibid, p. 420.
[368] Ibid, p. 431–432.

notified him: he just received Johannes Schober's letter. The chancellor informed the general that the Austrian government is immediately withdrawing its gendarmes from Western Hungary because it does not want to risk their lives needlessly. Hamelin's opinion was: "we must carry out this wish of the chancellor, although I admit, from a political perspective it carries a lot of weight." The ambassador replied: "I, too, feel that the situation is very grave." Then he added, that he will seek out Prime Minister Bethlen at noon in this matter. Hamelin: "Sir, please make it an especially important consideration that, if we deny Mr. Schober's request, the Hungarian rebels will undoubtedly oust the Austrian gendarmes from the country. If, on the other hand, we accede to the withdrawal of the gendarmes, we can expect all manner of surprises from the Hungarian rebels. Fact is, Austria is incapable of pacifying the territory. Austria is currently working on setting up volunteer free-forces similar to the Hungarians, so that these can be sent into the fray against the Hungarian rebels."[369]

The second battle of Ágfalva – as noted, the first battle of August 28 was the beginning of the insurrection – brought a significant change in the direction of the Western Hungary question. Its outcome was that the Entente generals in Sopron did not accede to Chancellor Schober's request, namely, either the dispatch of Entente forces or permission for the Austrian army to enter Western Hungary. The Inter-Allied Military Mission saw that permission for the entry of Austrian troops could have unforeseen consequences, such as the possibility of an Austrian-Hungarian war, leading to a foreign political crisis. Subsequently, the Chancellor informed the Hungarian ambassador, Szilárd Masirevich, that Austria had no intention of getting into an armed conflict with Hungary but would rather have a peaceful resolution. In these circumstances, Schober instructed Robert Davy not to expose the Austrian units to any danger and have them withdrawn. The provincial government should set up in Nagymarton, where control over the mail and telegram services should be secured.[370] The gendarmerie continued their total withdrawal, started the day before on the 8th, to the line of the millennial Hungarian-Austrian border. By the evening hours, several strategic settlements of western Sopron County were evacuated, including the villages of Kabold, Lakompak, Zárány, Zemenye and Cinfalva, along with the district center of Nagymarton[371] and border services were resumed in the traditional border zone.

Confirmation of the completion of the withdrawal came from a wiretapped telephone conversation on September 10 at 13:20 between the Austrian delegate to the Sopron Entente Mission, Hueber, and the gendarmerie Chief Inspector in Wiener Neustadt, Siskovics.

---

[369] Ibid, p. 422.

[370] Soós, 1971, op. cit., p. 148.

[371] MOL. K 26. 1388. csomó. 1922–„H" tétel, p. 427.

Hueber: What are you doing, then?
Siskovics: Guarding the old border.
Hueber: How did you get there?
Siskovics: We pulled back.
Hueber: According to orders?
Siskovics: Yes.

At 21:50, the head of the local Italian mission reported from the Nezsider district seat to Col. Ivaldi in Sopron: "The Austrian gendarmes have left Kismarton and its entire surroundings." Ivaldi: "Maintain public safety as well as you can. It is the same all over the area because the Austrians have left their positions everywhere." The following day, the 11th, the [Hungarian] gendarme headquarters reported: "Workers coming across the border post are saying that in Vienna and Wr. Neustadt the wall posters released by the Austrian government made public Western Hungary's remaining with Hungary and the withdrawal of the Austrian gendarmes yesterday."[372] This meant that, on the previous evening, the entire territory of Western Hungary earmarked for annexation was again under Hungarian administration.

A few days earlier, on September 9, PM Bethlen gave an account of his inspection tour of Western Hungary to the Cabinet. He told of the general calm in the Hungarian controlled zone 'B', while chaos reigned in zone 'A'. The rebels, who look upon their activities as a freedom fight, are joined by many of the local population. The situation is aggravated by the Serbs concentrating forces in the South, while the Czechoslovak authorities are expelling masses of Hungarians out of the areas they have occupied. The ambassadors of the Entente Powers have called on him, demanding that the Hungarian government put an end to the actions of the volunteer rebel forces. In response, he made two suggestions: the officers of the Entente Mission in Sopron, accompanied by Hungarian officers, travel to zone 'A' and try to 'convince' the rebels to disarm. The second: the Entente agree to have the Hungarian gendarmes move up to the historical border line, when the Hungarian government can offer assurance of the rebels disarming. The ambassadors rejected the second proposition because they felt that, with the advance of the Hungarian gendarmes to the former boundary, the Hungarian government would not evacuate Western Hungary. In the end, the ambassadors accepted the prime minister's first proposal.

The Cabinet then turned to a discussion of the response to be given to the Entente's September 6 memorandum. According to Bethlen, it must be stressed that we will evacuate the affected Western Hungary area but, in the meantime – and this is possible – we must gain time to restart negotiations with Austria. To that end, we should try to hand the area in question to the Entente, administered by the Hungarian government and our gendarmes would be stationed there. The Cabinet then decided on the text of the

---

[372] Ibid, pp. 269–270, 272.

responding memorandum. The gist: stress the interests of both the region's population, as well as of Austria and Hungary that the evacuation can not endanger the peaceful population by having "communist bands" devastate their lives. At the same time, the Hungarian government restate that it is ready to hand over the territory, however, citing the changed circumstances from the first plan, a new evacuation plan should be created with the inclusion of the Hungarian and Austrian governments.[373] The Hungarian government sent this reply memorandum to the Entente Powers on September 11.

On the morning of the previous day, Maj. Gyula Ostenburg had the casualties of the Ágfalva battle buried "with the greatest military pomp" in Sopron. The three Hungarian casualties – Elemér Szechányi, Gyula Machatsek and Ferenc Pehm – and the Austrian gendarme, Arnold Mosch, lay in state in the courtyard of the '48 Barracks. The assembled lined up, Ostenburg's gendarmes formed an honor guard, attended by the entire teaching staff of the academy, with the students in uniform. At the request of the next of kin, the body of Ferenc Pehm was taken to Szombathely after the ceremony to be buried there. Antal Sigray was present in the funeral procession, as well as Mayor Mihály Thurner of Sopron and an Austrian attaché from the Budapest embassy. The Austrian commander of the Ágfalva gendarmes took part in the graveside ceremony; members of the Entente Mission – presumably fearing a demonstration – stayed away.[374]

In his report of the next day to the Minister of Defense, Sándor Belitska, Lt.Gen. Pál Hegedűs analyzed the event: apart from the battle of Ágfalva, what shook the confidence of the Entente generals staying in Sopron was the fact the Maj. Ostenburg buried "with full military honors" the two academy rebels who were fighting "in defiance of the government," an honor due only to fallen members of the active military. "The burial had a political hue and carried the feature of a demonstration: entire school turned out, girls' schools in national costumes, patriotic speeches, etc. Count Sigray attended in his official capacity."[375] The general continued his intrigue in the report, saying: Maj. Ostenburg sent a detachment of 40 gendarmes to Kismarton, abandoned by the Austrian gendarmes, to prevent disorder and looting, allegedly at the request of the local mayor and now he refuses to leave.[376] In contrast to the previous, the Entente Mission requested from Commissioner Sigray on the day of the funerals that the Ostenburg battalion continue to safeguard Ágfalva and Brennbergbánya, as well as post squads West of the 'A' line in the area of Fertőmeggyes – Kelénpatak – Sopronkertes – Somfalva – Lépesfalva – Récény – Lakfalva – Doborján – Szabadbáránd. Past the last village ran the boundary of the 'A' zone.

On September 11, Chancellor Schober held talks in the Austrian border

---

[373] MOL. K 27. Minisztertanácsi jegyzőkönyv, 1921. szeptember 9.

[374] Krug, 1930, op. cit., pp. 81-86.

[375] MOL. K 26. 1388. csomó. 1922–„H" tétel, p. 415.

[376] Ibid, p. 416.

village of Landegg, near Eberfurth, with Entente generals Gorton, Ferrario and Hamelin, regarding the situation after the withdrawal of the Austrian gendarmes. The chancellor received their permission for the Austrian military to occupy certain Borderland areas and villages. Thus, the next day, the villages of Lorettom, Szarvkő, Büdöskút, Völgyfalu, Pecsenyéd and Savanyúkút on the western edge of Sopron County came under Austrian control, cutting off two strategic rail and border stations, Lajtaújfalu and Lajtaszentmiklós. Furthermore, in Moson County, a 3km. zone East of the traditional border, covering the villages of Császárkőbánya, Királyhida, Lajtaújfalu, Lajtakáta, Lajtakörtvélyes, Nemesvölgy and Köpcsény. Of these, the most important was Királyhida, a railway station and border checkpoint. To secure it, a unit of the *Volkswehr* from Bruck, along with a gendarme unit, crossed the Lajta River and took control of the Királyhida border crossing railway station and the military barracks.

According to the September 13 report of the Investigation Bureau of the Interior Ministry, the local Germans in the village of Mosonújfalu threw a festivity with the newly entered Austrian gendarmes, which they did not allow the local Croats to attend. "At that, the Croats went to another pub and sang Kossuth songs, which the Austrians wanted to stop. A fight broke out, during which the Croats kept yelling: We want to stay Hungarian. Throw out the Austrians." It was also reported from the 80% Croat-populated Mosonújfalu that: "The population is Croat and is not satisfied with Austrian rule. Increasing the bitterness is the fact that the Austrians promised them cheap sugar and collected the money for it but there is no sign of the money or the sugar." In any case, the magistrates of the villages of Mosonújfalu, Pándorfalu, Lajtaújfalu and Köpcsény "sent a memorandum to High Constable [of Moson County] dr. István Zsembery for transmittal to the Entente, in which the villages petition the Entente to leave them with Hungary and permit the Hungarian gendarmes to return."[377]

Although the Sopron Entente Mission had expressed its dissatisfaction with Sigray since the end of August, the removal of the Chief Government Commissioner only happened as a result of Prime Minister Bethlen's directive of September 11.[378] The government thus satisfied the demand of the Sopron generals to remove Sigray – his deputy, Villani, as noted previously, had already been demoted – because, according to them, he colluded with Maj. Ostenburg, field commander Prónay, Capt. Ranzenberger and the rebels. Sigray immediately turned to Bethlen with a personal letter. "Dear István, the division of the responsibilities of the chief government commissioner, as governed by the rules conveyed this morning, makes my position completely untenable to the degree that I will probably tender my resignation from Sopron, – something I did not wish to say to you this morning in the presence of others – that is why I said that the associate (and not subordinate) military

[377] Ibid, p. 478.
[378] Ibid, p. 459.

commander's position will make it very difficult to address the issues, since *de facto* power is in the hands of Hegedűs, because without military (...) [illegible word: creativity? flexibility?] in the present situation makes action impossible."

Earlier that morning, PM Bethlen redefined the responsibilities of the Chief Government Commissariat for Western Hungary with regard to the territory to be handed over. He left Count Sigray in charge of 'civilian matters, meaning public administration but took away direction of military and police bodies, which were assumed by Lt.Gen. Hegedűs. At the same time, both were directly to report to the Hungarian government, stating: "they should proceed with complete agreement, support and keep each other informed." However, "only Lt.Gen. Hegedűs will maintain contact with the generals of the Allied Mission in Sopron."[379] The last instruction showed the refined tactical sense of Bethlen because Hegedűs, as an army officer, was much better at talking to the high ranking Entente officers than Sigray, the nobleman-turned-politician. Col. György Köller was named as chief of staff for Hegedűs; previously he acted as military advisor beside the Chief Government Commissioner. In the end, Sigray did not resign his post.

On September 12, the prime minister again instructs Count Sigray and Lt.Gen. Hegedűs that he has received a short note from the Parisian Council of Ambassadors, through *chargé d'affaires* Iván Praznovszky, which "again places all responsibility on the Hungarian government." Moreover, it called upon him to evacuate Western Hungary because "otherwise, it would be forced to take forcible measures." Bethlen also informed that he called together the Budapest ambassadors of the Entente and explained to them that the Hungarian government received this most recent Paris note without them being aware of the contents of the previous Hungarian response memorandum. That is to say, in that we did not refuse the evacuation of zone 'A'. The ambassadors were willing to accept that Hungarian public administration return to zone 'A', after Hungarian forces have restored order, but only if the battalions of Ostenburg and Ranzenberger have had no part in the restoration of order. This means that the two units must be withdrawn from the area awarded to Austria. The PM then instructed Count Sigray and Lt.Gen. Hegedűs to make the necessary preparations in this regard. Finally, he asked Sigray, appealing to his 'patriotism,' to continue in his post, within the new area of responsibility.[380] In the evening, Maj. Ostenburg also reported by telegram to the prime minister. Among other things, he informed that "all day we have been receiving urgent requests for gendarme squads from the evacuated villages, such as Nagyhőflány, Lajtaszentgyörgy, Szárazvám, Kishőflány, Felsőkismartonhegy and Kismartonváralja, as well as Királyhida and Parndorfból [Pándorfalu] (...) [because] Communists bands are entering and threatening the population with looting and robbery, who are without any

---

[379] Ibid, pp. 450–451, 559.
[380] Ibid, pp. 470–471.

form of protection under the current order to withdraw."[381]

After the complete reoccupation of zone 'A', the creation of an integrated command over the rebel forces became more urgent. Citing 'higher orders,' Gyula Gömbös had made several attempts at taking over command of all the volunteer free-forces but was rebuffed by them, holding Hussar Lt.Col. Baron Pál Prónay as suitable. The reason was that it was he who organized the armed resistance in the central and southern areas of the western Hungarian territory earmarked for annexation, and it was there that his rebel forces were active. The situation was rectified by having Prónay officially released from the Hungarian National Army on August 28, "at his own request," for his already mentioned actions.[382] In the evening of September 6, Prónay arrived by train in Sopron from Budapest as a retired, non-serving lieutenant-colonel, meaning that he was independent of the government. There he held talks with Count Sigray and Maj. Ostenburg, where they agreed that Maj. Ostenburg would be in command of the rebels in the Nagymarton-Kismarton sector, while Prónay would command the free-troops in the rest of the territory.[383]

Two days later, on September 8, Commissioner Sigray escorted Prónay, under the alias of Pál Doborján, to the village of Nagyszentmihály, where he assumed command over the rebel forces. The headquarters were located, not by accident, nearby in the almost completely Hungarian-populated center of the Felsőőr district, from where he directed subsequent military operations. The rebel forces operating since the end of August, Lt.Col. Prónay organized into separate units, whose operational areas, leaders and initial strengths were have already written.

Prónay officially assumed overall command of the rebel forces on September 16 and he divided his forces into five units. The *1st Rebel Army* was commanded by Lt. v. Árpád Taby, Knight of the Order of Maria Theresa, former commander of the attack battalion of Magyaróvár, and was headquartered in Felsőőr in Vas County. Subsequently, it was commanded by rebel Lt. Antal Héjjas. The *2nd Rebel Army* was commanded by rebel Capt. Miklós Budaházy, former officer of the Szekler Division, garrisoned in the village of Felsőpulya, later Lakompak (both in Sopron County).[384] The *3rd Rebel Army* was commanded by rebel Lt. v. Endre Molnár, later by rebel Capt. Lajos Thurzó, garrisoned in Németújvár (Vas County). The *4th Rebel Army* was commanded by rebel 1st Lt. Iván Héjjas. This was a rapid

---

[381] Ibid, p. 468.

[382] *Honvédelem*, year III, issue 36, 1921, September 4.

[383] Prónay, 1986, op. cit., pp. 31–32.

[384] The secretary of Miklós Budaházy (according to Prónay, his aide), rebel Capt. József Szabó (1887-1934?) who, with Budaházy, recruited in the area between the Danube and Tisza Rivers, and took part in organizing the first Western Hungary uprising on August 28. Békés, Márton: A fegyveres revízió útja Nyugat-Magyarországon. Szabó József százados felkelőparancsnok válogatott iratai elé [The path of armed revision in Western Hungary. Preamble to the selected writings of rebel commander Capt. József Szabó]. In: *Vasi Szemle*, 2007, issue 4, pp. 418–426.

deployment unit. His deputies were rebel Capt. István Bacho (Bakó in some sources) and Franciscan priest Fr. Lajos Bónis, better known as Archangel Bónis, military chaplain. The unit was garrisoned in Pándorfalu in Moson County. The 5th *Rebel Army* was commanded by Capt. Viktor Maderspach (Ret.), the commander of the Officer Company of the Sopron Academy (after September 24 by rebel Captain Pál Gebhardt). His deputy was rebel 1st Lt. Elemér Székely. The unit was based in Nagymarton, Sopron County. The *Friedrich rebel unit*, based in nearby Kismarton, came under the command of the 5th Rebel Army, while the *Friedrich-Gebhardt unit* reported to Maj. Gyula Ostenburg.[385]

The total number of the northern and southern armies based in the 'A' zone of Western Hungary according to Jenő Héjjas, brother of Iván Héjjas, was around 3,500 – 4,000. This small, mobile but determined force defended a western front of about 200 kms., from the Czechoslovak border in the North down to the South Slavs in the South. The units were made up of farmers from the Great Plains, university students and demobilized officers. In their ranks were about 300 Bosnian and Albanian Muslim soldiers, who had fought in the Austro-Hungarian Monarchy's army during World War One, including Maj. Hussein Durics Hilmi (1887-1940). The ideological organizer of the insurrection was the already mentioned National Assembly representative György Adonyi Hir who, with others (captains Iván Héjjas, Miklós Budaházy and József Szabó, former officers of the Szekler Division; Fr. Lajos Bónis; chief district magistrate Lajos Förster) recruited members of the volunteer force all across southern Hungary in August of 1921.

The organizational structure of the rebel forces, given the size of the effective force, was as simple as possible. It was divided into two parts: front line and police / gendarme units. The smallest unit of fighters was the squad, of 3-4 men, then patrols of 10-15, platoons of 40-60, company sized units of 160-250, and finally the army [in reality between battalion and regiment size-*ed.*] of 650-1,000. The units were based on multiples of four.

Apart from this, commander-in-chief Prónay organized the so-called rebel gendarmerie, under the command of Maj. Count Tamás Erdődy,[386] who filled the post – as cited in Lt.Col. Ferenczy's report – beginning on September 8. On orders issued September 23, Prónay set up two gendarme districts, north and south of a horizontal line drawn across lower Lake Fertő. The northern one was commanded by Tibor Héjjas, headquartered in Pándorfalu, the

---

[385] Missuray-Krúg, 1935, op. cit., pp. 168–169.

[386] Count Tamás Erdődy (1868–1931) had a great role in the secret negotiations during WWI between the Emperor and the West. Queen Zita's brothers, Sixtus and Xavier, took part in secret talks between Feb.-April 1917, unbeknownst to Germany, between the Austro-Hungarian Monarchy and the Entente Powers. The separate peace agreement was rejected because Italy clung to possession of South Tyrol. A year later, French PM Georges Clemenceau publicized the letters in a treacherous move, forcing Austria to sign a long-term alliance with Germany. Erdődy played an important role in both of Charles VI's 1921 attempts to regain the throne.

southern by Tamás Erdődy,[387] headquartered in Felsőőr. At the same time – covered by the same directive – a 'rebel police force' began its activities in the village of Rödöny, near Pinkafő, under the command of Miklós Potyondi.[388] With this instruction, Prónay not only bolstered the rebels' fighting strength but also created the basis for an independent, sovereign power. The gendarmes of Lajta-Banate wore an armband, which carried the differentiating symbol in a rectangle. In the middle was a flattened circle, encircling it was the text: WESTERN HUNGARY / BURGENLAND.[389] On September 21, Prónay issued a proclamation of summary court proceedings on charges of robbery, violence against natural and legal persons, and treason against Lajta-Banate.

In the midst of reorganizing his forces – Prónay divided the students' Officer Company into two units on September 16 and 17 – visited zone 'A' under his jurisdiction, the sectors bounded by Fraknónádasd – Nagymarton – Darufalva and Kelénpatak – Kismarton – Sérc – Szentmargitbánya. Lajos Krug, a member of the second unit, wrote thus of their activities: "All of us were supplied with armbands printed with '*Home Guard -- Bürgerwehr*' (The necessary 80 armbands were made by my sisters; the writing was printed by us in ink.) Our goal was to organize civic guards in certain villages and thus ensure complete order and public safety. And for us to check that by simple patrols. We thus achieved that a substantial portion of the population took our side with confidence."[390] The Officer Company visited the local civic guards a few days later and noted that they were working well, to the satisfaction of the population. The armed force of the students took over direction of public administration within their defined operational perimeter in Sopron County, after the withdrawal of the Austrians. Within their operating zone, they set up their command post in Nagymarton, in the Posta Hotel. The head of the newly instituted visa department was overseen by 1st Lt. Károly Obendorf, mining student; the censorship and postal affairs was handled by Lajos Krug, forestry student; and dr. Károly Dobrovits became head of the customs department. The staff platoon of the students was located in Kismarton. By the end of September, they kept under control to two of the important stations along the historic Hungarian-Austrian border, Savanyúkút and Lajtaújfalu, and in a matter of days stopped the smuggling of goods.

In the meantime, Count Sigray notified the prime minister on September 13 that the Entente generals in Sopron read to him the notice of the Council of Ambassadors. The gist of it was that the Austrian and Hungarian government come to an agreement with regard to the Western Hungary question before September 27. According to the Commissioner, "it is likely that the Austrians will make use of the shortage of time and will keep the entire territory."

---

[387] Héjjas J., 1929, op. cit., pp. 65-67.

[388] Missuray-Krúg, 1935, op. cit., p. 172.

[389] Zsiga, 1990, op. cit., p. 136.

[390] Krug, 1930, op. cit., pp. 93-94.

Bethlen's response: then we will state that "under the Trianon treaty terms that are most favorable to us, we will ask not only for the handing over of Baranya County but also that Austria pay us, in cash or give us guarantees we can accept, their debts of the mutual assets. Perhaps we can also raise the counter-value of government assets on the territories to be handed over. All in all, we can raise a lot [of issues] with which we can drag out the negotiations."

In the Commissioners next report, still in the morning of September 13, the Hungarian public administration is working undisturbed in the zone 'A' emptied by the Austrians but that trains are only running to the Austrian border. What is more, the Entente generals are of the opinion that "the armed rebels, as civic guards and patrols, are maintaining flawless order."[391]

During these days, in mid-September, politicians once again raised the possibility that, to prevent the annexation of Western Hungary to Austria, an 'autonomous Burgenland' be proclaimed. In his September 13 morning report, Sigray also informed the PM that the question "from certain quarters, has been raised seriously before me. The plan would be that, in a few days in Sopron, the representatives of the villages, etc. would proclaim an independent Burgenland. They would petition to be a protectorate of Hungary and to keep the gendarmes and authorities until the natives [i.e.- the people now living in the Borderland about to be annexed-*J.B.*] could replace them. At the same time, they would ask the Hungarian government for financial and other assistance. The people in question believe that this would help in the Hungarian government's position. I replied that, in its present state, I would lodge a protest against the proclamation of such a Burgenland. (…) I asked them to take up get in touch with the government and present their plan there, as a possible expedient, if all else becomes impossible. As far as I know, representative Huber [János Huber of the National Assembly] will go up and will present himself with this, and other plans with the prime minister." Shortly afterwards, PM Bethlen again telegraphed Count Sigray, who he informed that if the Entente ambassadors had a new condition for the handover of the territory, meaning the replacement of Maj. Ostenburg and Capt. Ranzenberger, "we will of course agree (…) as to the autonomous status of Burgenland, I too consider that as the *ultima ratio* [last resort-*ed.*]."[392]

At 11:00 on the following day, the 14th, secretary Maróthy reported from the Commissariat in Sigray's name to the PM: "According to reliable sources, the Vas and Sopron county rebels and free-troops stated to Hungarian and Entente officers that the Hungarian government, which is willing to give up Western Hungary or a portion of it, no longer commands them. They will not evacuate the region. They consider the sending of Lt.Gen. Hegedűs as the sign of a potential disarmament… They trust that Hungarian forces will be loath to disarm Hungarian rebels who are protecting their country. It is a possibility

---

[391] MOL. K 26. 1388. csomó. 1922–„H" tétel, pp. 481–482, 484.
[392] Ibid, pp. 485–486.

that certain rebel units will resist being disarmed. The consequences are inestimable, since the Hungarian forces are naturally sympathetic to the rebels. The rebels are still upholding exemplary order. They would like to proclaim an independent Burgenland and organize its armed force. (...) Before a disarmament plan initiated by the Hungarian side is considered, the method should be carefully considered in light of the above. (...) if the government is able to point also to accomplishments, it could lead to greater success than the beginning of inflexible military action."[393]

Lt.Gen. Hegedűs also filed a telegram report regarding the September 14 events: the delegation of Kabold and Veperd villages called on the Entente Mission in Sopron where they asked for Hungarian gendarmes to maintain public safety. In the village of Savanyúkút, an Austrian Oedenburger Infanterie Regiment [Infantry Regiment of Sopron] was formed, conceivably from the "émigré rabble of Lt.Col. Faragó." At noon, PM Bethlen informed Lt.Gen. Hegedűs of the following: "I wish to reassure Commissioner Sigray that the cleansing of the rebels in zone 'A' has not been decided yet. We will only decide this if an agreement becomes possible regarding all of our questions, which also serves our interests. We cannot do such foolishness that we disarm Hungarians in such an area that we handed over to Austria. To do such a service to Austria, then evacuate zone 'B' and hand it, too, to Austria. Thus, there will either be an agreement regarding all questions, in which case we will undertake to evacuate zone 'A' (...) or there will not be an agreement, but then we will not do a special favor for Austria. (...) If we cannot reach an agreement and are forced to march out of zone 'B' due to compelling circumstances, the proclamation of independent Burgenland is a matter of the local population and the rebels, in which we cannot even get involved. Thus, the Hungarian government cannot officially consider this matter."[394]

During the following days, the attempts of Robert Davy, governor of the province of Burgenland, to relocate his offices to Sopron raised the interest of the Hungarian government and public opinion. In all likelihood, the aim was to underline that Austria has not given up its claim to the city.

In his noon report on September 15, Lt.Gen. Hegedűs informed that Chancellor Schober's request regarding this matter was read to him by the Entente generals when he was conferring with them. The Vienna government asked for assurances that Davy "would not receive any abuse from the Sopron population" and he promised to look after his security. He could not, however, assure that "he would not be verbally insulted on the street."

The matter of the Austrian governor was also touched upon in the September 17 report sent by Villani. The Entente's reply to the Hungarian memorandum announcing his arrival was: "Until Davy is in Sopron, Hungarian liaison officers cannot be in zone 'A' with the Entente sub-missions. This reply of the generals is without logic because, in my opinion,

---

[393] Ibid, p. 500.
[394] Ibid, pp. 502–503.

you cannot construct a link between Davy's whereabouts and the assignment of the Hungarian liaison officers. Especially since the generals' committee requested it at the time. The recall of the liaison officers has already been ordered. Their task, which we informed the generals' committee beforehand, they were naturally enough unable to complete, despite their best efforts."[395]

The situation was further complicated by the continued push of the Austrian government of the Davy matter. Foreign ministerial adviser Villani reported from Sopron at 11:00 on September 18 that the Entente generals had sent a telegram to the Council of Ambassadors in Paris. In it they asked that the council take action that Davy, as representative of the Austrian government, can stay in Sopron permanently and the guarantee of his personal safety be the responsibility of the Hungarian government. Regarding the potential Sopron activities of Davy, as *Landesverwalter* [provincial head, or chief-*J.B.*], forced Lt.Gen. Hegedűs to raise a objection with the generals, stating: "It is extremely difficult to guarantee his personal safety because the population connects him to the arbitrary actions and atrocities carried out by the Austrians. Namely: the dissolution of the village representative bodies, sacking the elected district and village civil servants, the taking and mistreatment of hostages. Since everybody here is convinced that Dr. Davy is responsible for these acts, the bitterness against him is so great that we would be able to protect his person from insults only if we always accompany him. With armed men or at least several secret police bodyguards, which he might not find very pleasant, either." Finally, Villani reported that he had a long conversation with Baron Stefan Neugebauer, ministerial advisor and 'on very good terms' with Chancellor Schober, – the content of which he will report to the Foreign Ministry – who was also working on removing Davy. Next he asked the prime minister's approval to start a disinformation action against Davy, making use of his close contacts at several Viennese newspapers. They would evaluate the work of the provincial governor and demand his removal for Austria's interest. PM Bethlen agreed to the anti-Davy steps "especially in the Austrian press. But if the generals were to allow him into Sopron, I ask caution, lest any physical violence or demonstrations be done against Davy that might be taken as disorderliness, to be able to be used against us."[396]

Earlier, Lt.Gen. Hegedűs reported in the evening of September 15: a delegation led by former mayor of Sopron, Károly Töpler, visited him and asked that Maj. Ostenburg and his battalion continue to remain in Sopron because the planned relocation of the unit "caused great agitation among the population." The local police have received information that former prime minister István Friedrich, Pál Prónay and Iván Héjjas are once more in Sopron, "for which there is no need, and not particularly desirable." Lt.Gen. Hegedűs suggested that, through Count Sigray, the government request them to leave the city. This had indeed happened because, according to the

---

[395] Ibid, pp. 518, 520, 543.
[396] Ibid, pp. 549–552.

Commissioner's daily reports – based on informants – Prónay was already in the vicinity of Felsőpulya on September 16th and by the 18th was in Felsőőr, in zone 'A'.[397]

Still on the same day, the 15th, Col. Lehár showed up in Szombathely with the stated objective: to gather familiarity of the "mood" of the Western Hungary population. In reality, he arrived as the agent of the Hungarian government but who was arrested the following day by Prónay in the vicinity of Felsőőr and was only released four days later by the intercession of Count Sigray.[398] Prónay justified himself by saying that Lehár "is an Austrian spy" and he received orders for the arrest.[399] The Entente generals in Sopron were of the opinion that the colonel was arrested because he was a "Karlist," meaning a follower of the former Habsburg ruler, Charles IV. Gyula Gömbös became embroiled in the solution of the Antal Lehár matter, as the following telegram shows: "The arrested former colonel, if he gives his word of honor never to enter into the district, is to be escorted to zone 'A' and released without any harm. (Signed) Jákfai."[400] Col. Köller, Chief-of-Staff of Lt.Gen. Hegedűs, sent the following telegram on the following day, September 16: "The situation is unchanged and calm everywhere in Western Hungary."[401]

At noon the following day, the 17th, Köller again informed: "In front of the Italian captain located in Nezsider, the people of Királyhida arrested and carried off as hostages, not released to this day by the Austrians, are exposed to the most horrible brutality." The management of the Hungarian Railways /MÁV/ turned to PM Bethlen in a telegram sent in the early afternoon because the Austrians cut the railway's only telegraph line along the Bruck–Királyhida–Pándorfalu line. "Our technician sent to effect repairs to the line has been rudely prevented from doing it. As a result, we are unable to communicate with the Bruck–Királyhida stations at this time." In early evening, a telegram sent by Villani to PM Bethlen, on instructs of Commissioner Sigray, disclosed: "Count Sigray begs Your Excellency that the government accept ambassador Kánya's view that it will not be us who clear the territory of rebels but leave it to the Austrians. And that, generally, we will not accept responsibility for the results, as the free-troops will not obey the government. Removal by armed force will meet with great difficulty (…) Hungarian soldiers would have to fight against Hungarian patriots."[402]

---

[397] Ibid, pp. 523, 525, 555, 558.

[398] Zsiga, 1988, op. cit., p. 126.

[399] Fogarassy, László: Lehár ezredes a Prónay-felkelők fogságában [Col. Lehár in the captivity of the Prónay rebels]. In: *Soproni Szemle*, 1975, issue 4, pp. 348–351.

[400] MOL. K 26. 1388. csomó. 1922–„H" tétel, pp. 548, 553–554. Gyula Gömbös used the alias 'Jákfai' in this period, after his family's estate in Jákfa.

[401] MOL. K 26. 1388. csomó. 1922–„H" tétel, p. 539.

[402] Ibid, pp. 541–542. Kálmán Kánya was, at this time, Secretary of State for Foreign Affairs, permanent deputy of the Foreign Minister, as well as his chief secretary. The 'ambassador' title refers is to the fact that he conferred several times with leading Austrian politicians regarding Western Hungary. [In Hungarian, 'ambassador' also

In the meanwhile, Marquis Della Toretta, Italian Foreign Minister, went to Vienna on September 11 and asked Gaetano Castagneto, Italy's ambassador in Budapest, to join him. The marquis informed Chancellor Schober that the Hungarian government asked him to mediate. It was during these talks that the so-called Sopron formula was created, which Castagneto took to Budapest, as well as the September 14 suggestion by Foreign Minister Miklós Bánffy, which became the basis for future negotiations. The crux of the latter was: the Hungarian government will immediately evacuate and hand over to Austria the questionable Western Hungary strip to the indicated Trianon border, if it receives assurance for the permanent retention of Sopron and its surrounding, and receives a prospect of a just border designation. Bánffy's proposal was handed to Chancellor Schober on September 15.[403] This was taken by the Austrian government that the sole means of relinquishing was after a plebiscite. On the same day, the secret Austrian-Hungarian negotiations began, with Italian mediation, which shortly resulted in the outlines of the later so-called Venice Protocol. However, in this situation, the Hungarian government had to take definite steps to disarm the rebels.

On September 18, Lt.Gen. Hegedűs informed PM Bethlen in the late evening hours: "According to a report of the district command in Szombathely, Lt.Col. Prónay is alleged to be in Felsőőr. Thus, he is in zone 'A', which is at this time outside my jurisdiction. This in spite of the fact that the local [Entente] generals' mission demanded the withdrawal of the Hungarian liaison officers from zone 'A', which I have already ordered yesterday. I will send Lt.Col. Ferenczy to Felsőőr tomorrow and, as per Your Excellency's orders, will request Prónay to immediately depart from the *Anschluss* territory [the portion intended to be annexed to Austria-*J.B.*]." Moreover, Ferenczy will also hand to the high command of the rebels, in the form of a 'Warning,' the government's similar decision and that it be publicized immediately not only in Felsőőr but other places under the control of the rebels. The general closed his report that he will once more suggest to the Entente generals tomorrow to permit again the dispatch of Hungarian liaison officers to the Entente sub-missions in the field.[404] The settlement of the local situation and the promising Hungarian-Austrian negotiations in Vienna were both disrupted by unexpected events.

We have not as yet pointed out that the activities of the rebels only spread over the central and southern portions of the to-be-annexed Western Hungary. North of this, in Sopron County, was under the control of Maj. Ostenburg's battalion. As a result, the area West of Lake Fertő and Moson County was free of clashes. This territory was controlled by the battalion and Hungarian army units charged with border duties. They had strict orders to halt and expel any potential rebels behind the designated Trianon border. Iván Héjjas and his

---

carries the meaning of 'go-between'-*ed.*]
[403] Ormos, 1990, op. cit., pp. 131–132.
[404] MOL. K 26. 1388. cs., 1922–„H" tét., pp. 558, 547.

forces had no intention of attacking these units as "they are Hungarians, too."

The line from the town of Ruszt on the western shore of Lake Fertő to Wiener Neustadt was controlled by Austrian troops and this sector of the front was especially reinforced. Iván Héjjas resorted to a military stratagem and with 50 rebels (plus two machine guns and two grenade launchers) went around the northern end of the lake, through the village of Magyaróvár [later amalgamated with Moson and now called Mosonmagyaróvár-*ed*.] and appeared unexpectedly in the village of Zurány (Zurndorf). The attacked at night from here and, without opposition, captured and disarmed the Austrian patrol in the nearby important railway junction of Pándorfalu (Parndorf). They moved into the nearby Harrach Castle, just across the border in Lower Austria, where they set up their headquarters. On his orders, the rebels stopped everyone, even escorting a traveling group of Entente officers from Sopron to their commander for identification. Héjjas signed their passports and they were free to leave with their car. The previous day, too, his men escorted a British and two French officers, and their car, to the castle. The rebel commander treated them in similar manner.

The rebels treated the Italian members of the Entente Mission differently, not checking their papers, because they had expressed sympathy towards Hungary, and even the Hungarian free-troops. They respected their bravery for standing up to the territory expropriating intruders. In secret, the Italian officers gave, or sent, medical supplies to tend to wounded rebels. Jenő Héjjas could justifiably cite the old saying: "Only lions have friends, not crawling bugs."[405] As a matter of fact, the Prónay rebels operating in the central and southern part of the Borderland regularly checked the identity papers of the Entente officers, mostly French and British, passing through areas controlled by them. No special complications arose from them.

With the raid on Pándorfalu, the clashes began in Moson County, too, that ended on September 29, between the Héjjas rebels and the Austrian units attempting to take possession of the Lake Fertő area. During this time, Lt.Gen. Hegedűs, accompanied by an Italian and a French officer, called on Héjjas in Pándorfalu to convince him to leave the area, which he refused to do. Gyula Gömbös telegraphed Héjjas to withdraw immediately from Moson County, also without results. In fact, the rebel commander kept getting newer and newer reinforcements, even having the Magyaróvár rebels join him under the command of Col. István Inzelt [in some sources Inselt-*J.B.*].[406] Thus was the 4th Rebel Army born, under the command of Iván Héjjas.

In the dawn hours of September 24, units of the Héjjas brigade attacked the guards of the bridges over the Lajta River [the traditional boundary between Hungary and Austria-*ed*.] at Királyhida, as well as the Austrian

---

[405] Héjjas, 1929, op. cit., pp. 63, 71-73.
[406] Fogarassy, László: A nyugat-magyarországi kérdés katonai története. III. rész. 1921. szeptember–november [The military history of the western Hungarian question. Part III, 1921 September-November]. In: *Soproni Szemle*, 1972, issue 2, p. 123.

battalion stationed in the village's military encampment. The soldiers fled to the other side of the river and Lajta Canal in panic, to Austrian territory. The routed occupation force was reinforced in the afternoon with a bicycle-mounted battalion and an infantry company and were able to retake only the railway station and the park around the castle from the rebels, who retreated to Pándorfalu with a significant amount of arms and ammunition. The surrounding high-ground was continued to be held by the Héjjas rebels. In fact, on the "march home" that afternoon, they took the center of Nezsider district. After the clash in Királyhida, the Austrians blockaded the railway at #159 watch-station and arrested 60 railway workers, including the station master, on the charge of having provided armed aid during the night to the rebels. They were taken to an internment camp north of Vienna, to Niederhollabrunn, and only released after the signing of the Venice Protocol on October 13.

The units of the 4th Rebel Army, led by Iván Héjjas, completed successful engagements against the Austrian occupiers in the closing days of September, who were substantially halted and forced back, capturing village after village from them. Thus, a sector of the historical Hungarian-Austrian border, formed by the chain of the Lajta Mountains, came under the control of the Héjjas force, along with the area northwest of Lake Fertő. They carried out raids from their headquarters in Pándorfalu to far flung settlements in Moson County, to Mosonújfalu, Nemesvölgy, Köpcsény, even as far as Pozsonyligetfalu. In this last village, they attacked a Czechoslovak patrol and forced it to turn tail. As well, they kept the pressure on the Austrian bridgehead at Királyhida and the villages on the Austrian side.[407] Thus, by the end of September, all of zone 'A' was in the hands of the five rebel armies, with the exception of the strong Austrian bridgeheads at Lajtaszentmiklós, Lajtaújfalu and Királyhida.

During the second half of September, the monarchist supporter former prime minister, István Friedrich, and his circle once again began robust organizing, based in part on the organization that was begun on August 30, the Western Hungary National Defense Organization [Nyugatmagyarország Országvédelmi Szervezete / Orszvé]. One of their flyers published at the time, *Magyarok!*, contained the following: "Our brotherly peace, our marriage of a thousand years is disturbed by the brutal incursion of the Entente Powers when, *like cattle, mocking our right to self-determination, without asking us, against our wishes want to herd us to a rotting, destructive, syphilitic Austria subsisting on alms.* (…) the honor of our people will not tolerate this degradation, *we will live with our right of self-determination, will turn with protest to the people of the world, and will defend our ancient land with weapon in our hand. We will not concede, we will never give up.* We, Germans, Hungarians and Croats of Western Hungary, with eternal loyalty to the millennial country, ask you Hungarian brethrens, do not leave forsake us,

---

[407] Héjjas, J., 1929, op. cit., pp. 74–89.

give us your support in our life and death struggle. Men, who want to fight for our ancient land, stand by us with arms in your hand and help out. We have formed our National Defense Organization, those not afraid and willing to fight, join our ranks! (…) Western Hungary National Defense Organization / [Signed[Supreme Command."[408] In the interest of realizing these goals, Friedrich sent armed units to Kismarton and co-operated with Maj. Ostenburg, too.

Kedves Szabolcs! Ide kellene betenni az eredeti, 2008-as könyvemből (234. old.) „Az 1921. évi nyugat-magyarország harcok" aláírású térképet!

On September 24, representative István Rakovszky raised a question in the National Assembly with regard to the fate of Imre Egan, former High Constable of Békés County, who was a leader of a rebel unit and who was wounded and taken captive in the September 2 clashes around Pörgölény (Pilgersdorf). Since his capture, Egan was held in Vienna, in the Lower Austrian Provincial Court Jail, charged with inciting revolt. In this matter, Rakovszky said: "Austria, in spite of the Hungarian government complying within the time set by the Trianon Treaty, could not establish its authority (imperium / imperial power) there [meaning the territory to be annexed-*J.B.*], therefore, from a legal perspective, the territory where Egan was captured was not under Austrian authority and, hence, the case against him of inciting rebellion against Austrian authority cannot proceed. (…) any time these free-forces captured Austrians in Western Hungary, their first act was to hand the captives over to Hungarian authorities on Hungarian territory. The Hungarian government then released or turned over to Austrian authorities these captured soldiers and gendarmes, without harm. In fact, I know that the Ostenburg detachment immediately released the captured and disarmed Austrian gendarmes and returned them unharmed to Austria." Rakovszky finally posed the following questions to PM Bethlen: "One, does the Prime Minister know that the Austrians are holding Imre Egan captive in the Viennese provincial jail and are charging him with inciting rebellion? Two, is he willing, on legal and humanitarian grounds, to raise the matter with the Austrian government and, citing Egan's patriotic reasons, ask for his direct release and freedom to return home?"[409]

In his response, the prime minister first clarified the legal standing of the Hungarian government in zone 'A' of Western Hungary. "We have, naturally, evacuated the territory but, until the handover document is signed by me, the territory is not deemed to have been handed over to Austria. Thus, it is still Hungarian territory today. In light of the fact that we have withdrawn from the territory all our police, gendarme and military power, we are not in a position to take a governmental stand against anyone, not the Austrians, not

---

[408] MOL. K 26. 1388. csomó. 1922–„H" tétel, p. 515.
[409] Nemzetgyűlési Napló, XIII. köt. Budapest, 1921. Athenaeum nyomda, p. 71.

free-forces, not against the local population. Hence (…) I want to make it absolutely clear, we cannot, and will not, take any responsibility for the events there. (…) we have knowledge of the capture by Austrian gendarmes of Imre Egan, former High Constable of Békés County, and that presently he is being held in Vienna, in the Lower Austria *Landesgericht* [provincial court jail]. We have already taken diplomatic steps with the Austrian government; the Hungarian Foreign Minister has protested violently with the Austrian government in this regard, and not only in the case of Imre Egan but in many others, too, since the Austrian gendarmes have taken hostages in zone 'A', captured Hungarian citizens and began proceedings against them. Therefore, the Hungarian government has taken diplomatic steps in this matter and wastes no time to raise the matter again.".[410] The answer to the question from the floor was acknowledged by Rakovszky and parliament.

In the meanwhile, the Hungarian-Austrian negotiations continued. Hungarian *chargé d'affaires* in Paris, Iván Praznovszky, forwarded to Foreign Minister Miklós Bánffy on September 23 the latest text of the memorandum from the Council of Ambassadors, which instructed the Hungarian government to vacate within 10 days the Western Hungary territory awarded to Austria. Otherwise, the Entente Powers will be forced to use extreme measures against Hungary without notification. The Hungarian government was unable to fulfill the terms of the ultimatum completely because it had power of arms only in the eastern zones 'B' and 'C', not in zone 'A', which was under the control of the rebels.

Primarily, it was the danger of another attempted return to the throne by Charles IV – which soon took place – that prompted PM Bethlen to oppose the proclamation of the state of Lajta-Banate. The prime minister instructed Gyula Gömbös at the end of September to prevent the possible proclamation of independence by the territory. On September 29, Gömbös met with supreme commander Prónay and informed him that the government must give up Western Hungary but that there would be a plebiscite in Sopron and its surrounding. Hence, he asked Prónay to take over public administration over the entire territory, except the noted district, without proclaiming a "separate imperium."

In these critical days and weeks, to keep the events of Western Hungary in hand, the Hungarian government made use of censorship, against which the National Assembly opposition, and the minority pro-monarchist party, put up spirited resistance. One of their targets was ministerial advisor Tibor Eckhardt (1888-1972), head of the prime ministerial press department, who regularly showed up in the parliament's gallery. In his September 24 speech on the floor of Parliament, representative Rakovszky also commented that "hardly a week goes by that the outrages of censorship are not raised here. (…) with bullying and cunning, free expression is suppressed. Newspapers that do not give in to censorship are eradicated, discarded. (…) Is the Prime Minister

---

[410] Ibid, pp. 71–72.

willing to act, to order media chief Tibor Eckhardt to handle censorship unbiased, and not use it for the dissemination of his own political views, and not for the persecution and discrediting of opposing views and those who hold them?"[411]

In response to the questions posed by Rakovszky, PM Bethlen read out the instructions given to the media publicity office with regard to the matter: "In the matter of the question of Western Hungary, all communiqués are banned that would upset our relations with our neighbors. Thus, it is especially not permissible to call for organizing or resistance against Austrians, as well as military threats, or voicing intent to support against Austria. Furthermore, calls or proclamations, which call on the population to volunteer or offer military resistance, and generally prevent the handover of Western Hungary by armed conflict, is not to be published. This ban is primarily aimed at those proclamations, whose publication and distribution has already happened over the signature of the Supreme Command of the Western Hungary National Defense Organization."[412] The prime minister promised an unbiased review in the matter of censorship.

The Italian Foreign Minister, Marquis Pietro Tomasi Della Toretta, invited the representatives of Austria and Hungary to Venice on October 1 to settle the Western Hungary question. Shortly after, on October 3, the Entente Mission generals and Lt.Gen. Hegedűs signed an agreement in Sopron. Its substance was that Hungary has handed over to Austria the territory specified in the Entente memorandum of September 23. The representative of the Austrian government did not sign the document saying: "Zone 'A' is still under rebel control. The agreement is in *pro forma* agreement that Hungary has fulfilled Austria's request for prior evacuation, which was a precondition to Hungarian-Austrian talks."[413] In all likelihood, Austria raised an objection because it felt tacit support from Prague. In a report sent from Prague on the following day, the 4th, there were two Czechoslovak divisions stationed in and around the city. "In the Austrian *Reichswehr* units on the border of Western Hungary are a large number of Czech soldiers in Austrian uniform who were transported over from [the former] Northern Hungary."[414] With the handing over of the territory to be annexed by the signing of the *pro forma* agreement, the long drawn out Western Hungary question seemed to be solved. The protocol permitted Hungary to continue to exercise control over Sopron and its surroundings by Gyula Ostenburg's battalion as the "Sopron Territorial Police" force.

As we have written previously, the morning telegraph exchange of September 3 between PM Bethlen and Deputy Commissioner Villani, the latter also reported: "The rebels have most recently issued stamps with the

---

[411] *Nemzetgyűlési Napló*, XIII. kötet. 1921, pp. 72, 74.

[412] Ibid, pp. 75–76.

[413] Zsiga, 1989, op. cit., pp. 127–128.

[414] MOL. K 26. 1264. csomó. 1921–XLII–6959. szám, p. 16. The correct name of the Austrian force in question was *Bundesheer* [Allied military force].

overprinting of '*Rebel Occupied Hungary*'."[415] There were several reasons for this. When Hungarian authorities evacuated zone 'A', the Royal Hungarian Mail also took with it its supply of postage stamps. The postal service which arrived in the territory with the advancing Austrian gendarmes also fled after the outbreak of the insurrection and the once-again Hungarian post offices were without stamps. Thus, until the arrival of official supplies from Hungary, the rebels were forced to look after stamps for their own letter writing needs. Hence, the representatives of the free-forces made use of the stocks of Hungarian stamps with various overprinting. The stamps were then carried by the rebel patrols to those village post offices which ran out of stamps. The overprinting not only served as value distinctions but also as a warning to the Austrian invaders. The rebel forces censored mail and post card traffic in their areas of control, stamping the cleared items with their seals. It also served to authenticate and legitimize their overprinted postal stamps. Due to the campaign situation, military camp postcards were also issued.

Those issued by the 1st Rebel Army were printed on September 2 but were released into circulation on the 5th when an order covering them took effect. The stamp series featured a black overprint with the text: *Rebel Occupied Part of Hungary, Aug.-Sep. 1921*. On September 18, the 5th Rebel Army (Gyula Ostenburg's detachment) issued the Mining and Forestry Academy's rebels' stamp series, overprinted with a black skull and crossbones and the text: *Rebels of Western Hungary, Sept. 1921, zone 'A'*. The Officer Company of the Sopron students made an inspection round of the local civil militias on September 20 and visited the post offices in several villages in the Nagymarton and Kismarton districts. They removed the yellow mail boxes left behind by the retreating Austrian authorities and replaced the Royal Hungarian Mail's boxes. They also burned the stamp inventories the Austrians left behind and supplied adequate numbers of the rebel's "death's head" stamps for use. In all, the rebels printed nine series of stamps but only seven were released.

---

[415] Ibid, 1388. csomó. 1920–„H" tétel, p. 364.

Chapter 7: The State of Lajta-Banat
October 4 – November 4, 1921

At noon on October 4, in the main square of the Felsőőr district center, Felsőőr (Oberwart), the center of an area populated by Hungarians since the Conquest at the end of the 9th century, Pál Prónay, commander of the insurrection, proclaimed the independent, sovereign and autonomous state of Lajta-Banate in front of a large crowd made up of people from the town and delegates of the neighboring villages. His act was a response to the memorandum signed in Sopron regarding the handover, as well as Austria's rejection of it. Subsequently, Prónay sent his units into the eastern zone 'B', evacuated by the Hungarian government's military, adding it to his zone of control in the western zone 'A'. With it, with the exception of Sopron and its surrounding area, the entire territory earmarked to be ceded to Austria, between the Trianon and the historical borders, came under the sovereignty of the free-troops and the new state. The events of the flag-festooned proclamation in Felsőőr are revealing. After an outdoor Mass, the white silk flag of the city of Kecskemét was dedicated. The patron of the flag was Countess Aimee Pálffy, Prónay's wife, who handed the standard to the commander of the 1st Rebel Army, Árpád Taby, after enthusiastic words. Following the ceremony, the representatives of the villages and the county entered the Felsőőr County Courthouse, followed by the commanders of the rebel armies, where they held a Constitutional Meeting, under the chairmanship of Béla Bárdoss. The minutes of the meeting were recorded by Dr. Ferenc Lévay. We now quote from the recorded minutes:

The president, Béla Bárdoss, opened the meeting with the following speech: "The Hungarian government officially handed over to Austria on October 3, 1921, at six in the afternoon, areas to be evacuated under the terms of Article 27, paragraph 1 of the peace document of Trianon. Austria, however, did not accept these areas. Thus, the right of self-determination reverted to us, which is why we must make a decision over our future."

Next, Bárdoss asked the supreme commander of the defensive forces of Western Hungary, Baron Prónay, to make his submission.

Prónay: "Honored Constitutional gathering! At this moment, every Western Hungary settlement in Moson and Sopron and Vas counties deemed for handing over to Austria is awaiting its fate to turn for the better. The shortsighted Trianon peace has torn from Hungary these Hungarian, German and Croat speaking people who have lived together in peace for a thousand years. Not one village wishes to be annexed to communist Austria. Hence, let Western Hungary be independent and free!" (*General and repeated shouts of agreement.*)

The president of the meeting next asked the lawyer Ferenc Lévay to read the *Declaration of Independence*. "We, who have been torn from our ancient country without our consultation and thrown as prey to the communists of a defeated Austria, to salvage our honor, our family, our property, our religion, our principles from the flood of the Red tide, in the name of the peoples of our communities we proclaim our independence, freedom and universal neutrality." (*General agreement and enthusiastic hurrahs*.)

The president went on to say: "I respectfully request that the reading of the Proclamation of Independence be acknowledged." (*General, endless shouts of agreement*.) Next, the presiding official asked Dr. Lévay to present the *Proposition of Recognition*.

"We request and authorize the Commander-in-Chief of the Western Hungary uprising to publish the independence proclamation in our name, form a responsible governing council, and have a draft constitution prepared."

At the request of the meeting's president – amid general agreement and hurrahs – the conference unanimously accepted this decision proposal. Following it, the rebel units swore their allegiance to the commander. The standards, blessed by the Catholic and Protestant chaplains, were presented to the rebel units, after speeches in Hungarian, German and Croatian. Finally, with the words "May God's blessing be upon the independence of our liberated country and people," the president concluded the constitutional meeting that took place "in the most enthusiastic of atmosphere." The record of the minutes was closed, signed by all the peoples' representatives and a stamped and sealed copy of the Declaration of Independence was amended.[416]

The minutes and the text of the declaration later appeared in the October 30 issue of the *Lajtabánság Hivatalos Lapja* [Official Paper of Lajta-Banate][417] in Felsőőr, published by the Governing Council of Lajta-Banate. Hungarian, German and Croat language versions of the Declaration were printed and posted in the villages of Western Hungary intended for annexation.[418]

The complete text of the manifesto poster is as follows:

"Proclamation to the people of the world!

While proclaiming the principle of self-determination of nations, the dictated Trianon treaty, without consulting us or asking us, wish to throw this territory we have held in mutual agreement for a thousand years, as prey to the Communists of a defeated Austria.

This forcible annexation is in opposition with law and rights, omitting our right to self-determination and penalizes us as the defeated.

It deeply affronts out national self-esteem and historical traditions, which have, over the centuries, bonded our Hungarian, German and Croatian fellow

---

[416] Missuray-Krúg, 1935, op. cit., pp. 159–161.
[417] *Lajtabánság Hivatalos Lapja*, I. évf. 1. szám. 1921. október 30.
[418] One of the few copies can be found in the Jurisich Miklós Múzeum Helytörténeti Adattára (Kőszeg) [Annals of Miklós Jurisich Museum of Local History (Kőszeg)].

citizens to the love of their country through a hatred of Austria.

In the interest of maintaining open, just and honest international relations, to ensure the rule of law in the mutual exchange between free peoples and to ascertain and to have guarantee of the ethical respect in all manner of international obligations, we have taken up arms and now stand with no enemy on our ancient land.

To keep and ensure our achieved freedoms, we proclaim and form the independent, sovereign and neutral state of Lajta-Banate, comprised of the people in the territories to be evacuated [by Hungary-*ed*.] under the terms of Article 27, paragraph 1 of the Trianon peace document.

The prerogatives of Head of State will be vested in the Viceroy, who shall be elected by the Constitutional Assembly. Executive power will be exercised by the Viceroy through a six-member, responsible Governing Council. The official language of the Banate is Hungarian; however, every citizen is free to use his mother-tongue in all official and private matters.

Laws and directives are to be publicized in the Hungarian, German and Croatian languages. Provisionally, the laws of the Hungarian state shall remain in effect.

Every citizen of the Banate, without regard to his nationality, language or religious affiliation, is equal before the law and enjoys the same political and civil rights and responsibilities.

The terms in this declaration of independence we accept as binding, which we will respect, and have others comply with, as attested by affixing our signatures and seals.

Dated the fourth day of October, 1921 in Felsőőr.
The Constitutional Assembly of Lajta-Banate."[419]

According to the terms of the proclamation, the head-of-government and executive powers were exercised by a Viceroy [Bán] elected by the Constitutional Assembly, and assisted by a six-member Cabinet and the government. Provisionally, the office of Viceroy was filled by Pál Prónay, as Commander-in-Chief of the unified – on this day – five rebel armies. The following day, the six-member Lajta-Banate cabinet was constituted. Its elected president (as well as being temporarily minister of the Religious Affairs and Public Education portfolios), was Capt. László Apáthy. Members: Ferenc Lévay, External Affairs (and temporarily Justice), Béla Bárdoss,

---

[419] Missuray-Krúg, 1935, op. cit., pp. 161–163.

Internal Affairs, György Hir, Economic Affairs, as well as Pál Prónay, military advisor. The post of overall commander of the insurrection forces was also assumed by Lt.Col. Prónay (ret.), who named Maj. Count Tamás Erdődy (ret.) as head of the Western Hungary gendarmerie, as Police Commissioner.

Legally, the leaders of Lajta-Banate primarily referred to the fact that, although the Trianon peace pact awarded Western Hungary – which was evacuated by the Hungarian army – to Austria but that territory the Austrian authorities did not immediately take into their possession. The reason was that the Viennese government could not curb the political chaos in its country and the emerging Leftist movements. As a result, the power vacuum in Western Hungary was filled by Hungarian patriots, the armed units of the national rebels. The Cabinet of Lajta-Banate also referred to the basic principle of the Paris Peace Conference, the right of self-determination of people – a principle which the decision makers in Paris decided not to apply to a significant portion of Hungarians living in Hungary! As a result, under the terms of the Trianon Treaty, one-third of Hungarians living in the Carpathian Basin, approx. 3.5 million ethnic Hungarians, were transferred under a foreign government – Czechoslovak, Romanian and South Slav – while at least half the territory this population inhabited was linked intrinsically to the core Hungarian ethnic area.

On the same day, the Szombathely publication, *Vas County*, ran a special edition that reported the event.[420] On the same date as the proclamation in Felsőőr, similar events took place in the Hungarian-speaking settlements of Felsőpulya, Kismarton, Nezsider, Lakompak and Nagyszentmihály. Posters appeared on the streets of Felsőőr later the same day, on the following day in the other Borderland settlements.

"People of Western Hungary!

The proclamation of the independence, sovereignty and neutrality of the territory evacuated under the terms of the Trianon peace has taken place at noon on October 4, 1921 in Felsőőr and the supreme command of the rebel forces in the evacuated territory has been set up. The population of Nezsider, Kismarton, Felsőpulya and Németújvár districts endorse the independence declaration and the memorandum of the same, signed by the councils of the villages and each village's seals affixed thereto, has been sent to the supreme

---

[420] *Vasvármegye*, 1921, October 4 issue. The owner and publisher of theSzombathely newspaper, National Assembly representative Albin Lingauer, under the laws in effect at the time, was responsible for presenting the pre-publication text of the special edition to the Royal Public Prosecutor's Office for clearance. As he did not do so, he ran afoul of article § 27 of law XIV of 1914. The prosecutor wanted to open proceedings against him and petitioned the National Assembly to lift his parliamentary immunity privilege. In: *Nemzetgyűlés Irományai*, XIII. kötet. Budapest, 1922, p. 360.

council in Felsőőr.''[421]

The constitution of Lajta-Banate was written by Dr. Ferenc Lévay, based on the Hungarian and Swiss models. The entire text was not published at the time, and was in manuscript form into the 1930s.[422]

On the day after the proclamation of Lajta-Banate, October 5, the Constitutional Council issued a directive:

To all state and local council offices
At their offices

On the authority of the Constitutional Assembly, I have assumed the office of head of state until such time as a Viceroy is elected.

My goal is the protection of the independence, sovereignty and neutrality of the people in the territory of the state the rebels' arms have won and protect.

Equal and equivalent responsibilities and rights accrue to every citizen of the state without ethnic or religious discrimination.

My greetings all of the country's civil servants and local council officials, and ask them to stay at their posts and be kind enough to support us in the work of these present hard times.

May God's blessing follow the independence of Lajta-Banate and its people!

Felsőőr, 1921, October 5
Pál Prónay, Commander in Chief[423]

Also on the same day, the following announcement was released by Viceroy Prónay, exercising his executive power:

Notice!

The people of Western Hungary have unanimously announced, amidst the greatest enthusiasm, their independence, sovereignty and neutrality.

The formative work has quietly begun and now everyone is working in accord, shoulder to shoulder.

There is no place among us for opposing agitation, destructive propaganda

---

[421] Missuray-Krúg, 1935, op. cit., p. 163.
[422] Ádám T., 1935, op. cit., p. 131.
[423] *Lajtabánság,* Felsőőr, year I, issue 1, 1921, November 3, p. 4.

and stirring of regressive politics against stated goals.

Hence, I direct every person in the territory of Lajta-Banate, who voices tenets against state or class in the interest of agitating against the existing order and peace, attempting to bring down public order and attempt to influence the attitude of the population in contravention of the October 4, 1921 resolution, to leave within 24 hours or face arrest.

Said local persons I will bring up in front of a summary court and have their property confiscated.

The decree to take effect on the day of its announcement.

Felsőőr, 1921, October 5
Pál Prónay, Commander in Chief.

The army of Lajta-Banate made public a notice, shortly after the declaration of independence:

Notice!
Soldiers, brothers!

Your brothers, who have taken up arms in defense of the country, appeal to you from the frontiers. Heed us while it is not too late!

Do not break your oath you made in the country's constitution [more accurately 'on' the constitution-*J.B.*] and to our foremost brave comrade, the governor. Place no belief in the cowardly, lurking liars who want to sell our country out of personal interest and use you for material gain. Do not forget that we hold traitors as greater enemies than Austrians. There is no pardon, no clemency for those. Woe to those who fall into our hands. All should beware of the fist of the frontline troops. Stay on the path of righteousness, do not be break your oath, do not change colors!

Accept the extended friendly hand and let us fight together against the internal and external enemies of the country. With you, if possible; against you, if necessary!

The rebel forces[424]

The newspaper of the rebels, *Lajtabánság*, reported the official public administrative divisions of the new country, based on the Hungarian census carried out on December 31, 1920. Incorporated council town: Kismarton

---

[424] Ádám T., 1935, op. cit., p. 97.

(area – 3,027 cadastral acres / 4,304 acres, 2,917 population). Boroughs: Nezsider (134,948 c.a., 19 villages, 33,119 pop.), Nagymarton (36,539 c.a., 19 vill., 27,556 pop.), Felsőpulya (69,509 c.a., 36 vill., 29,237 pop.), Felsőőr (83,722 c.a., 60 vill., 43,038 pop.), and Németújvár (74,938 c.a., 50 vill., 32,687 pop.). In total, 402,683 c.a., or 2,317.3 km², containing one town and 184 villages, with a population of 168,554. Each borough (or district) had a chief district magistrate. The free royal town of Ruszt (3,477 c.a., 1,402 pop.) close to Lake Fertő and the Kismarton borough were not mentioned in the administrative division. Probably because they were, at the time, under the authority of the Friedrich rebels and Prónay's authority did not yet extend over the area. According to the public administrative directive, villages reassigned from Hungarian boroughs to Lajta-Banate are to be supervised by the nearest borough.[425] This latter instruction was aimed partly at the boroughs contiguous with the Hungarian-Austrian border, and ordered to be ceded to a lesser or greater degree, of the western areas of Sopron (44,708 c.a., 21 vill., 24,580 pop.), Kőszeg (53,432 c.a., 36 vill., 18,692 pop.), Szentgotthárd (43,550 c.a., 32 vill., 24,645 pop.) and Rajka (39,203 c.a., 7 vill., 11,325 pop.). Partly also at the parts of the boroughs of Magyaróvár (14,708 c.a., 2 vill., 3,974 pop.), Szombathely (13,036 c.a., 11 vill., 4,608 pop.) and Körmend (6,469 c.a., 5 vill., 2,290 pop.) also destined for annexation from Hungary. The totals of these last were 215,106 c.a., or 1,237.8 km², containing 114 villages, with a population of 90,114.

The area of Lajta-Banate grew in the second half of October 1921 because the district of Kismarton (75,641 c.a., or 435.3 km², 26 vill., 34,779 pop.), where the Friedrich units were active (they had their headquarters in Kismarton), joined the Prónay-led Lajta-Banate. (The Ostenburg rebels of Nagymarton district, headquartered in Nagymarton, came under the command of Prónay in September. As noted in the previous chapter, they formed the 5th Rebel Army.) After driving out the invading Austrian forces, since September 10 the rebels controlled the parts of zones 'A' and 'B' from Királyhida in the north to Gyanafalva in the south to the new border specified in the Trianon Treaty. This was the territory over which they proclaimed the new country of Lajta-Banate on October 4. According to the available data, its area in October of 1921was 3,990 km², consisting of the town of Kismarton (excepting the town of Ruszt, which, while not mentioned in the public administrative division, logically belonged there), 298 villages and a population of 258,668.[426] With the addition of the town of Ruszt (20 km²,

---

[425] *Lajtabánság*, 1921, November 3, issue 1, p. 4.
[426] Az 1920. évi népszámlálás. Első rész. A népesség főbb demográfiai adatai községek és népesebb puszták, telepek szerint [The 1920 census. Part I. Major demographic data according to villages, settlements and farms.]. In: *Magyar Statisztikai Közlemények*. Új sor. Vol. 69. Budapest, 1923, pp. 286–303. Also: *A népmozgalom főbb adatai községenként – Die Grundlegenden Angaben der Bevölkerungsbewegung nach Gemeinden 1828-1920. Burgenland*. Magyar Központi Statisztikai Hivatal / Ungarisches Statistisches Zentralamt. Budapest, 1981, p. 254.

1,402 pop.), Lajta-Banate comes to 4,010 km^2 and a population of 260,070. Remember that the Saint-Germain Treaty signed on September 10, 1919 awarded 4,364 km^2 of Western Hungary, with 345 settlements, to Austria, along with three towns (Sopron, Kismarton and Ruszt). According to the 1910 census and settlement boundaries, the to-be-annexed territory had a population of 345,082. The patriotic resistance of the rebels reclaimed the majority (92%) of this area by a feat of arms more than a year after the June 4, 1920 Treaty of Trianon. It was no fault of theirs that the Borderland (Burgenland), or a large part of it, that Austria wished to amalgamate could not remain a part of Hungary.

The political and literary periodical magazine of the free forces, *Lajtabánság*, published numerous new measures regarding the organization of the new country. The *Economy* column made known to the public the territorial divisions of Lajta-Banate, as written previously. It also disclosed that regulations governing public administration and the administration of justice were under way. Provisionally, Hungarian laws would remain in force. Everyone would be able to use their mother tongue, in official business and private life; laws and measures are to be published in Hungarian, German and Croatian. Police matters will be handled by the gendarmerie of Lajta-Banate and local home guards; inside Lajta-Banate, the population has the right of free travel, travel documents to be issued by the appropriate authorities, countersigned by the local gendarmerie. People working in Austrian or Hungarian factories will have permanent documents provided; people of Lajta-Banate are permitted to ship animals for sale to Hungarian markets, as well as make purchases there. The column also covered the new customs regulations. The bottom line was that imports were duty free, while exports to Hungary were at preferential rates. The *Public Food Supply* column criticized the Venice Protocol and promised that the public would be looked after.

The columns containing *News* reported (as already covered previously) the minutes of the Constitutional Assembly meeting, the makeup of the provisional governing council, the description of the boundaries of Lajta-Banate, the draft constitution, as well as interim notices and decrees. It further reported that the command center of the armed forces, along with the central offices, have moved from Felsőőr to Nagyszentmihály, where buildings could house them more comfortably.

The most interesting column of the 'rebel newspaper, *Review of the Media*, refuted in three articles the charges of the Viennese *Neues Wiener Tagblatt* (New Vienna Newspaper) and the falsehoods of one of its articles (The Rule of the Bands), according to which a Lt. Bocskay has ordered illegal conscription in Köpcsény. We are clear on the relation of the Austrian press to the Western Hungary insurrection: in their usage, the Hungarian rebels are always referred to as 'bandits.' However, it is worth noting that the review

---

Area conversion calculation: 1 km^2 (100 hectares) = 173.7726 cadastral acres = 247.1 acres.

extended critical words elsewhere, too. The 'rebel paper' pointed the finger at Hungarian media, which, for unknown reasons of higher instructions, began a smear campaign against Lajta-Banate, poisoning public opinion and, wherever possible, calling the heroes of the freedom uprising a 'band of thieves and compromising their integrity.' "We can expect the press that, if they do not publish our communiqués due to censorship, at least they not compromise their ideals of integrity by publishing falsehoods. The Governing Council of Lajta-Banate has warned the papers in official telegrams to cease their undermining activities against the country, else all Hungarian newspapers will be banned from the country."[427]

An important function of organizing statehood is the introduction of postal and telegraphic traffic, which entails the issuance of stamps valid over the entire area. The latter was regulated by György Hir, counselor for economic matters on the Governing Council, in his directive issued on October 5 (G.ü. 5/1921), with the following justification. "In its proclamation of independence of October 4, 1921, the Constitutional Council of Western Hungary declared the territories of zone A and B to be the territory of Lajta-Banate. I now order Lt. László Szendey to assume interim responsibility for all matters relating to the postal service of Lajta-Banate. I direct the creation in Felsőőr for an independent stamp collecting and stamp issuing office. The stamp supplies in all the post offices of zone A and B to be over stamped with 'Lajta-Banate', with the exception of the 100 Korona stamps. These over stamped stamps are to be issued at a 50% surcharge, to cover previous debts, to the post offices requiring them. I instruct Mr. Szendey to make a report to me in three days regarding the execution of my directive. As well, I ask for his report on the time that existing stocks of stamps in the post offices will suffice to meet demand. / György Hir / Counselor for Economic Matters / Governing Council / Place for Seal"[428]

In the southern area controlled by the rebels, the stamps appeared on October 5, overprinted on the front in black with 'Lajta-Banate' and on the back with '50% surcharge. Supreme Command'. This was the first official stamp of the new country, in 12 values, printed in Felsőőr.[429] This issue was valid for the entirety of Lajta-Banate, however, it was mainly used by the post offices of the central and southern sectors. The issuance of the overprinted stamps was reported and registered in the appropriate international offices. We quote:

"*Supreme Command of the Western Hungary Insurrection*
International Union of Postal Union
Bern

---

[427] *Lajtabánság*, 1921, November 3, (issue 1), p. 4.
[428] Jászai, Emánuel János: A magyar bélyegek katalógusa [Catalogue of Hungarian stamps]. Budapest. 1927, p. 160; Prónay, 1986, op. cit., p. 131.
[429] Tóth Alajos, 1932, op. cit., p. 109.

170

Western Hungary has declared itself independent by an October 4, 1921 decision of its Constitutional Assembly and will issue its own stamps as the sovereign state of Lajta-Banate. Until new stamps are ready, the postal service of Lajta-Banate will issue Hungarian stamps with overprinting, as well as the 5 Fillér Harvest stamp will be overprinted to the new value of 2.50 Korona.

The undersigned Supreme Command, which is charged with governing and handling of issues, as decreed by the independence decision, attaches the required 37 samples of each value of the overprinted stamps and considers this official notification of the issuance of the stamps.

We await confirmation of our report.

Pál Prónay
Supreme Commander"[430]

The 5th Rebel Army, fighting under the command of Iván Héjjas in Moson County, issued its own series of stamps on October 10, with black overprinted text announcing *Hungarian Uprising Northern Army 1921*. When the overprinted stamps got into circulation, Lt. Szendey reported that the number of stamps printed would be adequate for about 20 days. Hence, György Hir, on receiving the report, issued another directive (G ü. 10./1921) authorizing 1st. Lt. Károly Verő to design three new stamps and have the draft drawings available for review in three days. The new Western Hungary stamps were ready on October 11. They were printed in Vienna (!) with the printing of 'Lajta-Banate Post' in various colors and 11 denominations. Some sources contest the October 11 date as Prónay recalled it as October 5. The first large shipment from the Viennese firm of Paulussen and Partner was sent on November 9, and in circulation after November 11. On November 17, the Vienna authorities seized the printer's stock and charged the company with fraud and treason.[431]

The Friedrich rebels issued their own stamps on October 12 with the overprinting: *Nyugat-Magyarország Orszvé. / Westungarn Orgland*. The Friedrich group issued a proclamation on September 30 in Kismarton in which it stated that a month earlier, on August 30, the National Defense Organization (Országos Védelmi Szervezet, ORSZVÉ) was formed. It also stated that it assumed authority of the Western Hungary area intended for annexation. The organization made it fairly clear that its goal was to recall Charles IV to the Hungarian throne. With the issuing of the stamps, it sought to strengthen its financial position. The stamps were ordered on September 27

---

[430] Jászai, 1927, op. cit., p. 161.

[431] The Austrian Attorney General suspended proceedings against the printer on January 17, 1922 since, at the time of printing, Austria had not extended its sovereignty over Western Hungary, making the case without foundation.

from a printing press in Budapest, which arrived in Kismarton on October 12. Postal authorities in Kismarton notified the executives of Hungarian Mail and Telegraph the next day of the release of the stamps into circulation. The stamps were in use for a limited time only, around Kismarton and Nagymarton, as immediately before the second *coup d'état* attempt of Charles IV, the numerically superior forces of Iván Héjjas attacked the Friedrich rebels, forcing them to retreat to Nagymarton.

Mail, parcels and periodicals with rebel stamps affixed were accepted by the Czech, Romanian and South Slav post offices, and other foreign countries. Not so by the Royal Hungarian Mail, which only delivered the items after having charged a postal surcharge.[432] The rebels feared – with good reason – that if the stamps are printed in Budapest, the authorities will confiscate them. That was the reason for having had them printed in Vienna. News of this leaked out and the Austrian government confiscated the printed supply. The Paulussen Press was only able to deliver stamps after the October 13 signing of the Venice Protocol, even though the stamps were ready two days before.[433]

In the meanwhile, Prime Minister Bethlen was fearful, on the one hand, that the proclamation of independence by Western Hungary would strengthen the royalists' overt aim of restoring Charles IV to the throne and, on the other hand, weaken Hungary's international position. He alluded to it in his telegram of October 4 to the high command of the Western Hungary insurrection. He objected sharply to the creation of an independent country in Western Hungary. He asked Prónay to cease the movement and alter their resolution. Knowing the intractableness of the commander and the high command, the government censored out all news of the Lajta-Banate proclamation from Hungarian papers and ordered the border to Western Hungary closed.

The prime minister also issued instructions to the police and other authorities that rebels *en route* to Western Hungary were to be arrested in Budapest and returned to their place of residence. Resisters were to be interned. Prónay, however, refused to budge as disclosed in his letter of October 7 to the prime minister. In it he stated that he insists on the proclaimed independence, sovereignty and neutrality of Lajta-Banate. Behind their backs, the Hungarian government should only hold talks with Austria regarding trade matters. On the same day, Prónay also imparted to Chief Commissioner [of the western counties] Sigray that they refuse to negotiate with either the Hungarian government or Austria with regard to the territory

---

[432] The Royal Hungarian Mail decreed the Lajta-Banate stamps as not acceptable for postal usage. The directive (2849, *Posta és Távírda Rendeletek Tára*, 1922) was issued on February 13, 1922, long after the fighting. Much later, in September of 1932, ignoring the directive, it began selling the stamps to collectors, in essence, making them official.

[433] Missuray-Krúg, 1935, op. cit., p. 202.

of Lajta-Banate but would "hold out to the last bullet, to the last breath."[434]

Also on October 7, at the Cabinet session PM Bethlen announce that the representatives of the Entente Powers delivered the invitation to the Italian mediated Hungarian-Austrian meeting in Venice. It was Vienna's stated request that Sopron and its surrounding decide on their affiliation by plebiscite. According to the PM, that stance clashed on two points with the Hungarian point of view. One, that Hungary wants to retain the city and its surrounding without a plebiscite; two, the question of border adjustment, which the Austrians totally rejected. Thus, in Venice, the Hungarian government strongly raised the situation of the civil servants and the question of payment of pensions, as well as stipulating a general amnesty for the participants of the rebellion. Bethlen then remarked that Western Hungary had already been handed over to the representatives of the Entente Powers. This, however, will only become reality if an agreement is reached in Venice. The Entente – more than likely – will demand that the rebels be removed from the territory. Hence, it is already important to prevent the free-forces from getting fresh reinforcements and be resupplied with new equipment. In the session, Interior Minister Gedeon Ráday stated that he will issue the necessary instructions.[435] The Cabinet ordered a strong military cordon along the Trianon border.

At the determined tone of the Hungarian government, Prónay took a more conciliatory position. In the name of "the high command of the free-forces," he wrote a new letter to the PM on October 10. Among other things, he stated that: Lajta-Banate was proclaimed "to free the government from the responsibility for the actions of the free-forces." He deems the new state to be "an independent territory" *vis a vis* the Entente Powers, the countries of the Little Entente (Czechoslovakia, Romania and the Kingdom of Serbs-Croats-Slovenes) and Austria but insists on the territorial integrity of Lajta-Banate. On the other hand, he will carry out the government's expectations and representatives should be sent to the high command, with "financial and monetary support" from the Budapest government to enable it to function. Finally, he asked that the Hungarian government prevent the insurrection to be used by some for insignificant political goals.[436]

Clashes between the rebels and Austrian gendarme units continued after the proclamation of independence. Col. Köller made a report on October 13 that, according to information received from Nezsider, Austrian forces attacked rebel units observing the border settlement of Császárkőbánya but the intruders were forced back. In the village of Gyanafalva in the borough of Szentgotthárd, a post of the free-forces was assaulted by a 40-strong group of émigré Hungarian Communists who were also successfully repelled. They continued to shout: "Wait, you cross-spiders," alluding to the rebels wearing

---

[434] Soós, 1971, op. cit., p. 159.
[435] MOL. K 27. Minisztertanácsi jegyzőkönyvek, 1921. október 7.
[436] Soós, 1971, op. cit., p. 159.

the double-cross insignia on their clothing. The flag of Lajta-Banate was red with a superimposed [apostolic-*ed.*] double-cross in white.

Prónay was, at this time, in Nagyszentmihály with Count Tamás Erdődy, the chief of the rebel gendarmes and a few other officers, and "all behaved impeccably," There was all the more trouble with the commander of a local rebel unit. "French Lt.Col. De Ligny is feeling very awkward in Gyanafalva, and complaining. (…) Jakula, the local commander, yesterday ordered that travel was only permitted with his written authorization and De Ligny, who wanted to go to Németújvár this morning [October 13], was hampered and, when he objected, had a rifle pointed at him by a rebel who spat at him: *Schwein entente Offizier* [Pig of an Entente officer]. He turned back at this and protested with Jakula who expressed his regrets and sent him an identification document. De Ligny does not know what to do with it: if he accepts, the Entente's prestige suffers, if he doesn't, he is unable to move. He complains that he gets no instructions from the Entente generals [in Sopron] and does not know the context in which to operate. He would very much like to relocate to Szentgotthárd but does not want to suggest it, lest he be seen as a coward. He does not know the numbers of the rebels, they are very secretive. He saw nothing of yesterday's clash. Only heard that both sides believed that the other attacked and that began the shooting. Otherwise, the situation is unchanged."[437]

Two detectives from the police department of the Interior Ministry, Sándor Hollósi and Károly Baláskovits, graphically described the functioning of the country of Lajta-Banate in their report of October 29. "The population of Western Hungary treat the rebels with due respect and confidence. The rebels earn the respect and confidence by maintaining order and good public safety over the territory in their jurisdiction. The rebels have their own gendarmerie, customs and finance officers, who collect duties on exports and imports. (…) They have their own laws and regulations for resistors and anti-Hungarian persons. (…) In conversation with one rebel, their goal is: categorical retention of the territory awarded to Austria for Hungary. (…) they will be able to retain the territory in question against the Czechs because, they expect an irredentist movement to arise in the occupied area. There is now a Bosnian company in the rebel forces. Initially, there were acts of robbery and blackmail by the rebels against the locals. These abuses were committed by bands formed under individual officers, at their initiative, which, after the reorganization of the rebel forces, their commander, former-Major Prónay [actually Lieutenant Colonel-*J.B.*], brought to an end with severe regulations and a few instances of hanging. Now, the rebels form a reliable, disciplined military force. In some villages, the small garrison units of rebels are fed by the people. Those assigned to border duty maintain themselves from the collected customs duties. The rebels are mostly royalists but not Habsburg supporters. The attempted *coup* of a few days ago [meaning Charles IV's

---

[437] MOL. K 26. 1264. csomó. 1921–XLII. Tétel, pp. 3–5. old.

second return attempt-*J.B.*] was distinctly rejected by them and expressed their delight at its failure."[438]

It was not by accident that Hungarian diplomacy urged a plebiscite for the contested area of Western Hungary regarding their affiliation, a move Austria hotly rejected. This clearly indicated the belief of both sides that the population would decide with staying a part of Hungary, in spite of the fact that the area in question had a minority ethnic Hungarian population. The government of Lajta-Banate issued its Declaration of Independence based on the representatives of the local populace and the apprehensiveness of the affected villages of a Social Democratic–Communist Austria. It is important to remember that the proclamation of sovereignty by the new state was made in the name of all three nationalities living in the area – Germans, Croats and Hungarians – and not merely based on their mother tongues. Although the official language of Lajta-Banate was declared to be Hungarian, all three languages were deemed to be acceptable in official and private usage. As well, laws and regulations were prescribed to be published in all three languages. It was based on this that the organization for the setting up of the infrastructure of the new state was begun, which, unfortunately, lasted a mere month. However, it is a fact that the proclamation of Lajta-Banate speeded up the resolution of the Western Hungary question.

According to the terms of the Venice Protocol, the Hungarian government began to disarm the rebels in the second half of October, whom they sternly instructed to lay down their arms. "A separate notice was addressed to Hungarian functionaries and Hungarian officers who took part in the insurrection to return home or face court action. A proclamation was aimed at students of academies to return to their schools or face the loss of half of an academic year. The population was warned not to support the rebels with either money or arms, or face legal consequences. Finally, an appeal was made to the enlisted men, and others not part of the mentioned groups, mainly officers and non-commissioned officers, and other parties, to lay down the arms, otherwise face legal charges of insurrection."[439] Former prime minister Friedrich was first to return permanently to Budapest; however, his unit came under the command of commander Prónay. Prime Minister Bethlen tried to convince the commander of the Lajta-Banate forces in a long October 17 letter that all further resistance was futile and continued fighting was especially dangerous for the results obtained in the Venice Protocol. In his reply two days later, Prónay attempted to bear out that he was in no position to comply with the government's request.

The Hungarian government finally conceded Western Hungary, in return for a plebiscite for Sopron and its surrounding area, which sealed the fate of Lajta-Banate. The second return attempt of Charles IV (October 20 to 24)[440]

---

[438] Ibid, 1921–XLII–9260. szám, p. 3.

[439] Ádám T., 1939, op. cit., pp. 81–82.

[440] To be covered in more detail in the next chapter.

only temporarily disrupted the disarmament of the rebels active in Lajta-Banate and the government's evacuation of Western Hungary. Gen. Árpád Guilleaume, commander of the Szombathely district, was assigned the execution of those two tasks. The district command counter-intelligence section only notified Governor Horthy and the Hungarian government at 04:30 on October 22 of the return of Charles IV and the prior events. Since Gen. Guilleaume did not want to swear allegiance to the king, Commissioner Sigray relieved him of his post in the afternoon of October 21. At a special session of the Cabinet the following morning, the decision was taken to relieve Commissioner Sigray of his position and replace him with Gen. Guilleaume. However, the influence of Charles IV was stronger in Szombathely and the commander of the military district, Gen. László Horváth had Gen. Guilleaume arrested. After the failure of the monarchists at Budaörs, Gen. Guilleaume resumed his post the same afternoon.[441]

With the agreement of the Entente generals, the Ostenburg battalion was withdrawn from the plebiscite-intended area of Sopron and its surrounding. Gyula Ostenburg was arrested a few days earlier, after the unsuccessful clash at Budaörs, and his unit's positions were taken over by a battalion of the Nagykanizsa regiment.

One of the problems arose from the fact that the rebels thought that the results of the Venice Protocol were not enough. Governor Horthy and the Hungarian government ordered commander Prónay for consultations to Budapest on October 31, who arrived with several of the leaders of the insurrection (military bishop István Zadravecz, father 'Archangel' Bónis, Bacho Bónis, Károly Pröhle and Aurél Héjjas). Horthy attempted to convince them that further resistance would cause immense international damage to the country. PM Bethlen tried to reason that a government based on law has no need for rebels.[442] Finally, in a private meeting with Horthy, Prónay promised to disarm his forces by November 6 and leave Lajta-Banate. In the meantime, Viktor Ranzenberger demanded on November 2, in the name of the "rebel commanders" that: the government notify them in writing to evacuate the area and assume financial responsibility for it. The government gave its assurances the following day.

On November 4, infantry Gen. Baron Pál Nagy (1864-1927) already reported to Bethlen that the southern group of rebels has finished their withdrawal. Prónay had already issued his order to disarm and withdraw on the 4th, two days before the date he promised to Horthy, and left his command center of Nagyszentmihály, departing for Szombathely. "The rebels, who fought valiantly against the Reds and drove them out of Western Hungary, do not wish to fight against the mother country and, after a short delay, laid down their arms in the village of Torony, west of Szombathely, on November 4,

---

[441] Békés, 2007, op. cit., pp. 101–102.
[442] Zadravecz, 1967, op. cit., pp. 173–176; Prónay, 1986, op. cit., pp. 309–312.

1921, exactly a month after the inauguration [of Lajta-Banate—*J.B.*].''[443]

In the central and northern zones judged for annexation, the free-troops also began a planned withdrawal. On the following day, the 5th, the order was essentially completed and their disarmament was "in progress," reported Gen. Nagy to the prime minister. He also reported that a portion of the rebels are of foreign nationality [i.e., from areas annexed under the Trianon Decree, having come from Transylvania, Northern Hungary and Vojvodina to fight in Western Hungary-*J.B.*] and "being without a livelihood, came to Budapest. (…) Their discontent is to be prevented." Gen. Nagy instructed that, within his sphere of influence, the 40 rebels – "for most part Serb and Croat army deserters" – be held in the collection camp for prisoners-of-war in the Keleti [Eastern] Train Station in the Budapest military region "to be fed and housed." He also informed that, according to reports, more rebels of similar background can be expected. Thus, he asked Bethlen to issue instruction regarding their situation and have jobs found for them. The military command group led by him, he went on, "having completed its special mission," will be transferred to Group III of the Defense Ministry beginning November 7, 1921 and "will no longer be able to influence the remedy of the rebels' requests."[444]

Smaller groups still lingered in the former Lajta-Banate. The free-troop unit recruited from around Sárvár, based in the villages of Királyfalva and Ercsenye in the Szentgotthárd district, only marched out of the area ceded to Austria on November 6. In fact, a squad of Hungarian gendarmes from Szombathely were ordered to Felsőőr and Szentelek on the 16th to expel a 1st Lt. Sala and a few of his rebels. Rebel units were disarmed by units of the regular Hungarian army. Collection camps were set up for those disarmed and held 525 in Magyaróvár, 600 in Kapuvár, 800 in Szombathely and 200 in Körmend, for a total of 2,125. However, only 1,400 weapons were collected from them. The rest, according to the rebels, were left with Hungarian-friendly locals in Burgenland for safekeeping for a possible second insurrection. In his diary, Prónay admitted that most of the missing weapons were hidden in Szombathely by an Oszkár Renner on his secret instruction.[445] (At the time of the insurrection, Renner was the director of the Lajta-Banate Railways. Later, Prónay awarder him the silver Lajta-Banate Commemorative Medal – number 18, as listed in his diary.)

The report quoted above clearly illustrates that the Hungarian government made strenuous efforts to look after the demobilized Western Hungary rebels who were without a livelihood. The director of the State Employment Agency in Budapest informed the PM's office on December 24 that, of the 72 former rebels sent to it, jobs were found for 32, 38 cases were closed due to the applicant not showing up in the office and were searching for jobs for 2. The work found for the 32 consisted of: 25 factory jobs or casual labor, 2 servants,

---

[443] Ádám T., 1939, op. cit., p. 82.

[444] MOL K 26. 1264. csomó. 1921–XLII–9394. szám, p. 3.

[445] Prónay, 1986, op. cit., p. 320.

2 horse grooms and 3 coachmen.[446]

Although the Venice Agreement decided in favor of Hungary, more could have been achieved with a little cleverer diplomacy. Among the Hungarian delegates – according to the rebels – several made criminal omissions.[447] According to the rebels, if not the entire annexed territory of Western Hungary but much more of it could have been retained. Their view is supported, in large part, by the speech made by former Chief Commissioner Sigray on "The Western Hungary resistance" in front the National Assembly on January 19, 1922. We quote: "We lost Western Hungary when the Foreign Ministry, after the exit of the Teleki government [April 13, 1921-*J.B.*], took a position of territorial concession and, having begun to make concessions, began to negotiate downwards, point by point. (…) While the [Bethlen] government bid downwards in the matter of the handover of Western Hungary areas, the people, associations and nationalistic-hearted population continually (…) raised caution against the handing over of the territory. (…) is the Hungarian government had insisted on its position on not retreating from the A-line, [then] the entire A-line [the area lying west of it-*J.B.*] could have been kept, since the Austrians could have just as easily given it up as they did Sopron, since the losing of Sopron made their Burgenland idea worthless to them. [Sopron was intended to be the provincial capital of Burgenland-*ed.*] (…) Chancellor Schober admitted later, as did the Hungarian government, that he was forced to go to Venice only because of the rebels and not because he was forced by the various showy diplomatic negotiations and tricks. It is possible that Chancellor Schober would have sought a peaceful arrangement with Hungary with an eye to the future, too, given the trade dependence, in which Austria's food supply is dependent on Hungary but he could not because he found continuous opposition in the parties, especially the Greater Germany parties, which always demanded that the entirety of the so-called Burgenland, all the Germans of Burgenland be attached to Austria and then, essentially, annexed to Germany.

That is why the downward negotiation was so damaging (…) – continued Count Sigray – whose end result was the retention of Sopron and ceding the rest of the territory; it was damaging because it did not make use of the successes of the rebels. (…) [and] return to a previous weaker offer, which did not make best use of the great successes of the rebels. How much this is so, Honored House, I wish to prove by the declaration of the Greater Germany Party, the same party in Austria that always opposed concessions to Hungary, the Greater Germany party, which, as we shall see, was itself convinced that it could never gain sway over Western Hungary if the Hungarian government does not enter into the Venice Protocol. Here, allow me to read a short section from the December 30 speech in Linz of the president of the Greater Germany Party, Dr. Dinghoffer, which contains the following passage (*he reads*): 'With

---

[446] MOL. K 26. 1921–XLII–9394. sz., p. 2.
[447] Ádám T., 1939, op. cit., p. 76.

regard to the criticism in the matter of Western Hungary, that the Greater Germany Party did not reject the Venice Protocol from the beginning, we answer that we did not want to create a government crisis, because otherwise Austria could not have expected to keep anything of Western Hungary, not Sopron, nor the other parts of the territory.' Hence, we can see that the Venice Protocol, which the government holds up as a prestigious gain, is seen on the other side, too, as a fortunate solution, and avers that, if the Venice Protocol had not happened, in that case, it is likely that the Austrians probably would have got nothing of Western Hungary." [448]

The private edition added the commentary to Count Sigray's speech: "The Foreign Minister, Count Miklós Bánffy, replied to the speech but neither he, nor the head of the government [PM Bethlen] refuted any of the assertions, in fact, they were forced to admit that the speech essentially covered the truth. Thus, it is clearly evident that the saving of Sopron is not attributable to the government but thanks to the local authorities, patriotic population and the resistance of the rebels! *The government had no merit in the deed! And the responsibility for losing the rest of Western Hungary rests with it!*"[449]

Further proof from an extant document, according to which another ten Moson County villages (Barátudvar, Boldogasszony, Féltorony, Ilmic, Mosonbánfalva, Mosonszentandrás, Mosontarcsa, Mosontétény, Pomogy and Valla), mainly German populated, and six more in the vicinity of Sopron (Cinfalva, Fertőmeggyes, Kelénpatak, Somfalva, Sopronkeresztúr and Zárány), three German and three Croat speaking settlements, would also have been included in the plebiscite area. The latter six, similar to Kópháza, would almost certainly have voted to remain with Hungary. They were excluded from the area covered by the plebiscite because, according to Ernő Träger, the Foreign Minister did not involve appropriate experts in drawing up the boundaries.[450]

Lajos Krug, a participant in the insurrection, bitterly remarked: "It is a firm fact that the first, unforgivable blunder was made by Foreign Minister Count Bánffy, when he made statements to the effect of being willing to give up parts of the territory of Western Hungary. First, Moson County came under the downward bidding, then slowly the energetic Hungarian stance shriveled to nothing! (…) the events of August [1921] completely overshadowed Count Bánffy until, finally, only the immediate surrounding area of Sopron was discussed behind the scenes."[451]

A total of 24 Hungarian rebels and one gendarme lost their lives in the Western Hungarian insurrection between August 28 and November 4, 1921.

---

[448] Speech of Count Sigray on the resistance in Western Hungary. (Private edition.) Athenaeum Irodalmi és Nyomdai Részvénytársulat nyomása. Budapest, 1922, pp. 3, 4, 13, 15. (Source: National Assembly minutes. Budapest, 1922, vol. XV)
[449] Ibid, p. 17.
[450] Fogarassy, László: A soproni népszavazás [The Sopron plebiscite]. In: *Soproni Szemle*, 1971, issue 4, pp 335-336.
[451] Krug, 1930, op. cit., p. 30.

They gave their lives for their country against the predatory, territory-hungry invading forces of Austrian, for land that was Hungarian for a thousand years, for the city of Sopron and the 18 settlements that were, ultimately, retained. Their sacrifice was not in vain; they all deserve the eternal thanks of a grateful nation.

Aside from those who fell in battle, commander Prónay had László Sátori, student of the Magyaróvár academy and reservist officer, Lt. Bakonyi and Cadet Bokor shot in Felsőpulya on September 13.[452] The latter two were executed by the commander for killing and robbing local Jews during the insurrection. In his memoirs, Prónay only remarks with contempt on one of his soldiers, a Jewish officer from his former White unit. Not for his origins but for his inhumane acts of reprisal.[453] Sátori and his associates were brought up in front of a court martial at the behest of Miklós Budaházy, commander of the 3rd Rebel Army. It became clear later that Sátori was executed in the place of another rebel, based on erroneous or intentionally false testimony.

On the Austrian side, casualties came to a total of 30 soldiers, 13 gendarmes and one civil servant.

On September 18, 1922, shortly after second insurrection, a memorial plaque was unveiled in Szombathely for six of the men from Vas County who gave their lives in the battle for Western Hungary / Borderland. Coincidentally, it was the date of Hungary's entry into the League of Nations. In the hallway, beside the entry into the county's council chamber, is a marble slab with their names: Ákos Gubicza, Ferenc Károly Hanus, Imre Kalocsay, Ferenc Nemetz, Kornél László Párvy and Ferenc Pehm.[454]

Eight years after the Western Hungary insurrection, in 1929, Prónay had a Lajta-Banate Commemorative Medal struck. The commemorative text read: "The Lajta-Banate medal was struck by the high command on the eighth anniversary of the insurrection in Western Hungary in the year 1921 for those who took up arms and fought for the integrity of our country, saving the honor of the Hungarian nation, and recovered Sopron for the mother country. This medal, which must not only symbolize the intransigent patriotism of the past but which, as a link, must hereafter unite the camp of the truly committed Hungarians, can be claimed and given by the high command to all those: Firstly, who can positively prove that, in the timeframe mentioned, were serving under the command of Lajta-Banate and served the insurrection selflessly and steadfastly to the end. Secondly, the commander-in-chief offers it to all noble patriots who supported this exalted goal with self-sacrifice, even if indirectly, and aided the work of the insurgents. Those who defiled and thwarted the noble aims of the sacred ideal of irredentism, can have no claim on the medal. In fact, the medal will be withdrawn from those who acquired

---

[452] Missuray-Krúg, 1935, pp. 204–214.
[453] Kovács, Tamás: Horthy és a zsidók. Sommás ítéletek, bonyolult valóság [Horthy and the Jews. Summary verdicts, complex reality.]. In: *Nagy Magyarország*, year II, issue 1, 2010, February, pp. 77–78.
[454] Ádám T., 1935, op. cit., p. 270.

them without authorization or those who become unworthy to wear it. The medal, designed by sculptor Hugó Keviczky (1879-1944), shows the rebel commander in military regalia on one side and, on the other side, a relief of the coat-of-arms of the independent and sovereign state of Lajta-Banate. The ribbon shows the colors of Lajta-Banate: a white cross on a red field. The medals are numbered on the back, 1-30 struck in silver for the commanders of the insurrection, the rest bronze [approx. 3,000]. The recipients of the medal not only receive a commendation scroll but have their information recorded in an official roll. The commendations are only valid with the personal signature of the supreme commander. (Budapest, 1929, June 1. Hq.)"[455] Prónay had the medals struck "in secret" in the Royal Hungarian Mint.

Some collectors have always supposed that one of the Lajta-Banate commemorative medal was minted in gold for Regent Horthy. However, the Regent refused to accept it and Prónay kept it for himself. In truth, a gold version was struck but with the variation that the front did not have Prónay's face, rather it carried four lines of text: For our beloved / commander / rebels / of Western Hungary. The gold medallion was presented to Prónay at a gala dinner by Miklós Budaházy, former commander of the 2nd Rebel Army, "on behalf of the insurrectionist camp."

Prónay did not secure the permission of the authorities for the awarding of the commemorative medal. The rebel medal was first presented in a ceremony on August 19, 1929 at the Officers Club in Budapest that was attended by several hundred former rebels. The medals were pinned on the chests by Prónay himself. The event was reported the next day by the paper, *Magyarság*,[456] and the article drew the attention of the highest circles of authority. The article informed the reader that, at Prónay's initiative, the approximately 3,000-strong veterans association of the Western Hungary insurrection had a medal struck. The awarding of the medal came unexpectedly, even Governor Horthy was informed only through the newspaper. Subsequent to the article, the Cabinet Office ordered an investigation. The Interior Ministry officials found out that Prónay and associates had already planned in 1921 the release of a similar medal but lacked the means. This implementation of the medal was not solely Prónay's merit but was also helped by Count Antal Sigray, Nándor Urmánczy, István Friedrich, Iván Héjjas and others. The cost of creating the medals was borne by Count Sigray.[457] The report of the investigation raised the possibility that, perhaps, Prónay acted unlawfully in creating the Commemorative Medal. The president of the Royal Hungarian Mint, Samuel Michaelis, was held responsible for not notifying the "appropriate authorities" of Prónay's order.

In the end, the Prime Minister's Office took the stance that, since the medal is neither a Hungarian or foreign decoration, nor does it carry the status

---

[455] Missuray-Krúg, 1935, op. cit., pp. 173–174.
[456] *Magyarság*, 1929, August 20.
[457] Makai, 1977, op. cit., pp. 335–336.

of a decorative medallion, therefore no permission is required to wear it. This was not unintentional; the governing circles felt it best to leave an insulted and forgotten-by-the-public Prónay in peace. In the meantime, the former commander had other goals; he travelled the cities and towns of the country. In his diary, he wrote: "At various events arranged for the awarding of the medals to the former rebels, I also organized the larger camp of western irredentists." A detailed list was maintained of the awardees, counting on them for a later "nation rescuing action." In spite of Prónay's efforts, the former Western Hungary rebels were still not united into an independent group or organization by the 1930s. one reason was that the various political parties attempted to draw them into their ranks for reasons of their own. The usual outcome was that if anybody attempted to call the former rebels to action, he could count on the antipathy of not only the media but a segment of the former insurrectionists, as well. There was but one exception, the founding of the group by Prónay in 1929 to create the commemorative medal.

Between the two wars, there were several memorials erected in and around Sopron to the Battle of Ágfalva, e.g.- the garden of the Mining and Forestry Academy, on Széchenyi Square, and a memorial column in Ágfalva.[458] A life-size statue of an armed rebel was erected in the „Cemetery of the Fallen" in Szombathely.[459] Later, on September 8, 1943, a memorial plaque was unveiled in Sopron by the *Hungarian Association of Sopron* in honor of the two Sopron students who fell in the anti-annexation fight of Western Hungary. The organization of the strongly anti-*Volksbund* movement was initiated and supported by the entire teaching staff and student body of the Academy.

On the 80th anniversary of the annexation of the Western Hungary territory, Ferenc Gyurácz published 16 period photographs of the significant events and everydays of the insurrection – pictures of self-esteem of a nation. In the introduction, he wrote: "If we look at these pictures closely and objectively, we get some small amount of balm for our wounds aching since 1918-20. (…) What do I mean? That our people – bled dry and demoralized by the annexing forces of countries, urged on and supported by Great Powers to expropriate Northern Hungary, Transylvania and Vojvodina, and our 'revolutionary governments' serving foreign interests that had no real willingness – were unable to resist. (When it became apparent that Aurél Stromfeld would be able to retake Northern Hungary, the 'internationalist' Béla Kun ordered him back.) What was without precedent for a thousand years, we voluntarily – without firing a shot – gave up our ancient territories, among them our culture's cultic land: Transylvania. This is an eternal shame for our nation. (…) However, as these pictures show, matters turned out differently in Western Hungary. Here, in 1921, men were found who took the

---

[458] *Vasvármegye*, 1922, September 19, p. 1; Sopron and …, 1934, op. cit., p. 28/a, 28/d. (photographs)
[459] Ádám T., 1935, op. cit., p. 256/b. (photograph)

principle seriously, which every nation of healthy disposition espoused earnestly for thousands of years, i.e., the nation's soil must be defended, even at the risk of our lives. That members of the resisting Hungarian free-forces opposing Austrian arms came from other parts of the country is as normal as the likelihood that the proportion of locals among the Austrians executing the occupation was likely even smaller. (...) For reasons of foreign policy, the government of Hungary was unable to express support at the time for the freedom fighters of Western Hungary and political needs still prevents suitable fostering of their memory. These, of course, may be justified but cannot have primacy in an intellectual existence. Hence, it is with an easy conscience that we ignore them and bestow unreserved reverence to the memory of our heroes. How large a role in the return of Sopron and its surroundings is due to their willingness to sacrifices, history has not adequately recorded. (...) But, it is beyond doubt, it had a role in salvaging our damaged national self-esteem and has a role still."[460]

The Hungarian media of the day (and internationally, mainly Austrian) paid close attention to the events of the Western Hungary insurrection. Some newspapers of the '20s and '30s gladly devoted space to nostalgia pieces. The publisher and editor of the *Nemzeti Élet*, László Budaváry (1889-1962) often took up the cause of annexed Western Hungary and the free-forces. Later, he regularly published the rebellion-themed short stories of István T. Ádám. The events of the Western Hungary insurrection provided themes for a number of books (memoirs and literary), articles and poems until the country was overrun by the Red Army in 1945. A film, *Impostors*, was made in 1969, based on the diary of Pál Prónay.

In conclusion, we must again state: the Western Hungary insurrection that broke out on August 28, 1921, and the proclamation of the independent state of Lajta-Banate on October 4, compelled the holding of the December 14-16 plebiscite, whose outcome was favorable for Hungary.

---

[460] Gyurácz, Ferenc: A nemzeti önbecsülés képei [Images of national self-esteem]. In: *Vasi Szemle*, 2001, issue 6, p. 678. Photographs pp. 679–686.

Chapter 8: From the Venice Protocol
to the Sopron plebiscite
October 11– December 14-16, 1921

A week after the proclamation of an independent Lajta-Banate, the Hungarian-Austrian meetings[461] began in Venice on October 11 under the presidency of the Italian Foreign Minister, Paolo Tommaso della Toretta. It was attended by Austrian Chancellor Johannes Schober, Hungarian Prime Minister István Bethlen and Foreign Minister Miklós Bánffy.[462]

In regard to the annexation of Western Hungary, an unknown fact was recorded by Bánffy in his diary. After the first day's discussions, the Foreign Minister invited the Italian ambassador to Hungary, Gaetano Castagneto, also in attendance, to dinner. "I mentioned how well disposed I found Toretta. 'I see your influence in it!' I said to Castegnatto (sic!). 'No, not entirely,' said the ambassador, laughing, 'there is a deeper reason.' And now what he said surprised me. 'At the time of the peace treaty, Toretta was an ambassador in Vienna. Maybe, because he was afraid of the [Western Hungary] Czech-Yugoslav corridor, he invented Burgenland!' He, Toretta! Yes, he! 'He specifically went to Paris because of it. Since the insurrection, perhaps he is a bit ashamed that his creation brought such a dangerous result. Now he is trying to rectify it. That is what I suggested to him two weeks ago. But he was reluctant. What was decisive was your latest turning to Beneš. Hence, the specter of the Czech-Serb corridor rose again in him'."[463]

According to the minutes of the Venice meeting[464] dated two days later on the 13th, the aim of the conference was "a mutual agreement to define the question of the boundary of Western Hungary granted to Austria by the treaties of Saint-Germain and Trianon." This was the first instance that the Entente Powers initiated an international summit to settle their prior decision made in two treaties. Italy had a decisive role in it because – although at the

---

[461] Bánffy, 1993, op. cit., pp. 80–86; Parragi, György: A velencei egyezmény megkoronázza Sopron megmentését [The Venice Agreement sanctions the rescue of Sopron]. In: *A "Sopronvármegye" Népszavazási Emlékalbuma*. Rábaközi Nyomda és Lapkiadó Vállalat. Sopron, 1934, pp. 59–65. (A továbbiakban: Népszavazási Emlékalbum.); Sopronyi-Thurner, Mihály: A magyar igazság kálváriája [The tortuous path of Hungarian legitimacy]. In: Sopron and …, 1934, op. cit., pp. 41–43.

[462] Count Miklós Bánffy (1873-1950), parliamentary representative from 1901 to 1918 and the country's Foreign Minister between April 14, 1921 and December 29, 1922. He had a significant role in Hungary's entry into the League of Nations in 1922. In 1926, he moved to his estate in Bonchida in Transylvania and took Romanian citizenship. When part of Transylvania was again re-annexed to Hungary by the Second Vienna Award, he was a member of the Upper House of the Hungarian Parliament (1940-1944). In 1949, he moved to Budapest, where he died shortly after.

[463] Bánffy, 1993, op. cit., p. 83. The Italian ambassador was alluding to the meeting between Bánffy and Beneš on June 23-24 in Marienbad.

[464] Halmosy, 1983, op. cit., pp. 179–183.

time the Paris Peace Conference rejected it – in the fall of 1921, it held out for the possible creation of some sort of a Czechoslovak-South Slav corridor in the west of Trans-Danubia. As well, the imminent danger that, in the interest of retaining Western Hungary, Austria would yield to the pressure exerted by Beneš. At this time, Beneš was attempting to draw Austria into an alliance, as the fourth county of the Little Entente. His plan was, through the support of Czechoslovakia for the annexation of Burgenland to Austria, to gain Austria's rapprochement toward the Little Entente, possibly to create an alliance. Thus, the political and military ring around Hungary would be completed in the West.[465]

The Venice Protocol of October 13 made it the responsibility of Hungary to proclaim to the entire population that: "An equitable agreement has been reached and, thus, all Hungarians are called upon to observe this agreement as their most patriotic duty." A notice is to be made to the rebels that: "Arms are to be laid down immediately under threat of the most serious penalty" and non-residents of Western Hungary should immediately leave the area. Within ten days, the same holds for civil servants and serving or retired officers. Those who comply with the notice will not be punished for acts committed during the insurrection, and will get a general amnesty. The latter, however, does not extend to ordinary crimes committed. Students who took part in the uprising – also within ten days – are responsible to show up at their schools or academies, else forfeit their semester. Those who continue to support the rebels will be punished to the fullest extent of Hungarian law dealing with illegal recruiting.

The deadline for the previous decrees is three weeks. When the affected area was evacuated by the rebels, Austria is to take possession. At the instructions of the Italian Foreign Minister, the Entente will send forces to Sopron and hold the plebiscite; first the city, then the surrounding area but the final result will be as the combined result of the two. The protocol defined exactly the boundary of the plebiscite: the semi-circle of Fertőrákos–Sopron–Ágfalva–Harka–Kópháza–Nagycenk, also Balf, Fertőboz and Sopronbánfalva, nine settlements in all. Finally, Austria and Hungary committed themselves to abide by the results of the referendum. Eight days after the announcement of the results, the affected territory is to be handed over to the entitled country.[466]

The day before the signing of the Venice Protocol, PM Bethlen specifically obliged himself in a separate memorandum to send in the Hungarian military if the rebels do not withdraw from Western Hungary. This undertaking, until its possible use, was not to be made public. On October 13, Bethlen and Toretta made another secret agreement. In it, the Italian Foreign Minister agreed to use all his influence to sway the Entente committee to be

---

[465] Ádám, Magda: A kisantant és Európa 1920-1929 [The Little Entente and Europe 1920-1929]. Budapest, 1989, pp. 126–127; Halmosy, 1983, op. cit., p. 186.
[466] Halmosy, 1983, op. cit., pp. 179-183.

cognizant of Hungarian claims when deciding on the border definition. Bethlen reported on the Venice dialogue and the two secret agreements at the Cabinet meeting held on October 16. He specifically stressed that the disarming of the rebels was an "obligation of honor," if they do not obey the order, they must be disarmed by force. After the representation, the Cabinet unanimously accepted the Venice Protocol and asked the heads of the Interior and Defense ministries to issue the necessary instructions to execute the agreed terms.[467]

The Austrian foreign affairs committee discussed the agreement after Chancellor Schober's report on October 19. Position taken by the group declared that the stance of the Entente Powers has shifted since the signing of the Trianon Treaty and seem not willing to execute the territorial decision in its entirety that favored Austria. Hence, the committee authorized he government to continue the negotiations begun in Venice. The decision was officially brought to the attention of Foreign Minister Bánffy by the Austrian ambassador in Budapest two days later. The Hungarian government's response was that the Venice Protocol charged the Entente generals to arrange the Sopron plebiscite; hence, there is no need for direct meetings between the two countries. The Council of Ambassadors in Paris ratified the Venice Protocol on October 27.[468] In return for the plebiscite in Sopron and surrounding area, the Hungarian government completely renounced claims to Western Hungary, sealing the fate of the territory and Lajta-Banate. Disarming the rebels, however, brought countless problems.

This situation was exploited by the monarchists, the supporters of Charles IV and launched a new attempt to seat the king on the Hungarian throne. In the meantime, the 'legitimists' held a meeting on October 17 in Szombathely, in the palace of Roman Catholic Bishop, Count János Mikes. In the preparation for, and execution of, the second royal *coup*, significant roles were played by István Rakovszky, president of the National Assembly, Lt.Gen. Pál Hegedűs, Count Gyula Andrássy jr., the last foreign minister of the Monarchy, Ödön Beniczky (1878-1931), one of the leading personalities of the Christian National Unity Party (KNEP) and National Assembly representative for Szombathely, Count Albert Apponyi, head of the Hungarian peace delegation to Paris in 1920, Col. Antal Lehár and Maj. Gyula Ostenburg. The politicians sent a letter inviting the former king back after a secret meeting in Sopron on October 18, which a courier of Ostenburg took to Switzerland. Charles IV, and his wife, Queen Zita,[469] landed at 4pm on October 20 in their Junker-13 plane on the Vas County estate near Dénesfa of

---

[467] MOL. K 27. Minisztertanácsi jegyzőkönyv, 1921. október 16.

[468] Soós, 1971, op. cit., pp. 163–164.

[469] Princess Zita of Bourbon-Parma (1892–1989) married Charles IV on October 21, 1911. Brook-Stepherd, Gordon: Az utolsó Habsburg [The Last Habsburg], 1968. A series appeared in the Hungarian press: Megszólal Zita, az utolsó királyné [Zita in her own words, the last queen]. In: *Magyar Hírlap*, 1968, November 22 – December 5 (parts 1–13).

Count József Cziráky, High Constable of Vas County and current Government Commissioner of Western Hungary.[470] The plane was purchased in Switzerland by embassy secretary Aladár Boroviczény – Charles Habsburg's secretary at the time of the *coup* – for 50,000 Swiss Francs from the Ad Astra Aero Co. in Frankfurt.[471]

A car was sent for them from the mansion and, after a brief stay, Charles and his wife, accompanied by Antal Sigray, travelled to Sopron. On the way, in another car, they were joined by former [and future-*ed.*] prime minister Pál Teleki and József Vass (1877-1930), a Catholic priest and Minister of Religious and Educational portfolios. Of some interest is that the car of the royal couple was driven by Count László Almásy, reserve Air Force first lieutenant, the later famous African explorer [of the movie *The English Patient-ed.*].[472] In the city fated for annexation, Charles Habsburg began his next attempt at regaining the throne the following day. He appointed István Rakovszky as Prime Minister. The government formed was made up of Ödön Beniczky, Interior portfolio, Gyula Andrássy, Exterior, Gusztáv Gratz, Finance, and Col. Lehár, Defense, who was also promoted by Charles to major-general. Pál Hegedűs was named commander-in-chief of all armed forces, Gyula Ostenburg was promoted to full colonel and placed in command of a 1,500-strong unit called the Royal Guard Combat Regiment. The Sopron garrison, under Pál Hegedűs, swore allegiance to the king, joined by the units of Ostenburg, Lehár and Friedrich.[473] Although Prónay and his insurrectionist forces did not attack the units that switched sides to Charles Habsburg, he did not join the royalists.[474] A number of the students' Officer Company

---

[470] Katona, Imre: Az ún. királypuccs részletei egy könyv ürügyén [The details of a so-called royal coup on the pretext of a book]. (Vágvölgyi, Tibor: Junkers F–13. Közlekedési Dokumentációs Vállalat. Budapest, 1990) In: *Soproni Szemle*, 1991, issue 4, pp. 320–323.

[471] *Nemzetgyűlési Napló*, XIV. kötet. 1922, p. 84.

[472] Krizsán, László: A sivatag titkait kutatta. Almásy Lászlóról [He searched the secrets of the desert. About László Almásy]. Magyar Nyugat Könyvkiadó. Vasszilvágy, 2005, p. 10.

[473] See, *IV. Károly visszatérési kísérletei*. Op. cit., vol. I, 1921; also, *A nemzetgyűlés mentelmi bizottságának jelentése gróf Andrássy Gyula, Rakovszky István, gróf Sigray Antal és Beniczky Ödön nemzetgyűlési képviselők mentelmi ügyében* (379. szám). In: *Nemzetgyűlés Irományai*. Vol. XII. 1922, pp. 109–114; Zsiga, Tibor: A második királypuccs és Nyugat-Magyarország (1921) [The second royal coup and Western Hungary (1921)]. In: *Vasi Szemle*, 1981, issue 2, pp. 273–292.

[474] According to recent opinions, Prónay was not a monarchist and Charles IV supporter during the insurrection. See secret report by Folkusházy, Lajos – Bengyel, Sándor: Az 1921. évi királylátogatás katonai műveleteinek leírása [The description of the military maneuvers of the 1921 royal visit] Budapest, 1922, p. 189. It is also a decisive fact that no court proceedings were started against Prónay. His *Diary* offers proof that he was a supporter of Governor Horthy and would have joined the monarchists only after Horthy had done so. Prónay requested that Horthy set up a court of honor where he can clear his name of monarchist accusations. His defense

demobilized; of those who stayed in active status, the commander, Capt. Pál Gebhardt, organized a 15-man bodyguard unit for the personal protection of the royal couple. The majority swore allegiance and took part in the later clashes.

The king set out for Budapest on October 21 with the units of Lehár and Ostenburg in four railway trains. The Royal Guard Combat Regiment, as the primary unit of the legitimists, reached Budaörs in the outskirts of Budapest, on October 23 and routed an 80-strong unit of volunteers made up of medical students. Although Charles IV had a force of about 5,000 soldiers, he wanted to enter Budapest without bloodshed, which is why he declined to order an attack. The Hungarian government had, at this time, a mere 2,000 armed men but, after a recruiting speech by Governor Horthy on the same day, their ranks swelled to three-fold. A significant role in this increase was played by Gyula Gömbös, who organized several companies from the Hungarian National Defense League (Magyar Országos Véderő Egyesület), the Awakening Hungarians Association (Ébredő Magyarok Egyesülete / ÉME) and the volunteer security units of the universities. In the meantime, military units called in arrived by trains from the cities of Debrecen, Miskolc and other places. The diplomatic representatives of the Entente Powers, too, called on the Hungarian government to resist and the deposition of the former ruler. Czechoslovakia and the Kingdom of Serbs-Croats-Slovenes ordered partial mobilization.[475] The government named infantry General Pál Nagy as commander plenipotentiary of all military forces. After the successful counterattack of the government forces in Budaörs, and the victorious clash on October 23, Charles IV ordered a retreat. By morning of the next day, government forces encircled the 'monarchist forces." As a result of the defeat and unsuccessful truce, Charles' units began to disintegrate and surrendered at Budaörs with their commander, Gyula Ostenburg.[476] The king fled to the Esterhazy castle in Tata where he was taken into custody with his wife, Rakovszky, Andrássy and Gratz on the 24th. They were taken to the Benedictine monastery of Tihany.[477] Charles and Zita were handed over to the representatives of the Entente Powers on November 1, who exiled the royal couple to the island of Madeira. They were taken there on board a British

---

documents, see Fogarassy, László: Legitimista lett-e Prónay Pál a nyugat-magyarországi felkelés folyamán [Did Pál Prónay become a legitimist during the Western Hungary insurrection]? In: *Soproni Szemle*, 1990, issue 1, pp. 12–19. The court handed down its decision on March 11, 1922, finding that Prónay did not commit any acts "contrary to his oath to the Governor or against the national interests."

[475] Report. In: *IV. Károly visszatérési kísérletei.* I. füzet. 1921, pp. 215–220.

[476] Gyula Ostenburg was arrested on October 23 after the clash in Budaörs. He spent several months in jail for his role in the monarchist coup until his release in July of 1922, when the military officially retired him.

[477] Bánffy, op. cit., pp. 97–105.

warship.[478] Col. Antal Lehár fled the country at the strong urging of Charles IV and lived out the rest of his life in Austria and Germany.

On the day of Charles' arrest, the 24th, Governor Horthy issued a proclamation in which he drew the conclusions of the events. "The Hungarian nation lived through momentous hours. Unscrupulous persons misled Charles IV, convincing him to return unexpectedly to Hungary to exercise his regal prerogatives, although they must have known that it would clearly lead to civil war, foreign occupation and the destruction of the country. (…) Thanks to the loyalty of the national forces and the sobriety of the Hungarian people, this attempt, that would have sealed the fate of the country forever, failed."[479] The proclamation was also signed by Prime Minister Bethlen.

After the second unsuccessful 'visit' by the former king, a peculiar exchange of telegrams took place between Governor Horthy and commander Prónay. "The army of the Lajta-Banate delightedly greets Your Excellency that, through personal valor and exemplary perseverance, You were able to deflect the long-time danger threatening the Country. / (Signed) Prónay." Horthy did not personally respond to the commander's telegram but replied through his aide-de-camp, Maj.Gen. László Magasházy (1879-1959). "His Excellency, the Governor, ordered that I express the warmest heartfelt thanks to You and your subordinates for the salutations sent to him. / Maj.Gen. Magasházy."[480]

The Foreign Minister, Miklós Bánffy, remarked thusly in his memoirs of the second royal return attempt, "the mad adventure of king Charles,": "He utterly ruined our relationships with the successor states, foreign policy-wise, and cut off any path to reconciliation. It was as a result of the royal *coup d'état* that the Little Entente was created. They were on relatively good footing with each other but no agreements bound them together and everybody had freedom of action, as the Marienbad discussions proved. Now, instead of a Hungarian-Austrian-Czechoslovak bloc, the Little Entente came to be, aimed exclusively against us, under the leadership of Beneš. (…) Our immediate loss, however, showed in Burgenland. The Venice Protocol, as I have said, orders that, until the plebiscite and the finalizing of the borders, our gendarmes provide public safety services, under [the direction of] Gen. Ferrario. [Col.] Lehár, however, withdrew them and under false pretexts led them against Budapest [i.e., Horthy and the Hungarian government-*J.B.*]. Here, they scattered. As a result, their place has been taken by foreigners, mainly Italian carabinieri,[481] which raised the assumption of the population that we have given them up. Although the plebiscite held in Sopron and surrounding area turned out well, *but the border adjustment, which we accomplished in Venice based on the* [Millerand] *accompanying letter, which*

---

[478] Charles IV died on April 1, 1922 at his place of exile, the island of Madeira.

[479] In: *IV. Károly visszatérési kísérletei*. I. füzet. 1921, p. 213.

[480] *Lajtabánság*, 1921, November 3, p. 4.

[481] Carabinieri: Italian military police arm. In this case, Italian units ordered by Gen. Franco Ferrario as president of the Inter-Allied Military Mission in Sopron.

would have significantly corrected the insane border in our favor, was absent and only much later, when the Austrians took possession of it, did it gain a final resolution in 1922, to our and the population's detriment.[482]

In the meantime, the Hungarian Parliament stripped not only Charles IV but the House of Habsburg of their right to claim the Hungarian throne by passing Law XLVII on November 6, 1921.[483] Thus, legally, the 400-year reign of the House of Habsburg came to an end in Hungary. Against those active in the attempted royal *coup*, the National Assembly began proceedings to strip their parliamentary immunity or started court proceedings. The immunity committee's report of November 22, 1921 (Report #379[484]) in the cases of Count Gyula Andrássy, István Rakovszky, Count Antal Sigray and representative Ödön Beniczky was heard by Parliament on December 16. The submission proposed to the House that "having noted with concurrence the government steps taken in this matter and granting the lifting of immunity for the government's action in regard to the same, the National Assembly ratify it"; the four representatives' "right to immunity was not impaired by their arrest, and furthermore recommends to the National Assembly that the parliamentary immunity of representatives Andrássy, Rakovszky, Sigray and Beniczky be lifted in regard to this matter."[485] Governor Horthy, however, had already granted an amnesty to the participants of the royal *coup* attempt on November 3, and to the organizers on December 31, 1921.

While these events were unfolding, the Entente generals headquartered in Sopron notified Austria on November 10, 1921 of the evacuation of the territory and called on it to take control of Western Hungary. The occupation intentionally proceeded slowly because the Austrian government did not really believe the rebel pullback. The slow progress was also an attempt to draw attention to their dissatisfaction with the Venice Protocol and that they did not deem it as final. Austria primarily wanted to compel the withdrawal of Hungarian troops from Sopron for the duration of the plebiscite. In the end, the Austrian occupation of Western Hungary took three phases. The military units of Austria took an unjustified, draw-out 23 days to take control of the western area of Vas, Sopron and Moson counties awarded to them by the Trianon Decree. The Entente Military Mission scheduled two days in August for its accomplishment. The obvious reason for the Austrian behavior, the intentional impediment to the terms of the Venice Protocol, to wit, the holding

---

[482] Bánffy, 1993, op. cit., pp. 108–109. (Bolding mine–*J.B.*)

[483] In: *IV. Károly visszatérési kísérletei.* II. füzet. A trónfosztással kapcsolatos külpolitikai anyag ismertetése 1921. október 22-től november 13-ig. Kiadja: Magyar Kir. Minisztérium. Budapest, 1921. Budapesti Hírlap nyomdája, p. 32.

[484] Nemzetgyűlés Irományai. XII. kötet. 1922, pp. 109–120.

[485] Ibid, pp. 119–120. The immunity committee's vote was a narrow 9:8. A minority opinion was filed to report #379 by representative István Somogyi. In it, he recommended that the four representatives "had their immunity infringed and the National Assembly order their immediate release from arrest." Ibid, p. 121. It was rejected.

190

of the plebiscite eight days after the occupation. Three units of the *Bundesheer*, each with 100 gendarme administrators attached, occupied the area around Lake Fertő on November 13 (Nezsider, Kismarton and Nagymarton). A similar sized detachment marched into the central portion of the Borderland on November 25 (Felsőőr, Németújvár és Gyanafalva).[486] The population of the northern Borderland, although not openly welcoming towards the Austrian soldiers, did not offer them any resistance, either.

It was at this time that the Austrian Postal Service's directive 127, dated August 27, 1921 took effect. According to it, Hungarian postage stamps were to stay in circulation in the annexed Western Hungary territory for 14 days after the originally planned occupation date of August 28-29, until September 4. After the outbreak of the insurrection – since Austrian forces were forced to withdraw – the Austrian directive was not in effect. Later, after the actual handover in November and the second Austrian occupation, the terms of the directive permitted the usage of Hungarian stamps until December 11. Those, however, were not the stamps of the Royal Hungarian Mail but the overprinted stamps issued by an independent Lajta-Banate. The reason was that part of the inventory of Hungarian stamps was withdrawn from the area at the end of August and most of what remained was overprinted by the rebels. After the end of Lajta-Banate, the rebel forces sold the remaining inventory (78,000 Korona) to a Viennese firm. They authorized a person from Budapest, Lipót Schwartz, to ship it to Austria. Schwartz, however, was detained by the authorities in Sopron and, lacking an export permit, confiscated the stamps. In the name of the former Governing Council of Lajta-Banate, György Hir petitioned the Finance Minister for their return because, at the time, they paid cash for the inventory before being overprinted.[487] (Further outcome of the case is not recorded.)

On November 22, Foreign Minister Bánffy and the Austrian ambassador in Budapest signed the document worked out, by the Entente generals in Sopron, after a great deal of dispute, covering the details of the plebiscite. In the end, the recording of the referendum was not based on this document but on the decision of the Council of Ambassadors, which was brought to Sopron from Paris by French Gen. Hamelin and contained the final conditions of the plebiscite. (1) Persons eligible for the referendum in the plebiscite territory must have been born in the territory or over 20 years of age who have been permanently domiciled in the territory after January 1, 1919 and January 1, 1921. The roll of voters is based on the National Assembly election rolls of 1920, which must be used as the basis for necessary adjustments. (2) Voting is

---

[486] Jelentés a soproni népszavazásról és a magyar–osztrák határ megállapításáról [Report on the Sopron plebiscite and the Hungarian-Austrian border determination]. Szerk/ed.: Baron Frigyes Villani. Sopron, 1923, pp. 19–20. The 'Confidential', in fact 'Secret', report was only printed in 20 (perhaps 30) copies for internal use only. Also see, Missuray-Krúg, 1935, op. cit., p. 132.

[487] Király, 1982, op. cit., pp. 149–150. The plates used for the overprinting were destroyed by the Austrian authorities.

to take place in separate booths, where the ballot must be torn in half of the choice the voter does not wish to support, but both ballots must be replaced in the envelope, etc.[488] Events speeded up after that. The Austrian parliament debated, then accepted, the Venice Protocol. During the session, Chancellor Schober stated that "We are not in a position to relinquish Sopron."[489]

The agreements for handover of the annexed Western Hungary region – with the exception of Sopron and vicinity – were signed in the borough centers on December 2 by the Austrian military commanders and the Entente representatives. According to their summary, the Entente generals deemed the Hungarian area awarded to Austria to have been vacated on December 3 and called on the Austrian delegates to sign the memorandum of handover. With that, every obstacle was removed from the holding of the plebiscite. Afterwards, the military administration handed the occupied area over to Robert Davy, the first governor of Austria's newly-conquered territory. In Paris, the Council of Ambassadors decided – fulfilling a request by Vienna – to send Entente military units to the affected area. They arrived on December 8 and Hungarian military units withdrew from there on the 12th. The Entente generals in Sopron posted December 14 as the referendum date in Sopron, December 16 for the eight villages in the vicinity: Ágfalva, Balf, Fertőboz, Fertőrákos, Harka, Kópháza, Nagycenk, and Sopronbánfalva.[490]

What were Hungary's chances? Before the Venice talks, Frigyes Villani and Mihály Thurner, mayor of Sopron, responded to the query of the Hungarian government: the referendum will be a success for Hungary if the voting areas will be narrowly defined so that in them Hungarians, and Hungarian educated German middle class, will hold the majority of the votes. According to Villani, working with the Entente Mission in Sopron as the Hungarian government's representative, because of the atmosphere of the affected population, the expected outcome of the voting raised "the most serious unease." He felt that the reasons for it were: certain Hungarian directives restricted trade and border traffic, and curbed the use of the German language. The 'excesses' of the rebels exacerbated the general sense of the people, the troublesome military and public administrative acts. And not the least that the masses blamed the Hungarian government for the responsibility of the post-war troubles and privations.[491]

Before the referendum, the Entente generals officially forbade all acts of opinion influencing but the Austrians ignored it. Shortly after the signing of the Venice Protocol, the *Oedenburger Heimatdienst* (Sopron Home Service)

[488] Villani, 1923, op. cit., pp. 16–18.
[489] *Vasvármegye*, 1921, December 1, p. 1.
[490] *Népszavazási Emlékalbum* (1934): Gévay-Wolff Lajos, Sopron vármegye alispánja, pp. 13–16, Thurner Mihály, Sopron polgármestere, pp. 17–25, Traeger (sic!) Ernő, pp. 26–30, Parragi, György, pp 59–65, Schulz Ferenc, pp. 66–70. Also, Sopron and ..., 1934, op. cit.: Sopronyi-Thurner Mihály, pp. 38–43, 71–74; Krug, 1930, op. cit., pp. 31–58, Missuray-Krúg Lajos, op. cit., pp. 43–52.
[491] Villani, 1923, op. cit., pp. 14–15.

organization was created in the middle of October, which had as its main goal the mobilization in the city on the side of Austria. Among its founders was Dr. Alfred Wallheim, university professor in Vienna, according to tradition, the inventor of the Burgenland name and its fourth governor. Some others were Josef Rauhofer, court councilor and living in Nagymarton, Pál Eitler, teacher in Sopron and János Ambroschitz, columnist in the German-language paper of Sopron, the *Ödenburger Zeitung*. The organization published a paper, *Der Freie Burgenländer* (Free Burgenland), as well as printing several thousands of flyers and posters. The activities of the *Oedenburger Heimatdienst* was made significantly easier by the actions of a local citizen, Holzmann Gotlieb, who continued to deliver to the organization various news items, exact reports on the general feelings of the Germans, their thoughts and opinions. The agitation material for the Croat population of Kópháza was translated by József Vukovits into the mother tongue of the locals; in fact, issues of the *Der Freie Burgenländer* were printed in Croatian. The organizations active in Sopron were most likely financed by the Austrian government – the presence of court councilor Rauhofer strongly suggests it – because it had vast sums at its disposal, and the Austrian authorities provided strong moral support, too.[492]

Austrian propaganda in Western Hungary to side with Austria gained momentum when Hungarian public order enforcement units had to leave the plebiscite area on December 12. Until then, it was possible keep the 'neighbor's' contention to an acceptable level. Afterwards, almost impossible. The Entente generals in Sopron did almost nothing to curb the ever-growing potent anti-Hungarian Austrian agitation. It seems, though, that after a while their conscience took a turn because they overlooked the 'self-help' principle of the Hungarians. After the withdrawal of Hungarian soldiers and gendarmes from the plebiscite area, public administration remained under the direction of Hungary but there was a state of emergency in effect. As a result, between December 12 and 15, there was no Hungarian public safety force in the area, allowing free hand to the Austrian-side instigation. The protection of Hungarian interests was taken over by the students of the Sopron Mining and Forestry School – remember, most served during the war and demobilized as reserve officers, many were active in the insurrection --, the association of Sopron smallholder-citizens, and 40 detectives of state police from Budapest. First of all, they organized the permanent state of readiness for Sopron: they patrolled nightly in Sopron, checked the identities and detained the distributors of Austrian flyers and placards; resistors were roughed up.

The leadership of the Academy Youth Circle divided the city into 10 patrol districts and through "hard work" kept up an "increased surveillance" in the

---

[492] Miltschinsky, Victor: Der „Oedenburger Heimatdienst". In: *Burgenländische Heimatblätter*, 1926, p. 237. Miltschinsky's name was previously linked with the Carinthian referendum, where he was representative of the propaganda organization, *Kärntner Heimatdienst* (Carinthian Home Service). Most probably, he brought his experience to the *Oedenburger Heimatdienst*, created for the same purpose.

districts they held unreliable. According to Lajos Krug, this primarily meant that they sought out the hiding places of the "amazingly well organized, from the Austrian side, propaganda committee" and prevent their activities. They checked on the activities in the *Buschenschank*s, the little wine shops where the vintners offered their wines for sale, as these seemed to be the hotbeds of Austrian subversion. They continually removed the Austrian posters urging the vote against Hungary and prevented the distribution of flyers. At the same time, they placed Hungarian material on the streets. The students also mounted a defense along the new border and at the new border railway stations against the smuggling in of publications popularizing Austria and flyers. They searched most thoroughly incoming trains, wagons and passengers, confiscating thousands of Austrian flyers and wall posters, arresting numerous persons active in conducting Austrian political mobilization. Traffic at the train stations was continuously kept under surveillance – for months, the student / reserve officers were the stationmasters – and the students were also in command of the home guard units.[493]

The local press loyal to Hungary – the German-language *Christliches Oedenburger Tagblatt* (Christian Newspaper of Sopron) and *Sopronvármegye* (Sopron County) – asserted the advantages of staying with Hungary. Among other things, the press stressed that cross-border traffic would be easier, the Hungarian government will stimulate the economy, the German-language population will continue to be able to use freely its mother tongue, foster its culture. In the previously quoted report by Villani, the expectation was that the better-off citizenry, the tradesmen and craftsmen and intellectuals, who would remain loyal to the country in the plebiscite. A part of the locals who worked in Austria were under the influence of the Hungarian Communist – Social Democrat refugees in Vienna and behaved with hostility toward Hungary. The well-to-do Protestant farmers tended to side with Austria, saying they will be able to sell their produce there for higher prices. Hungarian reasoning tried to counter this group / argument by pointing out that the situation of Austria's economy is terrible, the money devalues, and great gains have been made in the country by the Communists. At the time, these were all too real facts. Of the settlements to hold the referendum, Ágfalva, Balf, Fertőrákos, Harka and Sopronbánfalva were anti-Hungarian, and seemingly impossible to win over. Hungarian propaganda here intimated to the locals that, in the case of an Austrian win, rebels would attack the villages. The people of Fertőboz, Kópháza and Nagycenk were decidedly in favor of staying with Hungary.[494]

It soon became apparent that assembling the list of eligible voters posed the greatest problem. As we have written, the roll of voters was based on the February 1920 National Assembly election lists but that was two years old

---

[493] Villani, 1923, op. cit., p. 26.
[494] Ibid, pp. 23–29.

and Sopron and vicinity experienced a lot of vicissitudes in the intervening time. All eight of the electoral committees found that the lists were out of date. One of the main reasons was that the civic authorities were only given eight days by the Entente Mission to update the rolls.[495] The Austrian government immediately attacked the process, saying that persons who fled from the rebels were not on the lists, while hundreds were being enumerated – according to Austria – who were ineligible to vote, e.g.- people who were temporarily staying in Sopron or have had some connection in the past to the plebiscite area. The Austrian agents went from house to house, checking the accuracy of the lists, reviewing the referendum rolls. A separate committee was formed to review the new data, which, due to the shortage of time, was only able to review and correct only a tenth of the lists by December 13 – according to Victor Miltschinsky, Austrian referendum commissioner.[496] "The number of electoral irregularities could not have been great since the Austrians began checking the voter lists already on December 4 and were joined by Entente officers on December 6."[497]

In the situation that developed, there was, indeed, a small amount of uncertainty and the Austrian government chose attack as the best defense. It urged the delay of the referendum until December 18 with the Council of Ambassadors in Paris, the Entente countries' ambassadors in Vienna, and the French and Italian governments. It based the request on the fact that Hungarian security forces left the area on the 12th, that the electoral rolls were forged, and that the plebiscite would not take place in a free and unbiased atmosphere. The Council of Ambassadors assented to the extent that it transferred the decision to the Entente generals in Sopron. They, in turn, made the delay contingent on the written agreement to the delay of the Hungarian government and PM Bethlen. The Hungarian government rejected the delay, saying it could make no more concessions to Austria. This view was also supported by the Entente ambassadors in Budapest. On the day of the withdrawal of Hungarian security forces, the 12th, the Austrian government notified the Entente generals in Sopron: it would take no part in the plebiscite starting on the 14th, and instructed its representatives to leave Sopron. On the evening of the same day, its decision was communicated to the Entente ambassadors in Vienna, as well as its decision not to recognize the result of the people's will.

The Sopron plebiscite, compelled by the Western Hungary insurrection begun on August 28, 1921 and the proclamation by Pál Prónay of an independent state of Lajta-Banate on October 4, ended favorably for Hungary. In his report afterwards, Frigyes Villani grasped the substance of it: "The logical progress of events could lead to no other solution than that Sopron was

---

[495] Ibid, pp. 20–21.
[496] Miltschinsky, Victor: Das Verbrechen von Ödenburg [The crime perpetrated on Sopron]. Wien, 1922, pp. 61–79.
[497] Ormos, 1990, op. cit., p. 195.

to stay with Hungary. From the moment that the Hungarians defied the totally authorized entrance of the Austrians in August of 1921, and the Allied powers omitted, from the very first days, to take military action to back up the terms of the peace agreement, Sopron could be said to be lost to Austria."[498]

The plebiscite was held on December 14 in Sopron and on December 16 in the surrounding eight villages, under the strict supervision of the Entente representatives. The number of eligible voters was 27,069, the majority of which, 19,164 voters, were to be found in the eight districts of Sopron and in Brennbergbánya, considered the 9th district of Sopron. The minority, 7,905 persons, resided in the surrounding eight villages. Of the total, 24,063 cast ballots (17,298 in Sopron, 6,765 in the surrounding villages) with a mere 502 spoiled ballots. Of the valid 23,561 ballots cast, 15,334 (65.1%) elected to stay with Hungary and 8,227 (34.9%) opted for Austria. It is important to note that the citizenry of Sopron decided referendum results favorable to Hungary: 72.8% of the city's electorate voted for staying with their ancient homeland, while only 27.2% voted against it. In the surrounding eight villages, the similar result was 45.5% for and 54.5% against.[499] As a result of the referendum of Sopron and the eight villages – Ágfalva, Balf, Bánfalva, Brennbergbánya, Felsőboz, Fertőrákos, Harka, Kópháza, and Nagycenk – a total of 256.82 km[2] was able to be retained by Hungary.[500]

According to the data of the 1920 census, the referendum area had a total population of 50,021, whose language distribution was: 19,525 (39.0%) Hungarian, 27,473 (54.9%) German, 2,472 (5.0%) Croat and 551 (1.1%) other. Of the total population of 50,021, 34,197 spoke Hungarian. Another important fact to note: of the 35,248 people of Sopron according to the census, 28,467 (80.8%) spoke Hungarian, while the linguistic make up of the city was 17,166 (48.7%) Hungarian, 16,911 (48.0%) German, 733 (2.1%) Croat and 438 (1.2%) other.[501]

In the days following the plebiscite, indeed to this day, Austrian public

---

[498] Villani, 1923, op. cit., pp. 30–31.

[499] Villani, 1923, op. cit., pp. 32–34.

[500] Ibid, p. 87; Horváth, Zoltán: Három ország versengése Nyugat-Magyarországért. A soproni népszavazás 50. évfordulóján. I. rész [The contest of three countries for Western Hungary. On the 50th anniversary of the Sopron plebiscite. Part I]. In: Kisalföld (Győr), 1971, December 14, p. 6; Part II, December 15, p. 5; Fogarassy, László: A soproni népszavazás helye Európa korabeli diplomáciai történetében [The position of the Sopron plebiscite in the diplomatic history of Europe of the day]. In: Soproni Szemle, 1991, issue 4, pp. 289–315; Mollay, Károly: A soproni népszavazás tanulságai. 1921. dec. 14–1991. dec. 14 [The conclusions of the Sopron plebiscite. Dec. 14, 1921 – Dec. 14, 1991]. In: Soproni Szemle, 1992, issue 2, pp. 97–105; Boronkai, Szabolcs: Az 1921. évi soproni népszavazás a korabeli sajtó tükrében. I. rész [The 1921 plebiscite in the mirror of the media of the day. Part I]. In: Soproni Szemle, 2003, issue 1, pp. 3–19; Part II, 2003, issue 2, pp. 124–142; Ormos, 1990, op. cit., p. 220; „Magyarok maradtunk" 1921–1996 [We stayed Hungarians 1921-1996]. Sopron, 1996, p. 112.

[501] Lőkkös, 2000, op. cit., pp. 358–360.

opinion asserted a "great fraud" by the Hungarians, when, according to them, Sopron was "fraudulently stolen" from Austria. The first to state this opinion was Viktor Miltschinsky, the Austrian referendum delegate, who published a book in 1922 in Vienna, recounting in detail the circumstances of the voting. In it, he openly calls the Sopron plebiscite as a crime (*Verbrechen*) because, in a perfect vote, according to him, 70-80% would have decided with Austria. He wrote that, on the day of the referendum, every street in Sopron, indeed every house, had trusted persons. To prevent disorder, they led groups of citizens to the voting stations, while attempting to prevent Austrian-friendly persons from reaching the ballot boxes.[502] The veracity of his assertions can be realistically questioned since, on the day of the voting, Miltschinsky was not in the city; the Austrian government, as noted earlier, had ordered its scrutineers home from Sopron two days earlier.

With regard to the previous assertions, we must add: "Those of the "great fraud" opinion forget to mention that an international committee, comprised of British, French and Italians, worked out the rules and organization of the plebiscite. It was accepted by both Austria and Hungary prior to the voting. The international committee reviewed every question and report, making necessary corrections. During the plebiscite, international troops occupied and supervised the area. Both sides were able to propagandize in a controlled manner. The international committee expelled from the area Austrian propagandists in the last days before the referendum for impermissible, harsh propaganda. Austria only began to debate the previously accepted rules when the expected plebiscite results began to take shape against their expectation. (...) The decisive factor in the plebiscite was that, amidst the crises of the day, the Austrian population was faced with an uncertain future at the time, while Hungary's change in government direction took place earlier, liberalization had begun and with it economic growth. (...) The population of annexed Western Hungary did not wish to live in an independent province. Due to the Austrian situation of political and economic crisis, a portion of them wanted union with Lower Austria or Styria, while another portion wanted to return to Hungary."[503]

The withdrawal of Austria from the plebiscite process "could not have altered the outcome at the last minute, since there was no presence of Hungarian power in the territory and order was entirely upheld by the units of the Entente (...) in all likelihood, a greater significance can be attached to the fact that the German-speaking or German–origin population of Sopron had no intrinsic ties to Austria. As with most city dwellers today, strong linguistic and cultural assimilation was the norm. The villages surrounding Sopron had sizable Hungarian blocs, also, partly, it was not in their interest to be

---

[502] Miltschinsky, 1922, op. cit., pp. 97–100.

[503] Szeberényi, András: Előszó [Prologue]. In: Zsiga, Tibor: Burgenland, vagy Nyugat-Magyarország? [Burgenland or Western Hungary] Published by: Burgenlandi Magyar Kultúregyesület, Oberwart / Felsőőr, 1991, p. 5.

separated from the city with which they were affiliated. (…) The foreign observers saw that, during the days of the referendum, total calm prevailed in Sopron and the surrounding villages. No disturbances took place and the Entente generals acted with complete meticulous strictness and impartiality. We can assume that their instructions did not transgress the bounds of objective practices and their reports bear evidence that, deep in their hearts, they all felt certain sympathy for the Hungarians in this difficult question. By then, they were very cognizant of the difficult circumstances that the Peace Treaty had dealt to the country. They were also aware that the former world war 'accomplice,' Austria, still received a very sizable piece of Hungarian territory, even without these few square kilometers."[504]

From the quoted referendum results, it is apparent that a portion of the German-speaking citizens of Sopron voted for Hungary. A reason was that nobody clearly defined in the city: who is Austrian and who is German? The German-speakers held themselves to be Schwabians and were convinced, based on centuries old traditions that their ancestors emigrated from various parts of Germany to Sopron or Western Hungary. [They settled along the western border for the immediate opening their German language gave them in selling their products in Vienna-ed.] A Hungarian citizen, whose ancestors came from a distant German province [or state-ed.], most certainly harbors some fraternal feelings towards Germans but the same cannot necessarily be said towards Austrians. It was also not coincidental that, at the Sopron victory celebrations the following day, Mayor Mihály Thurner said: 70 million Germans can be proud of the Sopron Germans because they are "good Germans and not scoundrels, Germans who did not betray their country."

It must be noted here that, precisely during the Sopron plebiscite, a Czechoslovak-Austria agreement was signed on December 16, 1921 in the castle of Lány near Prague, the residence of Czechoslovak President Tomáš Garrigue Masaryk. The first article of the Treaty of Lány,[505] named for the signing location, stipulated that the signing parties undertake to defend the *status quo* as defined by the Saint-Germain and Trianon peace treaties. Article two: "The two countries mutually guarantee each other's territory. (…) in the interest of maintaining peace and the guarantee of the integrity of the noted territories, they further oblige themselves to extend mutual support in the political and diplomatic arenas." Article three: "Both countries undertake the responsibility that, in the instance that one is attacked, and is forced to defend itself, will declare itself neutral."

The treaty was signed by President Masaryk and Foreign Minister Beneš for Czechoslovakia and President Hainisch and Chancellor Schober for Austria. The latter two signed as if the two month old Venice Treaty did not

---

[504] Ormos, 1990, op. cit., pp. 196–198.

[505] For the text of the Czechoslovak-Austrian political agreement, see: Halmosy, 1983, op. cit., pp. 186-188. The agreement lapsed on March 15, 1927. It was not renewed.

exist. They, however, had an inkling that, with the plebiscite under way, Sopron was already irretrievably lost for Austria. Thus, as a last attempt to create confusion among the Great Powers, they brought up the Treaty of Lány, after unsuccessfully petitioning the Council of Ambassadors for a delay in the referendum date.

The Treaty of Lány was greeted with great delight by Romania and the Kingdom of Serbs-Croats-Slovenes because, with its signing, Beneš was able to encircle and isolate Hungary, i.e., to force his neighbor, who was unwilling to accept the modifications, to its knees. "The ratification of the Trianon peace, the creation of the Little Entente, the unsuccessful attempt of Charles convinced the Hungarians that they must submit to our political direction," wrote the Czechoslovak Foreign Minister in his notes.[506]

Austria, in the meantime, could not come to terms with the referendum results. Between December 19 and 23, it sent a memorandum of objection to the Paris Council of Ambassadors, to the French government and the Entente ambassadors in Vienna, in which it lodged a protest against the referendum and the December 26 scheduled handover of the plebiscite area. As a complaint after the fact, Austria proclaimed loudly that certain abuses were committed when the rolls of the eligible voters was compiled and, thus, demands a repeat of the voting. By this time, the futile charges of the Austrian government greatly annoyed the Entente generals in Sopron. They sent a note to Paris on December 23 to the effect that, if the Council of Ambassadors does not send a note to Hungary by noon the following day, regarding the handover of Sopron and vicinity, then they will do it.

The Hungarian government received, in the meanwhile, assurances of support from Italy and Great Britain. In light of the referendum results, the reports of the Entente ambassadors in Budapest and the generals in Sopron, the meeting of the Council of Ambassadors on December 23 – after a long debate – formed the opinion a repeat of the plebiscite would not bring a different outcome and decided to accept the validity of the referendum result. Subsequently, the Council informed the Hungarian government that the handover of Sopron and vicinity was to take place on New Year's day, 1922, instead of the planned December 26. Finally, on December 28 – after the Council rejected Austria's newest, and final, objection – President Hainisch signed, thus ratifying, the Venice Agreement.[507]

When Hungarian citizens Dénes Kollár and Roland Lex arrived at Németújvár, on the territory annexed to Austria, to visit relatives over the Christmas holidays, Austrian authorities arrested and jailed him for no stated reason. This was clearly in contravention of the Venice Agreement. On their behalf, Albin Lingauer posed a question in the National Assembly, asking what the government intended to do so that "these transgressions will not poison the relations between the two countries and aggravate the mood of the

---

[506] Ádám M., 1989, op. cit., p. 152.

[507] Ormos, 1990, op. cit., pp. 198–202.

people living along the border?" Foreign Minister Bánffy rose and replied: "When we received the news, we immediately contacted Austria – these sorts of abuses have been perpetrated by the lower echelons of authority – and the Austrian government complied with our wishes. The unjustly arrested pair was immediately released on December 26. According to the Venice Agreement, no one can be persecuted for their political activities. The Austrian government has completely accepted this position, and we have, to date, offered protection to all in every instance where local authorities have acted improperly by abusing their power."[508]

On January 1, 1922, Sopron and its surrounding area were returned to the ancient homeland according to international law, ending the two years struggle to retain the Western Hungary / Borderland territory. A jubilant celebration took place on that day. At 11:00, a farewell march-past was formed by the Entente troops who were ordered into the town on December 8-9 from the Silesian plebiscite area – 40 British, 120 Italian and 150 French soldiers. After their march past, companies of Hungarian soldiers marched through the Old Fortress section of town, followed by the flag-carrying representatives of the referendum villages. Finally, the Entente and Hungarian units lined up, facing each other in front of the main Post Office, and the generals and Hungarian officials walked between them. At precisely noon, the handover document was signed by generals Gorton, Hamelin and Ferrario, as well as the representative of the Hungarian government, General Árpád Guilleaume, followed by ceremonial speeches.

In the following weeks, ceremony followed ceremony in the city. On January 6, the Mining and Forestry Academy students held a torchlight parade to City Hall, offering their congratulations to Mayor Thurner and the city that offered their school refuge three years earlier on their displacement from Northern Hungary. On January 10, a ceremony was held at the statue of Count István Széchenyi, in the presence of national and local leaders. The military units lined up tore off, on command, the black mourning bunting on their flags. In the Grand Hall of City Hall, a special ceremonial was held where the City Council said special thanks to the students "who have nothing but their mere lives, which they offered so freely for our city."[509]

The Hungarian government, to close the dispute peacefully, made a chivalrous gesture to the still-grumbling Austrian government. In a note, it expressed its regrets that it only got word too late, on December 14, of the Austrian wish to delay the referendum. Budapest expressed the hope that Vienna would finally put to rest the Sopron matter, giving an opportunity for the opening of dialogue leading to cordial relations between the two countries, something the Venice Agreement urged. In further two notes, Budapest hinted at considerations at the upcoming Hungarian-Austrian economic talks, which would greatly ease Vienna's situation. In the end, Austria recognized the

---

[508] Nemzetgyűlési Napló, XVII. kötet. 1922. P. 98.
[509] Krug, 1930, op. cit., pp. 153–163.

referendum results on February 20, 1922. The Hungarian Parliament also passed Lex XXIX, amending the city's coat-of-arms with a ribbon on the bottom that read: *Civitas Fidelissima* or Most Loyal City.

An interesting and valuable memento of the plebiscite is a silver spoon. The head of the Inter-Allied Military Mission was Italian General Carlo Ferrario, charged with overseeing the territorial handover and, later, arranging for the referendum. General Ferraro looked for suitable accommodations in the city, renting Templom (Church) Street 6 from a widow. The sizeable rent came in handy for the large family, in dire straits after the war. They were more than happy to move in with relatives for the required time. The Mission staff inventoried the entire house and contents, including bedding, linen, silverware and kitchen utensils. When the Entente Mission left after the plebiscite, one silver spoon was missing according to the inventory. Lost, stolen or accidentally thrown out? It could not be determined. A few days later, General Ferrario handed the lady of the house a silver spoon, with the monogram C.F. carved on the handle, made from a Lombard-Venetian silver Solidus.[510] The family still retains the unique memento.

[510] Kubinszky, Mihály: A népszavazásra emlékeztető ezüstkanál [The commemorative plebiscite silver spoon]. In: *Soproni Szemle*, 1992, issue 4, pp. 379-380.

Conclusion

The Hungarian national resistance, the self-defense had local results even after the change of government, the Trianon Peace Decree and the changes to the country's borders. For example, in the southeast corner of Szentgotthárd district of Vas County, the entirely-Hungarian populated village of 200, Szomoróc, could not become reconciled to being annexed, to the Serb military occupation. Earlier, on August 12, 1919, a unit of the South Slav kingdom had arbitrarily crossed the line of demarcation laid down by the Entente and occupied Szomoróc, while the neighboring village of 353, Kerca, also Hungarian-speaking, remained under Hungarian authority. The Trianon Decree of June 4, 1920 sanctified here, too, the *fait accompli* achieved by the rapacious Serb acquisition and drew the new border between the two villages. Two months after the signing of the treaty, at 23:00 on the night of August 1, the men of Kerca and Szomoróc, with the local Royal Hungarian border guard unit and its commander, Lt. József Ránkai, got together and attacked the Serb garrison. While the 17 Hungarian border guards intentionally fired into the air, the villagers, armed with scythes, pitchforks and fence pickets, attacked the Serb unit, which retreated from its post in panic.

As a result of the successful offensive, Szomoróc returned to Hungary but the enemy soon returned to its post in greater numbers. Their first act was to fly the Serbian flag from the steeple of the Reformed church. The Hungarian high command replaced Lt. Ránkai for his unauthorized action. Serb authorities arrested 11 residents of Szomoróc who took part in the event and shipped them to Muraszombat, where the police brutally beat and tortured them. Afterwards, they were thrown into the county jail facing the street. Since they were not fed, after several days, they began to yell from hunger. Some ladies of Muraszombat raised objections to the brutal measures, saying that in civilized countries even robbers and murderers are fed. Their answer was: they do not deserve food as the goal is for them to die of starvation. In the end, the local Hungarians bribed the jailers and smuggled food to the prisoners. The Hungarian patriots of Szomoróc spent a year in the Muraszombat jail, when a judge appointed from Belgrade reviewed their cases. After a new round of beatings, they were allowed to return home.[511]

The brave stand taken by the Szomoróc and Kerca men, and Lt. Ránkai and his men, was not in vain because the village of Szomoróc was reunited with Hungary on February 9, 1923 due to an Entente border adjustment mission's redrawing the border on the previous day. The people of the village commissioned a new bell from Sopron to replace one that was 'requisitioned' during the war. The bell was ceremoniously installed in 1923, on the first anniversary of the village being returned to Hungary. Also, a memorial tree

---

[511] Tiszai, László: Kercaszomor. A legbátrabb falu honvédő harca [Karcaszomor. The defensive battle of the bravest village]. In: *Nagy Magyarország*, year I, issue 2, 2009, August, p. 14.

was planted by the bridge over the creek flowing between the two villages, dedicated to the memory of the assassinated former prime minister, István Tisza. After the reunification, a memorial stone column was erected at its base as a reminder of the former boundary of 1919-1923. The plaque on the *stele* described the escape from Serb occupation.[512] February 9 became a village memorial day, which celebrated every year until 1945.[513]

During the years of the Communist dictatorship, the authorities did not look kindly on Hungarians remembering, in any form, either the territorial robbery of the Trianon Peace Decree or the days of glorious national resistance. The local residents had to stay mute of the ejection of the Serb occupiers. In fact, on the order of the local Party Secretary, the memorial column had to be destroyed in 1949, the Tisza memorial tree was chopped down. It was only in 2002, 82-years after the events, that a ceremony was again celebrated. The village petitioned the Council of Vas County to be granted the title *Communitas Fortissima*, or Bravest Village. A private member's bill was raised in Parliament in November of 2005 but was not accepted. Later, on November 20, 2008, it passed the House and since then, the village of Karcaszomor proudly displays the *Communitas Fortissima* label in its coat-of-arms.[514]

The Border Adjustment Committee visited the annexed parts of Vas and Zala counties, the Vend (Slovene) Region (also Mura Region), during the third year of Serb occupation on September 19-20, 1921. The population of the region massed with Hungarian flags and butonnieres alongside the roads that the commission's cars took. The convoy was stopped in many places and held up while the crowds sang the Hungarian national anthem and cheered Hungary, before letting them proceed. "Col. Cree, the head of the Committee, reported to the Council of Ambassadors of these stirring scenes. It was as a result of these demonstrations that the Committee brought down its decision, recommending a new border for the Vend Region. The Yugoslav government did not accept it. The sad result of the demonstrations was that the Yugoslav authorities went from village to village and arrested anyone they suspected of taking part: men, women, youths girls. They were all jailed. The jails and barracks of Muraszombat and Marburg (today Maribor in Slovenia) were full of those arrested. The Hungarian government, as well as Col. Cree and the Council of Ambassadors, intervened in an effort to gain their release."[515]

During the 1920s, those Vends (Slovenes) and Hungarians living in minority status would sneak across the border after receiving their draft notice from the Royal South Slav regiments and present themselves for military service at the Hungarian barracks in Körmend, Szombathely, Zalaegerszeg or

---

[512] Zsiga, 1996, op. cit., p. 153.
[513] In 1942, the villages of Kerca and Szomoróc were amalgamated into Kercaszomor.
[514] Tiszai, 2009, op. cit., p. 15.
[515] Fall, Endre: Jugoszlávia összeomlása. A Délvidék visszatérése [The collapse of Yugoslavia. The return of the southern region]. Budapest, 1941, p. 62.

Nagykanizsa.

Hungarians and Vends, who emigrated for economic reasons before WWI to the United States, gave numerous signs of their devotion to Hungary in 1919, and even afterwards. They held meetings and sent telegrams to the Supreme Council in Paris and the American government demanding that the Lendva region (by now called the Mura Region) be reunited to Hungary. Alas, their actions remained fruitless.

To these, we must add that they happened more than a year after the signing of the Trianon Peace Decree! This also proves our contention that, in the Fall of 1918, Hungary had vastly greater opportunities for armed resistance if then-Prime Minister Mihály Károlyi, Béla Linder and their associates, believing in the false Entente promises of a just peace, had not disarmed the 1.5 million Hungarian army soldiers returning from the fronts (including 816,000 Hungarians and 46,000 Ruthenians/Rusyns). As it happened, in the middle of November of 1918, the Károlyi government would have been able to field 200,000 – 300,000 Hungarian and Rusyn soldiers against an approximate force of 4,000 Czechs, 4,000 – 5,000 Romanians and 20,000 South Slavs (mainly Serbs). As they neglected to do so, Mihály Károlyi and his group committed a treasonable act.

It is an undeniable fact, too, that well after the September 10, 1919 Treaty of Saint-Germain and the June 4, 1920 Trianon Peace Decree, the armed insurrection in Western Hungary of Pál Prónay and Iván Héjjas (August 28 to November 4, 1921) and the proclamation of the independent state of Lajta-Banate forced the holding of a plebiscite in Sopron and eight surrounding settlements (December 14 – 16, 1921) that had a favorable outcome for Hungary, allowing it to retain a territory of 256.82 km^2 intended for annexation to Austria.

On the day of the ceremonial return of Sopron and the eight villages, January 1, 1922, Austria's ninth province, Burgenland, also came into official existence. This, in spite of the fact that the final border adjustment between Austria and Hungary was not finalized until December 22, 1922. The second anti-Austrian Western Hungary uprising attempt in July had an important impact on the adjustment process as the renewed struggle exercised a great impact on the Paris decisionmakers.[516]

With the revised border redrawing in 1922-1923, Hungary was able to reclaim 113.7 km^2 and 5,383 people from what was annexed away by the Trianon Decree – over and above the revision of Sopron plebiscite. (There was a minor adjustment in favor of Austria of approx. 1,800 acres and 471 people.[517]) The following villages were able to return to Hungary: Ólmod, Kisnarda, Nagynarda, Felsőcsatár, Alsócsatár, Magyarkeresztes,

---

[516] Botlik, József: Az őrvidéki magyarság sorsa 1922–1945 [The fate of the Magyars of the Borderland]. Magyar Nyugat Könyvkiadó ,Vasszilvágy, 2011, pp. 119–147.
[517] Villani, 1923, op. cit., p. 87.

Németkeresztes, Horvátlövő, Pornóapáti and Szentpéterfa.[518] The end result was that, through tough negotiating, Hungary was able to retain 8.1% of the territory and 16.1% of the population awarded to Austria by the Saint-Germain and Trianon treaties.[519] Adding the numbers reclaimed by the successful Sopron plebiscite, Hungary realized a gain of 370.5 km^2 and 55,403 Hungarians from its former ally and rapacious territorial claimant, Austria. This was, we must note, the first victory over the onerous terms dictated in Trianon.

Today, it is virtually unknown that, after the end of WWII, Austria again came forward with a claim for Austrian-Hungarian border adjustment, mainly for Sopron and vicinity. The new claim was championed by the Socialist Party of Austria in early October of 1945. The new, and former, Socialist chancellor was Karl Renner.[520] The other proponent of the annexation of Sopron and its vicinity to Austria was Ludwig Leser, governor of Burgenland from 1945 to 1950.[521] He was hopeful that Austria would be able to bring up the issue at the Paris Peace Conference.

The question of the border revision with Hungary was brought up openly by the paper of the Austrian Socialist Party, the Viennese *Arbeiter Zeitung*, in an article titled 'Das Burgenland wieder selbständig' (Burgenland independent again)[522] which was reported to the Hungarian Foreign Ministry by the Vienna embassy's Miklós Tóth. The article dealt with the fact that Burgenland became free on October 1945, after having lost its independent status as part of the Third Reich's Anschluss of 1938, and was once more a full fledged province of the Austrian federated state, the *Bundesstaat*. The author of the piece goes into great detail of one of the fundamental questions of the irredentist movement, Western Hungary. The writer goes on to state: "The Sopron plebiscite (...) took place under the terror of the reactionary Hungarian civil servants, by then allied to the Italians. The people of Sopron wanted to be a part of Austria – and want it today, too."

The embassy's Deputy Secretary, Tóth, had a meeting with ambassadorial counsel Seemann, head of the political department of the Austrian Foreign Ministry, also the official in charge of Hungarian issues. Seemann replied that, since the freedom of the press regulations came into effect on October 1, 1945, the government is not empowered to influence the editorial direction of certain newspapers. He assured Tóth that the Austrian government

---

[518] Ibid, pp. 63, 69–71; Schlag, 2001, op. cit., pp. 496–498.

[519] Villani, 1923, op. cit., p. 87.

[520] The Austrian People's Party won the 1945 November elections. Karl Renner was elected at President of the Austrian Republic, a post he held until his death in 1950.

[521] Környei, 1981, op. cit., p. 222. Even in 1924, Leser voiced that the natural center for Burgenland was Sopron. On the 10th anniversary of the province, he wrote in one of his articles: "Out with everything that is still Hungarian."

[522] *Arbeiter Zeitung*, 1945, October 2, p. 2. The author of the article – O.H. – was possibly Oskar Helmer, later Minister of the Interior and a leading figure in the Austrian Socialist Party.

"disapproved to the greatest extent the position of the *Arbeiter Zeitung*." The Deputy Secretary finally remarked in his report: "The circumstance should be noted that the article in question happened to appear in the paper of the socialist party, the party whose leading personage is Chancellor Renner, and so it is hardly probable that the party's paper would take such a differing position from its chief on such a delicate subject."[523] A semi-official, unsigned reply was sent to the Hungarian embassy in Vienna from Budapest on October 9. According to it, Hungarian politicians were greatly surprised by the article. The Foreign Ministry suggested to Tóth that he mention, in private conversations, how unfavorable impact the article had made, especially since it was also broadcast by the Austrian radio. The Ministry also noted that the Hungarian press will not respond to the article in the hope that similar provocations will not happen in the future.

The Wester Hungary question, and the issue of Sopron, again surfaced in the Austrian press and various political forums in May of 1946. Meinrad Falser, Austrian embassy counsellor reported on the Hungarian mood in his report on May 27 from Budapest to the Austrian Foreign Minister. He expressed that Hungarian politicians and public opinion were perturbed not only by the statements in the Austrian press but also by comments made in the Austrian Parliament during a budget debate with regard to Sopron. Several days later, on May 31, László Bartók, head of the Hungarian representation in Vienna, raised the question while making his introductory meeting at the Austrian Foreign Ministry.[524] As a result of all these actions, the Viennese government sharply isolated itself from the issue. The Austrian territorial claims against Hungary were not raised at the 1947 Paris Peace Conference, as it was not in 1918, either.

---

[523] Gecsényi, Lajos: Iratok Magyarország és Ausztria kapcsolatainak történetéhez 1945–1956 [Documents to the history of relations between Hungary and Austria 1945-1956]. Magyar Országos Levéltár. Budapest, 2007, pp. 56–57.
[524] Ibid, pp. 111–112.

Bibliography

Chapter 1: From allied country to territory claiming neighbor

A *Diaz-féle fegyverszüneti szerződés*. A páduai fegyverszünet. (Személyes tapasztalatok és hiteles okmányok alapján ismerteti Nyékhegyi Ferenc ezredes. Budapest, 1922.)

A magyarországi németek. (Szerk. Manherz Károly. Változó Világ, 23. köt. Budapest, 1998.)

Angyal, Dávid: *A boszniai válság története*. (Budapest, 1932.)

Apáthy, István: *Erdély az összeomlás után*. In: *Új Magyar Szemle*, III. köt., 2. szám. 1920. december

Arz, Arthur báró, vezérezredes: *1914 – 1918. A központi monarchiák harca és összeomlása*. (Budapest, 1942.)

Bajza, József: *IV. Károly és a délszlávok*. In: *Új Magyar Szemle*, I. évf. III. köt. 1. szám. 1920. november

Bertényi, Iván & Gyapay, Gábor: *Magyarország rövid története*. (Budapest, 1992.)

Böhm, Vilmos: *Két forradalom tüzében*. Októberi forradalom. Proletárdiktatúra. Ellenforradalom. (Verlag für Kulturpolitik. München, 1923.)

Brenner, Vilmos: *A hiénc néptörzs egykor és ma*. In: *Vasi Szemle*, LII. évf. 1998. 5. szám

Eördögh, István: *Erdély román megszállása (1916–1920)*. (Szeged, 2000.)

Fogarassy, László: *A Magyar Tanácsköztársaság vörös hadseregének köpcsényi védőszaka*. In: *Soproni Szemle*, 1960. 3. szám

Fogarassy, László: *A nyugat-magyarországi kérdés katonai története. I. rész: 1918. december – 1921. augusztus*. In: *Soproni Szemle*, XXV. évf. 1971. 4. szám

Fogarassy, László: *Kik ölték meg gróf Tisza Istvánt?* In: *Történelmi Szemle*, 1980. 2. szám

Fogarassy, László: *Sopron és az 1919-es hadszíntér*. In: *Soproni Szemle*, 1961. 1. szám

Fráter, Olivér: *Erdély Román megszállása 1918 – 1919*. (Logos Grafikai Műhely. Tóthfalu (Vajdaság), 1999.)

Gagyi, Jenő: *A nyugatmagyarországi kérdés*. (Budapest, 1921.)

Gelsei Bíró, Zoltán: *A Habsburg-ház bűnei. Magyarország négyszázéves szenvedésének története*. (Budapest, 1918.)

Gulya, Károly: *Az annexiós válság és az Osztrák–Magyar Monarchia balkáni politikája*. In: *Acta Universitatis Szegediensis. Acta Historica*, 20. [köt.] (Szeged, 1965.)

Harrer, Ferenc: *Egy magyar polgár élete*. I. köt. (Budapest, 1968.)

---

525 A bibliográfiában felsorolt források, könyvek és tanulmányok egy részére több fejezetben hivatkoztunk. A terjedelem kímélése érdekében a felhasznált művek leírását csak abban a fejezetben közöljük, amelyben először fordulnak elő.

Hronský, Marián: *Priebeh vojenského obsadzovania Slovenska československým vojskom od novembra 1918 do januára 1919.* In: *Historický časopis*, 1984. 5. szám. *Magyar nyelven:* Hronský, Marián: *Szlovákia elfoglalása a csehszlovák katonaság által 1918. novemberétől 1919. januárjáig.* Honvéd Hagyományőrző Egyesület. (Budapest, 1993.)

Incze, Kálmán, szárazajtai: *Háborúk a nagy háború után. A béke háborúi.* I. köt. (Budapest, 1938.)

Irinyi, Jenő: *Az osztrák–magyar hadsereg összeomlása.* (A volt főparancsnokság okmányai alapján). In: *Új Magyar Szemle,* I. évf. III. köt. 2-3. szám. 1920. december

Koréh, Endre: *„Erdélyért".* *A székely hadosztály és dandár története 1918–1919.* II. kiad. (Budapest, 1929.)

Környei, Attila: *Az osztályharc néhány kérdése Sopron megyében a polgári demokratikus forradalom időszakában (1918. november – 1919. március).* In: *Soproni Szemle,* 1969. 1. szám

Litschauer, G. Franz: *Bibliographie zur Geschichte, Landes- und Volkskunde des Burgenlandes 1800–1929.* (Band 1–3. Linz–Wels, 1933–1938. Band 4. Eisenstadt, 1959.)

Lőkkös, János: *Trianon számokban. Az 1910. évi magyar népszámlálás anyanyelvi adatainak elemzése a történelmi Magyarországon.* (Budapest, 2000.)

Magyarország története 1918–1919, 1919–1945. (Főszerk. Ránki György. Budapest, 1976.)

Mikes, Imre: *Erdély útja. Nagymagyarországtól Nagyromániáig.* (Sepsiszentgyörgy, 1996.)

Mollay, Károly: *Litschauer, G. Franz könyvészetéről.* In: *Soproni Szemle,* 1939. 1-2. szám

Nagy, Iván, dr. vitéz: *Nyugatmagyarország Ausztriában.* (Pécs, 1937.)

Nagy, József: *IV. Károly. Az utolsó magyar király.* (Budapest, 1995.)

Palotás, Zoltán: *Tisza István „délszláv missziója".* In: *Új Magyarország,* 1992. május 22.

Pölöskei, Ferenc: *Tisza István.* (Magyar História. Életrajzok sor. Budapest, 1985.)

Raffay, Ernő: *Erdély 1918-1919-ben.* (Szeged, 1988.)

Révai Mór, János: *Magyarország integritása és a wilsoni elvek.* (Magyarország Területi Épségének Védelmi Ligája. Budapest, 1920.)

Rubint, Dezső: *Az összeomlás.* (Budapest, 1922.)

Sarkotič, István báró: *Az összeomlás Boszniában és Hercegovinában.* In: *Új Magyar Szemle,* II. évf. I. köt. 2. szám. 1921. február

Schwartz, Elemér: *A nyugatmagyarországi németek eredete.* In: *Ethnographia,* XXXII. évf. 1921. 1-6. füzet

Soós, Katalin: *Burgenland az európai politikában (1918–1921).* (Budapest, 1971.)

Sopronyi-Thurner, Mihály: *A magyar igazság kálváriája.* In: *Sopron és Sopronvármegye ismertetője 1914 - 1934.* (Összeáll. Horváth László, Madarász Gyula, Zsadányi Oszkár. Sopron, 1934.)

Szakály, Sándor: *A magyar katonai elit 1938–1954.* (Budapest, 1987.)

Szász, Károly: *Tisza István. Élet- és jellemrajz.* (Budapest, 1921.)

Thirring Gusztávné, Waisbecker Irén: *A nyugatmagyarországi németek és a nemzetiségi kérdések.* (Budapest, 1920.)

Thirring Gusztávné, Waisbecker Irén: *Néhány szó a heancok eredetéről.* In: *Ethnographia,* XXXIII. évf. 1922. 1-6. füzet

Világirodalmi Lexikon 8. köt. (Főszerk. Király István. Budapest, 1982.)

Wlassics, Gyula: *Az eckartsaui nyilatkozat. A királykérdés.* I-II. rész. In: *Új Magyar Szemle,* II. évf. I. köt. 1. szám. 1921. január; *A trónöröklés.* III. rész. In: *Új Magyar Szemle,* II. évf. I. köt. 2. szám. 1921. február

Chapter 2: The annexing of the western parts of Moson, Sopron and Vas counties to Austria

A magyar béketárgyalások. Jelentés a magyar békeküldöttség működéséről Neuilly [s]/S.-ben [-sur-Seineben] 1920. januárius–március havában. I. köt. (Kiadja a Magyar Kir. Külügyminisztérium. Budapest, 1920., II. köt. Budapest, 1921.)

A vörös dúlás nálunk. Sopron és [a] vármegye a két forradalom alatt. (Összegyűjt. Mayer Géza. Sopron, év nélkül. [1920?])

Ajtay, József: *Külpolitikai helyzet – Nyugat-Magyarország.* In: *Új Magyar Szemle,* II. évf., II. köt. 3. szám, 1921. június

Amon, Karl: *Wer hat dem Burgenland den Nanem gegeben?* In: *Burgenländische Heimat,* 1926. július 11.

Bajzik, Zsolt: *Vasi kastélyok a tanácsköztársaság idején.* I. rész. In: *Vasi Szemle,* 2000. 5. szám, II. rész. 6. szám

Bellér, Béla: *Az ellenforradalom nemzetiségi politikájának kialakulása.* (Budapest, 1975.)

Beneš, Edvard: *Détruisez l'Autriche–Hongrie. La martyre des tcheco–slovaques à travers l'histoire.* (Libraire Delagrave. Paris, 1926.) *Magyar nyelven:* Beneš, Edvard: *Zúzzátok szét Ausztria–Magyarországot. A cseh–szlovákok áldozatának történelmi bemutatása.* (Ford., sajtó alá rend. Nagy Andrea. Kiad. JATE Történész Diákkör. Szeged. 1992.)

Botlik, József – Csorba Béla – Dudás Károly: *Eltévedt mezsgyekövek. Adalékok a délvidéki magyarság történetéhez. 1918-1993.* (Budapest, 1994.)

Feiszt, György: *Ahogy az iskolákból látták. 1919 Vas megyében.* In: *Vasi Szemle,* 1994. 4. szám

Flanner, Karl: *Bécsújhely volt 1919-ben a „fordítókorong" a Magyar Tanácsköztársaság irányában.* In: *Soproni Szemle,* 1988. 2. szám

Fogarassy, László: *A nyugat-magyarországi kérdés katonai története.* II. rész. 1921. augusztus – szeptember. In: *Soproni Szemle,* 1972. 1. szám

Fogarassy, László: *Nyugat-magyarországi bandaharcok. (1921. augusztus–november 4.)* In: *Soproni Szemle,* 1961. I. köt.

Gábor, Sándorné: *Ausztria és a Magyarországi Tanácsköztársaság.* (Budapest, 1969.)

Gergely, Ernő: *A proletárforradalom és a tanácshatalom Kárpátalján és Nyugat-Magyarországon.* In: *Jogtudományi Közlöny,* 1963. október–november

Horváth, Ferenc: *Magyarország vasútépítések 1900 és 1914 között.* In: *Magyar vasúttörténet.* 4. köt. 1900-tól 1914-ig. (Főszerk.: Kovács László. Budapest, 1996.)

Kiss, Lajos: *Földrajzi nevek etimológiai szótára.* IV. bőv., jav. kiad. I. köt. (Budapest, 1988.)

Kiss, Mária: *Gazdasági-társadalmi és politikai viszonyok 1918 és 1945 között.* In: *Szentgotthárd.* (Szerk.: Kuntár Lajos, Szabó László. Szombathely, 1981.)

Koncsek, László: *A bécsi és Sopron megyei ellenforradalom kapcsolatai 1919-ben.* I. rész. In: *Soproni Szemle,* 1956. 2. szám. II. rész. *A bécsi és soproni ellenforradalom kapcsolatai 1919-ben.* 1959. 1. szám

Környei, Attila: *Adatok az 1919. évi Sopron vármegyei osztályharcokhoz.* I. rész. *A tanácshatalom osztályjellege.* In: *Soproni Szemle,* 1973. 1. szám. II. rész. *Ellenforradalmi kísérletek.* 2. szám

Követeljük Burgenlandot. (Egyesült Magyar Nemzeti Szocialista Párt, Budapest, 1938.)

Kővágó, László: *A Magyarországi Tanácsköztársaság és a nemzeti kérdés.* (Budapest, 1989.)

Kranzmayer, Eberhard: *Die österreichischen Bundesländer und deren Hauptstädte in ihren Namen.* (Wien, 1956.)

Krug, Lajos: *Tüzek a végeken. Selmectől–Sopronig.* (Sopron, 1930.)

Kubinyi, Elek: *A burgenlandi németek.* In: *Magyar Szemle,* 1928. III. köt. 3. szám. (Magyar Nagylexikon. Főszerk.: Élesztős László. II. köt. 1994.)

Marosi, Endre: *Magyarok Burgenlandban.* In: *Unio,* 1989. augusztus

Nemeskürty, István: *Mi történt velünk?* (Budapest, 2002.)

Ormos, Mária: *Civitas fidelissima. Népszavazás Sopronban 1921.* (Győr, 1990.)

Ormos, Mária: *Padovától Trianonig 1918–1920.* (Budapest, 1983.)

Paál, Vince: *Ausztria identitásai.* In: *Nemzeti és regionális identitás Közép-Európában.* (Szerk.: Ábrahám Barna, Gereben Ferenc, Stekovics Rita. Piliscsaba – Budapest, 1999.)

Pálosy, I.: *Nem sértjük a magyar–német barátságot. Követeljük Burgenlandot a magyar haza szent testéhez.* (Budapest, 1939 körül.)

Palotás, Zoltán: *A trianoni határok.* (Budapest, 1990.)

Papp, István: *Az első magyar proletárforradalom és a Sopronba került Bányászati és Erdészeti Főiskola 1919-ben.* In: *Soproni Szemle,* 1969. 1. szám

Pozsonyi, Márta: *A saint-germaini osztrák békedelegáció és a területi kérdés*. In: *Történelem és nemzet*. (Tanulmánykötet Galántai József professzor tiszteletére. Szerk.: Kiss Károly, Lovas Krisztina. Budapest, 1996.)

Révai Új Lexikona, XI. köt. (Főszerk.: Kollega Tarsoly István. Szekszárd. 2003.)

Romhányi, Zsófia: *A saint-germaini békekötés és az osztrák sajtó*. In: *Történelem és nemzet*. (Tanulmánykötet Galántai József professzor tiszteletére. Szerk.: Kiss Károly, Lovas Krisztina. Budapest, 1996.)

Romsics, Ignác: *A trianoni békeszerződés*. (Budapest, 2001.)

Romsics Ignác: *Szláv korridor, Burgenland, Lajtabánság: koncepciók Nyugat-Magyarországról*. In: *Regio*, 1992. 1. szám

Schwartz, Elemér: *A Burgenland név*. In: *Magyar Nyelv*, 1927. szeptember-október (7–8. füzet)

Schwartz, Elemér: *A Burgenland magyar neve*. In: *Vasi Szemle*, I. évf. 1934. 3. szám.

Schwartz, Elemér: *A nyugatmagyarországi német helységnevek*. (Budapest, 1932.)

Soós, Katalin: *A nyugat-magyarországi kérdés 1918–1919*. (Budapest, 1962.)

Soós, Katalin: *Adalékok a Magyar Tanácsköztársaság és az Osztrák Köztársaság kapcsolatainak történetéhez. A nyugat-magyarországi kérdés 1919. március–augusztus*. In: *Soproni Szemle*, 1959. 4. szám

Soós, Katalin: *Menedékjog vagy kiszolgáltatás?* In: *Századok*, 97. évf. 1963. 2. szám

Soós Katalin: *Magyar–bajor–osztrák titkos tárgyalások és együttműködés 1920–1921*. In: *Acta Historica*, XXVII. köt. (Szeged, 1967.)

Szinai, Miklós: *A Magyar Tanácsköztársaság és Ausztria kapcsolataihoz. Otto Bauer levele Kun Bélához*. In: *Századok*, 103. évf. 1969. 2-3. szám

„Tisztemben csak a város érdeke és az igazság fog vezetni". A 120 éve született Thurner Mihály polgármester (1978–1952) emlékére. (Szerk.: Turbuly Éva. Sopron, 1998.)

Tóth, Imre: *Elméleti és módszertani megjegyzések a regionalitás kérdéseinek kutatásához. Regionális identitások Burgenlandban és Nyugat-Magyarországon*. In: *Arrabona* 45/1. (Kiad. a Győr-Moson-Sopron Megyei Múzeumok Igazgatósága. Győr, 2007.)

Turbuly, Éva: *Adatok Thurner Mihály polgármester személyének és szerepének jobb megismeréséhez a két háború közötti Sopron életében*. In: *„Magyarok maradtunk"*. 1921–1996. Konferencia a soproni népszavazásról. Sopron, 1996. december 12. (Szerk.: Turbuly Éva. Sopron, 1997.)

Thurner, Mihály: *Emlékirat Sopron magyarságának és németségének sorsáról*. (Rábaközi Nyomda, Sopron, 1919.)

Vádbeszéd gyilkosság, rablás stb. bűntettével vádolt Cserny József és társai bűnügyében. Elmondotta Dr. Váry Albert főállamügyész, a B[uda]pesti Államügyészség vezetője 1919. december hó 6-án a Budapesti

Törvényszék előtt. (Kiadja Rákosi Jenő Budapesti Hírlap Ujságvállalata R.-T. Budapest, 1919.)

Váry, Albert: *A vörös uralom áldozatai Magyarországon. Hivatalos jelentések és bírói ítéletek alapján.* (írta és kiadja Dr. Váry Albert koronaügyészhelyettes. Váci Kir. Országos Fegyintézet Könyvnyomdája. Budapest, 1922.)

Walheim, Alfred: *Wie das Burgenland zu seinem Nanem gekommen ist.* [Hogyan jutott Burgenland a saját nevéhez.] In: *Volkszeitung* ['Népújság'], (Wien, 1924. január 27.)

Zöllner, Erich: *Ausztria története.* (Budapest, 1998.)

Zsiga, Tibor: *„Communitas Fidelissima" Szentpéterfa. A magyar–osztrák határmegállapítás 1922-23.* (Szombathely, 1993.)

Zsiga, Tibor: *Horthy ellen, a királyért.* (Budapest, 1989.)

Zsombor, Géza: *Westungarn. Zu Ungarn oder zu Oesterreich?* (Corvina Verlag. Oedenburg / Sopron, 1919.)

Chapter 3: The occupation of the Vend region of Vas County by Serbs
– the Mura Republic

Bakó, Balázs: *Az ellenforradalmár püspök.* Eljárás gróf Mikes János szombathelyi püspök ellen 1918–19-ben. In: *Vasi Szemle,* 2007. 1. szám

Éhen, Gyula: *A felfordult ország.* In: *Vasi Szemle,* 1995. 1. szám

Éhen, Gyula: *A felfordult ország.* (Magyar Nyugat Könyvkiadó. Vasszilvágy, 2006.)

Fára, József: *Muraköz történetének rövid foglalata.* In: *Vasi Szemle,* 1942. 3-4. szám

Geml, József: *Emlékiratok polgármesteri működésem idejéből. 1914. VI. 15.– 1919. IX. 4.* (Helicon Könyvnyomdai Műintézet, Timisoara, 1924.)

Fogarassy, László: *A magyar–délszláv kapcsolatok katonai története 1918– 1921.* In: *Baranyai Helytörténetírás 1985–1986.* (Pécs, 1986. Baranyai Levéltári Füzetek 71. szám.)

Göncz, László: *A muravidéki magyarság 1918–1941.* (Lendva, 2001.)

Göncz, László: *Muravidék, 1919. A proletárdiktatúra időszaka a Mura mentén és a vidék elcsatolása.* In: *Vasi Szemle,* 2001. 2. szám

A magyarság települési viszonyai a megszállt Délvidéken. (Pogány Béla kiadása. Budapest, 1941.)

Székely, László: *Emlékezés Mikes János gróf szombathelyi megyéspüspökről.* (Vasszilvágy, 2009.)

Zsiga, Tibor: *Muravidéktől Trianonig.* (Lendva, 1996.)

Chapter 4: From the Treaty of Saint-Germain to the Peace Decree of Trianon

Békés, Márton: *A becsület politikája. Gróf Sigray Antal élete és kora.* (Magyar Nyugat Könyvkiadó, Vasszilvágy, 2007.)

Békés, Márton: *Egy vidéki „újságkirály" sorsa.* I. rész. In: *Vasi Szemle,* 2006. 1. szám, II. rész. 2. szám

Brenner, Vilmos: *Koronás urának hű szolgája volt csupán. Lehár Antal ezredes élete és szombathelyi működése 1918–1921 között.* In: *Vasi Szemle*, 2001. 2. szám

Czakó, István: *Gyorsírói feljegyzések a trianoni béke létrejöttéről. Egy amerikai memoár leleplezései.* I. rész. In: *Magyar Szemle*, VIII. köt. 3. szám. 1930. március, II. rész. 4. szám. 1930. április

Czakó, István: *A trianoni „békekötés" felelőssége.* (Budapest, 1933.)

Fogarassy, László: *Háború hadüzenet nélkül. Hadműveletek Magyarország területén a páduai fegyverszüneti egyezménytől a soproni népszavazásig.* II. rész. In: *Soproni Szemle*, 1990. 4. szám

Igazságot Magyarországnak. A trianoni békeszerződés következményeinek ismertetése és bírálata. Írták: Apponyi Albert gróf, Berzeviczy Albert és mások. (Magyar Külügyi Társaság, Budapest, 1928.)

Kelecsényi, Ferenc: *Párisban a békekonferencia idején.* (Budapest, 1920.)

Lehár, Anton: *Erinnerungen. Gegenrevolution und Restaurationsversuche in Ungarn 1918–1921.* (Herausgegeben von Peter Broucek. Verlag für Geschichte und Politik, Wien, 1973.) Lehár, Erinnerungen (Emlékezések) c. művének egy része (123–225. pp.) magyar nyelven is megjelent. Lehár, Antal: Egy katonatiszt naplója, 1919-1921. Bev. Sipos Péter. In: *História plusz,* XV. évf. (1993.), 11. szám, 7-48. old.

Romsics, Ignác: *Magyarország története a 20. században.* (Budapest, 1999.)

Sarkady, Sándor, ifj.: *A Nyugat-Magyarországi Liga. Egy területvédő szervezet tevékenysége 1919–1922 között.* In: *Soproni Szemle*, 2001. 1. szám

Sigray, Antal gróf: *Nyugatmagyarország az ellenforradalomban.* In: *Új Magyar Szemle*, II. köt. 2. szám. 1920. szeptember

Sigray, Antal Nyugat-Magyarország 1919-es szerepéről. Közzéteszi: Békés Márton. In: *Vasi Szemle*, 2006. 6. szám

Simola, Ferenc: *Horthy Miklós csapatszemléje Szombathelyen, 1919-ben.* In: *Vasi Szemle*, 2002. 6. szám

Sisa, István: *Magyarságtükör. Nemzet határok nélkül.* (Budapest, 2001.)

Soós, Katalin: *A Nyugat-Magyarországi Kormánybiztosság megszervezése.* In: *Acta Historica,* XXXIII. köt. (Szeged, 1969.)

Ullein-Reviczky, Antal: *Német háború – orosz béke. Magyarország drámája.* (Budapest, 1993. Első kiadása francia nyelven: Neuchàtel / Svájc, 1947.)

Zeidler, Miklós: *A revíziós gondolat.* (Budapest, 2001.)

Zsiga, Tibor: *A Nyugatmagyarországi Katonai Körlet Parancsnokság az ellenforradalmi rendszer újjászervezésében. A katonai szervezet létrejötte.* In: *Vasi Szemle,* 1978. 3. szám

Zsiga, Tibor: *A Nyugatmagyarországi Kerületi és Vasvármegyei Kormánybiztosságok, mint az ellenforradalmi állam első decentralizált szervei.* In: *Vasi Szemle,* 1978. 1. szám

Zsiga, Tibor: *Az ellenforradalmi rendszer hatalomra jutásának eszközei és sajátosságai Vas megyében (1919-1920).* In: *Vasi Szemle,* 1977. 3. szám

IV. Károly visszatérési kísérletei. I. füzet. (Kiadja a Magyar Kir. Minisztérium. Budapest, 1921. Budapesti Hírlap nyomdája.)

Ádám T., István: *Soprontól Munkácsig.* (Budapest, 1939.)

„A Rongyos Gárda harcai 1919 – 1939". Írta: egy Rongyos. (Budapest, év nélkül [1940?])

Bandholtz, Harry Hill: *Napló nem diplomata módra.* (Budapest, 1993.)

Bánffy, Miklós: *Emlékeimből.* (Kolozsvár, 1932.)

Bánffy, Miklós: *Huszonöt év (1945).* (Sajtó alá rend., bev., jegyz. Major Zoltán. Budapest, 1993.)

Barbalics, Imre János: *Sopron egy 1920. évi osztrák szükségpénzen.* In: *Soproni Szemle,* 1983. 1. szám

Breit, József: *A magyarországi 1918-19. évi forradalmi mozgalmak és a vörös háború története.* (Budapest, 1925.)

Dabas, Rezső: *„Burgenland" álarc nélkül. Történeti-földrajzi tanulmány az elrabolt nyugati végekről.* (Montréal, 1984.)

Fogarassy, László: *Hamelin tábornok egy titkos jelentés tükrében.* In: *Soproni Szemle,* 1981. 1. szám

Fogarassy, László: *Védelmi előkészületek Ausztriával szemben gróf Bethlen István kormányának hivatalba lépése után.* In: *Soproni Szemle,* 1994. 3. szám.

Gagyi, Jenő: *Nyugat-Magyarország átadása.* In: *Új Magyar Szemle,* II. évf. III. köt. 3. szám. 1921. szeptember

Héjjas, Jenő, dr.: *A nyugatmagyarországi felkelés. Kecskemétiek az 1921. évi nyugatmagyarországi harcokban.* (Kecskemét, 1929.)

Hiller, István: *Sopron harca a hajdani selmecbányai főiskola idetelepítésért 1919-ben.* In: *Soproni Szemle,* 1969. 2. szám

Hiller, István: *A soproni egyetemi hallgatók mozgalmai a két világháború között. Fejezetek a Soproni Egyetem történetéből. 1919-1945.* (Sopron, 1975.)

Kubinszky, Jenő: *A „M. kir. Nádasdy Ferenc 3. honvéd huszárezred" Sopronban 1921–1939.* In: *Soproni Szemle,* 1995. 3. szám

Laky, Dezső: *Csonka-Magyarország megszállásának közgazdasági kárai.* (Budapest, 1923.)

Mollay, Károly: *A Szövetségközi Katonai Bizottság bizalmas utasítása a hozzá beosztott antanttisztekhez. 1921. augusztus 1.* In: *Soproni Szemle,* 1991. 4. szám.

Mórocz, Zsolt: *Vereségek rejtett hálózata.* In: *Vasi Szemle,* 2000. 3. szám

Ormos, Mária: *„Soha, amíg élek!" Az utolsó koronás Habsburg puccskísérletei 1921-ben.* (Pécs, 1990.)

Péterfy, Károly, dr. vitéz: *A soproni M. Kir. Honvéd Főreáliskola története 1898–1921.* (Sopron, 1934.)

Prónay, Pál emlékezései az 1921. évi nyugat-magyarországi eseményekről. Közreadta Fogarassy László. 1-3. rész. In: *Soproni Szemle,* 1986. 1-3. szám

Simola, Ferenc: *Elfeledett fénykép IV. Károly Vas megyei tartózkodásáról.* In: *Vasi Szemle*, 2005, 6. szám.

Speidl, Zoltán: *IV. Károly két restaurációs kísérletének nyugat-magyarországi vonatkozásai (1921).* In: *Vasi Szemle*, 1971, 1. szám.

Tóth, Endre: *IV. Károly első magyarországi restaurációs kísérletének következménye: a csehszlovák–román szövetségi egyezmény.* In: *Kisebbségkutatás*, 2007, 1. szám

Träger, Ernő: *A soproni népszavazás. A szomorúság, bizakodás és hűség napjairól.* In: *Sopron. Civitas Fidelissima.* (Szerk. Thirring Gusztáv dr. Sopron, 1925.) Német nyelven: Träger, Ernst: Die *Volksabstimmung in Sopron. 14–16. Dezember 1921.* (Ödenburg, 1921.)

Zsiga, Tibor: *Az első királypuccs és Vas megye (1921).* In: *Vasi Szemle*, 1979, 2. Szám.

Zsiga, Tibor: *Szombathely az utolsó királyi székhely. IV. Károly első visszatérési kísérlete.* In: *Vasi Szemle*, 1991, 4. szám

Chapter 6: The Western Hungary insurrection

Ádám, T. István: *A nyugat-magyarországi felkelés története.* (Budapest, 1935.)

A Rongyos Gárda harcai 1919-1939. (Budapest, [1940?])

Békés, Márton: *A fegyveres revízió útja Nyugat-magyarországon.* Szabó József százados felkelőparancsnok válogatott iratai elé. In: *Vasi Szemle*, 2007, 4. Szám.

Endre, László, dr. vitéz: *Képek a nyugatmagyarországi fölkelésből.* In: *A Cél*, XVIII. évf., 1928. január-február.

Endre, László, dr. vitéz: *Nyugatmagyarország sorsa.* (Held János Könyvnyomda. Budapest(?), 1934.)

Fogarassy, László: *A nyugat-magyarországi kérdés katonai története. III. rész. 1921. szeptember–november.* In: *Soproni Szemle*, 1972. 2. szám

Fogarassy, László: *A Prónay–Ranzenberger pör (1930–1932).* In: *Soproni Szemle*, 1978. 1. szám

Fogarassy, László: *Lajtabánság.* In: *Legújabbkori Múzeumi Közlemények*, 1967. 1-2. szám

Fogarassy, László: *Lehár ezredes a Prónay-felkelők fogságában.* In: *Soproni Szemle*, 1975. 4. szám

Iratok az ellenforradalom történetéből 1919–1945. II. köt. A fasiszta rendszer kiépítése és a népnyomor Magyarországon 1921–1924. (Szerk.: Nemes Dezső, Karsai Elek. Budapest, 1956.)

Károlyfalvi, József: *A nyugat-magyarországi felkelés és Kecskemét.* In: *Kapu*, 2001. 10. szám

Király, Tibor: *A nyugat-magyarországi felkelőharcoktól a Civitas Fidelissima-ig. Négy hónap bélyegtörténete Sopronban és környékén.* (Sopron, 2001.)

Király, Tibor: *Négy hónap bélyegtörténete Sopron és környéke történetéből.* In: *Soproni Szemle*, 1982, 2. szám

Krug, Lajos, ifj.: *1921. A nyugatmagyarországi szabadságharc története.* In: *Emlékezés (1921-1931).* (Szerk.: vitéz Tóth Alajos. Magyar Kir. Bányamérnöki és Erdőmérnöki Főiskolai Ifjúsági Kör, Sopron, 1932.)

Maderspach, Viktor: *Élményeim a nyugatmagyarországi szabadságharcból.* In: *Magyarság*, 1926. 1-5., 7-38. szám (január 1. – február 17., 37 rész)

Maderspach, Viktor: *Élményeim a nyugatmagyarországi szabadságharcból.* (Szerk., dokumentumait gyűjt., könyvalakba rend. vitéz Ádám Jenő. Közlekedési Dokumentációs Kft., Budapest, 2000.)

Maderspach, Viktor: *Élményeim a nyugat-magyarországi szabadságharcból.* (Masszi Kiadó, Budapest, 2009.)

Maderspach, Viktor felkelőparancsnok emlékiratai. In: *Soproni Szemle*, 1978. 3-4., 1979. 1. szám. (Közreadta Fogarassy László.)

Missuray-Krúg, Lajos: *A nyugatmagyarországi felkelés.* (Sopron, 1935.)

Páter Zadravecz titkos naplója. (Szerk., bev. Borsányi György. Magyar Történelmi Társulat, Budapest, 1967.)

Prónay, Pál: *A határban a Halál kaszál... Fejezetek Prónay Pál naplójából.* (Szerk., bev. tan. Szabó Ágnes, Pamlényi Ervin. Magyar Történelmi Társulat, Budapest, 1963.)

Stelczer, István: *Kik vívták meg az ágfalvai ütközetet?* In: *Magyarság*, 1929. szeptember 19. (212. szám)

Széljegyzetek Missuray-Krug Lajos könyvein. In: *Vasi Szemle*, 1938. 1–2. szám, 104-105. old.

Zsiga, Tibor: *A nyugat-magyarországi felkelés és Vas megye 1921.* In: *Savaria.* (A Vas megyei Múzeumok Értesítője. 15. köt. 1981. Szombathely, 1985.)

Chapter 7: The State of Lajta-Banat

Baranyai, Lenke: *Machatsek Lúcia és alapítványa.* In: *Soproni Szemle*, 1998. 1. szám

Fogarassy, László: *A soproni népszavazás.* In: *Soproni Szemle*, 1971. 4. szám

Fogarassy, László: *„Lajtabánság: politikai és szépirodalmi időszaki lap".* In: *Soproni Szemle*, 1997. 3. szám

Gyurácz, Ferenc: *A nemzeti önbecsülés képei.* In: *Vasi Szemle*, 2001. 6. szám

Jászai, Emánuel János: *A magyar bélyegek katalógusa.* (Budapest, 1927.)

Lajtabánság (politikai és szépirodalmi időszaki lap, 1921. november 3., Felsőőr)

Lajtabánság Hivatalos Lapja, 1921. október 30.

Makai, Ágnes: *A Lajtabánsági Emlékérem.* In: *Soproni Szemle*, 1977. 4. szám

Kovács, Tamás: *Horthy és a zsidók. Sommás ítéletek, bonyolult valóság.* In: *Nagy Magyarország*, II. évf. 1. szám, 2010. február

Sigray Antal gróf beszéde a nyugatmagyarországi ellentállásról. (Athenaeum Irodalmi és Nyomdai Részvénytársulat nyomása, Budapest, 1922. Különlenyomat, a Keresztény Nemzeti Földműves és Polgári Párt kiadása)

Chapter 8: From the Venice Protocol to the Sopron plebiscite

IV. Károly visszatérési kísérletei. II. füzet. (Kiadja Magyar Kir. Minisztérium. Budapest, 1921. Budapesti Hírlap nyomdája.)

Ádám, Magda: *A kisantant és Európa 1920-1929.* (Budapest, 1989.)

Boronkai, Szabolcs: *Az 1921. évi soproni népszavazás a korabeli sajtó tükrében.* I. rész. In: *Soproni Szemle,* 2003. 1. szám, II. rész. 2003. 2. szám.

Fogarassy, László: *A soproni népszavazás helye Európa korabeli diplomáciai történetében.* In: *Soproni Szemle,* 1991. 4. szám

Fogarassy, László: *Legitimista lett-e Prónay Pál a nyugat-magyarországi felkelés folyamán?* In: *Soproni Szemle,* 1990. 1. szám

Folkusházy, Lajos & Bengyel, Sándor: *Az 1921. évi királylátogatás katonai műveleteinek leírása.* (Budapest, 1922. 20 térképvázlattal)

Gévay-Wolff, Lajos: *Csoda történ...* In: *A "Sopronvármegye" Népszavazási Emlékalbuma.* (Sopron, 1934. Rábaközi Nyomda és Lapkiadó Vállalat, 13-16. old.)

Horváth, Zoltán: *Három ország versengése Nyugat-Magyarországért. A soproni népszavazás 50. évfordulóján.* I. rész. In: *Kisalföld* (Győr), 1971. december 14., II. rész. 1971. december 15.

Jelentés a soproni népszavazásról és a magyar–osztrák határ megállapításáról. (Szerk.: Villani, Frigyes, báró. Sopron, 1923.)

Katona, Imre: *Az ún. királypuccs részletei egy könyv ürügyén.* In: *Soproni Szemle,* 1991. 4. Szám. (Vágvölgyi Tibor: Junkers F–13. Közlekedési Dokumentációs Vállalat, Budapest, 1990.)

Krizsán, László: *A sivatag titkait kutatta. Almásy Lászlóról.* (Magyar Nyugat Könyvkiadó, Vasszilvágy, 2005.)

Krug, Lajos, ifj.: *Sopron nagy napjai.* In: *A "Sopronvármegye" Népszavazási Emlékalbuma.* (Sopron, 1934. Rábaközi Nyomda és Lapkiadó Vállalat. 31-58. old.)

Kubinszky, Mihály: *A népszavazásra emlékeztető ezüstkanál.* In: *Soproni Szemle,* 1992. 4. szám

"Magyarok maradtunk". 1921–1996. Konferencia a soproni népszavazásról. Sopron, 1996. december 12. (Szerk.: Turbuly, Éva. Sopron, 1997.)

Megszólal Zita, az utolsó magyar királyné. In: *Magyar Hírlap,* 1968. november 22. – december 5. (1-13. rész).

Miltschinsky, Victor: *Das Verbrechen von Ödenburg.* (Wien, 1922.)

Miltschinsky, Victor: *Der "Oedenburger Heimatdienst".* In: *Burgenländische Heimatblätter,* 1926.

Missuray-Krug, Lajos: *A leghívebb magyar város történetének aranynapjai.* In: *Sopron és Sopronvármegye ismertetője 1914 - 1934.* (Összeáll. Horváth, László – Madarász, Gyula – Zsadányi, Oszkár. Székely és Társa Könyvnyomdai Vállalat, Sopron, 1934. 43-52. old.)

Mollay, Károly: *A soproni népszavazás tanulságai. 1921. dec. 14–1991. dec. 14.* In: *Soproni Szemle,* 1992. 2. szám

Parragi, György: *A velencei egyezmény megkoronázza Sopron megmentését.* In: *A "Sopronvármegye" Népszavazási Emlékalbuma.* (Rábaközi Nyomda és Lapkiadó Vállalat, Sopron, 1934, 59-65. old.)

Schulz, Ferenc: *A „megpróbáltatások városának" fia a „hűség városának" felszabadulásán.* In: *A "Sopronvármegye" Népszavazási Emlékalbuma.* (Rábaközi Nyomda és Lapkiadó Vállalat, Sopron, 1934. 66-70. old.)

Sopronyi-Thurner, Mihály dr.: *A magyar igazság kálváriája.* In: *Sopron és Sopronvármegye ismertetője 1914 - 1934.* (Összeáll.: Horváth, László - Madarász, Gyula – Zsadányi, Oszkár. Székely és Társa Könyvnyomdai Vállalat, Sopron, 1934, 38-43. old.)

Sopronyi-Thurner, Mihály dr.: *Mozgóképek Sopron mozgalmas idejéből.* In: *Sopron és Sopronvármegye ismertetője 1914 - 1934.* Összeáll. Horváth, László – Madarász, Gyula – Zsadányi, Oszkár. Kiadó: Székely és Társa Könyvnyomdai Vállalat, Sopron, 1934, 71-74. old.

Szeberényi, András: *Előszó – Die Vorgeschichte.* In: Zsiga Tibor: *Burgenland, vagy Nyugat-Magyarország? – Burgenland, oder Westungarn?* (Kiadja: Burgenlandi Magyar Kultúregyesület – Herausgeber: Burgenländisch-Ungarischer Kulturverein. Oberwart – Felsőőr, 1991.)

Thurner, Mihály dr.: *Pillanatfelvételek a magyar igazság kálváriájáról.* In: *A "Sopronvármegye" Népszavazási Emlékalbuma.* (Rábaközi Nyomda és Lapkiadó Vállalat, Sopron, 1934, 17-25. old.)

Traeger, (sic!) Ernő dr.: *Amikor az élő valóság legendává lesz...* In: *A "Sopronvármegye" Népszavazási Emlékalbuma.* (Rábaközi Nyomda és Lapkiadó Vállalat, Sopron, 1934, 26-30. old.)

Zsiga, Tibor: *A második királypuccs és Nyugat-Magyarország (1921).* In: *Vasi Szemle,* 1981. 2. Szám

Conclusion

Botlik, József: *Az őrvidéki magyarság sorsa 1922–1945.* (Magyar Nyugat Könyvkiadó, Vasszilvágy, 2011.)

Fall, Endre: *Jugoszlávia összeomlása. A Délvidék visszatérése.* (Budapest, 1941.)

Tiszai, László: *Kercaszomor. A legbátrabb falu honvédő harca.* In: *Nagy Magyarország,* I. évf. 2. szám. 2009. Augusztus

Other sources

1919. évi törvények gyűjteménye. (Budapest, 1919.)

Az 1910. évi június hó 21-ére hirdetett *Országgyűlés Képviselőházának Naplója.* XLI. kötet. (Athenaeum Irodalmi és Nyomdai Részvénytársaság Könyvnyomdája. Budapest, 1918.)

Az 1920. évi február hó 16-ára hirdetett *Nemzetgyűlés Irományai.* (Pesti Könyvnyomda. Budapest, III. köt. 1920.; XII., XIII. köt. 1922.)

Az 1920. évi február hó 16-ára hirdetett *Nemzetgyűlés Naplója*. (Athenaeum nyomda. Budapest, I., IV. köt. 1920.; XII., XIII. köt. 1921.; XIV., XV., XVII. köt.1922.)

Az 1920. évi népszámlálás. Első rész. A népesség főbb demográfiai adatai községek és népesebb puszták, telepek szerint. In: *Magyar Statisztikai Közlemények*. Új sor. 69. köt. (Budapest, 1923.)

A népmozgalom főbb adatai községenként – Die Grundlegenden Angaben der Bevölkerungsbewegung nach Gemeinden 1828-1920. Burgenland. (Magyar Központi Statisztikai Hivatal – Ungarisches Statistisches Zentralamt. Budapest, 1981.)

Burgenland településeinek nemzetiségi (anyanyelvi) adatai (1880–1991). (Összeáll. Pálházy László. Központi Statisztikai Hivatal, Budapest, 2000.)

Documents on British Foreign Policy 1919-1939. (Ed. by P. T. Bury–R. Butler. First Series. Vol. VII. London, 1958.)

Gecsényi, Lajos: *Iratok Magyarország és Ausztria kapcsolatainak történetéhez 1945–1956*. (Vál., szerk. jegyz. ellátta, bevezető tanulmányt írta Gecsényi Lajos. Magyar Országos Levéltár, Budapest, 2007.)

Győr-Moson-Sopron megye időszaki sajtójának bibliográfiája (1779-1995). (Szerk.: Horváth József. Győr. 2000.)

Halmosy, Dénes: *Nemzetközi szerződések 1918–1945*. (Budapest, 1983.)

Kocsis, Károly: *A Muravidék mai területének etnikai térképe*. Mérték, 1: 200,000. (Budapest, 2005.)

Kocsis, Károly: *Az Őrvidék mai etnikai területének térképe*. Mérték, 1: 350,000. (Magyar Tudományos Akadémia Földrajztudományi Kutatóintézet. Budapest, 2005.)

Magyarország Közigazgatási Atlasza 1914.; A Magyar Szent Korona országai. (Szerk. Zentai László. Baja–Pécs, 2000.)

Magyar Országos Levéltár fondjai: K 26. 1234., 1240., 1264., 1299., 1388., 1920. csomók; K 27. Minisztertanácsi jegyzőkönyvek 1918., 1921.; K 28. 1., 3. csomók.

Miller, David Hunter: *My Diary at the Conference of Paris with Documents*, Vols. I-XXII. (Author published. USA, 1929.)

Posta és Távírda Rendeletek Tára, 1922.

Tanácsköztársaság (Hivatalos lap, 1919.)

Tanácsköztársasági Törvénytár. V. füzet. (Szerk.: Pongrácz Jenő. Budapest, 1919.)

Cited magazines and newspapers

A Cél, Acta Historica (Szeged), Alldeutsche Tagblatt, Arbeiter Zeitung, Arrabona (Győr), Baranyai Levéltári Füzetek, Burgenländische Heimat, Burgenländische Heimatblätter, Christliches Oedenburger Tagblatt, Daily Mail, Der Freie Burgenländer, Ethnographia, Historický časopis, História plusz, Honvédelem, Jogtudományi Közlöny, Kapu, Kisalföld, Kisebbségkutatás, Lajtabánság (politikai és szépirodalmi időszaki lap),

Lajtabánság Hivatalos Lapja, Legújabbkori Múzeumi Közlemények, Magyarság, Magyar Hírlap, Magyar Kultúra, Magyar Nyelv, Magyar Szemle, Nagy Magyarország, Nép, Népszava, Neues Wiener Tagblatt, Ödenburger Zeitung, Pesti Hírlap, Posta és Távírda Rendeletek Tára, Regio, Savaria (Vas megyei Múzeumok Értesítője), Soproni Hírlap, Soproni Szemle, Századok, Tanácsköztársaság (hivatalos lap), Történelmi Szemle, Új Élet, Új Magyar Szemle, Új Magyarország, Új Nemzedék, Unio, Vasi Szemle, Vasvármegye, Vierburgenland, Volkszeitung.

Endnotes

József Botlik (1949-) PhD, researcher of minorities, historian, lecturer of the School of Philosophy of the Pázmány Péter Katolikus Egyetem [Peter Pazmany Catholic University]. He has been studying, for the past four decades, the turbulent history of the 3.5 million ethnic Magyars torn from Hungary by the June 4, 1920 Peace Treaty of Trianon. He has written 15 books and 200 papers on the subject, as well as 80 radio and television programs. His major research region has been Sub-Carpathia [Ruthenia] but his works also cover the changing situation of Hungarians in the former Hungarian territories of Northern Hungary, Transylvania and Vojvodina.

His current book takes the reader to western Hungary, which burst into flames in the aftermath of the unjust Trianon decision. Here, the territorial robbers of Hungary cast their eyes on an area, populated not only by Hungarians but also Germans, Croats and Vends (Slovenes), who never wanted to be separated from the country. Making use of all the printed and archival material, the well-written monograph clearly presents the plans and claims of not only the Entente Great Powers but also those of Austria, Czechoslovakia, Romania and Serbia. He outlines national political struggles of the country recovering from the shock of the two traitorous 'revolutions' of 1918-1919. He discusses in detail the glorious revolution of August-September 1921 in western Hungary, in legitimate response to the perfidious actions of its former ally, Austria. In contradiction to the earlier Marxist-Communist historiographic practice, this work does justice to the brave effort made by the state of Lajtabánság [Lajta-Banat-*ed*.] (October 4 – November 4, 1921), created after the Austrians were ejected from western Hungary.

Finally, it confirms the role of this brave national resistance in forcing the December 14-16, 1921 plebiscite in Sopron, as a result of which the town of Sopron and surrounding villages were returned to Hungary, and salvaging a small measure of national honor.